PRESENCES THAT DISTURB

Presences that Disturb

Models of Romantic Identity in the Literature and Culture of the 1790s

ૐ

Damian Walford Davies

UNIVERSITY OF WALES PRESS
CARDIFF
2002

© Damian Walford Davies, 2002

British Library Cataloguing-in-Publication Data.
A catalogue record for this book is available from the British Library.

ISBN 0–7083–1738–3

All rights reserved. No part of this book may be reproduced, stored in a retrieval system, or transmitted, in any form or by any means, electronic, mechanical, photocopying, recording or otherwise, without clearance from the University of Wales Press, 10 Columbus Walk, Brigantine Place, Cardiff, CF10 4UP.
www.wales.ac.uk/press

The right of Damian Walford Davies to be identified as author of this work has been asserted by him in accordance with the Copyright, Designs and Patents Act 1988.

Typeset at University of Wales Press
Printed in Great Britain by Dinefwr Press, Llandybïe

For Francesca

Contents

List of Illustrations	viii
Acknowledgements	ix
A Note on Texts	x
List of Abbreviations	xi
Introduction	1
1 Models of Solitude and Involvement: Tewdrig and David Williams	8
2 Models of Betrayal and Flight: Vortigern	55
3 Models of Defeat and 'Horrid Sufferance': Kosciusko	95
4 Models of Bardic Jacobinism and Gratitude: Edward Williams	135
5 Models of Fellowship and Fulfilment: Wordsworth, Coleridge, John Thelwall	193
Epilogue	241
Notes	243
Appendix: 'Yours, a true Sans Culotte' – Letters of John Thelwall and Henrietta Cecil Thelwall, 1794–1838	285
Bibliography	330
Index	357

Illustrations

	page
The Death of Tewdrig by John Evan Thomas and William Meredyth Thomas	14
David Williams by J. F. Rigaud	23
New Morality by James Gillray	30
John Thelwall, portrait attributed to William Hazlitt	80
Richard Warner by S. Harding after J. Williams	97
Thaddeus Kosciusko by Benjamin West	105
Edward Williams ('Iolo Morganwg')	138
Edward Williams, *Trial by Jury, The Grand Palladium of British Liberty. A Song*	144
'Cerrig-Enion': frontispiece illustration to John Thelwall's *Poems, Chiefly Written in Retirement*	233

Acknowledgements

An early version of Chapter 1 was delivered as a lecture to the Charles Lamb Society in 1996 and published in *The Charles Lamb Bulletin* NS 97 (January 1997). I am grateful to the editor, Richard S. Tomlinson, for permission to include this material here.

I am indebted to Lord Abinger for permission to quote from the Abinger–Shelley Papers held at the Bodleian Library, Oxford, and to the following institutions and individuals for permission to reproduce the John Thelwall and Henrietta Cecil Thelwall letters published in the Appendix: The Public Record Office; The Houghton Library, Harvard University; The Pierpont Morgan Library, New York; The National Library of Wales, Aberystwyth; The Carl H. Pforzheimer Collection of Shelley and his Circle, The New York Public Library, Aston, Lenox and Tilden Foundations; Birmingham City Archives; Harris-Manchester College, Oxford; The Trustees of the Wordsworth Trust, Dove Cottage, Grasmere. Full details can be found in the headnotes to the letters in the Appendix.

A number of friends and colleagues offered invaluable advice and encouragement during the writing of this book. Michael Scrivener generously allowed me to see numerous articles in manuscript and responded readily to queries about John Thelwall. Dorothy Thompson, Gregory Claeys, Penelope Corfield and Dawne Clively provided helpful information regarding Thelwall's correspondence. I also greatly appreciate the suggestions of Jane Aaron, Kelly Grovier, Richard Marggraf Turley, John Mee, Donald Reiman, Nicholas Roe, Jonathan Wordsworth and Duncan Wu, as well as those of the anonymous reader for University of Wales Press. The patience and assistance of the staff of the Manuscript Department at the National Library of Wales, Aberystwyth ensured that researching there was a pleasure.

My greatest debt is to Francesca Rhydderch for her unfailing support and encouragement throughout. This book is dedicated to her, with love.

A Note on Texts

All references to *The Prelude* are to William Wordsworth, *The Prelude, 1799, 1805, 1850*, ed. Jonathan Wordsworth, M. H. Abrams and Stephen Gill (New York and London: W. W. Norton & Co., 1979). Poems by Wordsworth and Coleridge from the *Lyrical Ballads* are cited from the Cornell edition, *Lyrical Ballads, and Other Poems, 1797–1800*, ed. James Butler and Karen Green (Ithaca and London: Cornell University Press, 1992). Other poems by Coleridge written and published in the 1790s were routinely revised for later editions (sometimes minimally, sometimes more significantly), and these later versions are the ones with which readers are, generally, most familiar from the editions by E. H. Coleridge (1912), John Beer (1963; revised edition, 1993) and William Keach (1997). J. C. C. Mays's definitive Bollingen edition of Coleridge's *Poetical Works* is about to appear as this book goes to press. Since I am concerned to locate textual dialogues at precise moments in the 1790s, the issue of exactly which versions were read is an important one. For this reason, poems by Coleridge not in the *Lyrical Ballads* are cited from letter/manuscript versions, early printed texts (such as newspapers and pamphlets) and collections published in the 1790s; these are clearly identified throughout.

Abbreviations

Biographical Anecdotes	*Biographical Anecdotes of the Founders of the French Republic*, ed. Alexander Stephens (2 vols; London: R. Phillips, 1797, 1798).
Borderers	William Wordsworth, *The Borderers*, ed. Robert Osborn (Ithaca and London: Cornell University Press, 1982).
CL	*Collected Letters of Samuel Taylor Coleridge*, ed. E. L. Griggs (6 vols; Oxford: Clarendon Press, 1956–71).
EY	*The Letters of William and Dorothy Wordsworth: The Early Years, 1787–1805*, ed. Ernest de Selincourt, rev. Chester L. Shaver (Oxford: Clarendon Press, 1967).
FiS	S. T. Coleridge, *Fears in Solitude . . . To which are added, France, An Ode; and Frost at Midnight* (London: J. Johnson, 1798).
Fenwick Notes	*The Fenwick Notes of William Wordsworth*, ed. Jared Curtis (London: Bristol Classical Press, 1993).
GJW	G. J. Williams, *Iolo Morganwg* (Cardiff: University of Wales Press, 1956).
GM	*The Gentleman's Magazine*.
HCR	*Henry Crabb Robinson on Books and their Writers*, ed. Edith J. Morley (3 vols; London: J. M. Dent, 1938).

Heath (1796, 1799, 1803)	Charles Heath, *The Excursion Down the Wye from Ross to Monmouth* (Monmouth: C. Heath, 1796, 1799 and 1803 editions).
Heath, *Tintern Abbey*	Charles Heath, *Historical and Descriptive Accounts of the Ancient and Present State of Tintern Abbey* (Monmouth: C. Heath, 1806).
Hist. of Mon.	David Williams, *The History of Monmouthshire* (London: H. Baldwin, 1796).
Heroic Elegies	William Owen (Pughe), *The Heroic Elegies and Other Pieces of Llywarç Hen* (London: J. Owen & E. Williams, 1792 [1793]).
Incidents	David Williams, *Incidents in My Own Life which have been Thought of Some Importance*, ed. Peter France (Brighton: University of Sussex Library, 1980).
Ireland, *Confessions*	William Henry Ireland, *The Confessions of William Henry Ireland* (London: Thomas Goddard, 1805).
Ireland, *Vortigern*	William Henry Ireland, *Vortigern: An Historical Play; with an Original Preface* (London: Joseph Thomas, 1832).
Keats, *Letters*	*The Letters of John Keats 1814–1821*, ed. Hyder E. Rollins (2 vols; Cambridge: Cambridge University Press, 1958).
Keats, *Poems*	John Keats, *The Complete Poems*, ed. John Barnard (2nd edition; Harmondsworth: Penguin, 1977).
Lamb, *Letters*	*The Letters of Charles and Mary Lamb*, ed. E.W. Marrs Jr. (3 vols; Ithaca and London: Cornell University Press, 1975–8).
LB	*Lyrical Ballads, and Other Poems, 1797–1800*, ed. James Butler and Karen Green (Ithaca and London: Cornell University Press, 1992).

Lectures 1795	S. T. Coleridge, *Lectures 1795 on Politics and Religion*, ed. Lewis Patton and Peter Mann (Princeton: Princeton University Press, 1971).
Life	Henrietta Cecil Thelwall, *The Life of John Thelwall* (London: John Macrone, 1837).
LL	*The Liber Landavensis, Llyfr Teilo, or the Ancient Register of the Cathedral Church of Llandaff*, tr. W. J. Rees (Llandovery: William Rees, 1840).
LY i, ii, iii, iv	*The Letters of William and Dorothy Wordsworth: The Later Years, Part i, 1821–1828*; *Part ii, 1829–1834*; *Part iii, 1835–1839*; *Part iv, 1840–1853*, ed. Ernest de Selincourt, rev. Alan G. Hill (Oxford: Clarendon Press, 1978, 1979, 1982 and 1988).
MoH	Jonathan Wordsworth, *The Music of Humanity* (London: Nelson, 1969).
MM	*Monthly Magazine*.
MY ii	*The Letters of William and Dorothy Wordsworth: The Middle Years, Part ii, 1812–1820*, ed. Ernest de Selincourt, rev. Mary Moorman and Alan G. Hill (Oxford: Clarendon Press, 1970).
NLRS	*New Letters of Robert Southey*, ed. Kenneth Curry (2 vols; New York: Columbia University Press, 1965).
NLW MS	The National Library of Wales, Aberystwyth, Manuscript Source.
Notebooks	*The Notebooks of Samuel Taylor Coleridge*, ed. Kathleen Coburn (6 vols; New York: Routledge & Kegan Paul, 1957–73).
Peripatetic	John Thelwall, *The Peripatetic; or, Sketches of the Heart, of Nature and Society; in a series of Politico-Sentimental Journals* (3 vols; London, 1793).

PL	John Milton, *Paradise Lost*, ed. Alastair Fowler (London and New York: Longman, 1971).
PLP	Edward Williams, *Poems, Lyric and Pastoral* (2 vols; London: J. Nichols, 1794).
Poems	John Thelwall, *Poems, Chiefly Written in Retirement* (Hereford: W. H. Parker, 1801).
PRO	Public Record Office.
Prose Works	*The Prose Works of William Wordsworth*, ed. W. J. B. Owen and J. W. Smyser (3 vols; Oxford: Clarendon Press, 1974).
PW	*The Poetical Works of William Wordsworth*, ed. Ernest de Selincourt and Helen Darbishire (5 vols; Oxford: Clarendon Press: 1940–9).
SCPB	*Southey's Common-Place Book*, ed. J. W. Warter (4 vols; London: Longman et al., 1849–51).
Table Talk	S. T. Coleridge, *Table Talk*, ed. Carl Woodring (2 vols; Princeton: Princeton University Press, 1990).
The Prelude	William Wordsworth, *The Prelude, 1799, 1805, 1850*, ed. Jonathan Wordsworth, M. H. Abrams and Stephen Gill (New York and London: W. W. Norton & Co., 1979).
Tribune	John Thelwall, *The Tribune* (3 vols; London, 1795–6).
Waring	Elijah Waring, *Recollections and Anecdotes of Edward Williams* (London: Charles Gilpin, 1850).
Warner, *Walk*	Richard Warner, *A Walk Through Wales, in August 1797* (Bath: R. Cruttwell, 1798).

Warner, *Recollections*	Richard Warner, *Literary Recollections* (2 vols; London, 1830).
Watchman	S. T. Coleridge, *The Watchman*, ed. Lewis Patton (Princeton: Princeton University Press, 1970).
WC	*The Wordsworth Circle*.
Wu, *1770–1799*	Duncan Wu, *Wordsworth's Reading, 1770–1799* (Cambridge: Cambridge University Press, 1992).
Wu, *1800–1815*	Duncan Wu, *Wordsworth's Reading, 1800–1815* (Cambridge: Cambridge University Press, 1995).

Introduction

> And I have felt
> A presence that disturbs me . . .
> (Wordsworth, 'Tintern Abbey')
>
> O Presences
> That passion, piety, or affection knows . . .
> (Yeats, 'Among Schoolchildren')

This book examines the ways in which personal, political and cultural identities were constructed in the 1790s in relation to certain emblematic human presences – both historical and contemporary – with whom Romantic writers identified as instructive exemplars, monitory models and haunting second selves. Considering both the broad cultural impact of these models and the ways in which their presence is inscribed in specific texts, I contend that such acts of identification take place characteristically at moments of personal and public crisis and anxiety resulting from revolutionary upheaval and political disillusionment. Participants in the debates of the 1790s viewed these figures as paradigms of many of the master themes which the French Revolution had raised as central ideological issues and reified in actual experience: the relative claims of political involvement and domestic retirement; betrayal; violence; State repression; moral and political justice. For Wordsworth, Coleridge, Keats, John Thelwall and others, such human *foci* offered a means of defining and dramatizing personal anxieties and political allegiances.

Historical and cultural recovery is at the heart of my project: I argue that these figures, as well as a number of those whose responses to them I interrogate, deserve a far more prominent place than has been accorded them in accounts of the cultural and political contexts of Romanticism. As well as offering a historicist account of Romantic self-definition, I am also concerned to reposition the canonical literature of the period in relation to a marginalized Welsh topos. These 'presences that disturb', and many of the writers who responded to them, stand in some significant relation to Wales, the ideologically troubling space of the Wye Valley and Welsh cultural history (actual and invented). I see the Wye Valley – a motif in this study – not merely as a place thronged in the 1790s by tourists, antiquarians, connoisseurs, painters and poets and specifically associated with Gilpin's theory of the picturesque which strives to cleanse the landscape of its more disturbing aspects. I excavate it as a space haunted by political pariahs, masterless men and historical ghosts – in short, as one of the crucial, formative sites in which Romanticism came to terms with history. The climax of English Romanticism's pre-eminent account of subjectivity, *The Prelude*, is located in Wales, but critical attention to a specifically Welsh, or Welsh-inflected, influence on Romanticism has been minimal. This book seeks to address that need and to enrich our understanding of how other cultural histories condition the contours of English Romanticism and those of the English Romantic self. To read the margins is not to read marginally; it is to widen the critical aperture through which Romanticism has hitherto been viewed and allow other significant voices into the canon. Wales itself is revealed in this book to be a presence that disturbs and energizes the Romantic Imagination.

I contend that the receptive culture of the 1790s recognized defining paradigms of identity as readily in distant British history as in the grounds of Alfoxden House. The models profiled in *Presences that Disturb* range from the Dark Age hermit-king Tewdrig and the infamous Dark Age traitor Vortigern, to contemporaries such as the political philosopher David Williams, the Polish patriot-General Thaddeus Kosciusko and the radical 'Bard of Liberty', Edward Williams or 'Iolo Morganwg'. I seek to restore these influential but neglected figures to the critical narrative of Romanticism. The final 'presences that disturb' are Wordsworth and Coleridge themselves, who are invoked as models of fulfilment against which the harried jacobin John Thelwall – who only recently has begun to receive the critical attention he deserves – dramatizes his exiled self in a series of elegies written on the banks of the Wye in 1800.

Clearly, the figure of Kosciusko, for example – public, international, painted by Benjamin West – is a different *type* of model from Wordsworth and Coleridge or the hermit Tewdrig, and will therefore be mediated by the culture of the 1790s in a different way. His presence in literary texts will also, therefore, be differently marked. Throughout this study, then, I seek to discriminate between various registrations or modalities of 'presence' in the literary and non-literary writing of the 1790s by examining explicit negotiations with these models; broader indices of cultural influence and debt; culturally embedded figurations; cryptic, historically ramifying references; ghostly traces; and intertextual allusions which encode, emplace, inscribe or imply a presence.

Those terms I have just cited are carefully chosen; they serve to define my methodology against what might be termed the deconstructive historicization of certain incarnations of New Historicism as practised on Romantic texts. This study shares New Historicism's drive to recover the original historical contexts (or subtexts) of literary works. But the agenda of many New Historicist readings of canonical Romantic poems has been to foreground troubling absences and elisions — to emphasize how a poem displaces or erases history in the service of an imaginative idealization of experience. Critics such as Marjorie Levinson and Jerome J. McGann have sought to expose Wordsworth's poems, for example, as allegories of absence that have been 'purified' out of their socio-political context by 'different sorts of artistic means' which 'occlude and disguise their own involvement in a certain nexus of historical relations'.[1] Levinson's reading of 'Tintern Abbey' as a 'disingenuous', 'fiercely private' and, in the final analysis, incorrigibly escapist poem that is 'artfully assembled by acts of exclusion'[2] is well known. Textual absence is privileged over textual presence; a 'reconstructed alterity' (that which the poem has repressed) is imported from the realms of the extratextual to highlight the evasiveness of the poem's 'manifest discourse'.[3] Romantic lyrics are seen to perform apostatic 'swerves' and become political poems *manqué*. Alan Liu's interpretation of Book VI of *The Prelude* in *Wordsworth: The Sense of History* (1989) attends more subtly to the poet's background 'inscription' and acknowledgement of historical and political realities. But Liu also sees history as ultimately disavowed and 'denied' by Wordsworth, 'written over' by Nature and by what Liu sees as the magnificent fiction of the unhistorical, transcendent, autogenetic Romantic self. Such readings have achieved an orthodoxy which this study seeks to contest.

Presences that Disturb offers culturally nuanced interpretations of canonical Romantic poems which emphasize that such works are inhabited not by troubling absences but by disturbing *presences* which mark an insistence on history, not an evasion or denial of it. Though it is only one of a large group of texts under discussion in this book, the capacious frame of 'Tintern Abbey', which occupies a crucial place in the geography of Wordsworth's historical imagination, provides a key example of how Romantic writers negotiated rather than euphemized history as they responded to the example or registered the influence of the models I am considering. As I argue in Chapter 1, Wordsworth's reading of the Wye landscape in 'Tintern Abbey' recognizes that Nature could not represent an escape in a post-revolutionary world. Landscape, as David Williams's topographical and historical writing had shown Wordsworth, was dramatically the site of history. As a landscape poem and poem of the self, 'Tintern Abbey' is not 'doctrinally surefooted':[4] it is a poem of 'thoughs', 'ifs', yets', 'nors' and 'mays', one whose very syntax enacts disturbance. Nature itself – as a text bearing the disruptive imprints of history – emerges in my discussion as another of those presences that disturb.

'Valency' is a recurring term in this book. In the discourses of chemistry and linguistics, it is used to describe the power of an atom or a grammatical element to govern or combine with others and form 'collocationary patterns'. By analogy, I employ the term to describe the manifold cultural, political and literary nuances of my paradigms. I shall show how inscriptions of these archetypes of the Romantic self in literary works represent sites of rich cultural confluence which mark the interchange between various discourses of the 1790s: literature, political writing, antiquarianism, Bardism, topographical history, county history, the tour. Such sites dramatically embody the exchange of ideas and reveal the network of formative 'conversations' which make up what I refer to as the *reticular* nature of 1790s culture. I am concerned to locate canonical works as part of this contextual fabric. The image of a net or web is an appropriate one to figure, say, the relation between Coleridge's 1794 sonnet on the iconic Kosciusko, Keats's 1817 sonnet to the hero and various determining utterances in the wider discursive field such as John Thelwall's political lectures in *The Tribune* and Leigh Hunt's political essays in the *Examiner*. It will be seen that I am often concerned to excavate allusions, identify implied auditors and reconstruct the conversations of the age from traces left in literary works. Allusiveness is the literary inscription of cultural interconnectedness; what it imports into a text is a cultural model.

By rereading canonical poems in the context of their paratextual frames – that is, 'the writing that surrounds a work, title, prefaces, mottoes, and the like'[5] – Paul Magnuson has sought to reconfigure Romantic lyrics as part of what he calls 'public' Romanticism. Paratexts, Magnuson argues, are gateways to the public discourse; through such intersections, a poem can be seen to resonate beyond its verbal boundaries and generic frame, enter into dialogue with other utterances and address 'subjects of social and political concern'.[6] Magnuson's focus differs from mine, but his analysis of 1790s culture as a 'Corresponding Society' – a neat pun which identifies the cultural 'conversations' of the age with the fostering of radical debate by the London Corresponding Society (fronted by Thelwall) – is one I share and wish to supplement. Reading the interconnectedness of poems, tuning into this 'multiplicity of voices', involves recovering a text's precise material and cultural 'location'. 'Location is all,' Magnuson declares: a statement I echo in mapping the discursive circuits of the age in relation to resonant models of identity, but with the important additional meaning of 'location' as literal geographic space. I offer dialogic readings of literary works that stress the debts they owe to other literary productions, to non-literary writing and to conversations over dinner (for this last, see Chapter 3). To read Romantic texts at a remove from their locations is to restrict their freedom of association and speech. In this way, the rehistoricizing drive of the book seeks to enlarge our sense of the texts, experiences and figures that are 'proximate' to canonical Romanticism and condition its modes of representation.

'Perhaps we should read the English romantic story', Judith Thompson remarks,

> neither as the epic song of a visionary company, nor yet as a drama of appropriation, displacement and defacement, but rather as a record of poetic answer and provocation, or as Thelwall would have it, of 'sweet converse', 'Agreeing, or dissenting – sweet alike, / When wisdom, and not victory, the end'.[7]

Here, Thelwall, in July 1797, is speaking to Wordsworth and Coleridge. He would soon be ventriloquizing them in poems written from disillusioned retirement – 'dissenting' in a particularly interesting way. Although the 'sweet converse' of 1797 appears to become the *converse* – dark soliloquy – in these poems, Thelwall's response to the models offered by Wordsworth and Coleridge preserves the dialogue in a Thelwallian redefinition of the conversation poem. Such readings of the literature and culture of the 1790s, then, invoke presence, commonality, exchange, vocal plenitude and dialogue as its touchstones, rather than absence, exclusivity, privacy and soliloquy. One might say (and Magnuson's pun implies as much) that such values are in the spirit of the 1790s radicalism that provides the context for this study.

A critique of this kind forces a reappraisal of the public rhetoric and ideological freight of poems whose political valency remains unacknowledged when these works are read in cultural isolation. Allusion and dialogue are not to be seen in terms of a literary game or as marking merely 'literary' influence; they work to proclaim political positions and to extend political debate. For example, in positing two poems by Edward Williams as significant influences on Wordsworth's 'A Poet's Epitaph' and 'Simon Lee' in Chapter 4, I identify Williams not only as a literary model for Wordsworth but also, in the light of his construction of himself as an exemplum of Bardic Jacobinism in the early 1790s and his relations with William Godwin, as a political one. 'A Poet's Epitaph' and 'Simon Lee' become political (in this case anti-Godwinian) poems, the latter drawing its political resonance from a particular social bond celebrated in the Welsh poetic tradition. To recognize – or even subtly sense – the presence of such models as Williams, Vortigern or Kosciusko in Romantic poems is immediately to configure these works as more politically aware, more public and more complex. It is to locate the interface between the literary and the social and political, the moment at which lyric utterance becomes public intervention. My account in the final chapter of Thelwall's rewriting of the poetic templates offered by such canonical poems as 'The Dungeon', 'The Nightingale', 'Tintern Abbey', 'This Lime-Tree Bower my Prison' and 'The Thorn' serves not merely to provide fascinating co-texts for these works and thus diversify the canon, but also to enrich and problematize our readings of Wordsworth and Coleridge, since what Thelwall's dark reconfigurations also offer are interpretations of, and commentaries on, these focal poems. Thelwall's response to his poetic models reveals their subtexts, agendas and dislocations.

Recovering the plenitude of a Romantic text's relations with its culture involves recapturing an original reading experience which has been lost. It also involves deciding to what extent the complex resonance of certain figures, utterances or images in certain contexts would have been registered by contemporary readers. In some cases, the 'initiated' readership to whom the full cultural meanings of such figurations are accessible will constitute a circumscribed coterie audience rather than a wider 'public'. But my analysis of the reticular, allusive texture of 1790s culture seeks to establish the currency, availability and comprehensibility of such meanings which preclude their amounting to a private language. The political significance of the hermit of 'Tintern Abbey', for example – a figure mediated to Wordsworth by David Williams – would certainly not have been understood by every reader of the *Lyrical Ballads* in 1798. However, readers like Coleridge, Thelwall and others familiar with the works of Williams and with the model he offered his culture would certainly have been alive to the public issues figured by such an image.

The precise trajectories of my five chapters are briefly outlined in the prefatory remarks at the head of each. Presented in the Appendix is a collection of eleven letters by John Thelwall and his second wife, Henrietta Cecil, spanning the years 1794–1838, to which reference is made throughout this book. These letters provide an important documentary context for my discussion of Thelwall (and others) and contribute to the recovery of the conversations and dialogues of a troubled decade.

1
Models of Solitude and Involvement: Tewdrig and David Williams

> O! might my soul
> Henceforth with yours hold converse, in the scenes
> Where Nature cherishes Poetic-Thought,
> Best cradled in the solitary haunts
> Where bustling Cares intrude not, nor the throng
> Of cities or of courts. Yet not for aye
> In hermit-like seclusion would I dwell
> (My soul estranging from my brother Man)
> Forgetful and forgotten . . .
> (John Thelwall, 'Lines, written at Bridgewater'; *Poems*, 128)

This chapter seeks to re-establish the seminal importance and complex resonance in the political and literary culture of the 1790s of a neglected figure whose valency as an instructive model is at once immediately apparent and profoundly subtle. That valency operates to differing degrees across a range of cultural productions, from political discourse to topographical history to poetry. My concern, therefore, is to analyse the ways in which this figure – the political theorist David Williams – impacted on the consciousness of the culture at large and made his presence felt in more specific, local contexts. It is with one of those individual sites of signification that I begin. Focusing initially on a central Romantic image of tranquillity and retirement, of solitude voluntarily embraced – that of the hermit in Wordsworth's 'Tintern Abbey' – I restore to it, in Marjorie Levinson's phrase, a 'manifold of contemporary meanings'[1] through which the example of David Williams can be seen operating at a deep, embedded level. Against an overwhelming critical orthodoxy, I interpret this hermit as far more than a mere picturesque prop, and suggest that Wordsworth would have encountered him in one of Williams's influential works, *The History of Monmouthshire* (1796). The nature of those 'contemporary meanings' is then established in detail as the chapter broadens into a consideration of the works and activities through which Williams became a paradigm of political commitment, disillusionment and retirement for the culture of the 1790s more generally. Williams became an important exemplar and second self in the political, cultural and religious experience of such eminent contemporaries as George Dyer, Brissot de Warville, Madame Roland, William Godwin, John Thelwall and Coleridge. The full extent and significance of his involvement in the political debates of the 1790s needs to be explored before the more subtle cultural spaces he inhabits can be fully appreciated.

The kind of topographical history and landscape vision offered by Williams in *The History of Monmouthshire* was emphatically a product of his political experience in a revolutionary decade, and I argue that Wordsworth's own landscape vision in 'Tintern Abbey' and other poems of the late 1790s is importantly informed by Williams's career and by the politicized picturesque he articulates. The cultural embeddedness of 'Tintern Abbey' is thrown into relief when the poem is read in the light of the model David Williams offered Wordsworth, the political lineage in which Williams can be located and the specificity of the historical hermit he brought to Wordsworth's attention. The poet's projection of the hermit onto the banks of the Wye in the summer of 1798 is to be viewed not as a purely imaginative or escapist sleight-of-hand but as part of a politically and socially aware vision inherited from Williams – and from Coleridge – which helped Wordsworth tune into the 'the still, sad music of humanity'. These new insights into the political meanings encoded in the poem serve as a corrective to the classic New Historicist claim that it is one of the most disturbingly depoliticized poems in the language. What I want to stress in the following discussion is the need to read Romantic poems from a position more squarely within their complex, reticular culture.

Sensing him to be something of an incongruous presence, critics have been much exercised by the hermit of 'Tintern Abbey'. He is part of an imaginative surmise which reads the 'wreathes of smoke / Sent up, in silence, from among the trees' as giving

> . . . some uncertain notice, as might seem,
> Of vagrant dwellers in the houseless woods,
> Or of some hermit's cave, where by his fire
> The hermit sits alone.
>
> (*LB*, 116; ll. 18–23)

The figure has been variously interpreted. By 1798, Wordsworth's hermit would have been seen as part of the picturesque furniture of poetry and topographical prose. John Dixon Hunt has shown how landowners would often employ someone 'to do their meditation for them', to act out the rôle of a hermit in a purpose-built hermitage in the grounds of the great estate.[2] Describing Tintern Abbey in his *Observations on the River Wye* (1782), William Gilpin imagines that 'a man of warm imagination, in monkish times, might have been allured by such a scene to become an inhabitant of it'.[3] Mary Jacobus argues that 'Gilpin's fantasy makes it impossible to dismiss the hermit . . . merely as a picturesque prop' and that Wordsworth would have recognized in that fantasy 'a parallel for himself'.[4] Geoffrey Hartman sees the hermit as 'Wordsworth's prophetic figure *par excellence*', as 'an image of transcendence . . . the symbol, probably, for the pure or imageless vision'.[5] Richard J. Onorato regards the movement towards the hermit in 'Tintern Abbey' as one 'from the actual through the imaginative to the "imaginary"' and the hermit himself as having been 'wishfully projected on this actual landscape', a figure 'symbolic of [the] real but unacceptable psychic wish' of 'renounc[ing] the world and withdraw[ing] into the landscape and from it into . . . "more deep seclusion"'.[6] Furthermore, New Historicism has read the image as part of the poem's sublimating drive away from socio-historical and psychic pressures towards an idealized picture of self and Nature: for Marjorie Levinson, the hermit is 'Wordsworth's self-projection', a 'hollowed-out emblem of uncompromised consciousness' figuring 'the private, meditative poet' who is 'in flight from a dreaded reality'.[7] She argues that by equating the vagrants with the hermit, Wordsworth 'discredits the factual knowledge' of the state of the poor at Tintern while Kenneth R. Johnston contends that the image removes the 'possibly unsettling associations' of the 'vagrant dwellers in the houseless woods'.[8] The hermit emerges from these readings as a symbol of retreat from active involvement into sequestered privacy. It is a view which I wish to counter in this chapter.

Harold Bloom reads this 'curiously placed figuration' in terms of Wordsworth's fraught relation to Milton: 'the Hermit stands, through the fixation of a primal repression . . . for the blind contemplative Milton of the great invocations . . . The Hermit is the synecdoche for Milton's hiddenness, and so for Milton's triumphant blindness towards anteriority'.[9] With Bloom, Robert A. Brinkley sees the hermit as representing Milton. He also interprets the image as part of the Romantic Ideology ('What the imagination seems to displace is a potential engagement with social reality – even as the hermit displaces the vagrants'[10]), but asks: 'Is the hermit who appears to displace the vagrants a figure without political commitments? . . . can we interpret the substitution of hermit for vagrants, as a response to, not an evasion of, social and historical realities?'[11] Citing Milton's presentation of himself as a hermit in 'Il Penseroso', he politicizes the image by suggesting it embodies Milton's political faith. Nicholas Roe views the hermit as 'of course thoroughly at home in a picturesque prospect', whereas the 'vagrant dwellers in the houseless woods' give 'more cause for unease'.[12] Roe's touchstone here is the 'Miltonic Picturesque' – a *frisson* whereby picturesque theory strives to idealize the landscape, cleansing it of its more uncomfortable aspects, while certain verbal, allusive details pull in the opposite direction and activate the disturbing associations of place 'overlooked in picturesque theory' – namely, 'the vicissitudes of human history'.[13] Roe's formula emerges from his argument that William Crowe's topographical poem *Lewesdon Hill* (1788), a precedent for 'Tintern Abbey', is itself haunted by a disturbing precedent – the 'hilltop vision of post-lapsarian history granted to Adam by the archangel Michael' in Book XI of *Paradise Lost* which 'revealed no "sweet variety" but the future history of "a world perverse" subject to time, change, and the "many shapes / Of death"' (*PL*, XI, 467–8).[14] The 'Miltonic Picturesque', therefore, is a means of encoding haunting prototypes that politicize the picturesqueness of superficially harmonious scenes. The 'vagrant dwellers in the houseless woods' give 'more cause for unease', then, since they embody an allusion to what Roe sees as 'the most impassioned attack on social injustice in English Literature' – *King Lear*:

> Poor naked wretches, wheresoe'er you are . . .
> How shall your houseless heads and unfed sides . . .
>   . . . defend you
> From seasons such as these? O, I have ta'en
> Too little care of this.[15]

But Roe's discussion bypasses the hermit as a similarly resonant figure in the landscape. For Roe, the figure is wholly of the 'Picturesque' and does not partake of the stringent, more open-eyed 'Miltonic'. I wish to draw attention to the more disturbing significance of the hermit. A full understanding of the valency of this figure depends on a detailed exploration of the models of flesh-and-blood who haunt that superficially tranquil image of untroubled solitude.

Tewdrig: 'Patriot and Saint, and Sage' (Coleridge on Joseph Priestley in 'Religious Musings')

My argument is that the hermit of Wordsworth's poem is a historical figure. Enshrined in the *Liber Landavensis* – the *Book of Llandav* – whose Latin text was compiled between 1120 and 1140 (though some of its documents may be older) is the story of Tewdrig Fendigaid, 'The Blessed', a sixth- to early seventh-century king of Morgannwg and saint, around whom many myths have accrued.

The Tewdrig story has been described as 'one of the most beautiful tales in the whole of Celtic hagiography'.[16] Having 'less regard for temporal than eternal power', the *Book of Llandav* states, Tewdrig 'gave up his Kingdom to his son Meurig, and commenced leading a hermitical life among the rocks of Tintern'.[17] Much has been made of the political and personal resonances for Wordsworth of the subtitle-date of 'Tintern Abbey', 13 July 1798 – the eighth anniversary of the day he had first landed in France with Robert Jones (whose home at Llangynhafal, north Wales, he was heading for when he first walked past Tintern in 1793); the fifth anniversary of the murder of Marat, which, in the event, served to precipitate the rise of the jacobins and, ultimately, the Terror; and the anniversary of the eve of the Fédération ceremonies Wordsworth had witnessed in France in 1790 and 1792.[18] That the *main* title – 'Tintern Abbey' – embodies history (and more specifically, as we shall see, conflict) has gone unnoticed. 'Tintern' is a corruption of the Welsh *Din Teyrn* – 'fort of the king' – the modern Welsh for 'Tintern' being *Tindyrn*.[19] The reference is to King Tewdrig the hermit; indeed, Tintern might possibly have acquired its name from the moment Tewdrig retired there.

Significantly, however, Tewdrig was soon called out of his contemplative retirement. The *Book of Llandav* relates that while he was resident at Tintern,

... the Saxons began to invade his land against his son Meurig ... And the angel of the Lord said to him ... 'Go to-morrow to assist the people of God against the enemies of the church of Christ, and the enemy will turn their face in flight, as far as Pwll Brochwael ... and afterwards for the space of thirty years they will not dare ... to invade the country ... but thou wilt be wounded by a single stroke in the district of Rhyd Tintern, and in three days die in peace'.

... and being armed, he stood in the battle on the banks of the Wye, near the ford of Tintern, and on his face being seen, the enemy ... betook themselves to flight; but one of them threw a lance, and wounded him therewith ... After his son Meurig returned victorious ... he requested his father to come with him, who thus said, 'I will not depart hence until my Lord Jesus Christ shall bring me to the place ... where I shall like to lie after death, that is, in the island of Echni'. And early in the morning, two stags yoked, and ready with a vehicle, were seen before the house where he lodged, and the man of God knowing that God had sent them, mounted the carriage, and wheresoe'er they rested, there fountains flowed, until they came to a place near a meadow towards the Severn. And when they came there, a most clear fountain flowed, and the carriage was completely broken. He then immediately commended his spirit to God, and ordered the stags to depart; and having remained there alone, after a short space of time, he expired.[20]

The battle of Tintern probably took place around 595,[21] and although there is no hard evidence of a major battle having been fought there, E. T. Davies admits that while the bare bones of the Tewdrig story 'cannot now be proved or disproved ... historical probability is in its favour'.[22] What is certain is that a skeleton with a fractured skull ('one of them threw a lance, and wounded him therewith') now lies in a stone coffin under the chancel of the church at the 'place near a meadow towards the Severn' referred to in the *Book of Llandav*. This place is modern-day Mathern, a few miles below Tintern.

It is important to note that the Tewdrig story had a currency beyond the confines of arcane and specialized antiquarian interest. A number of late eighteenth- and early nineteenth-century guides to the Wye Valley, for example, refer to it. James Baker's *Picturesque Guide through Wales and the Marches*, published in Worcester in 1795 but also sold in London, (mis)quotes 'a wretched scrawl on the plaistered wall, in the chancel of Mathern church' – the epitaph erected by Bishop Francis Godwin (1562–1633), Bishop of Llandaff from 1601 to 1617,

The Death of Tewdrig: bronze by John Evan Thomas and William Meredyth Thomas which won first prize in the Abergavenny Eisteddfod of 1848. The wounded but victorious Tewdrig, his Bard and his daughter Marchell are depicted as a dramatic *pietà* (*by permission of the Brecknock Museum and Art Gallery and Peter Lord*).

author of *The Man in the Moone* (1638), antiquarian and friend of Camden:

> Here lieth the body of Theoderick King of Morganock, of Glamorganshire, commonly called Sir Theoderick, and was accounted a martyr, because he was slain in a battle against the Saxons, being then Pagans, and in defence of the Christian Religion. The battle was fought at Tintern, where he obtained a great victory. He died here, being in his way home, three days after the battle, having taken order of Maurice, his son, who succeeded him in the kingdom, that in the same place he should happen to decease, a church should be built, and his body buried in the same; which was accordingly performed in the year 600.[23]

In his *Historical Tour in Monmouthshire* (1801), William Coxe (whose *Travels in Switzerland* (1789 edition) helped guide Wordsworth on his 1790 tour[24]), also quotes Bishop Godwin on the Tewdrig story. Godwin, who resided in the Bishop's Palace at Mathern near the parish church, is writing around 1614:

> St. Theodoric, as he is usually called, having resigned his crown to his son, embraced the life of a hermit. The Saxons invading the country, Theodoric was reluctantly called from his hermitage to take command of the army; he defeated them near Tintern upon the Wye; being mortally wounded in the engagement . . . he expired at a place near the conflux of the Wye and Severne; hence, according to his desire, a small chapel being erected, his body was placed in a stone coffin. As I was giving orders to repair this coffin, which was either broken by chance, or decayed by age, I discovered his bones, not in the smallest degree changed, though after a period of a thousand years, the skull retaining the aperture of a large wound, which appeared as if it had been recently inflicted.[25]

Charles Heath in his *Historical and Descriptive Accounts of the Ancient and Present State of Chepstow Castle* (1801), also refers to the story in a chapter dedicated to 'Matherne'. The old name of the parish was *Merthyr Tewdrig* – 'the burial-place, the grave, of Tewdrig'; the present name derives from *man + teyrn* – 'the place of the king'. In his *Historical and Descriptive Accounts of the Ancient and Present State of Tintern Abbey* (1806), Heath dismisses the fanciful elements of the *Book of Llandav* account – 'we now smile at such fables' – but gives credence to the historicity of the story.²⁶ Having referred to Wordsworth as 'the great Druid of the Wye, the poet of nature internal and external' and printed 'Tintern Abbey' in *The Wye and its Associations: A Picturesque Ramble* (1841), Leitch Ritchie comments: 'The only event unconnected with the monastery which is assigned to this locality is a *battle*. Whether it was fought on the hills above, or whether the demon of war actually intruded within the charmed circle of Tintern . . . we cannot tell'.²⁷

Would Wordsworth, and others closely involved in the cultural ferment of the 1790s, have known the story, part history, part myth? What exactly would the valency of this model of solitude, patriotic commitment and heroic engagement have been for them at a time when political identities were being forged and reforged in response to revolution and repression? The answer ultimately lies in an exploration of the career of the political theorist and writer of topographical history, David Williams, who offered his own political identity as a troubling and educative mirror for the culture of that decade.

The David Williams Connection: George Dyer and *The History of Monmouthshire*

Having reminded us of Wordsworth's debt in the opening description of 'Tintern Abbey' to Gilpin's *Observations on the River Wye*, which Wordsworth and Dorothy carried with them to Tintern in July 1798, Mary Jacobus in her note ' "Tintern Abbey" and Topographical Prose' refers to 'two other descriptions of the Wye Valley which Wordsworth is likely to have known'.²⁸ One of them is Richard Warner's *A Walk Through Wales, in August 1797*, published at Bath in 1798, whose genesis we shall return to in Chapter 3. 'Wordsworth is less certain to have known David Williams's *History of Monmouthshire* (1796)', Jacobus writes, 'but an interesting literary connection makes it possible that he did.' She refers to an article in the *Monthly Magazine* for December 1796, signed 'G.D.', which discusses the relationship between topography and poetry and which, she implies, led Wordsworth to Williams's book.²⁹ She contends that 'it is presumably the work of Coleridge's friend and correspondent, George Dyer'.

The article is unquestionably Dyer's. In 1812 he published *Poetics: or, a Series of Poems, and Disquisitions on Poetry* which contains a chapter on 'The Use of Topography in Poetry'. His preface states that 'Part of

Chapter VIII, On the Use of Topography in Poetry, I have improved from two papers communicated by me to the Monthly Magazine, in Essays on Topography, with the signature G.D. for July 1796, and a following month'.[30]

Dyer in the December issue of the *Monthly Magazine* quotes David Williams's *History of Monmouthshire*:

> 'The beauty of Monmouthshire', Mr Williams justly observes, 'is not dependent on single scenes, or particular features; it is the result of all the circumstances which form the whole surface of the county . . . The whole county forms one exquisite landscape . . . one general and extensive scene, which is wonderfully picturesque . . .'[31]

Wordsworth's 'composite scene' at the beginning of 'Tintern Abbey', Jacobus contends, might owe something to Williams's 'comprehensive' view of landscape. She then quotes Williams himself on Tintern's 'contemplative atmosphere':

> The abrupt and lofty banks, clothed with woods, sometimes obtruding barren rocks, dispose the mind to contemplation, to imagine all the possible purposes of this sublime retreat. From the grounds at Persfield, the transition to this sequestered spot, has something like the imagined effect of enchantment . . .[32]

Although Jacobus does not argue for the direct influence of Williams's landscape vision and his description of Tintern on Wordsworth's poem, she does suggest that an emphasis on Tintern's 'contemplative atmosphere' was characteristic of the period's topographical prose and that such an emphasis might be informing Wordsworth's picture of the

> . . . steep and lofty cliffs,
> That on a wild secluded scene impress
> Thoughts of more deep seclusion . . .
> (ll. 5–7)

But Jacobus does not mention Dyer's earlier (July 1796) contribution to the *Monthly Magazine* in which he discusses topographical history, the fine arts and 'the improvement of political society' and speaks highly of *The History of Monmouthshire*. Dyer's article is central to the cultural connections I am seeking to tap into. Having discussed the 'uninviting aspect' of some topographical histories, Dyer states that he has before him 'the History of Monmouthshire, by Mr David Williams', 'a writer of distinguished talents. This production is the reverse of those already described. I intend to make one or two remarks on topographical history, in a way of cursory observation, not of regular criticism, on this excellent work.'[33] William Enfield's 'Brief Retrospect of the State of Domestic Literature' in the same July issue also brings Williams's book to the attention of 1790s readers, characterizing it as a political work:

> The 'History of Monmouthshire', by Mr D Williams, recommends itself to general readers by a force of style, and a depth of historical and political research, by no means usual among those dry compilations, which, for the most part, appear under the title of County Histories. It is splendidly adorned with views, ex[e]cuted by the Rev. Mr Gardnor, in *aqua tinta*.[34]

Another important piece of information that Jacobus does not cite is the fact that Wordsworth is certain to have read Dyer's discussions of *The History of Monmouthshire* since in March 1797, James Losh sent Wordsworth 'Monthly Magazines from Feby to December 1796 inclusive'.[35] The March and April issues carried translations by William Taylor of Norwich of two poems by Gottfried August Bürger – 'Lenore' and 'Des Pfarrers Tochter von Taubenhain'[36] – which influenced 'The Idiot Boy' and 'The Thorn' respectively, while the September and October issues contained Coleridge's 'On a Late Connubial Rupture in High Life' and 'Reflections on Entering into Active Life' (later retitled 'Reflections on Having Left a Place of Retirement'),[37] to whose rejection of 'delicious solitude' and pledge to engage, 'active and firm' with 'the bloodless fight / Of Science, Freedom, and the Truth in CHRIST' we shall return.

Dyer's July and December contributions to the *Monthly Magazine* would undoubtedly have attracted the attention of a poet whose only two publications to date, apart from a sonnet in the *European Magazine*, were the topographical poems *An Evening Walk* and *Descriptive Sketches*. The essays might very well have led Wordsworth to *The History of Monmouthshire*. In the December issue Dyer announces that his design is 'to show how far the topographer may assist the poet'. The topographer, he remarks, is not 'a mere noter down of places, a reporter of curiosities, or the panegyrist of elegant seats . . . but one who describes the nature of places'. All of which leads him to ask: 'What advantage, then, does the poet derive from the topographer?' His answer is that 'By local descriptions, [the poet] may be brought acquainted with scenes to which he was before a stranger . . .' Homer might have written 'from nature, as his original', but does it follow, Dyer asks,

> that a poet may not enrich his mind from the stores of other observers? The views taken by any individual, in comparison with the whole range of nature, are inconsiderable and confined; and if poets are not permitted to increase their stock, by receiving a little on credit, many must be poor indeed.[38]

Dyer sanctions this borrowing by borrowing himself from Iago's speech on theft: 'But he that filches from me my good name / Robs me of that which not enriches him / And makes me poor indeed' (*Othello*, III. iii. 164–6). Topographical writing, he emphasizes, does more than unfold to the poet 'scenes that he never saw'. Since '[no understanding] recollects every stage of its enquiries', and since 'no eye embraces every scene', topographical history not only acts as a succour for the memory, a source of reference for the eye that *has* seen its Yarrow, but creatively modifies the poet's own vision: 'Topography . . . may assist a poet . . . by retouching, as it were, the objects already pictured in his eye; by completing the picture, and thus, by increasing the sensations, and strengthening the conceptions, the topographer may give energy and precision to the poet.'[39] Although it is the business of topography to be precise, it may also 'enliven the passions by moderate sallies of the fancy, and occasionally, elevate the mind with moral reflection'. David Williams's book becomes an invaluable companion to the topographical poet drawn, as Wordsworth was, to the fashionable landscape of Monmouthshire: 'the modern History of Monmouthshire that has been much admired for its general contents, seems also highly favourable to the views above-mentioned'.[40] It is at this point that Dyer quotes from *The History of Monmouthshire*. Arguing that the poet should use such works as a companion to his own vision, Dyer's articles might very well have led Wordsworth to Williams's book as an example of topographical history that could be of value to the topographical poet. The work was certainly widely, and for the most part, favourably, reviewed.[41]

But Williams's book provided Wordsworth and his contemporaries with far more than an awareness of the possible symbiosis between a work of topographical prose and a poem's imaginative vision. Jacobus makes no mention of the fact that Williams's *History of Monmouthshire* repeatedly refers to the hermit-king of Tintern and his decision to renounce solitude and engage heroically once more in active life. Appendix XXXVII relates the story in detail:

> We find in the book of Llandaff, that, about this time 596, Tudric King of Glamorgan, who was still victorious, is said to have exchanged his crown for an hermitage, till going in aid of his son Mourice, whom the Saxons had reduced to great extremity, taking up arms again, he defended him against them at Tinterne by the Wye; but he himself received a mortal wound.[42]

Tewdrig also appears in *The History of Monmouthshire* as the grandfather of 'the great Arthur of the British History' and as the ruler 'who is said to have first built a church at Llandaff',[43] a claim reinforced by Appendix XXIII, drawn up for Williams, as are many other sections, by his fellow Welshman and purported relative, Edward Williams (Iolo Morganwg, 'The Bard of Liberty') – jacobin, friend of Coleridge and George Dyer, and a cultural model I shall be considering later in this book:[44] 'Tewdric. See an account of him in Godwin's Account of the Bishops of Landaff: it is probable enough, that he might have built a place of worship at Landaff, which occasioned the Bishop's See to be there established.'[45] Appendix XVII describes the village of Mathern, the burial-place of Tewdrig, which appears as the gift of Tewdrig's son Meurig to the bishopric in memory of his father[46] and as the 'ancient palace of the See of Llandaff'.[47] The link with Llandaff and its bishops is also made in a number of contemporary guide books: William Coxe states that Mathern served as the episcopal palace of the see until the early years of the eighteenth century.[48] Wordsworth would surely have been interested in the connection between the Tewdrig story and the bishops of Llandaff: soon after his return from France, he had in early 1793 composed his radical *Letter to the Bishop of Llandaff*, Richard Watson. In 1789, David Williams had anonymously published his own letter to the bishop – *An Apology for Professing the Religion of Nature in the Eighteenth Century of the Christian Æra, addressed to the Right Reverend Dr. Watson, Lord Bishop of Llandaff*. The *History of Monmouthshire* would have crystallized in Wordsworth's mind the link between a former radical self, the hermit Tewdrig, and the career of David Williams, whose own status as a model for the culture of the

1790s we now need to consider before returning to the full resonance of the hermit-model, whose own political identity parallels Williams's in important ways.

David Williams, Priest of Nature

I want to suggest that a number of other links apart from Dyer's articles in the *Monthly Magazine* led Wordsworth to *The History of Monmouthshire* and also to an identification with the career of its author. Wordsworth would certainly have known of the Welshman David Williams (1738–1816).[49] Born at Waunwaelod, Watford, on the north slope of Caerphilly mountain in the parish of Eglwysilan, south Wales, and educated at the theologically heterodox Dissenting Academy at Carmarthen, nicknamed 'The Priest of Nature' and 'the English Rousseau' by his friend Benjamin Franklin, with whom he founded the deist 'Club of Thirteen' (or 'Wednedays Club') to which Josiah Wedgwood (father of Tom and Josiah Wedgwood, friends of Wordsworth and Coleridge, and the latter's benefactors), belonged, and satirized in 1781 in a long poem entitled *Orpheus, Priest of Nature and Prophet of Infidelity*, he was a polymath: preacher, deist (his creed was ironically said to be 'I believe in God, amen'), religious thinker, reformer of dissenting liturgies, educationalist, historian, translator of Voltaire, admirer of Rousseau, interpreter of Montesquieu, disciple and critic of Hartley, political theorist and pamphleteer, and founder of the Literary Fund. He was the author of *The Philosopher* (1771), which the Cambridge liberal John Jebb, one of the founding members of the Society for Constitutional Information, greatly admired; *A Treatise on Education* (1774), which Coleridge borrowed from Bristol Library in 1796; *A Liturgy on the Universal Principles of Religion and Morality* (1776), which was enthusiastically received by Frederick the Great of Prussia, Voltaire and Rousseau;[50] *Letters on Political Liberty* (1782), a classic of eighteenth-century political theory and a defence of the American colonists which Williams claimed influenced French revolutionary thought;[51] *Lectures on Political Principles* (1789); *Lessons to a Young Prince by an Old Statesman* (1790), the second edition of which contained a lengthy attack on Burke's *Reflections on the Revolution in France* and is likely to have been one of the 'master pamphlets of the day' (*The Prelude* (1805), IX, 97) which Wordsworth says he read; *Observations sur la dernière constitution de la France* (1793), an examination of the

French constitution of 1791 written at Paris in 1792–3; and, of course, *The History of Monmouthshire* (1796), into which, as I shall show, so much of his political experience is distilled.

Elijah Waring in his *Recollections and Anecdotes of Edward Williams* remarked that '[David Williams] was . . . one of those "odd fishes", that often turn up on the fluctuating surface of human affairs in times of agitation, and swim with particular buoyancy in the surge and swell of popular opinion',[52] while Julia Wedgwood's verdict in *The Personal Life of Josiah Wedgwood the Potter* was that he 'was one of those men who produce more effect on their contemporaries than posterity can readily account for'.[53] It is Williams's status as a model for the 1790s that I now want firmly to establish since 'posterity' has radically underestimated his seminal influence on many writers and thinkers of that decade, Wordsworth included.

It was as the author of *Letters on Political Liberty* and the *ad hominem* attack on the 'political Swedenbourg' Burke and his 'unintelligible enigmas' in *Lessons to a Young Prince*[54] – as one of the major polemicists of the Revolution Controversy, that is – that Williams was invited to Paris in November 1792 to take part in the debate on the French Constitution of 1791 and in the framing of a new constitution following the *journée* of 10 August 1792. In the great age of constitution-framing, therefore, it was Williams who was asked to help forge this archetype of France's new political system. He was already much respected in France, owing mainly to the high esteem in which he was held by Brissot de Warville, whom Williams had met in England in 1783–4 and 1788–9. It was Brissot who introduced his Girondin colleagues – Madame Roland amongst them – to Williams's political thought. In his article on Brissot in *Biographical Anecdotes of the Founders of the French Republic* (1798), Williams represents himself as Brissot's instructor, styling himself Brissot's 'English master', his 'English interpreter' and his 'mentor', and stating in his autobiographical *Incidents in My Own Life which have been Thought of Some Importance* (written 1802–3) that he was 'in some degree an instrument' for preparing Brissot for his rôle in the revolution. Brissot in turn, Williams claimed, referred to him as his 'oracle'.[55] In his memoirs, Brissot described Williams as 'of all English men of letters the one who seems to me to have the most universal philosophy and the most detached from all national prejudices'.[56] From an early stage, Brissot took a strong interest in Williams's work as an educationalist and political thinker and arranged for a French translation of the *Letters on Political Liberty* to be

David Williams by J. F. Rigaud (1774)
(*by permission of the Royal Literary Fund and the Paul Mellon Centre for Studies in British Art*).

made (by Anne Gédéon Lafitte, Marquis de Pelleport) for which he was imprisoned and interrogated in the Bastille in the summer of 1784. Brissot and Williams corresponded regularly during the early years of the revolution, with Williams offering advice on how to strengthen the political position of France. It was through Brissot that Williams, together with Thomas Paine, Richard Price, Joseph Priestley, James Mackintosh, William Wilberforce and George Washington, was granted honorary French citizenship on 26 August 1792; his gracious letter of acceptance was read out in the Convention on 13 November by Roland.[57] Wordsworth had just arrived back in Paris from Orléans. With Paine, Williams was asked to stand for the Convention. Paine accepted; Williams wisely declined.[58]

Williams arrived in Paris as a constitutional adviser during the first week of December 1792. Mary Wollstonecraft, who had reviewed Williams's *Lectures on Education* (1789),[59] was to arrive in Paris a matter of days later. Wordsworth might have left Paris for England as early as late November, but it is possible he was still in the city in early December; it is safe to assume that he had left by 22 December. Both men saw Paris at a crucial stage of the revolution. It was a time of upheaval. Williams's potential usefulness as a political mentor was from the first undermined by 'The general spirit of faction' which Williams perceived was rife:

> I had not been in Paris a week when I perceived I could be of no use. The Convention was dividing into factions, while the Commune of Paris was seizing its power and the whole country crumbling into anarchy. The trial of the King, the whole of which I attended, gave me a perfect knowledge of the talents and spirit of the Convention, which proceeding on no principle, either of a constituent, legislative, or judiciary assembly, led the way in the career of criminal confusion, which hazarded the existence of France as a nation.[60]

Only a few days after his arrival, he found himself in the middle of the Jacobin–Girondin struggle for power. On 7 December, a letter was produced by Chabot in the Convention informing the President that Citizen Williams, amongst others, wished to act as defence counsel to the King. The document caused a great stir. Upon examination, the signatures were found to have been forged. Robespierre, who, in the same breath, called Williams and Paine traitors and hypocrites, became thoroughly suspicious of the Welshman.[61] Despite the relative secrecy surrounding his business in Paris,[62] it is clear that Williams had a dangerously high profile in early December.

Amid all this intrigue, Williams was asked to 'write down [his] objections' to the Constitution of 1791; Paine at this time was also acting as an adviser to the Committee of Constitution. Williams delivered his report – later translated and published as *Observations sur la dernière constitution de la France* – to Brissot in January 1793, and his political thought can clearly be seen to inform the (ultimately abortive) new Girondin constitution.[63] Diplomatic relations between France and England were worsening by the day, and Williams was asked by Brissot, Roland and Le Brun to act as ambassador to London. He wisely rejected the offer but agreed to deliver 'in [his] own private character . . . any papers they chose to send into the hands of Lord Grenville, and say everything he would permit me to say to prevent a war'.[64] At the end of January, Williams was present at a council at Clavière's house to hear a draft of the report on diplomatic relations which Brissot was to deliver to the Convention the following day. He persuaded Brissot to remove 'most of the criminating passages, some of them being mistakes and others impolitic, the council professing a strong desire to avoid the war'.[65] The next day in the Convention, however, Brissot delivered the report unchanged, the immediate result of the speech being nothing other than the French declaration of war on Britain and Holland. Williams states that Brissot's hair 'literally stood on end, and he left the tribune with strong symptoms of despondency and horrour [*sic*]'.[66] That night at dinner, 'with expressions of dissatisfaction and even fear in his countenance', Brissot explained: 'It is done, the Committee would have it; if we had hesitated, the Mountain would have taken the business out of our hands.'[67]

On the same evening, it was again proposed that Williams deliver a letter to Grenville in which Le Brun, suggesting an alliance between the English government and the Girondins, revealed how a war might be averted. As Williams's namesake, the historian David Williams, remarks:

> This letter . . . is unique in the history of diplomacy unless there is another example of a foreign secretary on the day on which his country had declared war writing to the foreign secretary of the enemy country to express his regrets and make overtures for peace.[68]

Williams returned to England with this diplomatic commission in

February 1793 but got no further than Aust, the Undersecretary of State. 'I . . . did not press myself uselessly on Lord Grenville', Williams remarks, 'and I did not write to him, that the contents of my letter might not reach France and send the Girondist government instantly to the guillotine.'[69]

The frame of mind in which Williams returned to England was similar to that in which Wordsworth also left France, and the concurrence of their French experience lies at the heart of the model Williams offered Wordsworth from now on. Although Williams had defended a nation's right to cashier and execute its king in *The Philosopher*, he was shocked by the execution of Louis and the factional hatred of the Convention. Disillusioned with what he regarded as the Girondins' ignorance of human nature and of the laws governing political society, their rashness, and their failure to establish the government of France on a stable constitutional base that would guard against Jacobin usurpation,[70] he renounced an active rôle in revolutionary politics:

> I withdrew from the political arena, not from fear, though I had some reasons for fear, not from change of principles or connections, but from despair occasioned by the ignorance and impetuosity of those reformers to whom power seemed to have been delegated only by chance . . . From this chaos of good and evil, or of principles and passions, I withdrew into my own private circle, attending occasionally to the slow growth of an institution I had commenced for the establishment of a *literary fund*.[71]

'I was received on my return as a partisan of France', Williams remarks, and his visit to France made him notorious. His reputation was tarnished, his company shunned, his movements monitored and his servants and neighbours questioned. He was later to consider what his fate would have been had he not been a staunchly non-party man. Only his rigorously independent stance, he claims, saved him from the kind of persecution meted out to John Thelwall, driven westwards in late 1797 to Williams's Wales, and the other defendants in the 1794 Treason Trials:

> If my name had been found in the lists of any of the societies pretending to be patriotic, I should have been committed to the tower with Hardy, Tooke &c – and the man who first discerned the features

of Jacobinism in Europe, who first wrote against it,⁷² and who, on that account, had the honour of being calumniated by Chabot in the Jacobin Club of Paris as the messenger of Pitt, loaded with four millions sterling to save Louis XVI, would have been tried in England for high treason, and acquitted, to be spit [*sic*] upon as an acquitted felon by the foul mouth of a sanguinary partisan.⁷³

Here, Williams knows himself to be both a model for Thelwall, Hardy, Horne Tooke and other English radicals harassed by Pitt's repressive measures and a Thelwall *manqué*. He is recognizing in the phrase 'acquitted felon' both his proximity to and distance from those freed in the Treason Trials of 1794, to whom William Windham, then Secretary at War, referred in the House of Commons on 20 December 1794 as 'acquitted felons'.⁷⁴ In turn, Thelwall himself would have perceived Williams to be a haunting second self who ultimately escaped his own experience of defeat and exile, profiled in Chapter 5. From their 'retirement' at Stowey and Alfoxden, Wordsworth and Coleridge would surely also have viewed Williams's experiences as a parallel of their own trajectories.

Williams's contract with the miniaturist and entrepreneur Robert Bowyer to write a continuation of Hume's *History of England* fell through when Bowyer was informed that Williams had accepted French citizenship. Peter France remarks that the achievement of the *History of Monmouthshire* in 1796 seemed 'a port in the storm'.⁷⁵ Madame Roland's gracious remarks in her *Appeal to Impartial Posterity* (English translation, 1795) did much to rehabilitate Williams's public image as a model reformer in the late 1790s; on 12 October 1795, Joseph Ritson wrote to his nephew: 'I perceive he has a very advantageous character in the *Memoires* of *citoyenne* Roland.'⁷⁶ Wordsworth is certain to have read the *Appeal* shortly after Pinney brought a copy to Racedown in January 1796.⁷⁷ 'For cool discussion in a committee, or the regular labours of a legislator', Madame Roland states,

> I conceive *David Williams* infinitely more proper than [Thomas Paine]. Williams . . . was invited by the government to repair to Paris, where he passed several months, and frequently conferred with the most active representatives of the nation. A deep thinker, and a real friend to mankind, he appeared to me to combine their means of happiness, as well as Paine feels and describes the abuses which constitute their

misery. I saw him, from the very first time he was present at the sittings of the assembly, uneasy at the disorder of the debates, afflicted at the influence exercised by the galleries, and in doubt whether it was possible for such men, in such circumstances, ever to decree a rational constitution. I think that the knowledge which he then acquired of what we were already, attached him more strongly to his country, to which he was impatient to return. How is it possible, said he, for men to debate a question, who are incapable of listening to each other? . . . Williams is equally fit to fill a place in the parliament, or the senate, and will carry with him true dignity wherever he goes.[78]

Having suggested the value of seeing Wordsworth and Williams as in fundamental ways parallel cases, I would now like to offer a more detailed consideration of the relationship between them. If Wordsworth was still in Paris in early December, is he likely to have known of Williams's presence in the city? Might he even have met him there?

'The Virtue of one Paramount Mind': David Williams and Wordsworth in the 1790s

Nicholas Roe has argued that Henri Grégoire, President of Les Amis de la Constitution at Blois (whose meetings Wordsworth attended in early 1792), a delegate at the first sitting of the National Convention on 21 September 1792, and later President of the Convention, exercised a formative influence on Wordsworth.[79] Roe speaks of Wordsworth's 'proximity to – and perhaps his personal acquaintance with – the author of the French Republic', to whom Wordsworth was to refer in the *Letter to the Bishop of Llandaff* as 'a man of philosophy and humanity'.[80] Grégoire was himself an admirer of Williams's historic deist experiment at the Margaret Street Chapel in London (glanced at by Southey in his *Letters from England*[81]), where from 1776 to 1780 Williams established the first public service in Europe based on deistic principles. Williams's Margaret Street venture was accompanied by Williams's *Liturgy on the Universal Principles of Religion and Morality* (1776), which avoids all dogmatic statements of belief beyond an acknowledgement of the wisdom and goodness of a Supreme Intelligence and the moral obligations of a simple deism that celebrates Nature as implying the existence of God. The Margaret Street experiment was an event of European importance; it has been seen as in part a prototype of Hébert's Worship of Reason and Robespierre's cult of the Supreme Being in revolutionary France, and Grégoire was to emphasize its direct influence on French Theophilanthropy under the Directory.[82]

Hence the inclusion of David Williams in James Gillray's cartoon, 'New Morality; or The Promis'd Installment of the High-Priest of the Theophilanthropes, with the Homage of Leviathan and his Suite', published in the inaugural (July 1798) number of the *Anti-Jacobin Review and Magazine*.[83] Gillray depicts Williams, in the company of Paine, Thomas Holcroft, Thelwall, Robert Southey, Coleridge, Charles Lloyd and Charles Lamb, as a snake slithering over his 'Atheistical Lectures', paying homage to Larevellière Lépaux (president of the French Directory and patron of Theophilanthropy) in St Paul's Cathedral.[84] Accompanying the cartoon is a portion of George Canning's poem, 'The New Morality' (which had appeared in full on 9 July in the final number of the *Anti-Jacobin; or, Weekly Examiner*): 'TH—LW—L and ye that lecture as you go,/ And for your pains get pelted, praise LEPAUX!/ . . . All creeping creatures, venomous and low,/ PAINE, *W—LL—MS*, G—DW—N, H—LC—FT, praise LEPAUX!' (my emphasis). Grégoire and Williams finally met in December 1792 when Grégoire was president of the Convention. It is reasonable to suggest, therefore, that Grégoire expressed his admiration for Williams and emphasized the Welshman's status and influence as a religious thinker and pioneer of new forms of rational worship in Wordsworth's company at Blois.

John Oswald might also have been a link between Wordsworth and Williams.[85] We know that Williams knew Oswald, whom he met in London in the early 1780s. In a letter of November 1791 to Brissot, Williams referred to him as 'a man of Talents . . . with whom in England I have had some acquaintance',[86] and in April and May of the following year, Williams, the founder of the Literary Fund, was to provide financial support for Oswald and his family.[87] It is possible that Oswald translated Williams's *Lessons to a Young Prince* into French in 1791. David Erdman has argued that Wordsworth might have known Oswald too, and that he might have been involved during the autumn of 1792 in Oswald's plan to lead a cross-channel attack to liberate London.[88] These mutual acquaintances may have resulted in heightening Wordsworth's awareness of Williams.

But it is Brissot who provides the most probable link. On 19 December 1791, Wordsworth wrote to Richard Wordsworth: 'I was at the national assembly, introduced by a member of whose acquaintance

'New Morality' by James Gillray, published in the *Anti-Jacobin Review and Magazine* (July 1798) (*by permission of the British Library*).

I shall profit on my return to Paris'.[89] It has been suggested that this member was Brissot.[90] Brissot was a likely acquaintance of Charlotte Smith, who provided Wordsworth with letters of introduction before he left for France. J. R. MacGillivray has suggested that on his return to Paris in October 1792 Wordsworth actually lodged with Brissot and that they were 'under the same roof' when Brissot wrote to Williams on 11 November 1792 inviting him to take part in the constitutional debate.[91] Barron Field in his *Memoirs* of Wordsworth also claimed that Wordsworth had 'lived in the same house with Brissot'.[92] Although Wordsworth wrote 'a mistake' and 'There is much mistake here which I should like to correct in person' against this statement, it is fair to assume that, at this time, Wordsworth, like Wollstonecraft, was moving among the Girondins, with whom David Williams worked closely from early December onwards, and that he had some contact with Brissot in Paris towards the end of 1792.[93] It is perfectly possible that Wordsworth knew of David Williams's presence in Paris.[94] Through Brissot, they may even have been introduced.

Bearing these contacts in mind, it is tempting to believe that a high-profile and respected figure such as Williams would have provided Wordsworth with an example of political involvement that gave definition to his own political experience in the 1790s. Both men returned to England disillusioned with the course the revolution had taken and with the indecisiveness of the Girondins. Both were later to comment on the danger in which they left Brissot and his supporters – Williams in the *Incidents* and Wordsworth in *The Prelude*:

> I doubtless should have made a common cause
> With some who perished, haply perished too –
> A poor mistaken and bewildered offering . . .[95]
> (*The Prelude* (1805), X, 194–6)

As I have already emphasized, Williams was also in a dangerous position at this time. 'Yea, I could almost / Have prayed', Wordsworth says of his sojourn in Paris towards the end of 1792,

> that throughout earth upon all souls
> Worthy of liberty – upon every soul
> Matured to live in plainness and in truth –
> The gift of tongues might fall, and men arrive
> From the four quarters of the winds to do

> For France what without help she could not do,
> A work of honour . . .
>
> (X, 118–24)

Dramatically conflating Acts (2: 2–4) and Revelation (6: 2–8; 7: 1; and note Wordsworth's reference a few lines later to 'angels' and 'the end of things'), this picture of political annunciation – of the angelic, pentecostal arrival of political deliverers – relies for its effect on biblical models. I would suggest that the *full* valency of the image emerges if we also acknowledge the presence here of the contemporary model of David Williams and Wordsworth's knowledge of his mission to assist the Girondin government in framing a new constitution. Later in Book X, Wordsworth remarks that while in Paris he had not doubted that

> the virtue of one paramount mind
> Would have abashed those impious crests, have quelled
> Outrage and bloody power, and, in despite
> Of what the people were through ignorance
> And immaturity (and in the teeth
> Of desperate opposition from without),
> Have cleared a passage for just government
> And left a solid birthright to the state,
> Redeemed according to example given
> By ancient lawgivers. In this frame of mind
> Reluctantly to England I returned . . .
>
> (X, 179–89)

I suggest that David Williams provides a specific referent that grounds and gives identity to the powerful anonymity of 'one paramount mind': clearing a passage for 'just government' and leaving 'a solid birthright to the state' describe *exactly* the work of David Williams at this time in Paris.[96] It was in exactly 'this frame of mind', too, that Williams returned to England about a month and a half after Wordsworth. Furthermore, Williams's great admiration for what he called 'the astonishing genius of Alfred' and the 'perfect political liberty'[97] of the Saxon constitution (of which he kept reminding Brissot) might be informing Wordsworth's wish here to see a constitution 'Redeemed according to example given / By ancient lawgivers'.

'Mean as I was', Wordsworth states of his 1792 self,

and little graced with powers
Of eloquence even in my native speech,
And all unfit for tumult and intrigue,
Yet would I willingly have taken up
A service at this time for cause so great,
However dangerous.

(X, 131–6)

Wordsworth doubtless imagined an active rôle for himself in the Girondin–Jacobin power-struggle. At the time, David Williams – a fellow Briton, emphatically 'graced with powers / Of eloquence' and intimately engaged in 'a service . . . for cause so great' with all its attendant tumult, intrigue and danger – would have offered a palpable ideal and example to the young Wordsworth casting about for a political mission.

Williams's experience in France certainly dealt a blow to the radical in him. He greatly mistrusted political demagogues, was no political activist, and after 1793 became increasingly 'an abstract thinker on reform',[98] who, viewing politics as a science, deprecated political experimentation. His publications post-1793 adopt an increasingly conservative position. Like Wordsworth, whose ideological and geographical trajectories Williams's career follows so fascinatingly, the Welshman returned to France in October 1802 during the Peace of Amiens – not to visit a daughter, but to gauge the political climate of the Napoleonic regime as an agent of the British government.[99] But it is important to emphasize that, in spite of this marked falling off in his active intervention in radical politics, Williams certainly remained well known as a radical and freethinker in London's political circles during the 1790s. His presence in the summer of 1798 in Canning's poem, 'The New Morality', and in Gillray's subsequent illustration of it, is obviously to be interpreted in terms of his 'atheistical' writings on religious philosophy and his influence on French Theophilanthropy, but mentioned in Canning's poem in the same breath as Thelwall, Paine, Godwin and Holcroft, and surrounded in Gillray's cartoon by the foremost radicals of the day, the author of *Letters on Political Liberty*, *Lectures on Political Principles* and *Lessons to a Young Prince* is certainly foregrounded (literally) as a 'venomous' *political* presence to be reckoned with. Clearly, he was regarded as the originator of many of the ideas that forged radical identities in the 1790s. An anonymous anti-jacobin tract of 1791, *A Defence of the Constitution of England*, sets

Williams's 'genius, or learning, or knowledge' above Paine's, and refers to Williams and 'the American Spy' (Paine) as the most dangerous of the British radicals (pp. 1–7, 59). Another publication of the same year, *The Civil and Ecclesiastical Systems of England Defended and Fortified*, argues that passages in Paine's *The Rights of Man*, Part I, are clearly indebted to Williams's work (pp. 6–7). Referring in 1799 to Williams and the Literary Fund, William Gifford in the *Anti-Jacobin Review* commented: 'We have heard, indeed, that its founders were men neither remarkable for the purity of their religious tenets, nor for the soundness of their political principles.'[100] Discussing the Temple of Reason established by the 'Friends of Morality' in 1796 at Nichols' Salesroom in Whitecross Street, William Hamilton Reid in *The Rise and Dissolution of the Infidel Societies in this Metropolis* (1800) remarked that 'the lectures there delivered were generally compiled from the writings of Voltaire, David Williams, and other authors, distinguished for their rancour or prejudices against Christianity'. He added that:

> neither the gentleman, then known by the appellation of the Priest of Nature, and who delivered deistical lectures in his chapel, in 1775–6, nor his congregation, should, by any means, be ranked with those pestiferous clubbists of late date; although it unfortunately happened that this renewal of a dangerous profession of false philosophy continued the concatenation of Infidelity nearer to the aera of the French Revolution, which, afterwards co-operating with those principles, increased the number of English Infidels beyond all precedent.[101]

John Thelwall, writing from political exile at Llyswen, Brecknockshire, was to refer at some length to Williams in the context of Reid's account in an anonymous article enjoining religious toleration for theists published in the *Monthly Magazine* of September 1800.[102]

A short while after his return from France and his withdrawal from active political engagement, Williams's writings were praised by the young Joseph Gerrald in his *A Convention the only means of saving us from Ruin* (1793). After his own return from France, Wordsworth was to become well acquainted with London's radicals. He and Williams would have had a number of mutual radical acquaintances, and Williams and his writings are sure to have been often mentioned. Wordsworth first met Godwin on 27 February 1795 as an ardent admirer of *Political Justice*; Williams had met Godwin while *Political Justice* was still being written, and the Welshman was one of the radical thinkers with whom Godwin discussed his great work in progress. Godwin wrote in his journal for 1792:

> During this year I was in the singular position of an author possessing some degree of fame for a work unfinished & unseen – I was introduced on this ground to Mr Mackintosh, David Williams, Joel Barlow & others, – & with these gentlemen together with Mr Nicholson and Mr Holcroft; had occasional meetings in which the principles of my work were discussed.[103]

His entry for 9 September 1792 runs: 'Dine at Mr Holcroft's: tea Major Jardine's with Holcroft, D. Williams, Barlow, Major Derham'.[104] Holcroft, whom both Wordsworth and Coleridge were later to meet, already knew Williams since he had attended Williams's Margaret Street Chapel and its successor, the London Philosophical Society.[105]

George Dyer admired Williams as a political theorist and refers frequently to his political writings in his own work. Williams appears as 'an ingenious writer' in Dyer's *Inquiry* of 1792, which repeatedly cites Williams's *Lectures on Political Principles* (1789).[106] The *Lectures* are cited again in Dyer's *Complaints of the Poor People of England* (1793) and in his *Memoirs of Robert Robinson* (1796), in which Williams and Edward Williams appear as 'two well-informed' men 'among the modern Welch'.[107] Wordsworth certainly read the *Memoirs*: he was presented with a copy by Dyer in 1796 and was later to describe the work to Crabb Robinson as 'one of the best books of biography in the language'.[108] Under the heading 'Poverty and Distress of Men of Letters' in his *Dissertation on the Theory and Practice of Benevolence* (1795), which Wordsworth is also known to have read,[109] Dyer wrote:

> It is only a year or two that a SOCIETY TO SUPPORT AUTHORS IN DISTRESS was constituted. The plan of this society, is drawn up with much good sense, and, it is hoped, requires only to be more widely known, to be more generally encouraged.

He proceeds to quote the constitution of the 'society' – the Literary Fund – and remarks: 'The above constitution was drawn up by David Williams, the author of many excellent political writings'.[110] Williams appears once again as the framer of constitutions. Dyer at this time would have known of Williams's trip to Paris in 1792–3; by mentioning both the Literary Fund's constitution and Williams's 'political writings', Dyer's compliment seems deliberately to be raising political ghosts.

Radical Benevolence: David Williams and the Literary Fund

The Literary Fund, later the Royal Literary Fund, which still exists today, was the brainchild of David Williams. Williams's withdrawal 'from the political arena . . . into [his] own private circle' (*Incidents*, 24 and 37), occasioned by his experiences in France and by the climate of repression instigated by Pitt, should not be seen as a wholesale retreat from political commitment. After 1793, that commitment merely operated in a different form. Williams's influence on 1790s culture (and, as we shall see, on the poetry written squarely *out of* that culture) is further illuminated by an exploration of the way in which the Literary Fund's operations were rooted in the radical culture of the decade. Williams had broached the idea of a fund for needy authors as early as 1773, but it was not until the late 1780s that he began to pursue his project with vigour. 'The Friends of the Literary Fund' was established in 1788, and two years later the Fund became a reality. From 1793, a well-advertised programme of anniversary dinners including the recitation of poems, glees, numerous toasts and a band was devised in order to raise the Fund's profile. Despite the fact that over the course of the first decade of its existence political reactionaries such as John Reeves (founder in 1792 of the Association for Preserving Liberty and Property Against Republicans and Levellers) and William Thomas Fitzgerald were to become prominent officers of the Fund, a number of noted reformers sat on its Committee in the early 1790s, including James Martin, President of the Society for Constitutional Information, John Hurford Stone, Alexander Jardine and William Frend, Coleridge's mentor at Cambridge and George Dyer's friend.[111] Subscribers to the Fund included Gilbert Wakefield, Capel Loft and John Wilkes. John Nichols, publisher of *The Gentleman's Magazine*, played an important part in the establishment of the Fund and served as its printer. Dyer himself was closely associated with the venture in its early years and knew David Williams well. He did much to publicize the Fund, listed the cases for its brochure in 1795 and occasionally recited poems at anniversary dinners. In late 1801, when, as Lamb light-heartedly records in a letter to John Rickman, Dyer was neglecting to feed himself and had become a 'nipt carcase', the Fund 'voted him seasonably £20'. 'If I can help it', Lamb states, 'he shall spend it on his own carcase.'[112] In 1799, Dyer himself was to inform David Williams of the financial plight of Edward Williams, who had already received 10 guineas in 1795.[113] Dyer's letter to the Bard of Liberty fascinatingly locates the operations of the Literary Fund within the radical culture of the 1790s –

> I accidentally heard, that you was [sic] in distress on account of pecuniary matters. I mention'd it to David Williams and I proposed to him to procure you something from the literary fund. He thought you ought to state your case exactly; and if you was to send it to him, he would do what he could for you . . . I write this at Wakefields [sic], who is preparing to go to Dorchester jail for two years, on account of his Reply to the Bishop of Landaff.[114]

– as does another letter of 16 April 1801 to the Welshman on Literary Fund business, which refers to Thomas Fysshe Palmer, one of the 'Scottish Martyrs' sentenced to seven years' transportation in 1793 for disseminating reformist tracts, and again to Williams's friend, Gilbert Wakefield:

> With you and your family I exceedingly sympathize and wish it was in my power to do more than sympathize – The Literary Fund have voted you twenty pounds; – and would, I doubt not, repeat their attentions and civility if you would be open and unreserved in stating your case . . . (for you have many friends among them), and punctual in acknowleging [sic] the receipt of monies . . . David Williams informed me, that you had not acknowleged [sic] the receipt of the twenty pounds, which exceedingly perplexed him . . . From Palmer I have not heard a long time – He is likely to settle, I hear, in B[otany]. Bay. Wakefield was not well, when I heard from him.[115]

These two letters poignantly frame the tragedy of Wakefield, incarcerated (May 1799–May 1801) for writing a *Reply* (1798) to the Bishop of Llandaff's *Address to the People of Great Britain* – yet another answer to Richard Watson to set alongside those of Williams and Wordsworth. Less than four months after his release, Wakefield was dead.

In May 1796, Dyer apprised the Literary Fund Committee of the difficult financial situation of a twenty-four-year-old poet whose wife was expecting their first child. The young poet in a financial fix was Samuel Taylor Coleridge, and on 19 May the Fund presented him with 10 guineas.[116] It is significant that only a month later, on 13 July, at a time when he was considering various teaching posts as a means of supporting his wife and first child Hartley, who was to be born in September, Coleridge borrowed from Bristol Library Williams's first signed work, the Rousseauian *Treatise on Education* (1774), which Williams wrote when he and his wife, Mary Emilia, were expecting their first child.[117] One of the touchstones of Williams's pioneering experiential pedagogy was that the ideal school should function 'as much like well-regulated families as possible' (*Treatise*, 24); as a prospective teacher and father-to-be himself, Coleridge would have found some pertinent advice in Williams's book: 'The true idea of a tutor is the substitute of a good father; and the place of a pupil is in his family, and as much as possible as his child.'[118] Thelwall was right when, in a letter of 10 May 1796, he advised Coleridge: 'Your school project I believe to be also a very bad one; & if I know anything of human nature, you have too much genius & too intractable a spirit to make a good schoolmaster',[119] but Coleridge was to act on David Williams's advice two months after borrowing the *Treatise* by taking in Charles Lloyd as pupil and guest at his increasingly cramped house in Bristol and subsequently at his cottage in Stowey. This was the time, of course, at which Wordsworth and Dorothy were marking the progress under their tutelage at Racedown and Alfoxden of little Basil Montagu.[120] Williams's diffusive influence can once again be seen operating across a range of cultural concerns.

Dyer published the poem he delivered at the Literary Fund's dinner on 3 May 1798 in his *Poems* of 1801:

> Address to the Society for establishing a Literary Fund for Authors in Distress on Thursday, May 3, 1798, at the Free Masons Tavern*
>
> *[NOTE] For an account of this Institution, as founded by David Williams, author of various political works, and of the History of Monmouthshire, see my Dissertation on the Theory and Practice of Benevolence

> > WELCOME, ye generous circle, who, remov'd
> > From Party's froward bickerings, and the rage
> > Of the Blood-monster war . . .

>   . . . here social sit
> A little GOSHEN; round whose sacred seats
> Benevolence spreads wings, and Pity meek
> Sheds, as from heav'n, its gentlest dew-drops down.
> . . .
> Enough of 'evil days, and evil tongues';
> Oft have you heard the tale of wild distress . . .
> . . .
> Of suffering genius, by hard fortune gall'd
> Death-stung by envy, or, in perilous times,
> Heart-harrowed by some tyrant's iron hand . . .[121]

Dyer's reference to 'the Blood-monster war', 'perilous times' and 'some tyrant's iron hand' locates the efforts of the Literary Fund firmly within the political context of 1790s and its increasingly embattled radicalism. The pointed allusion to the danger in which republican Milton found himself after the Restoration – 'though fallen on evil days, / On evil days though fallen, and evil tongues' (*PL*, VII, 25–6) – deepens the political resonance of the piece. Clearly, Dyer's association with the Fund was rooted in his belief in the central importance of compassion and benevolence on which he wrote so sensitively – and for Wordsworth, Lamb and Coleridge, so influentially[122] – in his *Dissertation on the Theory and Practice of Benevolence*. 'True benevolence', he wrote,

> is desirous of advancing human beings to all the innocent comforts of which their nature is capable, and of mitigating those distresses, to which by their own frailties, or the injustice of others, they are exposed – Ignorance, slavery, imprisonment, sickness, disappointment, and old age, have their distinct claims, and form a separate interest in a good man's heart. (p. 21)

The passage could stand as the Declaration of the Literary Fund, which Williams founded specifically to *practise* benevolence and to 'mitigat[e] those distresses, to which by their own frailties, or the injustice of others, [human beings] are exposed'.

In Dyer's address of 1798, it is 'Benevolence' that spreads its wings around the Literary Fund's 'sacred seats', and it is no surprise that Dyer quoted the Fund's Constitution in the *Dissertation* and referred with his usual admiration to David Williams. Nicholas Roe reminds us that Dyer was completing the *Dissertation* when Wordsworth and Dyer first met on 27 February 1795 in the company of Godwin, Frend and Holcroft – all acquaintances of Williams.[123] Coleridge was already corresponding with Dyer, whom he had met the previous year. Roe conjectures that the subscription organized by Frend and James Losh, amongst others, for the defendants in the recent Treason Trials would have been a topic of conversation on 27 February; Dyer was to mention the subscription in the *Dissertation*:

> [The author] has been given to understand, that a plan is now forming among some respectable persons, to bring before the publick several of the above cases; and it is to be hoped, the plan will comprehend every case of real distress throughout the country connected with pretended treasons or sedition. (p. 58)

Once again, the parallels with the efforts of the Literary Fund are obvious. Significantly, Williams in his history of the Literary Fund, *Claims of Literature* (1802), was to declare: 'If [justice] cannot yet be rendered by the laws . . . we must endeavour to administer the best substitute for it we can afford, in the corrective humanity of the SOCIETY FOR A LITERARY FUND.'[124] At this moment, then, David Williams's brain-child represented an interesting literary reflex of the 'plan now forming' among some of the foremost radicals of the day. Dyer's involvement with the Fund was a reflex of his own radical beliefs. With this in mind, it is perfectly possible that that other fundraising body, Williams's Literary Fund, whose aim was likewise to 'comprehend every case of real distress throughout the country', was among the topics Wordsworth, Dyer, Godwin, Frend and Holcroft discussed on 27 February 1795. Williams's involvement with the Literary Fund should therefore be viewed as in no way a retreat from social and political commitment but rather a central expression of the nature of his dissent post-1793.

The History of Monmouthshire, Tewdrig, and 'the still, sad music of humanity'

The account of David Williams's status as an important model for his culture which I have just offered should allow us to recognize that his influence could be both clearly acknowledged (by such writers as Dyer and Godwin) and more subtly processed. In turning back to explore the influence of Williams's *History of Monmouthshire* on Wordsworth's (and Coleridge's) poetic productions of the late 1790s, I will argue that the distinctive landscape vision articulated by Williams in that work – one which comprehends notions of radical benevolence and political awareness – together with the valency of the hermit Tewdrig achieve their full and complex resonance only when we locate them in the context of both Wordsworth's and Williams's involvement in the political and literary culture of the 1790s.

Just as Coleridge had borrowed Williams's *Treatise on Education* from Bristol Library in July 1796, so Joseph Cottle, publisher of *Lyrical Ballads*, was to borrow *The History of Monmouthshire* from the same place on 10 September 1799.[125] It was Dr Thomas Hooper of Pant-y-Goitre, Monmouthshire, as early as 1791, who suggested to Williams that he write a history of the county. John Morgan of the august Tredegar family, who traced their lineage back to Ifor Hael ('Ivor the Generous'), the patron of the great medieval Welsh poet Dafydd ap Gwilym, became one of the chief sponsors. It is no ordinary county history. The variety of genres with which it flirts reflects the polymath in Williams. The product of his experience as an educator, preacher and political theorist, it is audaciously heterogeneous: now a work of history, now of political theory, now of philosophy. Edward Williams congratulated his friend on his achievement in a letter that appropriately brings together history, philosophy and landscape:

> I have read your History of Monmouthshire with more pleasure than I ever found in any thing historical relating to Wales that ever was known to me. your observation on the manners and characters of the different ages and periods that came in review before you are in my opinion extremely Just, and as the Abbe De Mobley justly observes of what some, not many Historians have done, the remarks are short and comprehensive, not so tedious as to detain the readers [*sic*] attention too long from the narrative[.] you, as it were keep on still in the track of History, and without quitting it, look about, observe the various different Sceneries, near and distant, and delineate them as they appear to the eye. this if my metaphor is in any degree correct is making History the vehicle of Philosophical research after Truth, at the same time not suffering Philosophy to quit its vehicle and stroll abroad into long winding and very often dark ways, quite out of sight, never properly returning to the point whence it wandered, and redundantly exhibiting [*sic*] delineations of things that are too remote to be seen from the path which ought to have been kept in . . .[126]

As we have already seen, William Enfield in the July 1796 issue of the *Monthly Magazine* made a point of praising the depth of Williams's political as well as historical research – 'by no means usual among those dry compilations, which, for the most part, appear under the title of County Histories'. The reviewer in the *English Review* found the book to be more the work of the philosopher in Williams than of the historian in him,[127] while the *Analytical Review* drew attention to the political writings that lie behind the *History*, describing Williams as 'a firm friend of civil and religious liberty'.[128] In the *Cambrian Register*, however, we find Theophilus Jones, author of *A History of the County of Brecknock* (1805 and 1809), commending the absence of 'revolutionary reveries' in the work:

> On this rock we expected the man whom the wary old *Franklin* coaxed and amused for his services, by calling him *the English Rousseau*, would have broken his neck. Despotism, priestcraft, and oppression! the very sounds, we thought, would have disordered his imagination, and led him into revolutionary reveries. The tendency of the whole history is of a contrary nature . . .[129]

Jones also teasingly implies that Williams has learned from his mistakes in France. It is certainly true that Williams's political perspective in the *History* is marked by a commitment to caution in political affairs –

> But the lessons of [a wise and benevolent] philosophy must be from history, not from romance . . . the disciples of Montesquieu row along the shore, and are perpetually entangled by shoals and bays; those of Plato and Rousseau sail directly into the ocean, and they all perish. The political compass is not discovered, or it is not generally known; and until the discovery be fully made, the chances of safety will be thought near the shore, and not on the ocean.[130]

– and such passages clearly reflect Williams's disillusionment with the rashness of the Girondins, the bloody zeal of the Jacobins and the more inflammatory pronouncements of the British 'Friends of Freedom'. In his laudatory letter to Williams, Edward Williams went on eloquently (perhaps taking his cue from the above passage from *The History of Monmouthshire*) to position the *History* and Williams's political work of 1790, *Lessons to a Young Prince*, in relation to a model of *gradual* political reformation:

nothing will take now but what flatters the Errors, the vices, the *Crimes* of this unfortunate age. but I hope it will not be always so. who knows what may take place, when a prince to whom in his youth a most excellent letter was addressed having profited by its advice, may be seen on the throne. at least I hope a change for the better, and that a gradual amelioration of some things will take place. I say gradual, for I am persuaded now and indeed have ever been since I began to think on such things, that and [*sic*] abrupt, excessive and violent alteration of things however bad they may be will hardly ever succeed, will be productive of more evil than good. the Sun's heat of July however more desireable [*sic*] than the frost of Winter, would kill us by coming abruptly upon us in January, whose cold *vice versa* would equally destroy coming suddenly in July. all the opperations [*sic*] and Changes of Nature are softly and benignly gradual. the gradations of Spring and Autumn, of the progress from infancy to manhood &c should be our models in that progressive reformation which we would endevour [*sic*] to introduce.[131]

But it is important to emphasize that despite *The History of Monmouthshire*'s comments regarding the dangerous unknowability of the political compass, Williams's concern with social injustice remains very much in evidence throughout the work. Passages of topographical description and historical analysis give way to a more general discussion of the principles of political justice:

The division of labor [*sic*], is the principle of perfection in all occupations; but it separates men into classes, and is the source of acts of injustice and pretensions of despotism. A species of rotation, in all employments, is probably the true principle and foundation of justice and liberty.[132]

Williams's decision to view Monmouthshire's history from the Roman occupation onwards from a philosophical and political perspective afforded him the opportunity of establishing principles of 'justice and liberty' at every turn. Indeed, the *British Critic* viewed *The History of Monmouthshire* as the work of an opportunist who was using topographical and county history for the purposes of political propaganda: 'We cannot be induced to think that a county history is a suitable field for the insinuation of political theorems or religious prejudices'.[133] Williams expertly brings various discourses of the 1790s to bear on one another, and county history and topographical description in Williams's hands emerge as surprisingly 'suitable' and effective fields for such 'insinuation'.

As well as influencing the 'composite' scene at the beginning of 'Tintern Abbey' and the poem's emphasis on Tintern's contemplative atmosphere, Williams's book would also have played a rôle in educating Wordsworth into the deeper historical vision of which the submerged presence of the hermit-king Tewdrig is part. And here, Nicholas Roe's term, the 'Miltonic Picturesque', is again relevant. As noted earlier, George Dyer in the *Monthly Magazine* approvingly quoted Williams's description of the landscape of Monmouthshire:

> The beauty of Monmouthshire . . . is not dependent on single scenes or particular features; it is the result of all the circumstances, which form the whole surface of the County . . . The whole County forms one exquisite landscape . . . thickets indefinitely diversified, where objects, as the traveller moves, seem perpetually to peep and retire; turrets rising in coverts, and ruined arches almost buried within them; mutilated castles and mouldering abbeys partially concealed; hamlets, churches, houses, cottages and farms, are blended into one general and extensive scene, which is wonderfully picturesque . . . (*Hist. of Mon.*, 9–10; *MM* 2 (1796), 866–7)

Superficially, it is a landscape of harmony, retirement, concealment; its man-made features, which Nature appears to be quietly appropriating, engage the tourist in a coy game of picturesque hide-and-seek. But this passage is followed in Williams's *History* by an important statement which Dyer does not quote:

> But the contemplation of these scenes, must be exchanged for the occurrences and events that have occupied them; the principal objects of the Author being the good and evil, the light and shadow, of human action. (*Hist. of Mon.*, 10)

The turn is striking. Williams's 'but' marks the moment at which the blent air of the Picturesque is exchanged for the moral *chiaroscuro* of the Miltonic, the point at which the theorist's unproblematic melding ('blended into one general and extensive scene') of human and natural detail is exchanged for the historical vision that comprehends the human suffering, the wars, which lie behind the landscape. Such a vision sees Nature as inescapably, perpetually 'occupied' (Williams's word, carrying appropriate political overtones) by history. Certainly, Williams does his bit for fashionable picturesque theory in the *History*, at one point even counselling the reader faced with a beautiful natural prospect near Caerleon to avert his 'imagination' from the disturbing socio-political realities represented by 'the views of ruined splendors, produced by oppression and shaded by the exhalations of human blood'.[134] In the passage quoted above, however, he sees in Nature the contours of history, recognizing the need for the kind of landscape vision which, in the words of 'Tintern Abbey', penetrates into 'something far more deeply interfused' (l. 97). This is the historically aware sense of place, the responsive and responsible act of reading the landscape as witness of human tragedy, imagined by the Pastor in Book VI of *The Excursion* –

> Ah! what a warning for a thoughtless man,
> Could field or grove, could any spot of earth,
> Show to his eye an image of the pangs
> Which it hath witnessed; render back an echo
> Of the sad steps by which it hath been trod![135]
> (*PW*, V, 212; ll. 806–10)

– and dramatically emphasized in Book VIII of *The Prelude* ('a sense / Of what had been here done, and suffered here / Through ages – and was doing, suffering, still – / Weighed with me') and in the second *Essay upon Epitaphs*.[136] John Thelwall's *The Peripatetic* (1793) articulates a similarly historicized view of landscape: 'But every scene is to the topographer a memento of the ravages of ambition, and the miseries of erroneous policy'.[137] This acute sense of Nature as historical memento, which emphatically rejects the 'oversights' of picturesque theory, is one of the distinctive features of Williams's *History of Monmouthshire*. Emphasizing the need to *textualize* Nature – to link her forms with the human history underlying them and read the moral and political meanings inscribed in the landscape – Williams, like Keats, sees into the 'eternal fierce destruction'[138] behind the natural scene and order. What I want to suggest here is that Williams's work played a part in the educative process which Wordsworth describes in 'Tintern Abbey':

> For I have learned
> To look on nature, not as in the hour

>   Of thoughtless youth, but hearing oftentimes
>   The still, sad music of humanity . . .
>   (*LB*, 118; ll. 89–92)

'The still, sad music of humanity' – one of the 'gifts' Wordsworth celebrates – is therefore not as abstract as it sounds; it is rooted in the referents I have been resurrecting. Wordsworth would have recognized Tewdrig, the hermit-king of 'Tintern Abbey', whose story he read in *The History of Monmouthshire*, to be part of the historicized vision articulated by David Williams. Likewise, Wordsworth's invocation of this image of solitude would have been understood by his contemporaries as mediating a wider public debate in the late 1790s concerning the claims of retirement and public duty, escapism and activism. George Dyer's contributions to the *Monthly Magazine*, stressing how valuable the topographical historian could be to the poet, had shown Wordsworth that Williams's work could 'assist a poet . . . by retouching . . . the objects already pictured in his eye; by completing the picture, and thus, by increasing the sensations, and strengthening the conceptions, the topographer may give energy and precision to the poet'. The hermit of 'Tintern Abbey' is a significantly overdetermined figure comprising various personae: he is an actual historical presence, a poetic self-projection, a representative of the sham hermits of the great eighteenth-century estates, a 'sally of the fancy'. By alerting Wordsworth to his historical specificity, Williams's *History of Monmouthshire* is, in Dyer's words, 'completing the [historical] picture' and 'increasing the sensations'.

Though submerged (just as 'the light and shade of human action' lie behind the beauty of the landscape for Williams), the hermit's significance as a patriot-king called out of retirement to defend his people against foreign invasion problematizes any interpretation of the figure as mere picturesque staffage, an image of tranquil contemplation or an escapist fantasy. Far from marking one of those spaces in 'Tintern Abbey' in which New Historicist critics see painful realities being 'displaced' or 'elided' by the 'private' poet, and far from figuring an abdication of responsibility on the part of a man, in Levinson's words, 'in flight from a dreaded reality', this hermit, who emerged from his retirement to face martyrdom in the cause of liberty, embodies political duty and 'the still, sad music of humanity' with all its 'solitude, or fear, or pain, or grief'.[139] Alan Liu's analysis of Wordsworth's negotiation with political realities in Book VI of *The Prelude* emphasizes the poet's ultimate denial of history, first by means of the deflecting mirror of Nature and climactically in the Simplon Pass episode by the triumphant 'objectified subjectivity' of the Romantic self/Imagination.[140] However, Liu's method here is more subtle than Levinson's on the issue of absence versus presence in that it acknowledges Wordsworth's struggle with history (in the shape of Napoleon), his *inscription* of 'background reminders of historicity' and the *presence of history in its denial* (though he remains evasive, I think, as to the self-consciousness or otherwise of such inscription). My reading of the hermit figure certainly shares some of Liu's methodology, but our conclusions differ in that I see no final overwriting of history by Nature or the Imagination at work in 'Tintern Abbey'. What the figure of the hermit marks is a conscious insistence on history, not a denial of it. The hermit is to be read – in *The History of Monmouthshire* and in 'Tintern Abbey' alike – as a presence whose political identity prefigures that of David Williams himself, whose active involvement in politics was renounced in disillusionment but whose political commitment continued to be expressed in subsequent projects and publications throughout the 1790s. The hermit, then, is a far more complex 'self-projection' than Levinson allows. Wordsworth locates him seated by his fire. While this initial 'contemplative' state suggests perhaps the Wordsworth of the 1798 tour – a man seeking 'tranquil restoration' after the shocks of political disillusionment – the hermit's future rôle as warrior-king, called out, like Williams, to face a culture of 'evil tongues', 'sneers of selfish men' and 'greetings where no kindness is', is a reminder of the active involvement in the revolution imagined by Wordsworth's former, radical self of 1793, of the writing of his radical *Letter to the Bishop of Llandaff* and of the rôle in the revolution played by David Williams. The hermit also embodies Wordsworth's recognition that a poet contemplating the great work of his life – broached by Coleridge in March 1798 and significantly entitled *The Recluse*[141] – ought to be ready to speak boldly from, or even be called out of, contemplative retirement in order to rally those who 'in consequence of the complete failure of the French Revolution, have thrown up all hopes of the amelioration of mankind, and are sinking into an almost epicurean selfishness, disguising the same under the soft titles of domestic attachment' (Coleridge to Wordsworth; *CL*, I, 527)[142] and to oppose the unjust aggression of the great European powers – England included – just as Wordsworth had opposed what he had perceived to be the aggression of England *against*

France in 1793. In addition, the very overdetermination of the hermit figure marks historical presence itself as unstable and embattled, something to be fought for, something that ought never to be erased.

The hermit of 'Tintern Abbey', then, is emphatically not the hermit of Book IV of the 1850 *Prelude* – a straightforward embodiment of a state of restorative, 'benign' solitude undisturbed by socio-political cares:

> When from our better selves we have too long
> Been parted by the hurrying world, and droop,
> Sick of its business, of its pleasures tired,
> How gracious, how benign, is Solitude;
> How potent a mere image of her sway;
> Most potent when impressed upon the mind
> With an appropriate human centre – hermit,
> Deep in the bosom of the wilderness;
> Votary (in vast cathedral, where no foot
> Is treading, where no other face is seen)
> Kneeling at prayers . . .
> Or as the soul of that great Power is met
> Sometimes embodied on a public road . . .
>
> (1850, IV, 353–66)

This hermit is safely at a remove from 'the hurrying world', or in the words of 'Tintern Abbey', 'the 'fretful stir / Unprofitable, and the fever of the world' (ll. 53–4). But it is significant that the human incarnation of solitude which is profiled next in Book IV, 'embodied on a public road', is a very different one: that of the deathly solitary that is the Discharged Soldier (a disturbing presence to whom I want to return in Chapter 3). The harmonious lines on the hermit in 1850 contrast starkly with, and are instructively undercut by, this image of desolation 'akin to solitude' (1805, l. 419) and symbol of the effects of contemporary conflict on the human frame and soul. Taken together, these two images of solitude conspire to produce a *frisson* similar to that generated by the presence of the hermit in 'Tintern Abbey' – one which once again questions the moral and political propriety of solitude and of a merely picturesque view of landscape oblivious to the human tragedy at its heart.

The interplay between 'Tintern Abbey' and two poems by Coleridge – 'Reflections on Having Left a Place of Retirement' (first published in the *Monthly Magazine* in October 1796 and included in *Poems*, 1797) and 'Fears in Solitude', written in April 1798 'during the alarm of an invasion' (which Wordsworth would have seen in manuscript[143]) – represents a wider contextual fabric against which the significance of the hermit figure should also be interpreted. 'Tintern Abbey' absorbs into itself the debates dramatized in Coleridge's two conversation poems. All three poems address a contemporary personal and political predicament in the context of a landscape poem. No critic has drawn attention to the fact that, broadly speaking, all three share a similar tripartite structural logic.[144] In the first movement of each, the poet gazes over an apparently blessed landscape; in the second, more troubling thoughts and recollections disturb the harmony of the scene, the need for active involvement in a world of strife and fear is emphasized, and 'delicious solitude' ('Reflections', l. 58) and complacent renunciation of the world are rejected; in the final movement, the poet reverts to a communion with a landscape of tranquil restoration, but now with a chastened awareness of duty and of the threat of future crises.[145]

In this sense, both Coleridge poems represent important templates for 'Tintern Abbey'. Like 'Tintern Abbey', the opening of 'Reflections' describes 'the little landscape round' which is 'green and woody and refresh'd the eye', before moving to describe the wider vista from the 'stony Mount' which reveals the winding river, 'the Abbey, and the wood, / And Cots, and Hamlets',[146] while 'Fears in Solitude' opens with 'A green and silent spot, amid the hills! / A small and silent dell!'[147] The spiritual forms and sounds of the landscape in 'Reflections' can be heard only 'When the Soul seeks to hear; when all is hush'd / And the Heart listens!', as is the case in 'Fears in Solitude', in which the 'senses' of 'the humble man' who reads 'Religious meanings in the forms of nature' are 'gradually wrapp'd / In a half-sleep' – compare the second verse paragraph of 'Tintern Abbey' in which the 'sensations sweet' of 'These forms of beauty' are 'Felt in the blood, and felt along the heart' and the 'blessed mood' is attained when one is 'laid asleep / In body, and become a living soul'. The final lines of 'Reflections' vow that the poet's spirit 'shall revisit thee, dear Cot!', which, as Paul Magnuson has noted,[148] is appropriated by Wordsworth in 'Tintern Abbey': 'How oft, in spirit, have I turned to thee / O sylvan Wye!' Specific phrases in 'Fears in Solitude' are also consciously echoed by Wordsworth: 'All sweet sensations, all ennobling thoughts', from a pantheist passage in which Coleridge articulates his debt to the landscape of his 'mother Isle', is echoed in Wordsworth's own expression of gratitude – 'I have owed to them, / In hours of weariness, sensations sweet' – while Coleridge's 'No speculation on contingency, / However dim and vague' is recapitulated in 'Tintern Abbey' as 'With many recollections dim and faint'. These verbal echoes and shared motifs remind us that Coleridge is yet another informing presence in 'Tintern Abbey'.

My point here is that Wordsworth's meditation in 'Tintern Abbey' gains stringency and amplified political significance from its negotiation (on both verbal and structural levels) with these Coleridgean models and also from the landscape vision of Williams's *History of Monmouthshire*, which would itself have reactivated and deepened the resonance in Wordsworth's mind of the central sections of the two Coleridge poems in which threatening contemporary realities are confronted. 'Was it right', Coleridge asks himself in the second movement of 'Reflections', transporting himself back to Clevedon:

> While my unnumber'd Brethren toil'd and bled,
> That I should dream away the trusted Hours
> On rose-leaf Beds, pamp'ring the coward Heart
> With feelings all too delicate for use?
> . . .
> Yet even this, this cold Beneficence
> Seizes my Praise, when I reflect on those,
> The sluggard Pity's vision-weaving Tribe!
> Who sigh for Wretchedness, yet shun the Wretched,
> Nursing in some delicious solitude
> Their slothful loves and dainty Sympathies!
> I therefore go, and join head, heart, and hand,
> Active and firm, to fight the bloodless fight
> Of Science, Freedom, and the Truth in CHRIST.
> (*Poems*, 1797, 103)

The example of Tewdrig, who had fought a *bloody* fight for 'Freedom, and the Truth in CHRIST', of David Williams himself, whose political disillusionment did not blunt his social and political conscience, and of the Coleridge who at the end of 1795 was about to re-enter the lists as editor of *The Watchman*, gives a deep political valency to Wordsworth's hermit and to the 'gift', partly Williams's, of having 'learned / To look on nature . . . hearing oftentimes / The still, sad music of humanity'. Coleridge's imaginative transfiguration of the landscape of his Quantock paradise in the central section of 'Fears in Solitude' –

> O my God,
> It is indeed a melancholy thing,
> And weighs upon the heart, that he must think
> What uproar and what strife may now be stirring
> This way or that way o'er these silent hills –
> Invasion, and the thunder and the shout,
> And all the crash of onset; fear and rage,
> And undetermined conflict . . .
>
> (*FiS*, 2–3)

– would have reminded Wordsworth of the forces that were in the summer of 1798, three months only after Coleridge wrote his poem, still threatening his own Wye paradise, and which had once encroached on Tewdrig's retirement on the banks of the Wye. And the hard-won 'chearful faith' of 'Tintern Abbey' notwithstanding, these lines would also have served to activate the need for the politically aware and penetrative landscape vision enjoined by David Williams in *The History of Monmouthshire*: 'But the contemplation of these scenes, must be exchanged for the occurrences and events that have occupied them; the principal objects of the Author being the good and evil, the light and shadow, of human action'.

Finally, the radical benevolence at the heart of the Literary Fund's operations is also relevant to the notion of political commitment enshrined in the hermit-model. Nicholas Roe has drawn attention to the contiguity in Coleridge's writings of the 1790s, Wordsworth's poetry of the late 1790s and Dyer's *Dissertation on the Theory and Practice of Benevolence* of ideas on the motivated relationship between landscape, moral behaviour and benevolence. On 10 March 1795, Coleridge wrote to Dyer:

> It is melancholy to think, that the best of us are liable to to be shaped & coloured by surrounding Objects – and a demonstrative proof, that Man was not made to live in Great Cities! . . . The pleasures, which we receive from rural beauties, are of little Consequence compared with the Moral Effect of these pleasures – beholding constantly the Best possible we at last become ourselves the best possible. In the country, all around us smile Good and beauty . . . (*CL*, I, 154)

In his *Dissertation*, published in the same month, Dyer wrote in a similar vein:

The GOOD MAN from the appearances of nature derives tender affections, generous principles, and humane conduct. From the glowing and variegated scenes around him he derives something which warms his heart, and throws a smile over his countenance . . . The good man thus acquires universal tenderness. (*Dissertation*, 19)

Wordsworth's blank verse fragment of March 1798, 'Not useless do I deem', a draft conclusion to 'The Ruined Cottage', similarly establishes a link between the contemplation of tranquil Nature and man's benevolent, active efforts on behalf of humankind:

> . . . the man
> Once taught to love such objects as excite
> No morbid passions, no disquietude
> No vengeance and no hatred, needs must feel
> The joy of that pure principle of love
> So deeply that . . .
> . . . he cannot chuse
> But seek for objects of a kindred love
> In fellow-natures, and a kindred joy.
> Accordingly he by degrees perceives
> His feelings of aversion softened down,
> A holy tenderness pervade his frame . . .
> . . .
> All things shall speak of man, and we shall read
> Our duties in all forms; and general laws
> And local accidents shall tend alike
> To quicken and to rouze, and give the will
> And power by which a [ ] chain of good
> Shall link us to our kind.
> (*MoH*, 269–70; ll. 3–14, 36–41)

Again, communion with Nature leads inevitably (there is much of David Hartley's philosophy here) to social involvement and action. As Roe notes, such spring 1798 lyrics as 'Expostulation and Reply' and 'Lines Written at a Small Distance from My House' are informed by the same notion. 'Here', Roe remarks, 'Wordsworth's joy in companionship resembled Dyer's belief that natural benevolence was a social virtue, realised through acts of practical compassion'.[149] Roe goes further and claims that the influence of Dyer's pamphlet operates also in a central passage of 'Tintern Abbey' at a 'moment of Romantic exultation' in which 'the kindly aspect of . . . Dyer's dissent is fulfilled in a vision of transcendent harmony'.[150] In that passage, it is to 'forms of beauty' that Wordsworth owes 'feelings . . . / Of unremembered pleasure':

> . . . such, perhaps,
> As may have had no trivial influence
> On that best portion of a good man's life;
> His little, nameless, unremembered acts
> Of kindness and of love.
> (*LB*, 117; ll. 32–6)

In the context of the profile I have offered of David Williams's *History of Monmouthshire* and his involvement with the Literary Fund, I would argue that not only Dyer's, but Williams's influence, too, is at work here. Williams was a central figure in the construction of a discourse of benevolence in the late 1790s. Williams's emphases in *The History of Monmouthshire* on the moral lessons of history, on 'habits of virtuous temper and beneficent activity', were surely in part developed in conversations with his good friend Dyer, who in 1794–5 was writing his *Dissertation*. Early in his work, Williams is careful to establish a link between the forms of Nature and the cultivation and practice of benevolence which was also being discussed by Dyer, Coleridge and Wordsworth around this time:

> It is not the intention of the Author, to rival the Tourist in description. Scenes certainly affect the temper. The beautiful and picturesque in nature aid moral causes, in inducing tranquillity, mildness, and benevolence, in the native inhabitants: while rocks, precipices, and torrents, are supposed, not without probability, to incline the mind to irritation and passion. (*Hist. of Mon.*, 6)

Those lines in 'Tintern Abbey' on the 'best portion of a good man's life; / His little, nameless, unremembered acts / Of kindness and of love', as well as the other Wordsworth poems cited above, can be seen to take their cue from the example of *The History of Monmouthshire*. Even more pertinently, of course, the model David Williams offered Wordsworth as founder of the Literary Fund – that high-profile organ of 'practical compassion' that was a central expression of Williams's political identity and involvement after his return from France – should also be seen as interfusing these passages. It is a model that would have clarified in Wordsworth's mind one of the central tenets of *The History of Monmouthshire*: that Nature's forms should not and do not offer an experience of escape and forgetfulness but rather one that 'quicken[s] and rouze[s]' one's social and political consciousness, conscience and memory.

2
Models of Betrayal and Flight: Vortigern

Speaking 'bare truth' to Coleridge in Book X of *The Prelude*, 'As if . . . in private talk', Wordsworth, in the context of his account of Robespierre's Terror, recalls the feelings of fear and guilt he experienced 'Through months, through years, long after the last beat / Of those atrocities':

> . . . in dreams I pleaded
> Before unjust tribunals, with a voice
> Labouring, a brain confounded, and a sense
> Of treachery and desertion in the place
> The holiest I knew of – my own soul.
>   (*The Prelude* (1805), X, 376–80)

And in the 1850 version:

> . . . a sense,
> Death-like, of treacherous desertion, felt
> In the last place of refuge – my own soul.
>   (X, 413–15)

Wordsworth is speaking both of the experience of having been betrayed by a revolution he initially welcomed but which soon turned bloody and of a confounding sense of his own insertion as treacherous accessory in the course that revolution had taken. As one would expect, acts of betrayal were central to the experience of many of the major political and cultural figures of a revolutionary decade, and in this chapter I want to identify a resonant model of betrayal in an emblematic figure to whom Wordsworth and others responded at moments of crisis during the 1790s. This prototype of betrayal is an illuminating example of how a culture of antiquarianism intersected with, and was co-opted by, radical discourse in a decade in which political disillusionment and recantation followed swiftly on the heels of an initial pledge of cheerful faith and hope.

As is the case with David Williams, the culture's negotiations with my second model range from explicit engagements to subtle, more elusive and allusive traces. And as with Williams and his hermit, this figure offered not one but many, multi-valent paradigms of identity. Once again, it is with what I see as one of the 'tremor[s] of anxiety'[1] in 'Tintern Abbey' that I wish to begin the identification of this archetype for the 1790s, since the context of Wordsworth's description at the exact centre of that poem of a troubled and traumatized former self is useful in focusing the significance of this figure in 'Tintern Abbey' as a whole and also in the wider culture in which the poem is embedded.

Significantly, tradition holds that one of the sites of this prototype's own political crisis was the Wye Valley – no scene, as I have already argued, of 'tranquil restoration' – and in considering his tragedy and trajectory, a picture emerges of that rifted, traumatized space as a haunted refuge not just for Wordsworth but for other hunted political pariahs aware of the area's links with disturbing avatars with whom they readily identified as second selves. The Wye Valley becomes a site of cultural confluences, unstable political and cultural identities, and 'awkward cross-currents of ideological loyalties'.[2] The perception and experience of Wales and its borderland in the 1790s cannot therefore be dismissed as merely 'touristic'; I have already stressed that the influential type of landscape vision enshrined in David Williams's *The History of Monmouthshire* was one which conflated politically aware and 'aesthetic' views of landscape and topography. The ways in which this second prototype was mediated to the receptive consciousness of 1790s culture reveal once again how the discourses of topographical history and the tour played a part in clarifying – and problematizing – contemporary cultural and political allegiances.

Acknowledging that 'Tintern Abbey' is a poem in which Wordsworth in the summer of 1798 'dare[d] to hope', Nicholas Roe has also focused our attention on the way in which the poem is haunted throughout by political disillusionment and by the 'misgivings and betrayal [Wordsworth] had endured five years before'.[3] 'Tintern

Abbey' emerges from Roe's critique as a fraught 'intersection of a meditative philosophic poem with the revolutionary experience of the decade'. The poem's subtitle-date, which, as already noted, activates a number of personal and political anniversaries and associations, its mode of 'assertion and simultaneous reservation' and its 'conditional mood' which disturb Wordsworth's 'repeated claims to faith', together with the haunting echoes in its opening lines of a poem written in 1793 at the Isle of Wight, discussed below – all these serve as 'subdued reminder[s]', ghostly presences, of personal loss and revolutionary failure. Roe establishes Wordsworth's experience of *betrayal* as central to the fabric of 'Tintern Abbey', remarking that the poet's claim that 'Nature never did betray / The heart that loved her' is 'modified by its implied recollection of other and earlier betrayals, even in the prayer of "chearful faith" with which the poem concludes'.[4]

Writing 'Tintern Abbey' in July 1798, Wordsworth recalls his late July/early August 1793 visit to Tintern by cryptically contrasting past and present selves:

> And so I dare to hope
> Though changed, no doubt, from what I was, when first
> I came among these hills; when like a roe
> I bounded o'er the mountains, by the sides
> Of the deep rivers, and the lonely streams,
> Wherever nature led; *more like a man*
> *Flying from something that he dreads, than one*
> *Who sought the thing he loved.*
> (*LB*, 118; ll. 66–73; my emphasis)

The identity of this 'something that he dreads' has been the subject of much discussion. Having returned from revolutionary France in late 1792, leaving behind Annette Vallon and the infant daughter he would not meet until August 1802, Wordsworth in the summer of 1793 was facing an uncertain future. A summer tour with William Calvert began inauspiciously. July 1793 was spent on the Isle of Wight, and with 'a spirit overcast, a deep / Imagination, thought of woes to come, / And sorrow for mankind, and pain of heart' (*The Prelude* (1805), X, 304–6), Wordsworth watched the British fleet gathering in the Solent for war with France, where his political sympathies and private attachments lay. The scene was described at the time in the poem 'How sweet to walk along the woody steep' – 'But hark from yon proud fleet in peal profound / Thunders the sunset cannon; at the sound / The star of life appears to set in blood' (*PW*, I, 308; ll. 15–17) – verbal echoes of which, as Roe has convincingly argued, haunt the opening passage of 'Tintern Abbey' and 'identify changes in Wordsworth himself' between 1793 and 1798.[5] In the 1842 'Advertisement' to 'Guilt and Sorrow', the revised version of 'Salisbury Plain' (composed 1793–4), Wordsworth stated that he left the Isle of Wight 'with melancholy forebodings. The American war was still fresh in memory. The struggle which was beginning . . . I was assured in my own mind would be of long continuance, and productive of distress and misery beyond all possible calculation.'[6] Back on the mainland, Calvert's carriage was wrecked when his horse dragged it into a ditch. Proceeding alone to visit Robert Jones at Plas-yn-Llan, Llangynhafal, in north Wales, Wordsworth crossed Salisbury Plain on his way to Tintern with very little food and in a feverish state of mind. The *Prelude* account of the experience graphically records a vision of ancient Britons, druids and human sacrifice at Stonehenge.[7] For Jonathan Wordsworth, it is these traumas, this sense of having betrayed and been betrayed, that lie behind Wordsworth's simile in 'Tintern Abbey'.[8] Referring likewise to Wordsworth's personal anxieties, Mary Moorman asks: 'And from what was he flying but from the torment of his own thoughts and memories?'[9] Richard J. Onorato argues that Wordsworth's bounding roe evokes an image of 'startled deer fleeing into a protective landscape' – 'The suggestion is of fleeing from man, as Wordsworth was at the time . . . after having had a dreadful experience of the world of men'[10] – while Harold Bloom, more questionably, writes: 'Why is Wordsworth so afraid of time in *Tintern Abbey*? Surely it *is* time that is the hidden reference in the enigmatic: "more like a man / Flying from something that he dreads than one / Who sought the thing he loved".'[11]

I, however, want to suggest a new interpretation of the lines from 'Tintern Abbey' by identifying a different 'hidden reference' in Wordsworth's image of himself as a fugitive. It is one which gives a deeper historical resonance to a simile whose cryptic generality is ordinarily glossed as embodying the emotional shocks of Wordsworth's personal and political experience in the early 1790s. A second self can be seen to inhabit the verse: the ghost of a political figure whom Wordsworth and his contemporaries viewed as a compelling model of their own experience of disillusionment, defeat and betrayal that 'haunted [them] like a passion'.

Tintern's associations with the hermit-king Tewdrig have already been explored. The Wye Valley around Tintern is also traditionally associated with another, more famous Dark Age figure: Vortigern. This early fifth-century Brythonic king – a historical figure around whom many myths have gathered – is known in Welsh tradition as the arch-traitor Gwrtheyrn, whose act of political betrayal resulted in the loss of Britain to the Saxons. He figures as the *superbus tyrannus* (proud ruler) of Gildas's *De Excidio Britanniae* (*c*.547), is mentioned by the Venerable Bede in the *Historia Ecclesiastica Gentis Anglorum* (731), and versions of his story are related at length by Nennius in the *Historia Brittonum* (*c*.796), and by Geoffrey of Monmouth in the *Historia Regum Britanniae* (*c*.1136).[12] In later centuries, as I shall show, the powerful historical exemplum of betrayal, flight and retribution enshrined in the Vortigern story was to claim the attention of historians, travel writers, poets and dramatists from Holinshed, Drayton and Milton to Goldsmith, Thomas Pennant, William Warrington, William Henry Ireland and John Thelwall.[13]

In Geoffrey's *Historia*, Vortigern has King Constans assassinated and usurps the throne, forcing the British princes Aurelius Ambrosius and Utherpendragon to seek asylum in Armorica. Beleaguered by the Picts, Vortigern enlists the military support of the newly arrived Saxons under Hengist and Horsa. At a banquet, he lusts after Hengist's daughter Renwein (Ronwen or Alice in other versions) whom he marries, conceding Kent to the Saxons. Having massacred the British nobility at a peace conference at Amesbury, the Saxons take advantage of their foothold and overrun the kingdom. The massacre became the subject of a potent myth known as 'The Treason of the Long Knives'[14] which was to rankle long in the Welsh consciousness,[15] and which, in other versions, was located at Stonehenge itself. Lines from 'Salisbury Plain' – 'Though treachery her sword no longer dyes / In the cold blood of Truce' (ll. 428–9) – attest that Wordsworth was familiar with this incarnation of the tale. The harried Vortigern is eventually pursued to the Wye Valley by a vengeful Aurelius Ambrosius, who has returned to claim the kingdom. I quote Aaron Thompson's 1718 translation of the *Historia*, and Geoffrey's Latin:

> And when the People were urgent to fall upon the *Saxons*, [Ambrosius] disswaded them from it, because his Desire was to pursue *Vortegirn* first. For the Treason committed against his Father so very much affected him, that he thought nothing done till that was first revenged. In

Pursuance therefore of this Design, he marches with his Army into *Cambria*, to the Town of *Genoreu*, whither *Vortegirn* had fled for a safe Refuge. That Town was in the Country of *Hergin*, upon the River *Gania* [super fluuium guaie], in the Mountain called Cloartius . . . Immediately . . . they set their Engines to work, and laboured to beat down the Walls. But at last, when all other Attempts failed, they had Recourse to Fire, which meeting with proper Fuel, ceased not to rage, till it had burnt down the Tower and *Vortegirn* in it.[16]

Geoffrey localizes the demise of the fleeing Vortigern in the Wye Valley:[17] Genoreu is present-day Ganarew, a few miles above Tintern Abbey; the river Gania ('guaie') is the Wye; Cloartius, overlooking Ganarew, is Little Doward Hill,[18] the site of a fine prehistoric fort. Wordsworth would have passed through Ganarew and seen the two prominent hills of Great and Little Doward in the summer of 1793, on 11 July 1798 on his way to Goodrich Castle, and again the following day on his way down to Chepstow. In addition, a number of contemporary guides to the Wye Valley focus the attention of tourists on the Doward Rocks; as I have already noted, Mary Jacobus[19] argues that Wordsworth is almost certain to have seen Richard Warner's *Walk Through Wales, in August 1797* (1798), which singles out the Doward hills as 'a very grand feature of the Wye'.[20]

Daniel Defoe in his *Tour through the Whole Island of Great Britain* (1724) noted that 'the stories of Vortigern, and Roger of Mortimer, are in every old woman's mouth' in 'the yellow mountains of Radnorshire'.[21] And in 1805, Theophilus Jones in his *History of the County of Brecknock* glossed the current Welsh proverb 'Sais yw ef, syn!' (He's a Saxon – Beware!) with reference to the Treason of the Long Knives myth:

> The treachery of the Saxons, whom the aboriginal Britons introduced into the island as friends and allies, and their cruelty in exterminating in cold blood the nobility of the antient [sic] inhabitants (as is said to have been done on Salisbury Plain) still rankles in the bosoms of the indigenous sons of freedom.[22]

Prys Morgan has drawn attention to the currency of the Vortigern story in Welsh literature and in the Welsh consciousness from the medieval period to the nineteenth century.[23] But would Wordsworth and his contemporaries have known of the strong associations of this part of the Wye Valley with the fugitive Vortigern, who also came to this spot 'among these hills', a few miles above Tintern Abbey, 'more like a man / Flying from something that he dreads, than one / Who sought the thing he loved'?

Wordsworth and Vortigern: The Evidence

Prior to 1798, Wordsworth would have encountered versions of the Vortigern story in Goldsmith's *History of England*,[24] Chatterton's 'The Battle of Hastings',[25] David Williams's *History of Monmouthshire*,[26] and possibly Drayton's *Poly-Olbion*.[27] He was obviously familiar with it by 1821 when the majority of the *Ecclesiastical Sketches* were composed:

> The Pictish cloud darkens the enervate land
> By Rome abandoned . . .
>   . . . Awed by her own knell,
> She casts the Britons upon strange Allies,
> Soon to become more dreaded enemies
> Than heartless misery called them to repel.
> (Part I, ix, 'Dissentions'; *PW*, III, 346; ll. 8–14)

As Duncan Wu points out, Wordsworth certainly knew Geoffrey's *Historia* in Aaron Thompson's translation by late 1814/early 1815 since Thompson's work is one of the acknowledged sources for 'Artegal and Elidure'.[28] Wu also notes that Wordworth – a fairly frequent user of Robert Southey's library – may have known Thompson's book before that date since, on 16 November 1807, Southey told C. W. Williams Wynn that he owned a copy of 'the English "Geoffrey of Monmouth"'.[29] An earlier acquaintance, again through Southey, with Geoffrey's work cannot be discounted. Southey's familiarity with the *Historia* is evident as early as 1796 when he contributed a piece to the *Monthly Magazine* of September 1796 correcting a correspondent who had signed himself 'Meirion' – the Welsh scholar and lexicographer William Owen Pughe – on a number of issues relating to the *Historia*.[30] Wordsworth, who had first met Southey the previous year, is certain to have seen this article, since in March 1797 James Losh sent Wordsworth 'Monthly Magazines from Feby to December 1796 inclusive'.[31]

Moreover, it is clear that during the 1790s, the Wye Valley's associations with the fleeing Vortigern and his army were known to tourists.

The 1799 edition of Charles Heath's *Excursion Down the Wye from Ross to Monmouth* tells of the discovery in 1700 of 'the bones of a man of very large and uncommon stature . . . in the cavity of a rock, part of the mound and fence of the antique camp on *Little Doward*'.[32] Heath goes on:

> it may not be thought a meer [*sic*] fanciful conjecture . . . to surmise, the bones of the tall man . . . might possibly belong to one of VORTIGERN'S OFFICERS, or great men, who fled from the defeat at the battle at *Amesbury* . . . and secreted himself . . . in the rock part of the encampment on *Little Doward*.[33]

After offering another localization of the tale ('We well know, that Vortigern retreated . . . into Radnorshire, where he immediately built for himself a Castle . . . and in which he was destroyed by fire'[34]), Heath provides a brief biography of Vortigern. The 1803 edition of the *Excursion Down the Wye* cites in addition the Galfridian version of the story:

> Vortigern was burnt by Aurelius Ambrosius and his army, by applying fire to the tower to which he had flown for security in the *Town of Genoreu*, which lies on the banks of the river WYE, near the town of Monmouth, which still retains its name.[35]

In the *Historia Brittonum*, Nennius gives another account of the fate of Vortigern: 'After . . . all the men of his nation had risen against him . . . and whilst he himself is wandering vagrant from place to place, at last his heart broke and he died without praise.'[36] It is perfectly possible that Wordsworth, who, as so much of the poetry of the 1790s attests, was fascinated by restless wanderers – 'Even something of the grandeur which invests / The mariner who sails the roaring sea / Through storm and darkness, early in my mind / Surrounded too the wanderers of the earth'[37] – heard of the area's links with the fugitive Vortigern as he passed through Ganarew in 1793 and 1798. Heath knew Coleridge, and included his 'Lines Written at the King's Arms, Ross, formerly the House of the Man of Ross' in the 1796, 1799 and 1803 editions of the *Excursion Down the Wye*.[38]

Paradigms of Romantic Identity/Models of Treason

What would have been the contemporary significance of the Vortigern tale? In the context of the shocks and betrayals of the 1790s, its valency would surely have transcended the merely 'antiquarian'. That Wordsworth, on the banks of the Wye again, contemplating a haunted self of 1793, is recognizing in the lines 'more like a man / Flying from something that he dreads, than one / Who sought the thing he loved' a parallel between his 1793 self and the fugitive Vortigern is a fascinating possibility. These lines, then, mark a different registration of historical 'presence' from that represented by the image of the hermit in 'Tintern Abbey' and by the landscape vision of the poem in which the presence of David Williams is to be detected. Here, a language of ghostly allusion, read in the context of the troubling associations of place, reveals a disruptive presence in the mode of absence. Bearing in mind the lessons of *The History of Monmouthshire*'s politicized Miltonic Picturesque, Vortigern, like the hermit Tewdrig, complicates Wordsworth's search for a tranquil retreat in Nature. In the lines from the 1850 version of *The Prelude* quoted at the beginning of this chapter, it is significantly Wordsworth's 'last place of refuge' that is haunted by 'a sense / . . . of treacherous desertion'. Wordsworth's identification with the traitor seems even more plausible given his divided loyalties in 1793. For the young Wordsworth in the summer of 1793, moving westward into Wales over Salisbury Plain and through the Wye Valley, his ideological and emotional loyalty lying with the enemy, Vortigern the hounded betrayer would have been a compelling prototype – a complex human focus ('an appropriate human centre', in the words of *The Prelude*[39]) of a contemporary crisis of both political allegiance and cultural identity. A matter of weeks later at Llangynhafal with Robert Jones, as Book X of *The Prelude* records, a treasonous 'conflict of sensations' was palpably felt on hearing the news of the English defeat at the Battle of Hondeschoote. Wordsworth proceeds to describe himself meditating darkly on revenge in a Welsh church in a passage that heralds the lines quoted at the head of this chapter:

> . . . I rejoiced
> Yes, afterwards truth painful to record,
> Exulted in the triumph of my soul
> When Englishmen by thousands were o'erthrown,

> Left without glory on the field, or driven,
> Brave hearts, to shameful flight. It was a grief —
> Grief call it not, 'twas any thing but that —
> A conflict of sensations without name . . .
> When in the congregation, bending all
> To their great Father, prayers were offered up
> Or praises for our country's victories,
> And, 'mid the simple worshippers perchance
> I only, like an uninvited guest
> Whom no one owned, sate silent — shall I add,
> Fed on the day of vengeance yet to come!
> (*The Prelude* (1805), X, 258–74)

The summers of 1793 and 1798 were both times of French invasion scares, and a motley French force had actually landed at Carreg Wastad, near Fishguard in Wales, in February 1797.[40] In August 1793, and in the restrospective glances of the above *Prelude* passage and 'Tintern Abbey', Wordsworth might well have been identifying himself with the fleeing traitor, in league with an alien nation, now hounded by invader and compatriot alike; Vortigern's betrayed Britain with the England Wordsworth was betraying; and the invading Saxons with the French.

But Vortigern would have emerged as an exercising and ambiguous model. Such an identification with Vortigern and with the narrative of cultural and political defeat of the Britons by the Saxons which his story embodies is, like the 'long knives' of that story, double-edged, offering not one set of superficial correspondences — a definitive paradigm — but several complex and contradictory ones that would have given a deep historical resonance to Wordsworth's 'Welsh' experience, and thrown into relief the problematic nature of his own 'British' and 'English' identities, haunted by betrayal, in the 1790s. The Vortigern story would surely have alerted Wordsworth to the status of the English nation once more as aggressor — in 1793 at war with French, as earlier with British, liberty. His French allegiance in this respect would have activated a subversive sympathy with that older, indigenous British nation driven westward, now surviving subsumed and marginalized under a hegemonic Anglo-centric, imperialist 'Britain'. Such sympathy was indeed to be made explicit later in *The Convention of Cintra* and the *Ecclesiastical Sketches*:

Perdition to the Tyrant who would wantonly cut off an independent Nation from its inheritance in past ages . . . Look upon Scotland and Wales . . . the flashing eye, and the agitated voice, and all the tender recollections, with which the names of Prince Llewellin and William Wallace are to this day pronounced by the fire-side and on the public road, attest that these substantial blessings have not been purchased without the relinquishment of something most salutary to the moral nature of Man: else the remembrances would not cleave so faithfully to their abiding place in the human heart. (*Prose Works*, I, 328)

> Mark! how all things swerve
> From their known course, or vanish like a dream;
> Another language spreads from coast to coast;
> Only perchance some melancholy Stream
> And some indignant Hills old names preserve,
> When laws, and creeds, and people all are lost!'
> (Part I, xii, 'Monastery of Old Bangor';
> *PW*, III, 347; ll. 9–14)[41]

The Vortigern story would have played a part in sowing the seeds of this empathy. As Linda Colley remarks, Britain at this time was 'an invented nation superimposed . . . onto much older alignments and loyalties'.[42] 'The troubled west' ('Salisbury Plain', l. 37) therefore becomes the site of a radical 'otherness' that would have foregrounded Britain's internal difference in the 1790s. In a recent article, Paul Wright has argued for the identification of the young Wordsworth during that decade 'through an elaborate set of images, figures, locations and associations' with a politically radical Wales experienced as a mirror of, and substitute for, radical France. This 'spiritualized political empathy' was, of course, one reflex of the practical necessity of having to confine one's tour to the shores of Britain since war with France had closed the Continent to tourists. Wright's primary focus is 'Wordsworth's own ambivalent attraction to the figure of the druidic bard' (an aspect of which I want to consider in Chapter 4), not the figure of Vortigern, but citing Wordsworth's 'Salisbury Plain' and *The Prelude* accounts of his experiences there, Wright at one point refers to the Treason of the Long Knives to contend that 'now, in a sense, Salisbury has joined France and America and become Wales, or at least a means of expressing Welsh discontent. This was a political discontent which Wordsworth shared . . . as he journeyed towards Wales in

1793.'[43] Alan Liu's insightful, if sometimes diffuse, postcolonial analysis of Wordsworth's 'Welsh' persona in the 1790s similarly identifies his 'subversion' as informed by a Welsh 'colonial discourse' empowered by a historical imagination, a new nationalist mythology, 'aware in every moment of the relation between *then* and *now*':

> in the early 1790s the poet honed his long knife of subversion specifically upon Welsh colonial discourse – a subversive 'language' . . . that protested [against] what it took to be English imperialism exerted upon a subordinate people in Britain itself . . . For a radical just back from France, to sojourn at length in Wales . . . was to be immersed in a fulsome language of subversion 'produced' in counteraction to the Pittite repression. The Celts, we may say, were Wordsworth's vision of British sansculottes . . . Welsh colonial discourse and 'Celtism' provide a first, a minimum explanation of the subversion the poet sought to model himself upon when he came home from France and cast about for a political stance.[44]

I contend that the figure of Vortigern would have been a focus for this 'vision' and 'model' Liu describes – one which provided Wordsworth with a 'native' archetype of subversion on which his political identity was grounded after his return from France. Complicating this subversive cultural and political sympathy with the Welsh nation, of course, is Wordsworth's personal identification with Vortigern *himself*, who now emerges as an *antitype* (I take the term, appropriately, from Joseph Cottle's *The Fall of Cambria* of 1808[45]), responsible for betraying the Britons. Indeed, fresh in Wordsworth's mind in 1793 would have been his defence in the *Letter to the Bishop of Llandaff* of the execution of a contemporary traitor-king who had betrayed his nation's trust.

Another cultural paradigm operates. The Vortigern story and the sojourn in Wales would surely also have honed Wordsworth's sense of his own *Englishness*, his own Saxon 'otherness', and his being culturally implicated in the crimes against, and the betrayal of, the ancient British nation. Language and accent would have betrayed him. Fascinatingly, in a letter of May 1829 to George Huntly Gordon, Wordsworth is clearly casting an altercation he had with a Welsh parson at the Montgomeryshire seat of Thomas Thomas, one of Thomas Pennant's neighbours, during his 1791 or 1793 visit to Wales in terms of an *inverted* 'Treason of the Long Knives' scenario. The knowing reconfiguration of the model establishes the essential difference and distance between an English Wordsworth and the culture of Wales-as-France (note Wordsworth's use of French in the following quotation). It is the 'Cambro Briton' who now turns the tables on a 'vile Saxon' Wordsworth:

> an event took place so characteristic of the Cambro Britons that I will venture upon a recital of it . . . One day we sat down une partie quarrée at the Squire's Table, himself at the head; the Parson of the Parish, a bulky broad-faced man between 50 and 60 at the foot and Jones and I opposite each other. I must observe that 'the Man of God' had not unprofessionally been employed most part of the morning in bottling the Squire's 'Cwrrw' anglisé strong Ale, this had redden'd his visage (we will suppose by the fumes) but I sat at table not apprehending mischief. The conversation proceeded with the cheerfulness good appetite, and good cheer, naturally inspire – the Topic – the powers of the Welsh Language. 'They are marvellous', said the revd Taffy. 'Your English is not to be compared especially in conciseness, we can often express in one word what you can scarcely do in a long sentence'. 'That', said I, 'is indeed wonderful be so kind as to favor me with an instance?' 'That I will', he answered. 'You know perhaps the word Tad?' 'Yes.' 'What does it mean?' 'Father' I replied. 'Well', stammer'd the Priest in triumph, 'Tad and Father there you have it' – on hearing this odd illustration of his confessed notions I could not help smiling on my friend opposite; whereupon, the incensed Welshman rose from his chair and brandished over me a huge sharp pointed carving knife. I held up my arm in a defensive attitude; judge of the consternation of the Squire, the dismay of my friend, and my own astonishment not unmixed with fear whilst he stood threat[e]ning me in this manner and heaping on my poor English head every reproachful epithet which his scanty knowledge of our language could supply to lungs almost stifled with rage. 'You vile Saxon!' I recollect was one of his terms, 'To come here and insult me an ancient Briton on my own territory!'[46]

Wordsworth here is the Saxon betrayer and invader, but the long knife is being wielded by the aggressive 'ancient Briton'. A sense of the wrong done to Wales/France cohabits in Wordsworth's reworked paradigm with an awareness of threatened Englishness and of the need to defend a 'poor English head'. The passage dramatizes a sense of anxiety and identity surely not confined to his later conservative English nationalism but operative also in the early 1790s as an element of his fraught identification with Vortigern.

I have been arguing that by the time he came to write 'Tintern Abbey', the Vortigern story would have been available to Wordsworth as a paradigm of betrayal which embodied and helped focus a complex crisis of political and cultural identity experienced by the poet in 1793. This second self, whose ghostly presence in the lines 'more like a man / Flying from something that he dreads, than one / Who sought the thing he loved' is another of those sites of disturbance that Roe shows troubling the surface tension of 'Tintern Abbey'. The example of Vortigern proved valuable to the poet as an instructive model through which he could get a purchase from the perspective of the summer of 1798 on the 'conflict of sensations' experienced by a former self. By July 1798, of course, a war against French liberty had become a war against French aggression and expansion following the French invasion in early 1798 of the Swiss Cantons – a deeply troubling act that was an ideological watershed for both Wordsworth and Coleridge. Looking back to his previous visit to the Wye in the summer of 1793 in a poem that seeks to locate the distance between past and present selves ('Five years have passed . . .') as well as the contiguity between them ('I catch the language of my former heart'; 'Oh! yet a little while / May I behold in thee what I was once'), the multi-valent model offered by the Vortigern tale – traitorous subversive sympathy with France/Wales and an awareness of English allegiances – would have been useful in mapping the *distance* he had travelled ('Though changed, no doubt, from what I was') from that hunted figure he portrays. Shoring up hope for the future after revolutionary failure, Wordsworth's choice of words in the final movement of 'Tintern Abbey' is indeed telling: 'Nature never did *betray* / The heart that loved her' (my emphasis). Hearing the 'still, sad music of humanity' in the Wye Valley – the 'last place of refuge' of the traitor Vortigern – Wordsworth's prayer is motivated, significantly, by a fear of betrayal. The lines invoke Vortigern, whose presence, I contend, is also one of the 'recognitions dim and faint' (l. 60), part of the 'sad perplexity' (l. 61), with which Wordsworth's 'picture of the mind revive[d] again' in 1798. That recollection, which the disturbing associations of place and memory activate, troubles Wordsworth's search, amid fears of 'evil tongues', 'Rash judgements', 'the sneers of selfish men', and 'solitude, or fear, or pain, or grief', for a new 'anchor' and 'guide' (ll. 110 and 111) that will not in the future either betray him or incite thoughts of betrayal in him. As 'Tintern Abbey' emphasizes, Nature and an awareness of the One Life in Nature are to provide that 'anchor', but it is to be one forever haunted by 'the still, sad music' that will act as a chastening descant to Nature's more joyous songs. Nature – not considered in the abstract but viewed with David Williams's lessons regarding 'the occurrences and events that have occupied' it in mind – will now resonate for Wordsworth both with 'A presence that disturbs . . . with the joy / Of elevated thoughts' and with presences that disturb.

A Vortigern for the 1790s

My purpose so far has been to offer Vortigern as an illuminating referent in a number of profiles which Wordsworth offers of his jacobin self. In establishing Wordsworth's familiarity with that model, I have also suggested its availability and currency in the wider culture through topographical and antiquarian discourse. Wordsworth's negotiations with Vortigern should also be considered in the context of other, explicit contemporary engagements with this figure which can be seen to dramatize contemporary anxieties and political positions.

Vortigern was the subject of great interest in literary circles in the late 1790s. It was the nineteen-year-old William Henry Ireland's forged Shakespearean play *Vortigern* (performed 1796; published 1799) that gave the figure such a high profile. (As we shall see, literary forgery in the 1790s was a profoundly political enterprise which was perceived as a jacobin act of betraying history itself, of sabotaging the values and questioning the inviolability of the past.) Even Milton (as Ireland says he discovered later) had listed episodes from Vortigern's life 'in outlines for British tragedies'.[47] Indeed, the Vortigern tale can be seen to be the archetypal 'British' tragedy and narrative of the nation in that it is fundamentally about the demise of 'Britain' as a homogeneous cultural entity. Ireland's 'discovery' of a cache of Shakespearean manuscripts caused a great stir.[48] The forgeries – 'the astonishing artifices of this second Chatterton', as Joseph Ritson called them[49] – prompted many ardent defences and scholarly refutations, with the Shakespeare scholar Edmond Malone 'standing forth as generalissimo of the non-believers'.[50] *Vortigern* itself, which, as *The Briton* noted on 4 April 1796, 'from the peculiar circumstances attending it, has excited so considerable a degree of public attention', spawned a host of parodies and derivatives, such as the anonymous

Precious Relics, or the Tragedy of Vortigern Rehears'd[51] and Abraham Portal's tragedy on Vortigern's son, *Vortimer; or, the True Patriot* (1796).[52] In his *Confessions* of 1805, Ireland claimed he had gone to Holinshed's *Chronicles* for the Vortigern story, having been inspired by a copy made by his father, Samuel Ireland (who was, interestingly, to publish his *Picturesque Views on the River Wye* in 1797), of John Hamilton Mortimer's painting 'representing Rowena in the act of presenting wine to Vortigern'.[53] Indeed, during the period 1769–88, Henry Füseli, Angelica Kauffman, William Wynne Ryland, John Hamilton Mortimer and John Francis Rigaud all chose Vortigern and Rowena as historical subjects for their paintings and engravings.

After fraught negotiation between Samuel Ireland, who was also a victim of his son's imposture, and Richard Brinsley Sheridan, who from the outset was sceptical as to the play's authenticity,[54] *Vortigern* was staged at Drury Lane on 2 April 1796, with John Philip Kemble in the title rôle and Dora Jordan as Vortigern's daughter, Flavia. Kemble's sister, Sarah Siddons, was offered the part of Vortigern's wife Edmunda, but declined it, Ireland stated, 'on account of a cold under which she laboured'.[55] The theatre was packed since the newspapers had been awash with pre-performance speculation and argument; the February 1796 issue of the *Monthly Magazine*, for example, anticipated a lively debate regarding the play's authenticity. It was to remain the topic of conversation and newspaper articles during the following months[56] at a time (June–July) when Wordsworth was in London. Kemble, in league with Malone and the unbelievers, had pointedly attempted to produce the play on April Fool's Night, 'in order to pass upon the audience the compliment of *Fools All!*', as Ireland later repined.[57] The audience began to get increasingly restive during the third act, and tradition has it that they erupted during Vortigern's great speech on death in the final act when Kemble delivered the line 'When this solemn mock'ry is ended' ('And when this solemn mockery is o'er' in subsequent printings) in 'the most sepulchral tone of voice possible' and with 'peculiar emphasis', before repeating it 'with even more solemn grimace'.[58] Ireland claimed in the *Confessions* that the line was 'the *watchword* agreed upon by the Malone faction for the general howl':[59]

> *Vortigern* Time was, alas! I needed not this spur.
>   But here's a secret and a stinging thorn,
>   That wounds my troubl'd nerves. O! conscience! conscience!

> When thou didst cry, I strove to stop thy mouth,
> By boldly thrusting on thee dire ambition:
> Then did I think myself, indeed, a god!
> But I was sore deceiv'd; for as I pass'd,
> And travers'd in proud triumph the Basse-court,
> There I saw death, clad in most hideous colours:
> A sight it was, that did appal my soul;
> Yea, curdled thick this mass of blood within me.
> Full fifty breathless bodies struck my sight;
> And some, with gaping mouths, did seem to mock me;
> While others, smiling in cold death itself,
> Scoffingly bade me look on that, which soon
> Would wrench from off my brow this sacred crown,
> And make me, too, a subject like themselves:
> Subject! to whom? To thee, O! sovereign death!
> That hast for thy domain this world immense:
> Church-yards and charnel-houses are thy haunts,
> And hospitals and sumptuous palaces;
> And, when thou wouldst be merry, thou dost choose
> The gaudy chamber of a dying King.
> O! then thou dost ope wide thy boney jaws,
> And, with rude laughter and fantastic tricks,
> Thou clapp'st thy rattling fingers to thy sides:
> And when this solemn mockery is o'er,
> With icy hand thou tak'st him by the feet,
> And upward so, till thou dost reach the heart,
> And wrap him in the cloak of lasting night.[60]

Although some parts of the play evince genuine power, *Vortigern* was that night laughed off the stage.[61] Coleridge, who in the March and April issues of *The Watchman* had referred at length to Ireland's forgeries and to *Vortigern* in particular, remarked: 'In theatrical phrase, it was completely DAMNED!!'[62]

The play itself became a model by the end of the decade, making Vortigern fashionable for forgers and those with antiquarian tastes. Charles Lamb informed Coleridge on 27 May 1796 that his friend James White's comic imitation of Shakespeare, *Original Letters, &c. of Sir John Falstaff and His Friends*, published in the summer of 1796, 'took the hint from Vortigern'.[63] Lamb probably had a hand in the book's 'Dedicatyone, To Master Samuel Irelaunde' (William Henry Ireland, that is, who occasionally used his father's name), and was later to ask

Coleridge to review the work.[64] On 4 March 1799, William Taylor of Norwich wrote to Robert Southey: 'Have you a mind for a piece of waggery at Bristol, to find up "More Reliques of Rowley"? I have half a tragedy in stanzas, with northern mythology, choruses, and the English mis-spelt, like Chatterton's "Goddwyn": the title is *Wortigerne*.'[65] In February 1800, Taylor suggested that the play be included in the second volume of Southey's *Annual Anthology*, 'with some equivocal words of advertisement, as if it were a real Rowley or more Chattertoniana'. Southey wanted to see it in the edition of Chatterton he was preparing. Eventually, a fragment of the play was published in the *Monthly Magazine* for January 1801, with Southey supplying 'a short undated, but signed introductory letter . . . throwing out a suspicion of their being Rowleyana or Chattertonia'.[66]

But it is clear that more *political* 'hints' could be taken from *Vortigern* in the 1790s. In early 1798, Daniel Stuart sent Coleridge Sir Henry Bate and Lady Mary Dudley's *Passages Selected by Distinguished Personages, on the Great Literary trial of Vortigern and Rowena; A Comi-Tragedy* (1795–1807), which uses passages purporting to be extracts from Ireland's play to satirize contemporary public figures.[67] Stuart sent the book to Coleridge as a prototype for similar satirical portraits which he wanted Coleridge to write for the *Morning Post*.

Indeed, Ireland's *Vortigern* is to be seen as far more than a literary and antiquarian curiosity. Chapter 4 will examine the way in which the pseudo-antiquarian Bardic forgeries of my fourth model for the 1790s, Edward Williams, were emphatically an expression of his jacobin sympathies; Ireland's forgery is another example of how antiquarianism was co-opted during that decade as part of contemporary political discourse. His account of the genesis of the forgery – historical portraiture inspiring a retreat into the black-letter source-material of the chronicles – throws a rather misleading antiquarian blanket over the affair and should be balanced by an awareness of how resonant the author would have known the Vortigern story to be to a society at war with external and internal enemies. It is hardly surprising that an audience and readership acutely aware of the jacobin threat were immediately sensitive to the political valency of the tale, whose themes are, after all, civil war, regicide and treason. Damned and jeered it might have been as a forgery and artistic success, but the politics of *Vortigern*, and the implicit politics of Ireland's wider project, were certainly taken seriously. It is clear that Edmond Malone and his admirer Burke regarded the Ireland forgeries not merely as a literary scam but also as pernicious jacobin imposture. For Malone, defending Shakespeare in the 1790s against shoddy scholarship and forgery was emphatically a political act – a literary reflex of the Burkean defence of a nation's sacrosanct 'inheritance'. Peter Martin is right to see Burke's support of Malone from the early 1790s (when he pointedly sent him a copy of his *Reflections on the Revolution in France* to acknowledge the achievement and wider cultural implications of Malone's *Plays and Poems of Shakspeare*[68]) as implying that 'in Burke's mind anti-revolutionary sentiment and . . . Malone's Shakespeare work . . . shared common intellectual-political ground. They were both efforts to reassert the sanctity and inviolability of the past'[69] – against spurious and destabilizing versions of it, that is, put to dubious use in the service of contemporary jacobin ideology. 'Burke, like Malone', Martin states, 'linked literary forgery with "the false pretence and imposture" of radical philosophies that would either turn their backs on or fraudulently distort the past'.[70]

Appearing on the eve of the ill-fated performance of *Vortigern*, Malone's monumental *Inquiry into the Authenticity of Certain Miscellaneous Papers*, which definitively discredited Ireland's forgeries, was shot through with anti-jacobin feeling. In it, Malone railed against the 'detestable doctrine of French Philosophy and the imaginary Rights of Man', accusing Ireland of supporting 'those modern republican zealots who have for some time past employed their feeble, but unwearied, endeavours to diminish that love and veneration which every true Briton feels . . . for ROYALTY'.[71] He dispatched a copy to Burke, who, as Martin notes, 'celebrated the *Inquiry* as honouring the nation and its ideals – exaggerated praise, to be sure, but reflecting the pressure of the revolution felt by all cultural discourse in the 1790s'. Ireland himself was well aware of the political resonance of his Shakespeare forgeries. On 21 February 1796, Thomas Caldecott wrote to Samuel Ireland to say that 'Edmund Burke is, I know, at the head of the combination against you and Malone is his instrument. Politically against you the first, and every way as against the other'.[72] On 8 September 1795, months before the play was actually performed, *The Times* was already considering the issue of the play's authenticity in terms of the revolution controversy:

> The *pros* and *cons* between *Vortigern* and Shakspear rest their arguments chiefly on the character of the Fool, which is strongly *Democratic.* One party contends that it cannot be Shakspear's, as all his writings are

peculiarly Loyal and Aristocratic; the other, that he always stuck close to nature, and that nothing can be more natural to a fool, than *Democracy*.

The Oracle of 18 February 1796 announced: 'we understand from good authority, that the Lord Chamberlain has refused to licence the play of the new Shakspeare, upon three distinct grounds of objection — that it is immoral, indecent, and Jacobinical.' *Vortigern* therefore occasioned a very public discussion during a decade of revolutionary upheaval and government repression of the cultural and political significance of that central model of English literary achievement — and bulwark against all things French — Shakespeare.

Viewed in the context of 1796, it is certainly a politically contentious play (and one is reminded of the uses to which Shakespeare's own *Richard II* had been put two centuries earlier). The usurper Vortigern's speech on death in Act V, quoted above, is essentially a meditation on the equality of kings and their subjects, and on the ultimate leveller — death — who comes like a violent revolutionary to destroy royal power. Ireland was in fact forced to cut King Constantius's lines in Act I, scene iv —

> Though thou hast plac'd me sovereign over men,
> And on my temples bound the diadem;
> Yet am I subject still to human frailty,
> And nought can boast more than my meanest vassal.[73]

— from the performed text since a jacobinical allusion to the 'frail' George III, haunted by madness and the threat of revolution, could too readily be construed (Constantius delivers these lines before the stage directions announce: 'Enter two murderers'). Aurelius's lines in Act III, scene v, though not cut, are deeply subversive both of kingly authority and of the subject's patriotic duty at a time of war:

> O God! why should I, a mere speck on earth,
> Tear thousands from their wives, children, and homes!
> O! wherefore, from this transitory sleep,
> That now doth steal from them their inward cares,
> Should I send thousands to cold, dreary death?
> 'Tis true, I am a king, and what of that?
> Is not life dear to them, as 'tis to me?

> O! peasant, envy not the prince's lot;
> Thy page in life's great book is not foul charg'd,
> And like to ours besmear'd with dying breaths.[74]

Significantly, two years later in 'Fears in Solitude', Coleridge was to make a similar comment on the ease with which the shared humanity of those sent out to die is dismissed, though he stressed that by 1798 the guilt was that of a whole nation:

>   forth
> (Stuff'd out with big preamble, holy names,
> And adjurations of the God in heaven),
> We send our mandates for the certain death
> Of thousands and ten thousands!
> . . .
>   . . . as if the wretch,
> Who fell in battle doing bloody deeds,
> Pass'd off to heaven, *translated* and not kill'd:
> As tho' he had no wife to pine for him,
> No God to judge him!
>   (*FiS*, 5–6)

Even though the end of *Vortigern* sees 'rightful' royal power restored in the shape of Aurelius, and the traitor-king Vortigern actually spared (as he is emphatically not in the received version of the story), Ireland's play is certainly seditious inasmuch as it places in the mouths of its kings – Aurelius, Constantius and Vortigern – lines in which they themselves question their claim to power, divest themselves of divine mystery and lament the crimes committed by them and in their name. Mair has commented on the 'anachronism' of the play's 'democratic sentiments' and on 'Vortigern's un-Elizabethan deference to the voice of the people'.[75] Moreover, Ireland's decision to locate the climax of Vortigern in London, the heart of a British state at war (a departure from Holinshed, who follows Geoffrey of Monmouth), adds to the contemporary relevance of the tale. An added political *frisson* is derived from the sporadic echoes of *King Lear* (unsurprising, of course, in a forgery masquerading as genuine Shakespeare), which begin in the first act with Constantius's 'To thee one half our pow'r we here resign', are enshrined in the person and speeches of the Fool, and are highlighted at the very end of the play in Aurelius's speech after the defeat of Vortigern –

> To-morrow, Lords, we'll meet at Westminster;
> For your ripe ages and experience,
> Must teach our young and giddy years the way,
> To sow content after these dismal times.

– lines which clearly evoke Edgar's speech at the close of *King Lear*: 'The weight of this sad time we must obey; / Speak what we feel, not what we ought to say. / The oldest hath borne most: we that are young / Shall never see so much, nor live so long' (V. iii. 322–5).[76] *King Lear*, of course, represents another profoundly suggestive paradigm for the 1790s, and Ireland would have been aware of the tendentious nature of his allusions to a play about the nature of royal authority, a king's terrible madness, betrayal, civil war, and, of course, a French invasion.

A Vortigern for Welsh Radicals

At exactly the same time as Ireland was using the Vortigern story as a means of mediating contemporary political issues, a Welsh political commentator of note was also enlisting the model as a focus for contemporary Welsh cultural and political anxieties, as viewed from the perspective of the radical culture of London out of which he wrote. It was in October 1795 that Vortigern surfaced in the explicitly political context of John Jones's racy Welsh Paineite tract, *Seren Tan Gwmmwl* (The Cloud-hidden Star). Jones (*bardicé* Jac Glan-y-Gors, 1766–1821), landlord, poet and noted radical, was a prominent member of the London Gwyneddigion Society which led the Welsh cultural and political renaissance of the eighteenth century; David Williams was elected an honorary member in 1790.[77] The subtitle of Jones's pamphlet runs: 'Some remarks on Kings, Bishops, Lords &c. and the Government of England generally. Written for the monoglot Welsh'. It was widely read in Wales, and occasioned a heated and protracted paper-war in the Welsh radical periodical, *Y Geirgrawn* (The Treasury of Words, 1796), which culminated in Jones's spirited riposte.[78] Tradition has it that the author was forced to fly to his native Cerrigydrudion, Denbighshire, in order to escape prosecution – another flight to Wales by a 'traitor' that replicated Vortigern's – and in his second pamphlet, *Toriad y Dydd* (The Break of Day, 1797), Jones reported that copies of *Seren Tan Gwmmwl* had been hunted down by his political antagonists: 'clywais eu bod yn cerdded o'r naill dy i'r llall, i losgi y llyfr a ysgrifenais' (I heard that they went from house to house to burn the book I had written).[79] Jones's significant debt to Paine's *The Rights of Man* is evident throughout *Seren Tan Gwmmwl* (some passages are straight translations); his enlisting of Vortigern in the service of 1790s radical propaganda, however, is his own. Citing as a source Theophilus Evans's famous historical work, *Drych y Prif Oesoedd* (The Mirror of Primitive Ages; 1716 and 1740), which gave the Vortigern story a new lease of life in Welsh, Jones locates Vortigern firmly in the radical discourse of the 1790s:

> I wish to draw attention to how much terror mankind has suffered on account of kings since the time of Nimrod to Louis XVI of France . . . Now I will remark upon the kings and princes of our own land; firstly, a king of our own nation – Vortigern.[80]

(In his strictures on the Two Acts of 1795, Coleridge had referred to William Pitt as 'the dark Nimrod'.[81]) It is the proud, lustful, drunken Vortigern, not the broken, hunted fugitive, who appears in Jones's pamphlet, since his aim is to castigate kingship, but betrayal is still at the heart of the point being made. Vortigern is here the archetype of *all* kings, and an audacious historical sleight-of-hand discredits Vortigern (who had shown that even native British kings are traitors) and the House of Hanover:

> the drunken, wicked and senseless king (as kings are generally) lusted after [Ronwen] and wished to sleep with her that night . . . It is likely that it was in his own land that Hengist learned that kings and princes loved to feast, and drink, and whore, since Hengist came from Germany, and similarly, people from Germany came here not so long ago, and their race still loves to drink and whore and run into debt. (pp. 12–13; my translation)

Jones then enlists the legend of the Treason of the Long Knives as part of a nationalist, as well as anti-monarchic, agenda. The loss of Britain to the Saxons and the subsequent political disenfranchisement of the Welsh nation are attributed to the vices of a king. At a time when Jones's fellow-radical Edward Williams, 'The Bard of Liberty', was busily forging and reinventing Wales's Bardic past in the service of a politicized cultural renaissance,[82] Jones, too, makes Welsh history count in the Revolution Debate of the 1790s. The Vortigern story is foregrounded as a cautionary tale for political reformers and the marginalized Welsh:

> Hengist placed the Welsh and English to sit next to each other at table, and, after the feasting, as he had promised, he gave the English a signal to draw their long knives from their sleeves, and to kill the man next to him. And so they did, with as little feeling as if they were slaughtering so many pigs. And therefore nearly all the Welsh nobility were murdered in that bloody feast because of the drunkenness, foolishness, naivety and lasciviousness of their king.
>
> That was the first time that the English got the upper hand on the Welsh, and it is clear enough, that such a tragedy was the fault of their king alone. But O! that our forefathers in that age (like the people of America in this) had been without a king, or any other man who wielded the power to harm his fellow countrymen. In Vortigern we have a king who has injured his nation to this very day. Who knows that the Welsh at present would not be in possession of the whole Island of Britain, if they had taken the advice of the Lord, and avoided the curse that is a king? (p. 14; my translation)

The tale is pared down and becomes a dramatic exemplum, while a clear gloss – a readily understandable political exegesis – is supplied in the second paragraph for a monoglot Welsh audience for whom political instruction of the sort Jones offers in *Seren Tan Gwmmwl* was a new experience. A historical model that would have been familiar to that audience becomes a means of mediating 1790s Paineite propaganda to the Welsh. The canny exploitation here of the *cultural* as well as political valency of the Vortigern tale serves to illuminate further Wordsworth's negotiations with the various paradigms of cultural identity offered by that same icon of betrayal.

Vortigern and the English Radicals: The Case of John Thelwall

The final chapter of this book will discuss the way in which the hounded jacobin polemicist, political philosopher and poet John Thelwall constructed himself in a series of poems written in 1800 as a dark second self of Wordsworth and Coleridge. Here, however, I want specifically to explore Thelwall's interest in the Vortigern story as a prototype of his own political crisis in the 1790s. We have already seen how the haunted Wordsworth in 1793 fled to the asylum of the Wye Valley; that troubled site, to which Thelwall was driven in the late 1790s, also provides the focus for Thelwall's identification with the hounded betrayer. As Roe has noted in his discussion of 'Tintern Abbey', it was 'an area of historical conflict that had significance for Wordsworth's own generation as a last resort of political defeat and isolation'.[83]

The background to Thelwall's flight needs to be rehearsed briefly in order to establish the nature of the crisis he experienced in late 1797. Thelwall was the most famous orator of the London Corresponding Society, the radical movement's foremost theorist in the 1790s, and certainly 'the most representative figure of state persecution'[84] of that decade – an infamous and tragic emblem of defeat. Together with other high-profile radicals such as Hardy, Holcroft and Horne Tooke, he had been charged with High Treason and acquitted in the State Trials of 1794. Soon afterwards, the man regarded by Pitt's government as one of the most dangerous of English jacobins was effectively gagged by the Two Acts (December 1795), designed specifically to shut him down. Exploiting a loophole in the law, he embarked on a series of lectures on classical history, focusing on abuses of political power in ancient Rome in a thinly veiled comment on the political situation of his own day – another example of history made politically resonant in the 1790s. Having escaped assassins, press-gangs and Church-and-King mobs during his 1796–7 lecture tour of the provinces, the broken radical visited Wordsworth and Coleridge at Nether Stowey and Alfoxden in July 1797 during a 'Pedestrian Excursion' through England and Wales in search of 'a peaceful retreat'. Harried by the repressive Pittite State as a traitor – 'He perceived, with anguish, that, from the fury with which he was pursued, every effort he made, instead of producing the Reason he loved, only irritated to the Violence he abhorred', as he later recalled[85] – Thelwall at this moment longed for a life of sequestered, Pantisocratic retirement with Wordsworth, Coleridge and Poole, as the famous anecdote in Coleridge's *Table Talk* attests:

> We were once sitting in Somersetshire in a beautiful recess. I said to [Thelwall] – 'Citizen John! this is a fine place to talk treason in!' 'Nay! Citizen Samuel!', replied he, 'it is a place to make a man forget that there is any necessity for treason!'[86]

John Thelwall, portrait attributed to William Hazlitt (1805) (*by permission of the National Portrait Gallery, London*).

In a letter of 18 July 1797 to his wife (presented for the first time in full in the Appendix), he describes the restorative time he was enjoying as part of a 'literary & political triumvirate' and 'philosophical party' at the 'Enchanting retreat' of 'the Academus of Stowey' and at the 'friendly retreat' of 'All fox den'. Thelwall's spelling emphasizes the den-like nature of this retreat to which the jacobin fox had effectively been pursued by the dogs of law. Although Coleridge realized that the broken Thelwall in the summer of 1797 was a man 'whose pocket is better adapted for a bundle of sonnets than the transportation or ambush-place of a French army',[87] he baulked at Thelwall's plans to retire among them. He was conscious of the fact that the persona of betrayer and traitor in which the State and its 'apparatus of threatened persecutions' had so successfully cast Thelwall might very well result in 'tumult', 'calumnies' and 'riots & dangerous riots' if Thelwall joined the poets near Stowey.[88] But in discouraging Thelwall from taking a cottage nearby, Coleridge was also anxiously distancing himself from his own 'traitorous' jacobin past. Chapter 5 will explore in detail 'the politics of friendship' between Thelwall and the two poets at this time.

Circumstances, then, conspired to drive Thelwall in late 1797, 'after many wanderings' ('Tintern Abbey', l. 157), into exile in the Wye Valley at Llyswen, Brecknockshire. As Thelwall was well aware, it is a place where 'vagrancy' is inscribed in the very landscape: the poetic name for the Wye being 'Vaga' – 'wandering' – which Thelwall himself makes use of in two elegies written at Llyswen after the death of his six-year-old daughter, Maria.[89] (Describing the Wye in 'Tintern Abbey' as 'Thou wanderer through the woods', Wordsworth would also have been aware of the way Nature in the Wye Valley served as a reminder of the human predicament of his 1793 vagrant self – a lesson learned partly from David Williams.) Thelwall was visited at his Llyswen farm (which gives its name to the 'sweet Liswyn farm' of Wordsworth's 'Anecdote for Fathers' in the *Lyrical Ballads*) by Wordsworth, Dorothy and Coleridge in August 1798, a matter of weeks after the composition of 'Tintern Abbey'.[90]

During his three years at Llyswen, Thelwall produced *Poems, Chiefly Written in Retirement* (Hereford, 1801) whose 'Prefatory Memoir', written in the third person, offers a fascinating portrait of a defeated radical's experience in the late 1790s and establishes an illuminating context for his identification with Vortigern. The rôle in which Thelwall repeatedly casts his proscribed radical self is that of the hunted animal. The 'Prefatory Memoir' pleads that Thelwall 'be permitted to walk in the uprightness of his own convictions, without being hunted, any longer, from society, by a proscription more ferocious than if assassination, or the other crime of Italy, had been proved against him'.⁹¹ At the same moment, Mary Wollstonecraft's novel, *The Wrongs of Woman* (1798), offered a powerful dramatization of pursuit and flight in the context of the politics of gender: 'The preserving her situation was, indeed, an important object to Jemima, who had been hunted from hole to hole, as if she had been a beast of prey'; 'But why should I dwell on similar incidents! – I was hunted, like an infected beast, from three different apartments'.⁹² Looking back at this period in *The Champion* of 6 June 1819 (which he edited between December 1818 and December 1821, turning the moderately reformist paper into an organ for radical reform as he once again entered the lists at a time of political instability following Peterloo),⁹³ Thelwall described himself as having been

> proscribed and hunted – driven like a wild beast, and banished, like a contagion, from society – during those reiterated attempts by armed banditti, to kidnap and to murder him, and by which he was chased like a worse than outlaw, and followed, and persecuted even in his miserable retreat – during all those monstrous atrocities at Yarmouth, at Lynn, at Wisbeach, at Derby, on the borders of Leicestershire – at Stockport, and at Norwich – atrocities the bare narrative of which would look like a libel upon an age of barbarism . . . Even in his way to this retreat, the yell of murderous persecution still pursued him . . . And did persecution and proscription end even here? – No: in his little isolated retreat, in the village of Llyswen, the toils of the peasant, and the meditations of the poet – nay, the child pangs of the faithful partner of his sorrows, were wantonly disturbed by the inquisitorial mandates and official myrmidons of the Duke of Portland.⁹⁴

In her 1837 *Life of John Thelwall*, Thelwall's second wife, Henrietta Cecil, recalled that he was 'hunted from society by persecutions incredible in these days' before he retired 'into the depths of Wales'.⁹⁵ 'I write to you on the subject of John Thelwall', Coleridge told John Chubb in August 1797, 'must his country *for this* be made a wilderness of waters to him?'⁹⁶ The autobiographical and narrative poems in Thelwall's *Poems, Chiefly Written in Retirement* repeatedly portray a pariah-figure 'in his native land, / Wander[ing] an exile'.⁹⁷ Even at Llyswen, an 'enchanted dormitory where the agitations of political feeling might be cradled to forgetfulness', the 'new Recluse',[98] as he represents himself, was watched by Home Office spies. The 'Prefatory Memoir' (truthfully) tells how a neighbour attacked him with a pickaxe, and how the hostility of the local population was excited against him by 'pointed and inflammatory allusions from the pulpit'.[99] He was eventually driven out in late 1800 when his landlord refused to execute the lease on the farm.

It is no surprise to find that Thelwall, like Wordsworth, was fascinated by restless wanderers, vagrants, pariah-figures, political exiles, refugees, felons, the disaffected, the displaced and their historical prototypes. During his 'Pedestrian Excursion', after 'toy[ing] with danger' and negotiating Salisbury Plain's 'inextricable labyrinths' in the trackless dark,[100] Thelwall stayed at Amesbury, where Geoffrey of Monmouth locates the Treason of the Long Knives which precipitated Vortigern's flight to Wales. And, most significantly, having finally been hunted to the Wye Valley, Thelwall (who in his youth had attempted a career in the theatre) began writing 'The Fairy of the Lake' – a verse-drama on the Vortigern story which appears in his collection of 1801.

This was not the first time that Thelwall had exploited the political relevance of the Vortigern story. And as was the case with Wordsworth, the valency of the figure for Thelwall would have been multi-faceted, functioning both as a prototype of his own hunted radical self and as a political antitype, in Cottle's phrase. The 'Prefatory Memoir' records that the young Thelwall had 'made considerable progress in compiling a history of England; for which . . . he made several rude drawings, as embellishments of the more striking incidents'. The Treason of the Long Knives from the Vortigern story would surely have been one of these. In *The Peripatetic* (1793), Thelwall had already taken 'the timorous policy of Vortigern', which resulted in 'extermination, personal slavery, and flight to the barren mountains of Wales', as the starting point for a strikingly contemporary political discussion of 'the folly and weakness of alliances, and other similar modes of calling in the assistance of mercenary troops' revolving around the *journée* of 10 August 1792 in Paris.[101] And in his *Rights of Nature* (1796), he had spoken forcefully of the depredations of the Saxon conquerors and the fate of the Dark Age, dispossessed Welsh:

> Were not the *seven kingdoms of the heptarchy*, with their Hengists, and

their Ellas, and their Cerdics at their head, thus founded . . .? Were they not afterwards melted into an individual state in the same crucible of blood and violence . . .? . . . The territory was seized by murder and rapine; the proprietors were dispossessed; such as escaped the general slaughter, were either driven into the mountains of Wales, or reduced to the most abject villanage; the lands were divided among the victorious banditti; society was split into its various orders, and the main distinction between *military freemen*, and *agricultural slaves*, was ultimately established in all its rigour. Such were the boasted institutions of our Saxon ancestors.[102]

A year later, this passage would of course resonate with tragic personal relevance.

'The Fairy of the Lake' itself is a curious hybrid – a conflation of 'savage Scandinavian mythology', in Edward Williams's phrase[103] (or 'runic mythology' in Thelwall's), Arthurian legend and the Matter of Britain (compare William Taylor of Norwich's own *Wortigerne*, written at exactly the same time – 'half a tragedy in stanzas, with northern mythology, choruses, and the English mis-spelt'). Formally, with its mythological machinery and frequent choruses of fairies, spirits and demons, it represents an interesting precursor of Shelley's *Prometheus Unbound* (1820). As Thelwall states in his notes: 'The Cambrian superstitions harmonize so readily with those of the Northern nations; and the mixed and illegitimate christianity of those times borders so closely upon paganism, that, I trust, the combination will not destroy the *poetical probability* of either' (*Poems*, 207). In the 'Prefatory Memoir', Thelwall mentions that while at Llyswen he had sent to London 'for some books, particularly such as might illucidate the early periods of British Story'[104] which were seized by the government at Hay-on-Wye and examined by the Privy Council before they were eventually returned – another dramatic 'appropriation' of Dark Age history in the 1790s. And, on 12 August 1801, Thelwall wrote to George Dyer referring to a number of historical and antiquarian works which Dyer had obviously recommended, including Holinshed's *Chronicles* and Aaron Thompson's translation of Geoffrey of Monmouth (see Appendix, Letter No. 6).

It is clear that Thelwall saw a parallel between the haunted, hunted Vortigern, reviled as a traitor, fleeing westward at a time of political strife, and his own experience in the 1790s, tried and hounded as a traitor. His verse-drama focuses on the love of Rowenna, the evil

Scandinavian sorceress, for the British champion Arthur; Vortigern himself remains a disturbing presence behind the scenes throughout the play until we see him carried across the stage in the final act, murdered by Rowenna. At the beginning of the piece, harried by British patriots and Britain's enemies, Vortigern flees westward:

> *Rowenna*: Whether [*sic*] fled
> The abject Vortigern?
>
> *Alwin*:   From bourg to bourg
> (By all alike rejected) with his suit,
> Westward he fled, towards his Cambrian wilds,
> A hunted fugitive: till join'd, at last,
> By those who 'scaped the slaughter, he attain'd
> The heights of bleak Farinioch. There he lurks,
> Hem'd by Gwrtheyrnion's towers, whose giant strength
> Frowns o'er the midway steep.
>
> (*Poems*, 10–11)

Ireland had located the climax of his play in Vortigern's castle in London; Thelwall locates the fugitive's demise in the 'Beacons of Brecknock (Farinioch)', stating in a note that 'This castle was, in reality, situated among the fastnesses of Plynlinmon, near the source of the Wye'. In relocating the climax of the tale in Brecknockshire, he brings the action closer to his own retreat at Llyswen, as if to emphasize the contiguity of ancient betrayer and contemporary radical. Standing first in Thelwall's poems, immediately after the 'Prefatory Memoir', 'The Fairy of the Lake', and specifically the figure of Vortigern, should be read as a politicized dramatization of Thelwall's own trajectory and of contemporary political strife. As Coleridge shrewdly asked Thelwall on 23 April 1801: 'You say no part of the contents of this Volume are to be political? – How is this possible if you give your Memoirs?'[105] Arthur's 'British' victory over Scandinavian Rowenna, which the end of the play celebrates, is complicated by an awareness of how the trajectories of the 'traitor' Thelwall and Britain's betrayer, Vortigern, parallel each other. The defeat of foreign foes in a play that would surely have been read in 1801 as 'patriotic', legitimizing a 'British' cause at a time of war, is subtly undermined by that inescapable identification.

Just as it focused Wordsworth's attention on internal cultural difference, so the Vortigern story would have further complicated Thelwall's sense of his own political and cultural identity. Many poses are struck in Thelwall's account of himself in the 'Prefatory Memoir'. While his identification in 'The Fairy of the Lake' with the fate of Vortigern seems obvious, Thelwall in the 'Prefatory Memoir' casts himself in the rôle of the unwelcome Saxon – a member of the race with which traitorous Vortigern aligned himself – as he speaks of 'the animosity which the Welsh are apt enough to entertain (without other reason) against every SAXON who intrudes, as a settler, among them' (*Poems*, p. xxxvii). Dark Age political enmities begin to resurface in and define 1790s relations in the Wye Valley: at a time of war in Europe, through his reading of British history and through his own experience, Thelwall, confronting a British 'other', became aware of deep-rooted internal, national differences *within* Britain beyond those on which the ideological battles between Paine and Burke, democrat and anti-jacobin, were based. For Thelwall, as for Wordsworth, it is the Vortigern story that focuses these enduring enmities. Fascinatingly, Henrietta Cecil Thelwall's *Life* records that 'JOHN THELWALL was descended from a Saxon family, part of which, as appears from the heraldic records of North Wales, took refuge in that country at the time of the Norman Conquest'.[106] Thelwall's retreat-as-Saxon into Wales was therefore a repetition of a former, harassed flight. Evident in Thelwall's late eighteenth-century negotiation with the Vortigern tale is the divided nature of Britain as a narrativized nation and of 'the British' as narrativized subjects.

Thelwall's identification with the troubling figure of Vortigern should also be read in the context of his negotiation with another prototype of betrayal and flight inscribed allusively in the tendentious 'Prefatory Memoir'. This model is William Godwin's jacobin novel, *Caleb Williams*, published in 1794 (the year in which Thelwall was put on trial), which, in its portrait of Squire Falkland's victimization of one who has discovered his terrible secret, stands as a dramatic political parable of radicalism hunted down by the *ancien régime*. It is a novel that is of course driven by the themes of betrayal and flight: impelled by his master-passion, curiosity, Williams betrays the trust of his mentor by spying on him; interestingly, the novel thereafter highlights his resolute *refusal* to betray Falkland's secret. Hounded by Falkland and the vengeful spy Gines, Williams at one point flees to Wales. Just as Thelwall described himself in *The Champion* as 'proscribed and hunted – driven like a wild beast . . . from society', so Caleb repines that 'The story of a flagitious murder shall be listened to with indifference, while an innocent man is hunted, like a wild beast, to the furthest corners of the earth!'[107] Just as Thelwall was to be watched by spies and his reputation tarnished by the village priest's 'pointed and inflammatory allusions', so Caleb is shadowed by Gines: 'The employment to which this man was hired was that of following me from place to place, blasting my reputation.'[108] The prototype seems obvious, but it can be seen working in a detailed way in Thelwall's *Poems*. The passage in the novel in which Caleb decides to fly to Wales is remarkably prophetic of John Thelwall's experience, and so closely parallels Thelwall's account of his own trials and his search for 'an elegible [sic] retreat' in the 'Prefatory Memoir' to his *Poems* that I want to suggest that Godwin here provides Thelwall with a literary model for his autobiography. It is worth quoting both passages at some length; the emphasis is mine:

> My next care was in regard to the scene I should choose as the retreat of that life which I had just saved from the grasp of the executioner . . . I knew not in what mode Mr Falkland intended to exercise his vengeance against me; but I was seized with so unconquerable an aversion to disguise, and the idea of spending my life in personating a fictitious character, that I could not for the present at least reconcile my mind to any thing of that nature. The same kind of disgust I had conceived for the metropolis, where I had spent so many hours of artifice, sadness, and terror. I therefore decided in favour of the project which had formerly proved amusing to my imagination, of withdrawing to some distant rural scene, **a scene of calmness and obscurity,** where for a few years at least, perhaps during the life of Mr Falkland, I might be hidden from the world, recover the wounds my mind had received in this fatal connection . . . **cultivate the faculties I in any degree possessed, and employ the intervals of these occupations in simple industry** . . . The menaces of my persecutor seemed to forebode the inevitable interruption of this system . . . I fixed upon **an obscure market-town in Wales** as the chosen seat of my operations. This place recommended itself to my observation as **I was wandering in quest of an abode** . . . **It was at a distance from any public and frequented road**, and had nothing which could deserve the name of trade. **The face of nature around it was agreeably diversified**, being partly **wild and romantic**, and partly rich and abundant in production. (*Caleb Williams*, 298–9)

Heralding the 'Llyswen' section of his 'Prefatory Memoir', Thelwall explains that

> The assistance of a few friends enabled him to stock a little farm, of about five-and-thirty acres, in the **obscure and romantic village** of *Llys-Wen*, in Brecknockshire . . . In the election of this spot, so far as it might be considered elective (for he had already devoted four months to **a pedestrian excursion, in unavailing search for an elegible [sic] retreat:**) Thelwall was principally influenced by the **wild and picturesque** scenery of the neighbourhood. For the village (embowered with orchards, and over-shadowed by grotesque mountains) is sweetly situated upon the banks of the Wye, at one of the most beautiful, tho least visited, parts of that unrivalled river; and the cottage itself, thro the branches of the surrounding fruit trees, catches a *glympse* – while its alcove (elevated on the remains of an old sepulchral tumulus) commands the *full view*, of one of the characteristic and more-than-crescent curves of that ever-varying stream; with its glassy pool sleeping beneath the reflected bank, its rapids above, and roaring cataracts below, bordered with plantations and pendant woods, and **diversified with rocks and pastures**. Such a retreat could not but appear, to an enthusiastic imagination, as a sort of enchanted dormitory, where the agitations of political feeling might be cradled to forgetfulness, and the delicious day dreams of poesy might be renewed: and as his wife's brother (who on account of his relationship, had been hunted, by a certain Lord of the Bed-chamber, from his farms in Rutland) accompanied him in this new establishment, Thelwall flattered himself that **agriculture, under the superintendance [sic] of the one, and the visitations of the Muse to the other, might secure that humble sort of subsistence to which he had determined to accommodate his desires**. In the choice of this situation he was, also, further influenced by **its remoteness from all political connection**. For, determined himself to observe the most inviolable silence respecting his opinions, he took it for granted, that there, where they had never yet been heard of, he should be equally out of the way of all solicitations to revive the discussion, and all the animosities they had excited against him. (*Poems*, pp. xxxv–xxxvi)

The parallel fates of Thelwall (who in the 1794 Treason Trials had also escaped 'from the grasp of the executioner' and had now been hounded from the metropolis into Wales) and the fictional Caleb Williams (a Welsh surname, of course, as is the 'Jones' of the first edition, altered in subsequent editions to 'Gines'), together with the verbal similarities, highlighted in bold above, between these passages, are too obvious to be ignored. The third person that Thelwall uses (to establish a sense of credible objectivity in the Memoir), strengthens the link: Thelwall is writing his autobiography, but with the potent prototype of Caleb Williams informing the writing, he is also fictionalizing himself, 'in personating a fictitious character', as Caleb himself had been forced to do in London. Thelwall's fate post-summer 1797 is a remarkable realization of Godwin's story, and the haunting inscription in the 'Memoir' of Godwin's narrative of the hounding of a 'betrayer' should be seen as further enriching the valency of the Vortigern figure in 'The Fairy of the Lake'.

The Wye's Wandering Jews

Another powerful archetype can be seen to inform the models Vortigern and Godwin offered Thelwall. I have shown how Wales and the Wye Valley in the 1790s became a place of refuge for a number of political pariah-figures, wanderers and exiles. In the context of his discussion of Southey's 1797 poem, 'For the Apartment in Chepstow-Castle where Henry Marten the regicide was imprisoned Thirty Years', the 'prison lyrics' of Coleridge and Wordsworth ('The Dungeon' and 'The Convict'), and their relation to the 'radical source of human renewal' enshrined as Nature in 'Tintern Abbey', Nicholas Roe has argued that 'For Wordsworth and other jacobins the most politically resonant edifice in the Wye Valley was Chepstow Castle',[109] which Wordsworth passed in both 1793 and 1798. Roe sees Marten, the seventeenth-century republican regicide, as another haunting presence in the Wye Valley. But as one of the most popular guidebooks of the 1790s makes clear, Chepstow Castle is also associated with the legend of the archetypal wanderer and outcast. James Baker's popular *Picturesque Guide through Wales and the Marches* (1795) records that Chepstow Castle

> consists of four courts, divided by screens, with gates, two on each side the keep, or citadel, which is a large square building, commonly called the Chapel, and was antiently feigned to have been built by Longinus, a Jew, the father of him who pierced our Saviour's side; who, for some crime was condemned to seek Britain, and to build something on the river Wye.[110]

This version of the legend of the Wandering Jew – another exemplum of betrayal and flight who haunted the imaginations of such contemporaries as Matthew Lewis, Shelley, Byron and De Quincey – further disturbs the politics of the Wye Valley in the 1790s and augments the valency of the other models of betrayal I have been considering.[111] The existence in the period of tales and printed accounts (such as *The Surprizing History of the Wandering Jew of Jerusalem with his arrival at Dover this year 1780*) telling of the appearance and peregrinations of the Wandering Jew attest to a popular fascination within the shores of Britain in the 1790s with the figure who insulted Christ and refused to let him rest on his way to Calvary.[112] In May 1797, Andrew Franklin's farce, *The Wandering Jew, or Love's Masquerade*, was performed at Drury Lane and appeared in published form in the same year. Hunted Caleb Williams adopts the disguise of a Jew in the metropolis, and, as Eric Rothstein notes, 'finds himself . . . a real Wandering Jew . . . [Caleb] has refused rest to Falkland, like the Jew who refused Christ rest'.[113] It is obviously the rôle of the Wandering Jew that Mortimer voluntarily embraces at the end of Wordsworth's post-Godwinian verse-drama *The Borderers* – situated, like 'Tintern Abbey', in a geographically ambiguous borderland country – which was read to Coleridge at Racedown in early June 1797 and to the fugitive, vagrant Thelwall under the trees at Alfoxden a month later:

> I will go forth a wanderer on the earth
> A shadowy thing, and as I wander on
> No human ear shall ever hear my voice,
> No human dwelling ever give me food
> Or sleep or rest, and all the uncertain way
> Shall be as darknesss to me, as a waste
> Unnamed by man! and I will wander on
> Living by mere intensity of thought,
> A thing by pain and thought compelled to live,
> Yet loathing life, till heaven in mercy strike me
> With blank forgetfulness – that I may die.
> (*Borderers* (1797–1799), V. iii. 265–75)

A few months after the composition of 'Tintern Abbey', Wordsworth, at Goslar, wrote his 'Song for the Wandering Jew': 'Day and night my toils redouble! / Never nearer to the goal; / Night and day I feel the trouble / Of the wanderer in my soul'. Furthermore, it is little mentioned that the Wandering Jew was the prototype of that other restless pariah whose crime was a betrayal of the One Life, the Ancient Mariner, as one of Coleridge's notebook entries of 1795–6 – 'Wandering Jew / a romance'[114] – and his *Table Talk* attest:

> It is an enormous blunder in these engravings of David Scott, brought here by Mr Aitken, to represent the Ancient Mariner as an old man on board ship. He was in my mind the everlasting wandering Jew – had told this story ten thousand times since the voyage which was in early youth and fifty times before.[115]

Judith Thompson has identified Coleridge's anxiety regarding Thelwall's status as vagrant in the autumn of 1797 and his guilt 'about his own lack of power, influence, and perhaps will to help him, in spite of continued appeals', as providing 'one subtext for the narrative of wandering, guilt, betrayed hospitality and failed sympathy that is the "Rime of the Ancient Mariner"'.[116] And centrally here, it is clearly in the rôle of the 'unblest' Wandering Jew that Thelwall, travelling westward, Cain-like ('a fugitive and a vagabond shalt thou be in the earth', Genesis 4: 12) towards Wales in August 1797, repeatedly casts himself in his *Poems, Chiefly Written in Retirement*:

> Yet must I leave
> Your social haunts – for not my unblest feet
> Yet may I rest, or my long wanderings close,
> Tho weary'd: but thro' many an untried scene
> (Perhaps from this how differing!) shape my way,
> Beneath my weight of sorrows . . .
>   ('On leaving the Bottoms of Glocestershire [*sic*]'; *Poems*, 138)

His cradle-song of October 1797 to his infant son John Hampden (named, like his eldest son, Algernon Sidney, after a seventeenth-century republican hero), portrays the same pariah:

> Ah! sleep on –
> As yet unconscious of The Patriot's name,
> Or of a patriot's sorrows – of the cares
> For which thy name-sire bled; and, more unblest,
> Thy natural father, in his native land,

> Wanders an exile; and, of all that land,
> Can find no spot his home.
> (*Poems*, 141)[117]

Thelwall's identification with the Wandering Jew amounted to so much more than a melodramatic poetic pose: it was an act of deeply felt imaginative sympathy that was both therapeutic (he had joined a historical and mythical fellowship of Wye Valley dissidents) and highly problematic. At work in the negotiation of Wordsworth, Thelwall and others with Vortigern and the Wandering Jew is a practice of self-mythologizing born out of crisis – a need to locate the embattled self in the context of larger narratives and histories that would offer wider perspectives on a claustrophobic present.

Finally, it might be appropriate to anticipate the discussion in the final chapter of the complex poetical dialogue which Thelwall's poetry of 1800 conducts with poems by Wordsworth and Coleridge by identifying a moment at which Thelwall's negotiations with Vortigern seem to inform Wordsworth's later verse. Wordsworth's familiarity with Thelwall's *Poems* is well attested; he probably read the volume in April 1802.[118] Wordsworth's 'Artegal and Elidure' (composed in 1815), which derives from Geoffrey of Monmouth's *Historia*, tells of the Vortigern-like flight of the deposed tyrannical King Artegal from his subjects and his search for 'a place of safe retreat' (l. 163). Thelwall's lines on Vortigern – 'From bourg to bourg / (By all alike rejected) with his suit, / Westward he fled, towards his Cambrian wilds, / A hunted fugitive' (*Poems*, 10), come back to haunt the verse:

> *From realm to realm* the humbled Exile went . . .
> In many a court, and many a warrior's tent,
> He urged his *persevering suit* in vain.
> (ll. 82–5; my emphasis)

Moreover, one hears in Wordsworth's later lines on the fugitive Artegal – 'How changed from him who, born to highest place, / Had swayed the royal mace' (ll. 94–5) – a recollection not only of the defeated Satan's lines to Beelzebub in *Paradise Lost* ('O how fallen! how changed / From him, who in the happy realms of light'; *PL*, I, 84–5) but also of those lines in Wordsworth's own 'Tintern Abbey' – 'Though changed, no doubt, from what I was when first / I came among these hills' – which herald the identification with Vortigern in the enigmatic simile 'more like a man / Flying from something that he dreads, than one / Who sought the thing he loved'. These allusions locate Thelwall and Wordsworth as the latest in a disturbing line of betrayers that includes Satan, Vortigern and Artegal; encoded here is a hellish heritage of betrayal for the 1790s. It is also noteworthy that another member of the Wordsworth–Coleridge circle, Joseph Cottle, seems to engage with Thelwall's lines on Vortigern in his epic on the thirteenth-century conquest of Wales by Edward I, *The Fall of Cambria* (1808), which is haunted throughout by the Vortigern story:[119]

> him, whose name the Briton execrates,
> The coward Vortigern, who, when beset,
> Rather than fight the battles of the brave,
> Sent fatally, for that opprobrious crew,
> The Saxon, and thus seal'd his nation's curse.
> But when he told how these illustrious chiefs,
> Ceaseless, pursued the traitor Vortigern,
> From haunt to haunt, and now incircled him
> In Cambrian castle, where the raging flames,
> At length, reduced his carcase, to the dust,
> Llewellyn, with a zest of transport cried,
> Whilst his young eye, shot ardour, rolling round,
> 'These were my countrymen!'
> (*The Fall of Cambria*, I, 22; Book 2, ll. 43–55)

Like Wordsworth's 'Artegal and Elidure', Cottle's *Fall of Cambria* here also makes use of the archetype of Satan and the impending Fall of Man, identifying the Saxons ('that opprobrious crew') with the host of rebel angels – '[Satan's] horrid crew' in Hell's 'dark opprobrious den of shame' (*PL*, I, 51 and II, 58) – and configuring Llewellyn ('his young eye shot ardour, rolling round') as a version of the confounded Satan – 'round he throws his baleful eyes' (*PL*, I, 56). In the poems quoted above, Wordsworth and Cottle invest the identities of their protagonists with a powerful Miltonic charge that invokes the arch-betrayer – Satan – as a prototype for Vortigern also.

Visiting Thelwall in August 1798, Wordsworth would have been reminded of the radical self that had fled to the Wye Valley five years previously – the self he had just resurrected so enigmatically in 'Tintern Abbey'. One wonders whether the conversation turned on Vortigern and the play Thelwall was contemplating or had by that time begun writing.

'[T]hus I entertain / The antiquarian humour, and am pleased / To skim along the surfaces of things, / Beguiling harmlessly the listless hours', remarks the disillusioned Solitary (in whom there is much of Wordsworth, of course) in Book III of *The Excursion* (*PW*, V, 79; ll. 133–6). I have been arguing in this chapter for the sort of political, cultural and psychological climate in which the figure of Vortigern, together with other prototypes of betrayal and treason which amplify that story, would not have been of merely antiquarian interest to a 'spirit oppressed by sense / Of instability, revolt, decay, / And change, and emptiness' (appropriately, the Solitary again, a few lines later). The contemporary significance of these models is the result of a historical vision that recognized that the past provided points of focus and complex paradigms that could dramatically figure, accurately reflect and usefully clarify contemporary crises of political and cultural identity.

3
Models of Defeat and 'Horrid Sufferance': Kosciusko

Political disillusionment, revolutionary failure and betrayal were at the heart of the cultural valency of the 'presences that disturb' considered in the first two chapters. These traumatic experiences are also integral to the resonance of my third model for the 1790s, the contemporary Polish patriot-General, Thaddeus Kosciusko – a potent symbol of heroic martial sacrifice and the international struggle for liberty. Like David Williams, Kosciusko has been unfairly neglected in accounts of 1790s culture and British Romanticism generally. Hero of two revolutions, the Pole figured as a monitory, educative model in the political consciousness of such figures as Richard Warner, Coleridge, Thelwall, Hunt, Keats and Wordsworth, and the intensely emotional response he elicited from these writers drew them into the decade's most important political debates and conversations. But the valency of Kosciusko is qualitatively different from that of the paradigms so far considered, in that 1790s culture responded directly to his iconic, broken body as the literal – and at the same time powerfully symbolic – *physical* site of the decade's conflicts. In such engagements, a language of historical haunting (as with Vortigern in 'Tintern Abbey') or one indicating deep cultural embeddedness and indebtedness (through which David Williams inhabits the poem) falls away. In person and in visual representations, Kosciusko was dramatically, accusingly *present*, urgently contemporary. However, that public presence could also be more subtly inscribed, as in Wordsworth's poetry of the late 1790s and early 1800s. Reconstructing conversations that are part of the contextual fabric of these poems allows us to detect an implied presence in absence.

The impact of Kosciusko on a figure who was himself a literary and political model for the 1790s – the Revd Richard Warner – provides a useful starting point. Warner's response to the hero is intimately bound up with the genesis of his popular volume of topographical description, *A Walk Through Wales, in August 1797* (1798), which represents a particularly interesting example of the interface of the political, literary and touristic experience of the decade. I then offer a profile of the General's paradigmatic place in the Romantic Imagination, focusing in particular on the responses of Coleridge and Keats, which illustrate well how a reticular culture of conversation and allusion constructed, debated and sharpened the relevance of such cultural models. Finally, I return to Warner and the Wye to reconstruct a fascinating, and typically 1790s, moment of cultural confluence involving Kosciusko, Warner and Wordsworth to suggest how this emblematic presence might inhabit the poetry of the period in less obvious – though no less instructive – ways.

Richard Warner: 'Ruffian of Republicanism'

At the turn of the nineteenth century, the Anglican priest and 'rigorous Whig' Richard Warner (1763–1857) was 'the best known man of letters' in Bath.[1] His enemies accused him of preaching 'foul democracy'; indeed, in 1801, the *Anti-Jacobin Review*, after savaging his *History of Bath* at great length, made no attempt to hide its prejudice against him in its summing-up:

> We thus finish our review of Mr Warner's History of Bath. We have not taken any unfair advantages against it, though we have been compelled to censure it at times. We were prejudiced against its author, we own, from the portrait of his person prefixed to it, and from the perusal of the sentiments occasionally in it. The portrait exhibited to our eyes a rector of a church in Bath, with his hair dressed *a la Brutus*; and so looking more like a ruffian of republicanism newly imported from France, than a sober divine of the Church of England.[2]

The reviewer surely has a model in mind – that 'political divine' who had launched the Revolution Controversy with a sermon, Richard Price, as he appears in Burke's *Reflections on the Revolution in France*: 'this arch-pontiff of the *rights of men* . . . this spiritual doctor of politics'.[3] In 1804, Warner published a sermon he had preached on 25 May of that year (a day of general fasting in support of the war with

Richard Warner by S. Harding after J. Williams: engraving published in Warner's *History of Bath* (1801) (*by permission of the National Portrait Gallery, London*).

France) entitled *War Inconsistent with Christianity,* and dedicated it to the Whig statesman, Charles James Fox.[4] For William Blake, it was a sermon that was to elevate Warner to the status of a model of mercy, wisdom and anti-imperialism: David Erdman has persuasively argued that the personified Cathedral City of Bath – 'benevolent Bath', one of the 'Friends' of suffering Albion – in Blake's *Jerusalem* is a tribute to Warner's moral voice from the west:

> ... at length was heard
> The voice of Bath, faint as the voice of the dead in the house of death –
> Bath, healing city, whose wisdom in midst of poetic
> Fervour mild spoke through the western porch, in soft gentle tears ...[5]

Erdman hears in Bath's speech to Albion echoes of Warner's sermon:

> Blake quotes 'Bath' at some length in an appeal to Albion which amounts to an anti-war sermon . . . urging mercy and inveighing against imperial selfhood or British national pride in almost Warner's terms: 'however high/ Our palaces and cities, and however fruitful are our fields/ In Selfhood, we are nothing' (*Jerusalem* 40 [45]).[6]

In 1798, Warner, who for four years had been William Gilpin's curate at Boldre near Lymington, had published at Bath his *Walk Through Wales, in August 1797.*[7] It proved to be a popular and influential work, reaching a fourth edition by 1801. Considering its success and influence in his *Literary Recollections* of 1830, Warner states:

> a demand for a second edition, very speedily followed the publication of the first . . . I may also say, that it originated a taste, among the younger part of my countrymen, for *pedestrian tours* into the principality: so that, since its appearance, the number of genteel *foot travellers* there, has, (as I have been informed) nearly equalled those, who have flown through its romantic and picturesque scenery, in the various vehicles of our country of everlasting migration . . . But my 'Walk' did more than this, for it animated the *old* to resume the use of their legs; and inspired the *fair sex*, with a desire to emulate my exertions; or, (which I would rather believe) to follow my example.[8]

It is in his *Literary Recollections* that Warner speaks of his poignant meeting in the summer of 1797 with Kosciusko – a meeting that is closely linked to the inception of the *Walk Through Wales*. At that historical moment, it is clear that for this 'political divine', Kosciusko would have been an inspiring model of anti-imperialism, encountered, in Blake's words, at 'the western porch' – not of Bath, but of nearby Bristol, from where the exiled Kosciusko was waiting to depart for America.

Warner and the 'Fallen General'

'In the beginning of the year 1798, I entered upon a new *Walk* in literature', Warner punningly recollects, 'and published a *Pedestrian Tour* into Wales, an agreeable excursion, which I had made with my friend Richard Cruttwell, Esq., during the preceding autumn. The circumstance which gave rise to this expedition is worthy a remark.'[9] Warner tells how he read in the local papers of the arrival in Bristol of Thaddeus Kosciusko (Tadeusz Andrezei Bonawentura Kosciuszko), the Polish patriot-General (1746–1817). He had arrived in London on 29 May 1797, and had met worthies such as Cartwright, Fox, Grey, Wilberforce and Sheridan. Under the heading 'Domestic Occurrences, Tuesday, May 30', *The Gentleman's Magazine* announced that 'The gallant General Kosciusko arrived in the river Thames on-board a Swedish vessel, attended by many Polish officers, who are going with him to America.'[10] Enthusiastic Londoners besieged his hotel, anxious to catch a glimpse of the hero. From London, he travelled west to Bristol, and remained there from 13 to 19 June.

By that time, the seasoned Polish soldier had become an icon of liberty and, more important, a dramatic embodiment of liberty's defeat. Having gallantly served in America under Washington in the War of Independence,[11] he became chief of the Polish Confederacy, and when Russia invaded Poland in 1792 with the support of the Confederation of Targowica, he held Dubienka for five days with 4,000 men against a Russian force of 18,000. He was made 'Distinguished Citizen' of revolutionary France on 26 August 1792 – the very day David Williams, Paine, Price and Priestley were granted honorary French citizenship; the accolade caused Pitt some unease when Kosciusko arrived in London. In January 1793, the year of the Second Partition of Poland, he went to Paris to seek support from both the Girondins and Jacobins for a Polish insurrection and may well have witnessed the execution of the King. His pleas ultimately fell on deaf ears, but dressed in national costume and surrounded by his infantry and artillery, he formally proclaimed the insurrection on 24 March 1794 in the ancient market square of Kraków, simultaneously issuing the Polish Act of Insurrection – an important document of rights resembling the American Declaration of Independence:

> I, Tadeusz Kosciuszko, swear before God and to the whole Polish nation, that I shall employ the authority vested in me for the integrity of the frontiers, for gaining national self-rule and for the foundation of general liberty, and not for private benefit. So help me, Lord God, and the innocent suffering of Thy Son![12]

On 7 May he issued the Manifesto of Polaniec, which abolished serfdom and offered the peasants protection from their landlords. After some initial success against the aggressors, notably at Raclawice, the Polish army was defeated in October 1794 at Maciejowice by Russo-Prussian forces; Kosciusko was badly wounded and taken prisoner. Following the capture on 4 November of Praga, the east bank suburb of Warsaw, by General Suvorov and the massacre of its inhabitants by the Cossacks, the city capitulated. Suvorov is said to have sent a three-word dispatch to Catherine the Great of Russia: 'Hurrah – Praga – Suvorov', to which the Empress responded with 'Bravo – Fieldmarshal – Catherine'. On being unhorsed at Maciejowice, Kosciusko himself is supposed (erroneously) to have uttered the ominous words 'Finis Poloniae' – 'This is the end of Poland'. It was indeed the end of Kosciusko's dream of an independent Poland: the Third Partition, ratified in 1797, and the abdication of the last king of an independent Poland, Stanislaw II Augustus Poniatowski, ensued. Kosciusko was taken to St Petersburg, and imprisoned in the Peter-Paul Fortress.

On being released from prison by Tsar Paul I on 19 December 1796, Kosciusko, following the westward trajectory of political defeat taken by so many harried liberals of the age, sought retirement in America, travelling first through Finland, Sweden and England. He was warmly received in Philadelphia and became a close friend of Thomas Jefferson, then Vice-President. On 5 May 1798, however, he secretly left for France, hoping once more to enlist French support in the cause of his beloved Poland. There he met with Napoleon, whose plans for Poland he repeatedly rejected as not going far enough to restore the country's national integrity. In exile at Berville, near Fontainebleau, he continued to campaign for an independent Poland, the restitution of pre-partition borders and a free constitution. After the fall of Napoleon, Tsar Alexander's personal pledge to Kosciusko regarding the future of Poland was cruelly betrayed at the Congress of Vienna (1814–15). The General died at Solothurn, Switzerland, aged seventy-one.[13] In the summer of 1797, still smarting from his terrible wounds, he arrived in England a tragic and palpable reminder of Poland's fate and of England's connivance in her demise. *The Gentleman's Magazine*, announcing Kosciusko's arrival in England, graphically describes his physical condition at this moment:

> He is incurably wounded in the head, has three bayonet-wounds in his back, and part of his thigh carried away by a cannon shot; and, with the excruciating torments those wounds occasion, as he cannot move himself, he amuses his hours with drawing landscapes. He . . . complains that his wounds were long neglected after he was made prisoner.[14]

As Miecislaus Haiman has remarked, however – interestingly, with an echo of 'Tintern Abbey' ('And I have felt / A presence that disturbs me'), Kosciusko may have been physically incapacitated, but he was also a troubling and accusatory human exemplum of the effects of imperialist aggression and of Pitt's foreign policy:

> [Kosciusko's] arrival in London . . . was rather inconvenient to the government of Pitt. The former American 'rebel', now an impotent invalid, but still politically dangerous, came like a reminder of the crime of the Partitions perpetrated on Poland with the tacit approval of England; his presence might disturb those guilty powers, their hands still covered with the blood of Poland, which Pitt now expected to win for a coalition to destroy revolutionary France. Still the Tory papers did not dare to attack the guest, and enthusiasm carried the people.[15]

Haiman rightly characterizes Kosciusko in the summer of 1797 as a politically resonant figure – 'dangerous to the pretenses of despotism' (Leigh Hunt's words in an *Examiner* essay of 1817 that cites Kosciusko, discussed below)[16] – on whose broken frame Pitt's guilt was inscribed in blood.

In his *Literary Recollections*, Warner proceeds to recall his meeting with this paradigmatic presence. 'All that man could effect, in the honourable and important post to which he had been raised, Kosciuszko performed', Warner writes, but the fiat had been passed, that Poland should be conquered and dismembered. On the 5th of October 1794, the unequal battle was fought, at Matchevitz in Poland, between the Baron de Fergen and his myriads, and the little patriotic band commanded by Kosciuszko, which decided the fate of the hero and his country . . . He was overtaken . . . by a party of Cossacks: one of whom, not aware of his rank, thrust a spear into his back, and he fell senseless to the ground. A monastery received him . . . he was sent a prisoner to Petersburgh . . . but at length being liberated he determined to retire to America, and proceeded to Bristol, in his way to the United States.[17]

Warner 'burned to see and converse with, so exalted a character'. Having 'obtained an introduction' to the Consul with whom the 'fallen General' was staying at Bristol, he set out on foot with Richard Shuttleworth Cruttwell (son of and successor to Richard Cruttwell, publisher of William Lisle Bowles's *Fourteen Sonnets* (1789) and of Southey and Lovell's *Poems* (1795)) in the hope of meeting him. It was during this walk to Bristol that the Welsh tour that would produce *A Walk Through Wales* was decided upon. The Welsh landscape beckoned on the way, a promised land to the west like the America for which Kosciusko was heading:

> The day was brilliant; the country beautiful; and from the heights which we ascended in our devious walk, the distant mountains of Wales, disclosed themselves in tempting perspective. We talked of the wonders and glories of this, to us, *terra incognita*: expressed a mutual wish to visit its mountains, rocks, and cataracts: agreed that a *pedestrian tour* through the principality, would be nothing more than the multiplication of a certain number of walks to Bristol and back again; and finally determined, ere we reached the Consul's house, on 'a walk through Wales'.[18]

Wales seems as much a New World as the United States. At the Consul's house, Warner and Cruttwell were immediately granted an audience with Kosciusko. Once again, it is a sense of the man's iconic status that emerges from Warner's affecting description:

> I never contemplated a more interesting human figure than Kosciuszko, stretched upon his couch. His wounds were still unhealed, and he was unable to sit upright. He appeared to be a small man, spare and delicate.

– A black silk bandage crossed his fair and high, but somewhat wrinkled forehead. Beneath it, his dark eagle eye, sent forth a stream of light; that indicated the steady flame of patriotism, which still burned within his soul; unquenched by disaster, and wounds; weakness, poverty and exile. Contrasted with its brightness, was the paleness of his countenance, and the wan cast of every feature. He spoke very tolerable English; though in a low and feeble tone . . . On rising to depart, I offered him my hand: he took it. My eye filled with tears: and he gave it a warmer grasp. – I muttered something about 'brighter prospects' and 'happier days'. – He faintly smiled, and said (they were his last words to me) 'Ah! sir, he who devotes himself for his country, must not look for reward on this side the grave!'[19]

The account should be compared with Southey's anecdote in his *Letters from England* of the meeting in the same room between Kosciusko and a Bristol baker (which shows the potential of the scene for sentimentalism[20]) and with his portrait in the 'Introductory Address' to Coleridge's *Conciones ad Populum* of another radical 'martyr', the incarcerated Joseph Gerrald.[21] Both Benjamin West and Richard Cosway painted the crippled Kosciusko during his stay in London in 1797 – the former from memory and the latter through a keyhole, since the disabled General proved a reluctant sitter[22] – and these powerfully iconographic portraits show him exactly as Warner saw him here: wan, emaciated, prone on a couch with a bandaged head and right thigh, surrounded by letters and books, his crutch beside him and his Magyar hat and sword (the latter a gift from the Whig Club) nearby. Outside the window in West's portrait, the dome of St Paul's reminds the viewer of the General's exiled state (and indeed of his recent incarceration in the Peter-Paul Fortress).[23] West presented Kosciusko with a drawing of *Hector parting from Andromache* which, as von Erffa and Staley note, 'translates into a Homeric vocabulary Kosciuszko's own role as a warrior in the doomed cause of his country's independence', thereby elevating the General to the status of epic hero.[24] Seventeen years later in the *Examiner*, Leigh Hunt (echoing Southey's description of Kosciusko in his *Letters from England* – 'his countenance pale, painful and emaciated') was to recall the General as he appeared in two other engravings executed by Anthony Cardon (1798) and William Sharp (1800): 'a man reduced almost to helplessness, and reclining on a couch with that pale and painful countenance, through which the eagerness of his noble character still looked out'.[25]

Thomas McLean has drawn a provocative parallel between West's image of the prone Kosciusko and the same artist's representation of a female nude in the Council Chamber of the Royal Academy at Somerset House, and between the 'even more ambivalent' engravings of the General by Cardon and Sharp and traditional artistic representations of nude, reclining females. Though an 'attractive and sympathetic portrait', McLean remarks, West's painting 'lacks the power and masculinity' visible in his other portraits 'of important men', and he implies that these contemporary images of Kosciusko would have questioned viewers' assumptions regarding the conventional — that is, strongly gender-marked — representations of such public 'heroes'.[26] The extent to which these portraits evoke, or were designed to evoke, the model of the female nude is debatable, but it might be suggested that one observes in them a process of *effeminization* that is part of the contemporary construction of a discourse of physical weakness, 'helplessness' (Hunt's word), 'delicateness' (Warner's) and emasculation surrounding Kosciusko. Significantly, Cosway has recourse to viewing his subject voyeuristically through the keyhole. Tyranny has 'reduced' Kosciusko to the status of a (somewhat exotic) female, these paintings seem to imply; he is produced by these artists as an unnerving spectacle for the public gaze.

Despite Kosciusko's flashing eye, the tired smile and the unquenched patriotic ardour emanating from him, Warner in 1797 is confronted with an image of complete physical defeat. All of Poland seems embodied in that one figure, propped up on a couch in Bristol, assailed by 'disaster, and wounds; weakness, poverty and exile'. But another potent model of Romantic identity can be glimpsed. Haunting this portrait of a broken and exiled 'rebel' is a prototypical image of physical defeat made bearable by a 'fixed mind' and 'unconquerable will': that of the arch-rebel-General Satan in *Paradise Lost*, himself initially prone on the burning marl:

>   . . . his form had yet not lost
> All her original brightness, nor appeared
> Less than archangel ruined, and the excess
> Of glory obscured . . .

>   . . . Darkened so, yet shone
> Above them all the archangel: but his face
> Deep scars of thunder had intrenched, and care

Models of Defeat and 'Horrid Sufferance' 105

The wounded Thaddeus Kosciusko in London, by Benjamin West (1797) (by permission of the Allen Memorial Art Museum, Oberlin College, Ohio).

> Sat on his faded cheek, but under brows
> Of dauntless courage, and considerate pride
> Waiting revenge; cruel his eye, but cast
> Signs of remorse and passion . . .
>
> Thrice he essayed, and thrice in spite of scorn,
> Tears such as angels weep, burst forth: at last
> Words interwove with sighs found out their way.
> (PL, I, 591–4, 599–605, 619–21)

Satan here provides a model for Kosciusko, and a number of parallels between 'fallen General' and fallen angel suggest that the image of Satan is in Warner's mind: the prone position, the wounded head, the wrinkled forehead and 'intrenched' face, the wan, faded cheek contrasted with the brightness of eye and form only partly obscured by recent trials, the unquenched passion, the difficult address, the tears. The multi-valent prototype of the defeated Satan allows likeness to coexist with difference: it serves to emphasize the heroic stature and suffering of the Pole whilst at the same time functioning ironically, alerting us to the fundamental difference between the two and distancing Kosciusko from the arch-rebel whose pride and ambition cost him Heaven. In the words of *Paradise Lost*, Satan's 'malice serve[s] but to bring forth' the 'Infinite goodness' of Kosciusko (*PL*, I, 217–18). Of course, the model Milton offers here is also, inescapably, an ideologically troubling one in that it evokes a satanic Kosciusko and a martyred Satan. But in doing so, it emphasizes that these, too, were received identities in the period, and allows Kosciusko to be seen from the perspective of his imperialist antagonists, and Satan to be viewed from a contemporary radical standpoint – that of Godwin and Hazlitt, for example – which regarded him as the prototypical republican, political hero and 'first Whig'[27] who rebelled against tyranny and arbitrary power.[28] In addition, Warner's invocation of Satan in his portrait of Kosciusko is used as a means of *self*-definition: it can be seen to encode Warner's sense – here, from the perspective of 1830 – of his having been regarded by those in power in the late 1790s as politically 'of the Devil's party' ('a ruffian of republicanism newly imported from France'), and knowing it. Warner's description is another illuminating example of the way in which such models suggest numerous paradigms of political and moral identity. Valuable here is Lucy Newlyn's observation in her analysis of the complex resonance of

Milton's own 'allusiveness' in the similes of *Paradise Lost*: 'To opt for one alternative or the other is to deny a conjunction of opposites in the poetry's meaning which is essential to its intellectual complexity.'[29]

Warner's embarrassment on leaving is poignantly registered by 'I muttered something about "brighter prospects" and "happier days" '. He struggles for something meaningful to say, trying to 'make off to advantage', as Keats puts it in a letter about the embarrassment of leave-taking.[30] The 'brighter prospects', however, are less (effetely) cliché than the immediate context might suggest. The recently-glimpsed − literal − bright prospects of Wales can be seen to lie behind Warner's attempt to take leave on a brighter note: 'The day was brilliant; the country beautiful . . . the distant mountains of Wales, disclosed themselves in tempting perspective.' The phrase 'brighter prospects' links the glimpse of the bright west of Wales with the brighter future awaiting the wounded General further west in a safe transatlantic haven for Europe's exiled patriots. Perhaps Warner also took his awkward cue in that room at Bristol from the landscapes which, as *The Gentleman's Magazine* reported, the General was sketching.

Literal 'bright prospects', then, may have informed Warner's words of comfort, but the phrase is painfully ineffectual. Its naïve idealism, its lameness in projecting a bearable future for the lame Kosciusko, do little to dispel the reality of past and present 'disaster, and wounds; weakness, poverty and exile'. The visit to the Consul's house where Kosciusko lay wounded is, for Warner, 'the circumstance which gave rise to [the Welsh] expedition'; the inception of the tour is closely associated in Warner's mind with the tragedy of Kosciusko's 'fallen' state and 'dismembered' State.[31] That association would surely not have been without its tensions. The meeting with Kosciusko and the heroic failure he embodied must in retrospect have complicated − embarrassed, perhaps − the innocent alacrity with which Warner had embraced the journey into Wales's *terra incognita* a short while before the emotional meeting. The wounded figure on his couch, poignantly and significantly 'drawing landscapes', would have bedimmed the 'tempting perspective . . . the wonders and glories' of the west which Warner glimpsed, disturbing them with the grim realities of a patriot cause overthrown and a continent at war. Kosciusko would also have served as a disturbing reminder of why he who wished to travel in the late 1790s had to confine himself to British shores.[32] In retrospect, then, Warner's 'view from the heights' becomes far more complicated. It can be read as an example of the Miltonic Picturesque − a vision of 'wonders and glories' now haunted by the precedent of the hilltop prospect of *Paradise Lost*, Book XI, in which Adam sees 'many shapes / Of death', 'fierce faces threatening war', and 'Death's ministers, not men, who thus deal death / Inhumanly to men' (*PL*, XI, 467–8, 641, 676–7).[33] With the relation I have just explored between the inception of the Welsh excursion and the experience of meeting Kosciusko in Warner's mind, the opening of the *Walk Through Wales*, which alerts the reader to the 'last stand' of liberty in a former age, cannot have failed to resonate with the tragedy of a contemporary 'chieftain', the ravages of whose 'last stand' Warner had just seen inscribed on his body:

> we have more than once amused ourselves with anticipating the pleasure we should receive, when leisure and opportunity would allow us to visit the country of the ancient Britons . . . to breathe the inspiring air where liberty made her last stand in these kingdoms, against the strides of Roman power, under the gallant Silurian and Ordovician chieftains.[34]

At the outset of the *Walk Through Wales*, Wales, like Poland, becomes a politicized site, the locus of imperial incursion and the death of liberty – a death still presided over by Pitt. Just as Wales 'became' France for the radical Wordsworth in 1793 through a complex process of historical-cultural identification, here Wales briefly images Kosciusko's Poland. Indeed, for Warner, the assassination of ancient British liberty might ultimately be construed as a factor in Kosciusko's tragic fate. The model of defeat embodied in Kosciusko would have also linked the fate of Wales and Poland with that of the radical cause in Britain between 1793 and 1798. As Warner knew well, Kosciusko was in the 1790s one of the great heroes of British liberals and jacobins – an icon who defined their radical identities in important ways. It is these formative negotiations with Kosciusko that I now want to examine.

Kosciusko and the Romantic Imagination

Like Robespierre and Napoleon – two other resonant presences of the 1790s and early 1800s – Kosciusko fascinated and exercised the imaginations of two generations of Romantic writers. To his contemporaries an inspiring symbol of 'honest patriotism' defeated by imperial tyranny, he became a popular literary subject. In his piece

'On Liberty', published in his *Poems* of 1792, which John Thelwall later chose to reprint among his political lectures in the second volume of *The Tribune*,[35] George Dyer lauds Kosciusko and his fellow-patriots:

> May tyrants ne'er, those murd'rers of the world,
> Austria's proud Lord, and Prussia's faithless king,
> Their blood-stain'd banners to the air unfurl'd,
> O'er freedom's sons the note of triumph sing;
> Still with the great resolve the Polish heroes fire,
> To live in thine embrace, or at thy feet expire.[36]

In her 'Hymn: "Ye are the salt of the earth"', written in the summer of 1794 and published in the *Monthly Magazine* for July 1797, Anna Laetitia Barbauld refers to the Reign of Terror in Paris, Kosciusko's insurrection (which had recently gained added impetus from the Polish victory at Raclawice on 4 April), and the imprisonment from May 1794 to September 1797 at Olmütz of the Marquis de Lafayette, whose plight would soon be that of the 'patriot martyr' Kosciusko (known also as 'The Polish Lafayette'):

> E'en yet the steaming scaffolds smoke,
> By Seine's polluted stream;
> With your rich blood the fields are drenched,
> Where Polish sabres gleam.
>
> E'en now, through those accursed bars,
> In vain we send our sighs;
> Where, deep in Olmutz' dungeon glooms,
> The patriot martyr lies.[37]

'Poor Poland!' Coleridge wrote to Southey from Wrexham on 13 July 1794, 'They go on sadly there'.[38] In the same year, as part of a series of sonnets on eminent contemporaries published in the *Morning Chronicle*, Coleridge addressed an emotional sonnet to Kosciusko.[39] In a letter of 5 February 1818 to James Perry, Coleridge recalled that it was this poem that prompted Thomas Holcroft to approach him on 16 December 1794 at a dinner hosted by Perry and Gray, the proprietors of the *Chronicle*. The sonnet to the fallen Kosciusko was therefore specifically the springboard from which Coleridge entered the seminal radical conversations of the 1790s:

I shall never forget, or recall without a smile . . . the impression which the stranger whom I found in the room before dinner, made on me. A striking countenance – poring on the Paper of that day and occasionally turned towards me – At last, he rose, advanced to me with the paper in his hand, & began – 'Sir! I apprehend, that you are the Author of this Sonnet on Koskiusko?' I bowed assent. 'Sir! it is a very bad composition – a very wretched performance, I assure you'. I again bowed: and with a smile that expressed a little surprize at the oddness, but no offence at the harshness, of this volunteer Address, made some modest reply admitting the too probable appropriateness of the Criticism. 'Nay, but, Sir! do not misunderstand me – It is a poem of genius – a proof of great Genius, Sir! You are certainly a man of Genius, Sir! My name is Holcroft – and I should be glad to see you at my House next Sunday, to dine with me – & meet with Mr Porson & Mr Godwin'.[40]

The meeting with Holcroft, and the subsequent meeting with Godwin, were to prove of paramount significance in the development of Coleridge's political and religious thinking. His assessment in a letter to Southey of 17 December 1794 of the meeting with Holcroft shows him at pains swiftly to define his own radical and metaphysical 'systems' against those of Holcroft:

Holcroft *opposes* [our system] violently – & thinks it not *virtuous*. His arguments were such as Nugent and twenty others have used to us before him – they were *nothing*. There is a fierceness and *dogmatism* of conversation in Holcroft, for which you receive little compensation either from the variety of his information, the closeness of his Reasoning, or the splendor [*sic*] of his Language. He talks incessantly of Metaphysics, of which he appears to me to *know nothing* – to have *read nothing* –/ He is ignorant as a Scholar – and neglectful of the smaller Humanities, as a Man –/ Compare him with Porson! My God! to hear Porson *crush* Godwin, Holcroft, &c – They absolutely tremble before him! I had the honor [*sic*] of *working* H. a little – and by my great *coolness* and command of impressive Language certainly *did him over* . . . He absolutely infests you with *Atheism*.[41]

As arranged, the meeting with Godwin, whose *Political Justice* Coleridge had already begun to 'set . . . at Defiance'[42] in his letters to Southey, took place on 21 December at Holcroft's. Coleridge's sonnet to Kosciusko was therefore the occasion of his introduction to two major radical figures of the 1790s. The important point here is that it precipitated the meeting with the atheist philosopher in reaction to whose system Coleridge's own Christianized radicalism of the 1790s in large part evolved. Just as Thelwall in *The Tribune* of 1796 remarked that 'it was not *Tom Paine* but *Edmund Burke* that made me so zealous a reformer',[43] so the atheistical jacobinism of Godwin and Holcroft helped galvanize Coleridge's committedly Unitarian political stance (an opposition discussed in the next chapter). In his diary for that Sunday, Godwin noted: 'talk of self love & God', which suggests that Coleridge took the opportunity of challenging Godwin's atheism – perhaps, as Roe remarks, by 'invoking Priestley and Hartley, Frend and Dyer to confound Godwin's arguments from *Political Justice* and Holcroft's "incessant Metaphysics" and *"Atheism"*'.[44] During the course of his Bristol lectures, in which his opposition to Godwinism was further expounded, Coleridge referred to the Poles' fight for freedom under Kosciusko and to the third partitioning of Poland in October 1795: 'a great people shall from hence become adequately illuminated for a Revolution bloodless, like Poland's, but not, like Poland's assassinated by the foul Treason of Tyrants against Liberty.'[45] He also printed 'Sketches from the Life of Kosciusko' from Stephen Jones's *History of Poland* (1795) in *The Watchman* on 13 May 1796.[46] Lamb wrote to Coleridge on 24 June 1797, a few days after Kosciusko had sailed for Philadelphia from Bristol: 'Did you seize the grand opportunity of seeing Kosciusko while he was at Bristol? I never saw a hero; I wonder how they look.'[47] Coleridge had not; he was with the Wordsworths at Racedown. Lamb here light-heartedly cultivates a tone of child-like awe in the face of the phenomenon that is Kosciusko, but both he and Coleridge would have been shocked by how this hero actually 'looked' in the summer of 1797.

In stating that Coleridge's sonnet to the hero was an important platform from which the young poet and political lecturer gained entry into the influential radical circles of the decade, it can also be shown in detail that Coleridge's subsequent immersion in that radical culture resulted in fascinating poetico-political 'conversations' which took that model of vanquished liberty as their subject. And in pointing up such 'conversations', I want to emphasize how the discourses of poetry and political writing creatively fed off and into each other in response to such a model. April 1796 marked the beginning of Coleridge's correspondence with Thelwall. As well as Dyer's 'To Liberty', Thelwall in 1796 reproduced in *The Tribune* Samuel Whitchurch's poem on Kosciusko entitled 'Farewell to the Year 1794', whose engagement with Coleridge's December 1794 sonnet to the Polish General developed over the next two years into a wider dialogue involving Thelwall's own response to Kosciusko in two *Tribune* lectures and Coleridge's own valediction to the dying year, 'Ode on the Departing Year' (late December 1796), which takes its tone from his 1794 sonnet. Again, Kosciusko brings Coleridge into the foremost radical conversations of the 1790s. The Whitchurch, Thelwall and Coleridge pieces quoted below – which deserve to appear at some length – can now be revealed to be part of a formative symbiotic relationship that extends from the echoes of Coleridge's and Southey's 'historic drama' *The Fall of Robespierre* (1794) in Thelwall's *Tribune* essay, 'On the Prospective Principle of Virtue' (May 1795), and Coleridge's defence of Thelwall (which the latter took amiss) in his Bristol lecture against the Gagging Acts, *The Plot Discovered* (December 1795), through Thelwall's use in a lecture of *The Plot Discovered*, Coleridge's strictures on Thelwall in *The Watchman* (17 March 1796), their formative correspondence (spring 1796 onwards), and Coleridge's eulogistic sonnet to Thelwall (May 1796), to their meeting at Nether Stowey (July 1797) which inspired Thelwall's 'conversation poem', 'Lines, written at Bridgewater', and ultimately to Thelwall's barbed marginalia to *Biographia Literaria*.[48] Verbal correspondences between the four pieces are highlighted in bold below. Coleridge's 16 December 1794 sonnet to Kosciusko (reprinted in his *Poems on Various Subjects* of 1796) sets up the dialogue:

> O! what a loud and fearful shriek was there,
> As tho' a thousand souls one death-groan pour'd!
> Great KOSCIUSKO, **'neath an Hireling's sword,**
> His Country view'd. – Hark! Thro' the list'ning air,
> When pauses **the tir'd Cossack's barb'rous yell**
> Of Triumph, on the chill and midnight gale
> Rises with frantic burst, or sadder swell,
> The dirge of murder'd Hope: while Freedom pale
> Bends in such anguish o'er her destin'd bier,
> As if from eldest time some Spirit meek
> Had gather'd in a mystic urn **each tear**
> That ever furrow'd a sad Patriot's cheek;
> And she had drench'd the sorrows of the bowl –
> E'en till she reel'd, intoxicate of soul!
>   (*Morning Chronicle*, 16 December 1794)

Certain phrases in the sonnet are clearly echoed in the following stanzas of Whitchurch's anti-war poem, 'Farewell to the Year 1794', initially published in 1795:[49]

> Too much of this was *Poland* made to feel,
> 'Gainst *Royal Robbers* forc'd in arms to rise;
> For, ah! **beneath the barb'rous *Cossack's* steel,**
> Her valiant KOSCIUSCO bleeding lies!
>
> Illustrious Chief! – *sure 'tis no treason here*
> **To pay an heart-felt tribute to thy worth;**
> **O'er suff'ring Liberty to drop a tear,**
> And curse **the bloody Tygress of the North.**
>
> Lo! *Ismael's* **brutal Conqueror,** from afar,
> Leads on his **myrmidons** in scent of prey;
> Train'd up to all the cruelties of war,
> To age, to sex, they no distinction pay!
>
> . . .
>
> **In vain the Mother's prayer – the Infant's cry –**
> **Nor prayers, nor tears, could move the furious band;**
> **Beneath the sword** ALL **undistinguish'd die,**
> For this the FIEND SUWARROW gave command![50]

Thelwall's engagement with Kosciusko and the plight of his dismembered Poland occurs in two powerful passages of anti-Pitt jacobin rhetoric – delivered initially in lectures of April and May 1795 and subsequently published in *The Tribune* of 1796 – which stand at the centre of the dialogue. Thelwall's comparison of Kosciusko and Pitt in the second extract should be seen as a companion-piece to the third of his *Tribune* lectures 'On the Prospective Principle of Virtue' (May 1795), which contrasts the characters of Robespierre and Pitt and also contains echoes of Coleridge's lines on Robespierre in his play of 1794:[51]

> late as it is, there is one subject I cannot pass over without some animadversion. I mean the conduct of the Minister of this country with respect to Poland; that country whose struggles for dawning liberty warmed the heart of every generous Briton . . . every spark of liberty has been trampled out; the **Hyaena of the North**, and the vultures of

Germany, have torn its mangled limbs; have feasted on its gore; and have been supplied, by British gold, with the means of this destruction and inhuman partition . . . And was [the Despot of Prussia] not thereby enabled to hold out against the vigorous exertion of the Poles, till the **Hyaena of the north** was ready to pour her **Barbarians** upon them, and to repeat the *massacres of Ismael in the streets of Warsaw*. Yes, this **tiger in human shape**, this royal savage, is one of the allies with whom our virtuous administration thinks a free people ought to coalesce, for the destruction of republicanism in France . . .[52]

Poor devoted Poland! . . . But for [Pitt's] subsidy, it is clear Prussia could not have resisted the brave efforts of the gallant *Kosciusko*. He did not resist them effectually at last. He felt (and trembled while he felt) the zeal, the ardour of that brave peasant. – Yes, *peasant* I will call him; for *Kosciusko*, like *Stanhope*, was an aristocrat only by birth: he could perceive that the peasantry are the life, the soul, the existence of society; and therefore he gloried in the character, and assumed the appearance: like a peasant he fought – like a peasant he conquered – and, at last, like a peasant fell, to *chains* indeed! to *anguish*! but not to *infamy*. No: he fell *from prosperity*; but he rose *to glory*. His name will be resounded; his memory will be beloved. Posterity will bow adoration to his bust, when *Pitt* and all his dependants, are swept down the tide of oblivion . . . O Poland! Poland! – Yes there was a time when the friends of liberty might flatter themselves with a hope, that not the General of the Poles, but the *despot* of Prussia **(for it is now no longer treason to speak of him as he deserves!)** would have felt the galling of chain . . . O Poland! O exhausted country! **O depopulated Warsaw!** . . . what heart bleeds not for thy fate! Behold the **fiend Zuwarrow**, hot from scenes of massacre and cruelty, where **Ismael's sons** groaned and bled, by thousands, at his command; **nor even Circassia's daughters, the beauties of the east, no, nor the smiling infants at the breast** escaped his butchering knife. Zuwarrow comes, and **Warsaw's streets groan** beneath his blood-stained steps. And thou, Imperial Daemon! **thou cursed Hyaena of the north**, thou pouredst thy savage fury in his soul, and gavest the dagger edge. Thus Poland fell.[53]

Coleridge's 'Ode on the Departing Year' develops the nascent visionary quality of his 1794 sonnet to Kosciusko and updates Whitchurch's poem to the departing year by recording the death, on 17 November 1796, of Catherine the Great, 'the Hyaena of the north':

> I mark'd Ambition in his war-array;
> I heard the mailed Monarch's troublous cry –
> 'Ah! wherefore does the **Northern Conqueress** stay?
> Groans not her Chariot o'er its onward way?'
>   Fly, mailed Monarch, fly!
>   Stunn'd by Death's 'twice mortal' mace,
>   No more on MURDER's lurid face
> Th'insatiate Hag shall gloat with drunken eye!
>   Manes of th'unnumbered Slain!
>   **Ye that gasp'd on WARSAW's plain!**
>   **Ye that erst at ISMAIL's tower,**
>   When human ruin chok'd the streams,
>   Fell in Conquest's glutted hour,
>   **Mid Women's shrieks and Infants' screams;**
>   Whose shrieks, whose screams were vain to stir
>   **Loud-laughing, red-eyed Massacre!**
>   Spirits of th'uncoffin'd Slain,
>   Sudden blasts of Triumph swelling
>   Oft, at night, in misty train,
>   Rush around her narrow Dwelling!
>   **Th'exterminating Fiend** is fled –
>   (Foul her Life and dark her doom!)
>   Mighty Army of the Dead,
>   Dance, like Death-fires, round her Tomb!⁵⁴

The interplay between the poems and the *Tribune* lectures is plain: compare ''neath an Hireling's sword' and 'the tir'd Cossack's barb'rous yell' in Coleridge's sonnet with Whitchurch's 'beneath the barb'rous *Cossack's* steel' and with Thelwall's 'barbarians'; the title of Whitchurch's piece with that of Coleridge's ode; the description of Catherine the Great in Whitchurch's poem – 'the bloody Tygress of the *North*' – with Thelwall's 'this tiger in human shape . . . thou cursed Hyaena of the north'; Whitchurch's 'brutal Conqueror' and 'the FIEND SUWARROW' with Coleridge's 'Northern Conqueress' and 'exterminating Fiend' and with Thelwall's own 'fiend *Zuwarrow*'. The dialogue is also evident in the shared dramatic narrative of imperial rapaciousness – inflated to the level of myth – that brings Suvorov, 'hot' from reeking Ismael in 1790 to Warsaw in 1794;⁵⁵ in the account of the fate of women and infants at Ismael; and in the echo of Whitchurch's (rather nervously phrased) compliment to Kosciusko – 'sure 'tis no treason here / To pay an heart-felt tribute to thy worth' – in

Thelwall's indictment of Frederick William II of Prussia – 'for it is now no longer treason to speak of him as he deserves'. The intertextual drama of these pieces illustrates well the reticular quality of the culture that produced them. It also shows how allusiveness – the literary inscription of such connectedness – was employed in the 1790s by a community of radical writers, profoundly responsive to each other's work, to cement and signpost shared political allegiances.

In *The Pleasures of Hope* (1799), Thomas Campbell lamented the downfall of Poland and the defeat of Kosciusko – 'Hope, for a season, bade the world farewell, / And Freedom shrieked – as Kosciusko fell!' – and was to mention him again in his 1831 'Lines on Poland'.[56] When Campbell was buried in Westminster Abbey on 3 July 1844 in the presence of Macaulay, Lockhart, Brougham and Peel, a guard of Polish nobles sprinkled a handful of soil from Kosciusko's grave on the coffin. The narrow room of the sonnet seems to have been for the Romantics an attractive form in which to articulate with succinct drama the tragedy and heroism of the General. On 19 November 1815, Leigh Hunt published a sonnet entitled 'To Kosciusko: Who took part neither with Bonaparte in the height of his power, nor with the Allies in the height of theirs' in the *Examiner*,[57] and on 16 February 1817, the *Examiner* published Keats's sonnet to Kosciusko, which links his name 'with Alfred's and the great of yore'. Countering Morris Dickstein's contention that the sonnet is an example of Keats's 'evasion of the political . . . evoking "a refreshing alternative world"', John Kandl has explored the 'allusive relationship' between this sonnet and essays by Hunt which cite Kosciusko as a figure 'of significance at that particular historical moment' as European monarchies were being restored post-Waterloo.[58] Hunt's *Examiner* essay of 12 January 1817, which pits the 'new Leviathan' of 'Popular Opinion' against divine right and kingly despotism, rails against the apostasy of erstwhile radicals – Coleridge is explicitly named – and refers to the 'great man' Kosciusko as 'the head' of a tribe of reformers and radicals who have 'stood foremost in the danger' and for whom the fight for freedom is an ongoing battle:

> Kosciusko, though not actually engaged with any set of men, may be considered as the head of them. That great man is still alive: – he fought against the first outrage on public justice: he fought against the *first* partition of Poland, when he had strength: and now, covered with scars, but still inflexible of heart, he sets his face in contemptuous

silence against the *second*. We may expect him to speak and act again, if the world go on as it promises.⁵⁹

Here, Hunt resurrects Kosciusko – at the time an old man of seventy-one – as a powerful contemporary icon for a new period of political struggle. Kandl locates Keats's sonnet as part of this contextual fabric, and sees Keats's poem as engaging also in dialogue with Coleridge's 1794 sonnet to Kosciusko. Keats's sonnet reverses 'Coleridge's dirge of shrieks and groans' and recasts 'Coleridge's failed "Kosciusko" as a figure of consistent faith in reform' and as 'a sound signifying . . . both Hope and Freedom'.⁶⁰

> Good Kosciusko, thy great name alone
> Is a full harvest whence to reap high feeling;
> It comes upon us like the glorious pealing
> Of the wide spheres – an everlasting tone.
> And now it tells me, that in worlds unknown,
> The names of heroes burst from clouds concealing,
> And change to harmonies, for ever stealing
> Through cloudless blue, and round each silver throne.
> It tells me too, that on a happy day,
> When some good spirit walks upon the earth,
> Thy name with Alfred's and the great of yore
> Gently commingling, gives tremendous birth
> To a loud hymn, that sounds far, far away,
> To where the great God lives for evermore.
> (Keats, *Poems*, 94–5)

Thomas McLean notes that the inspiration for the tintinnabulary trope of Keats's sonnet is another of Hunt's *Examiner* articles (3 July 1814), which announces that 'The very mention of the name of KOSCIUSKO, after having been compelled to ring the changes so often upon the BONAPARTES and the FERDINANDS, – the mighty tyrants and the mean, – is like a new music, coming to us in a summer wind.'⁶¹ Evident in these appropriations and constructions of Kosciusko is the substitution of a discourse of the visual for a discourse of the verbal and aural. McLean observes that, for second-generation Romantic writers, an obsession with the scarred, suffering body of Kosciusko – 'so central to earlier [that is, 1790s] representations' – is 'replaced by a powerful, ghostly and guilt-creating name'. And it is that name, with its 'almost transcendent force',[62] that is enlisted by Hunt and Keats in early 1817 to locate and indict Coleridge's political identity. Coleridge had just published the first of his 'Lay Sermons' in *The Statesman's Manual* (December 1816), whose reactionary ideology, obscurantism and 'cant' Hazlitt had already savaged in two *Examiner* reviews of September 1816 (a pre-emptive strike in which Coleridge appears as an 'arch-angel ruined'[63]) and December 1816. Hazlitt was to resume his attack on the turncoat Coleridge in the same 12 January 1817 issue of the *Examiner* in which Hunt, as we have seen, invoked the 'great man' Kosciusko as a consistent friend of freedom and berated Coleridge for his desertion. Kosciusko clearly emerges in Hunt's article as the antithesis of the apostate Coleridge: 'with all respect to Mr Coleridge's talents, and regret at the desponding turn of them, there are millions of younger souls and bodies more healthily wise than he, – millions who have all the desires and aspirations he once had'.[64] In the context of these criticisms of Coleridge and celebrations of Kosciusko, Keats's refiguring in his 1817 sonnet of Coleridge's gloomier 1794 poem would have served to point up in the minds of Hunt, Keats and Hazlitt the distance between the radical Coleridge of the 1790s and the increasingly conservative commentator recently ensconced at Highgate. As already demonstrated, Coleridge's earlier sonnet to the Polish hero had itself been part of a radical 1790s dialogue which strongly emphasized Coleridge's reformist contacts and commitment; by 1817, however, Keats's own dialogic engagement with Coleridge's sonnet emphasized Coleridge's rejection of a former radical self. Read in its wider *Examiner* context, therefore, Keats's sonnet is revealed to be more than an 'evasion of the political'. Not only does it resuscitate Kosciusko as a paradigm of unwavering principle and signifier of undaunted reformist commitment at another dark time for European radicals; it also marks shifts of political allegiance in others. The sonnet is a further instructive example of the way in which the contextual fabric of such a poem animates it with political meanings which would be difficult to trace if the sonnet were read in cultural isolation. We need to be alive to the reticularity of such texts if we are to defend works of the Romantic period from the charge of retreating from history into 'refreshing alternative world[s]'.

Moreover, the presence of Kosciusko in Keats's 'Sleep and Poetry', completed around the same time as the sonnet, further serves to counteract any evasion of the political. It is the scarred, defeated general, however, who appears here – an image that invokes earlier,

1790s representations. Keats again pairs the Pole and Alfred as he describes the bust of Kosciusko which Leigh Hunt kept in the library of his cottage in Hampstead. The concluding movement of the poem amounts, in Charles Cowden Clarke's words, to 'an inventory of the art garniture of the room':[65]

> Sappho's meek head was there half smiling down
> At nothing . . .
> Great Alfred's too, with anxious, pitying eyes,
> As if he always listened to the sighs
> Of the goaded world; and Kosciusko's worn
> By horrid sufferance – mightily forlorn.
> (Keats, *Poems*, 93; ll. 381–2 and 385–8)

Hunt's and Keats's veneration of the bust of Kosciusko bears out Thelwall's prognostication in *The Tribune* of 1796 that 'Posterity will bow adoration to his bust, when *Pitt* and all his dependants, are swept down the tide of oblivion'. More important to an examination of the valency of Kosciusko in the literary productions of the time is my contention that the lines on Alfred and Kosciusko should be seen as part of Keats's groping in this transitional poem towards the maturer knowledge and historicized imagination – soon to be arrived at in the letters, the Odes and 'The Fall of Hyperion' – that conceive of poetry as a healing but (a)stringent force that resists the 'fair / Visions of all places' ('Sleep and Poetry', ll. 62–3) and engages with the problem of human suffering. The lines on the couch-bound Kosciusko represent one of the sites of disturbance in a poem in which 'a sense of real things' (l. 157) – history's harsher conditions – come to disturb an escapist vision experienced 'upon a couch at ease' (l. 353). Significantly, the word 'forlorn' here – 'Kosciusko's worn / By horrid sufferance – mightily forlorn' – anticipates the pivotal 'forlorn' of the final two stanzas of 'Ode to a Nightingale', which functions as a hinge between an ultimately deceptive 'fancy' (l. 73) to which the poet yields, and the return to a painful consciousness of self in a world of 'weariness', 'fever' and 'fret' (l. 23) in which 'men sit and hear each other groan' (l. 24):

> The same [music] that oft-times hath
> Charmed magic casements, opening on the foam
> Of perilous seas, in faery lands forlorn.

> Forlorn! the very word is like a bell
> To toll me back from thee to my sole self!
> (Keats, *Poems*, 348; ll. 68–72)

No doubt the word would have tolled Keats back in May 1819 to his December 1816 lines on the General's 'horrid sufferance', establishing a link between the forlorn Keats and the forlorn Kosciusko.[66]

Another of those sites of disquiet in 'Sleep and Poetry' occurs earlier in the poem as Keats rejects the attractions of a classical-pastoral fantasy peopled by 'tame nymphs' and the temptation to 'rest in silence' in 'the bosom of the leafy world', declaring:

> And can I ever bid these joys farewell?
> Yes, I must pass them for a nobler life,
> Where I may find the agonies, the strife
> Of human hearts . . .
> (Keats, *Poems*, 86; ll. 122–5)

These lines are consonant with David Williams's injunction to the topographer/historian in *The History of Monmouthshire*: 'But the contemplation of these scenes, must be exchanged for the occurrences and events that have occupied them; the principal objects of the Author being the good and evil, the light and shadow, of human action.'[67] For the most part, however, Keats in 'Sleep and Poetry' is still in the Chamber of Maiden-Thought, where, as he told Reynolds on 3 May 1818, 'we become intoxicated with the light and the atmosphere . . . [and] see nothing but pleasant wonders, and think of delaying there for ever in delight'.[68] But in the sites of disturbance identified above – moments which offer an interesting parallel to the 'tremor[s] of anxiety' in 'Tintern Abbey' – we perceive the darkening of the Chamber of Maiden-Thought and the opening up of the 'dark passages' which for Keats were the result of 'sharpening one's vision into the heart and nature of Man – of convincing ones [sic] nerves that the World is full of Misery and Heartbreak, Pain, Sickness and oppression . . . We see not the ballance [sic] of good and evil.'[69] As that same letter to Reynolds attests, of course, Keats located the writing of 'Tintern Abbey' at precisely this tenebrous moment – 'To this point was Wordsworth come, as far as I can conceive when he wrote "Tintern Abbey"' – and went on to state: '[Wordsworth's] Genius is explorative of those dark Passages. Now if we live, and go on thinking, we too shall explore them.'[70] The lines on Kosciusko make 'Sleep and Poetry', in which the would-be poet's unhistorical imagination luxuriates in visions of 'heart-easing things', resonate briefly, but prophetically, with Wordsworth's 'still, sad music of humanity', or, in Keats's own words, with 'the sighs / Of the goaded world'. It is fitting that lines on the gravely wounded Kosciusko should anticipate the sharper vision of Keats the poet–physician.

Indeed, Keats's allusion to Kosciusko's 'horrid sufferance' can be traced to the clinical account of his wounds in lectures given by Sir Astley Cooper, the most flamboyant and accomplished surgeon of his day, which Keats attended as a young student at Guy's Hospital in 1815–16. Cooper himself would have politicized Keats's vision of suffering: a confirmed democrat in the 1790s, Cooper had visited revolutionary Paris in 1792, attended meetings of the National Assembly, and witnessed the September Massacres. He was intimate in the early 1790s with Thelwall (both attended the meetings of the Physical Society at Guy's Hospital of which Thelwall was a conspicuous member), and under Thelwall's influence, he became 'tolerably republicanized'.[71] In 1843, Bransby Blake Cooper wrote disapprovingly of his uncle's radical contacts:

> It is curious that we should find Astley Cooper thus again thrown into frequent communication with Mr Thelwall, to whose influence the best friends of the former had already attributed the taint in his political and religious principles ... Perhaps to the fact of his renewed intimacy with Mr Thelwall, more than to any other cause, may be attributed this delay in the hoped-for change, which to a certain extent seemed to have been promised, by his expressions of horror at the savage cruelties committed by the democratic leaders at Paris ... Many facts contribute to prove that Thelwall exercised a serious influence over the mind of Astley Cooper during the early period of his professional life.[72]

Cooper's lectures on the 'Principles and Practice of Surgery', which Keats attended and which were later published (1824–7), cite Kosciusko as a notable medical case. Cooper's account of Kosciusko's injuries is important since it would have radically *humanized* for Keats an archetypal Kosciusko who had by 1816 been elevated by two generations of Romantic writers to the status of myth:

> In a fracture of the thigh bone, by which the sciatic nerve was injured, so as to produce numbness in the limb below, the person recovered in

nine months. Koschiusko [sic], the Polish General, had his sciatic nerve injured by a spike, and when in this country, many months after receiving the wound, he had not got rid of the effects; and I have heard since, that he remained lame.[73]

Keats's lecture notes read: 'The Patriot K[osciusko] having had the Sciatic Nerve divided by a pike wound was a long while before his limb recovered its sensibility.'[74] Cooper's reference to Kosciusko would have been fresh in Keats's mind when he came to write 'Sleep and Poetry' and 'To Kosciusko' at the end of 1816. Perhaps Keats also recalled the ardour with which Cooper may have spoken of the man who achieved heroic status during his own radical years.

Kosciusko features prominently in Jane Porter's successful early historical novel, *Thaddeus of Warsaw* (1803), which led to a friendship with the General and in which Thaddeus, like Kosciusko, is driven as an exile to England after the Poles' defeat by Russia. Byron was to refer to Prince Mavrocordato of Greece as 'the only *Washington* or *Kosciusko* kind of man among them',[75] and the Pole appears as hero in *The Age of Bronze* and *Don Juan*.[76] Like Warner, to whom we shall shortly return in order to consider Kosciusko's impact on Wordsworth, Walter Savage Landor had 'seen and once conversed'[77] with Kosciusko as the wounded General passed through England in 1797. In Rome in 1860, the elderly Landor related the fascinating circumstances of that meeting to James T. Fields, who published the account in his *Biographical Notes and Personal Sketches*:

> I have seen some famous people in my time, and not the least among them was Kosciusko. A young girl who had heard him say he would like to see me brought me to his door. She knocked and said, 'General Kosciusko, I have brought a friend to see you'. 'I am sorry, my dear', he answered, 'but I can see no one'. 'I knew you wished to meet Mr Landor' – 'What, Landor?' – and in one instant he started from his couch and came forward to embrace me. He had been severely wounded in the head, and his pale face, bound about with broad black bands, gave him a look of deathly whiteness. He was reading, as he lay, a volume of my poems, and called my attention to the coincidence.[78]

Landor is surely embellishing the tale (would Kosciusko have been reading what can only be Landor's *Poems* of 1795?), but the emphasis on the stark contrast between the deathly pale face and the black silk bandages rings true and the description should be read alongside Warner's. As part of his *Imaginary Conversations of Literary Men and Statesmen* of 1824,[79] Landor published a fictional dialogue between the exiled Kosciusko and the Polish king, Stanislaw II Augustus Poniatowski. It is tempting to assume that it is informed by elements of the actual conversation Landor had with the Pole in the summer of 1797:

PONIATOWSKI
If we could but have saved our Poland! O! my comrade! . . . O with what enthusiasm would our legions follow you! why not return amongst us and command us?

KOSCIUSKO
Where is Poland?

PONIATOWSKI
She rises from her ashes with new splendour: in every battle she performs the most distinguished part . . . do you sigh at hearing it!

KOSCIUSKO
Poniatowski! her blood flows for strangers, and her heroism is but an interlude in the drama of Ambition. She is intoxicated from the cup of Glory to be dismembered with the less feeling of her loss.[80]

Landor might well be resurrecting aspects of his conversation with Kosciusko here. Interestingly, he might also be adding his voice to that earlier 1790s intertextual 'conversation' inspired by Kosciusko which has already been explored. The final sentence quoted above may be a reminiscence of the concluding lines of Coleridge's sonnet to Kosciusko and his soon-to-be-dismembered Poland, which Landor would have encountered in the version printed in Coleridge's *Poems* of 1796: 'And she had drain'd the sorrows of the bowl / Ev'n till she reel'd, intoxicate of soul!' Significantly, Coleridge's sonnet here echoes his personification of the September Massacres in *The Fall of Robespierre*: 'through the streaming streets / Of Paris red-eyed Massacre o'er wearied / Reel'd heavily, intoxicate with blood'.[81] The sonnet to Kosciusko recasts this horrific personification as a 'Spirit meek', intoxicated not with blood, but with a patriot's tears; Landor gives the image its latest incarnation in the form of a Poland that is not so much intoxicated as anaesthetized by evanescent glory, awaiting amputation.

In 1835, Landor was to raise Southey to hallowed company by declaring: 'A phrenologist once told me that he observed the mark of veneration on my head. I told him in return that I could give him a proof of it. I would hold the stirrup for Kosciusko, the brandy-bottle for Hofer, the standish for Southey.'[82] For a modern reader, Southey's ink-pot sits rather incongruously with Kosciusko's war-horse (three died underneath him at Maciejowice) and the Tyrolese freedom-fighter Andreas Hofer's battle-issue. In a posthumously-published fragment of 1895, Landor envisaged a mighty Polish–Tyrolese–American military triumvirate of iconic freedom-fighters:

> Kosciusko, Hofer, George
> The staid Virginian, standing side by side . . .
> To strike such men how vainly kinglets forge
> The brittle playthings of their puny pride.[83]

It was only against Washington, however, that kings proved 'kinglets' and their ordnance 'vain' and 'brittle'. The other two were, profoundly, symbols of heroic defeat.

Wordsworth also regarded the fallen General as a hero, and was to invoke the Pole's sacrifice in the cause of liberty in *The Convention of Cintra* (1808–9): 'The stir of emancipation may again be felt at the mouths as well as at the sources of the Rhine. Poland perhaps will not be insensible; Kosciuscko and his compeers may not have bled in vain.'[84] I want to suggest, however, that informing Wordsworth's 1790s experience is a deeper awareness of Kosciusko and his fate which I trace to another of those influential conversations of the 1790s – another of those fascinating sites of cultural confluence. Significantly, the conversation that is about to be reconstructed occurred in the summer of 1798, a matter of days before Wordsworth revisited the Wye Valley.

The 'Inner Conflicts' and 'Conversations of the Time'

Before embarking on their tour of the Wye Valley on 10 July 1798, Wordsworth and Dorothy visited James Losh at Bath, arriving there on the 8th. They took lunch, tea and dinner with him and other guests, as well as breakfast on the 9th.[85] Losh, like Wordsworth and David Williams, had seen revolutionary Paris in 1792, had been a member of the London Corresponding Society, the Society for Constitutional

Information and the Friends of the People, and an active campaigner for reform in the 1790s. Wordsworth and Losh may have met in Paris in 1792; there is some evidence to suggest they travelled back together.[86] In an attempt to map the psychological climate as well as the geographical trajectories of the time, Nicholas Roe asks: 'What did Wordsworth and Losh talk about on those two days at Bath?' He suggests that

> The conversation must have turned on the forthcoming *Lyrical Ballads* and projected trip to Germany; a little earlier in the year Losh had noted [in his diary] 'were there any place to go to emigration would be a prudent thing for literary men and the friends of freedom'. But if this much is a reasonable conjecture, they doubtless also touched on political affairs, mutual acquaintances, and shared experiences following their coincidence at Paris six years before in autumn 1792. As Wordsworth parted from Losh in July 1798 it seems highly likely that politics, poetry, his recent past and immediate future would have been much on his mind. On the evening of 10 July, perhaps, he arrived at Tintern and then or shortly afterwards began to compose his poem.[87]

As Roe summarizes in a later study: 'This meeting is important in that it suggests Wordsworth's memory of the revolution may have been an immediate context for his visit to the Wye.'[88] Referring to the pivotal year 1798 in his treatment of the themes of 'apostasy and disenchantment' in the political experience of Wordsworth, Coleridge and Thelwall during the 1790s, E. P. Thompson remarks: 'We get near to the conversations of the time from scraps of information in the diaries of James Losh . . . But how are we to reconstruct Wordsworth's inner conflicts at this time? There is little evidence.'[89] Getting 'near to the conversations of the time' and offering some new 'evidence' is what I propose to do here. I suggest that the conversation of another of Losh's guests might also have turned the poet's thoughts to some disturbing political realities, public and private betrayals, shortly before his arrival at Tintern and the composition of 'Tintern Abbey'.

What has not been stressed by commentators is that present at all three meals at Losh's on 8 July was Richard Warner, Losh's erstwhile lodging companion, with whom the Wordsworths also dined the next day. Warner's recently published *Walk Through Wales* carried a frontispiece aquatint of Tintern Abbey and would have been a likely topic of conversation, and Wordsworth would surely have seen it. One can fairly assume that, in addition to John Thelwall's articles on 'The Phenomena of the Wye, during the Winter of 1797–8' (which appeared in two instalments in the *Monthly Magazine* in May and July 1798),[90] Gilpin's *Observations on the River Wye*, and, as I have already argued, David Williams's *History of Monmouthshire*, Warner's conversation and his *Walk Through Wales* stimulated Wordsworth to return to Tintern and the banks of the Wye that summer.[91]

The influence on Wordsworth of the *Walk Through Wales* deserves to be highlighted. Mary Jacobus has suggested that the opening passage of 'Tintern Abbey' may well be indebted to Warner's description in the *Walk Through Wales* of the Wye Valley near Tintern:

> In Warner's description of Llandogo – situated, like his own poem, 'a few miles above Tintern Abbey' – Wordsworth would have found a landscape that anticipated his opening lines:
>
>> You must imagine . . . a lofty hill, whose indented side is mantled with deep woods, through which a multitude of small cottages, sprinkled over the declivity in an artless, whimsical, and picturesque manner, shew their little whitened fronts, and strongly impress the imagination with the idea of its being fairy land . . .
>
> Wordsworth's plots and orchards 'Which . . . Among the woods and copses lose themselves' (ll. 12–13) must reflect a real landscape, but their air of belonging to an enchanted natural world may well owe something to Warner.[92]

Jacobus also suggests that the meditative tenor of the poem is characteristic of the mood evoked in passages of topographical prose on the Wye Valley such as Warner's description of the Wye near Monmouth, north of Tintern:

> At the distance of little better than half a mile from Monmouth, the river makes another grand sweep to the right, and assumes a different character from that which it has hitherto observed. Dismissing its rocks and precipices, *it rolls through lofty sloping hills,* thickly covered with waving woods from their roots to their tops. All here is solemn, still, and soothing; a deep repose reigns around, *and attunes the mind to meditation.*[93]

'Wordsworth's lofty cliffs and rolling river', Jacobus writes, 'suggest not only the landscape, but also the mood, which his title alone' – 'Tintern Abbey' – 'would have led his readers to expect'.[94] Further debts can be posited. Describing the famous Doward Rocks just before this passage, Warner mentions the 'fine echo' produced by them, 'the *centrum phonicum* of which appears to be near a spreading beech tree in the middle of the meadow'.[95] Appropriately, operative here also is a fine echo in another sense. Warner's description of the vagrant Wye – 'Dismissing its rocks and precipices, it *rolls through* lofty sloping hills' – is echoed in Wordsworth's own description in 'Tintern Abbey' of waters '*rolling* from their mountain-springs / With a sweet inland murmur'. There is, of course, much pantheist 'rolling' in Wordsworth's poetry around this time: 'the blessed power that rolls / About, below, above' ('Lines Written at a Small Distance from My House'); 'Rolled round in earth's diurnal course / With rocks and stones and trees!' ('A Slumber did my Spirit Seal'); 'Winds blow and waters roll' ('September 1802'); 'And hear the mighty waters rolling evermore' ('Ode: Intimations of Immortality'). But what 'rolls' most famously and most impressively in 'Tintern Abbey' is 'A motion and a spirit' that, significantly, impels 'All *thinking* things, all objects of all *thought* / And *rolls through* all things' (ll. 102–3; my emphasis). Coleridge's 'Holies of God', the 'Monads of the infinite mind' of 'Religious Musings' that 'interfus'd / Roll thro' the grosser and material mass / In organizing surge!' (ll. 423–5) also lie behind Wordsworth's poem at this point. But perhaps it is Warner's picture of the Wye 'roll[ing] through' a landscape which 'attunes the mind to meditation' – his linking, that is, of the 'rolling' river and the particularly focused kind of 'thinking' represented by 'meditation' – that prompted Wordsworth to transfer, later in the poem, the attributes of those waters 'rolling from their mountain-springs' to the 'spirit' that 'impels / All thinking things, all objects of all thought / And rolls through all things'.

Apart from Warner's recent tour and book, then, what might he and Wordsworth have discussed during those two days at Bath? Warner's encounter with Kosciusko would have been fresh and sensational news in July 1798, and any talk in Wordsworth's company of the *Walk Through Wales* (whose genesis, as already shown, is so closely linked with Kosciusko) would surely have provided an irresistible opportunity to tell the tale, especially given the fact that Warner had already decided on a second tour of Wales on which he was to embark in a matter of weeks. Moreover, if, as Roe suggests, politics were also in the air during those meals at Losh's, the story would indeed have furnished a lively and relevant topic of discussion. 'Were there any place to go to emigration would be a prudent thing for literary men and the friends of freedom', Losh had remarked earlier in the year; Warner's encounter with the defeated hero who was at Bristol precisely in order to emigrate to America would surely have struck a chord with a number of those assembled at Bath in July 1798.

Just as the 'tempting perspective . . . the wonders and glories' of Wales would have taken on a darker colouring for Warner in the context of his meeting with Kosciusko, so the opening passage of 'Tintern Abbey', which shows the influence of Warner's *Walk* and which, as already argued, encodes a reference to the patriot-martyr Tewdrig, might also be haunted by the figure of that contemporary patriot-martyr, Kosciusko. I suggest that there is an inscription of him in 'Tintern Abbey' in a mode other than that of direct, or even self-conscious, invocation. A 'vagrant dweller' ('Tintern Abbey', l. 21) in England in the summer of 1797, bound for retirement after defeat, Kosciusko further enriches the valency of the hermit as a paradigm of patriotism called *out of* retirement to triumph over a foreign foe. The Pole also adds to the valency of those lines I considered in the previous chapter: like Vortigern, Kosciusko was also moving westward, 'more like a man / Flying from something that he dreads, than one / Who sought the thing he loved', and the wounded man who embodied the betrayals suffered by his dismembered country should also be seen as informing Wordsworth's wishful claim that 'Nature never did betray / The heart that loved her' (ll. 123–4), disturbed, as Roe has argued, by its 'implied recollection of other and earlier betrayals'. The 'healing thoughts' which Wordsworth shores against future betrayals and against 'solitude, or fear, or pain, or grief' in the final movement of 'Tintern Abbey' are also poignant reminders of the need for literal healing, and perhaps specifically of the crippled General, his wounds, as Warner would certainly have emphasized, 'still unhealed'. Significantly, that final movement was composed as Wordsworth walked down the hill from Clifton into Bristol – the place from which the wounded Kosciusko had recently departed into exile.

'O How Fallen!': Wordsworth's Broken Soldiers

Moreover, Warner's story would have fascinated a poet who only a few months previously had composed his own study of a vagrant, broken veteran, encountered a decade before but representative also of the effects of mid-1790s campaigns against the French:

> There was in his form
> A meagre stiffness. You might almost think
> That his bones wounded him . . .
> His visage, wasted though it seem'd, was large
> In feature; his cheeks sunken . . .
> From behind
> A mile-stone propp'd him, & his figure seem'd
> Half-sitting & half-standing. I could mark
> That he was clad in military garb,
> Though faded yet entire . . .
> He appeared
> Forlorn and desolate, a man cut off
> From all his kind, and more than half detached
> From his own nature . . .
> . . . in his very dress appear'd
> A desolation, a simplicity
> That appertained to solitude . . .
> Long time I scanned him with a mingled sense
> Of fear and sorrow. From his lips meanwhile
> There issued murmuring sounds as if of pain
> Or of uneasy thought . . .
> . . . From his resting-place
> He rose, & with his lean & wasted arm
> In measured gesture lifted to his head
> Returned my salutation. A short while
> I held discourse on things indifferent
> And casual matter. He meanwhile had ceased
> From all complaint – his station he resumed,
> Proppd by the mile stone as before, & when erelong
> I asked his history, he in reply
> Was neither slow nor eager, but unmoved,
> And with a quiet uncomplaining voice,
> A stately air of mild indifference,
> He told a simple fact . . .[96]

As was the case with Warner's description of Kosciusko and Milton's portrait of Satan, a comparison of Wordsworth's 'Discharged Soldier' and Warner's account of the Polish General reveals some fascinating points of contact. The 'meagre stiffness', the wounds, the 'propp'd', 'half-sitting & half-standing' position, the high forehead, the wan and wasted visage, the low voice, and the vagrant isolation ('cut off / From all his kind') are common to both soldiers. Kosciusko's faint and tired smile as Warner takes his leave of him is strangely akin to the 'languor', 'strange half-absence' and 'indifference' (ll. 119, 143–4) which contribute so much to the disturbing ontological status of the soldier-solitary Wordsworth met above the Windermere Ferry in 1788. Furthermore, even both soldiers' valedictions are consonant: the discharged soldier's reproof, delivered with 'ghastly mildness' – 'My trust is in the God of Heaven, / And in the eye of him that passes me' – finds a parallel in Kosciusko's own mild reproof – 'Ah! sir, he who devotes himself for his country, must not look for reward on this side the grave!'

Both men appear as disquieting archetypes: Roe remarks that the 'ghostly figure' of Wordsworth's discharged soldier 'has acquired an emblematic presence beyond the "simple fact" of his personal history' (and, one might add, beyond his nominal political – that is, British – allegiance). Roe locates him in a 'distinguished line' of literary 'deathly archetypes' which include the 'olde man' resting on a stile in Chaucer's 'Pardoner's Tale', Spenser's Malegar in *The Faerie Queene* and, significantly, Milton's Death in the encounter at the Gates of Hell in Book II of *Paradise Lost*.[97] It is also the emblematic presence of Kosciusko in Warner's description that emerges so forcefully: in the words of *The Prelude*, Book VII, which relate Wordsworth's encounter with the blind beggar – another 'propped' and injured individual, 'Neglected and ungratefully thrown by' – Kosciusko appears as 'a type / Or emblem' of defeated radicalism. In the light of Warner's account, which would have alerted Wordsworth to the similarity between their encounters with these veterans, the 'Discharged Soldier' would have resonated in his mind with a startling proleptic symbolism and an added contemporary political charge.

In addition, the poet who was to write 'On the Extinction of the Venetian Republic', 'Thought of a Briton on the Subjugation of Switzerland', and the homage to another incarcerated 'miserable chieftain', Toussaint L'Ouverture, would surely have been much affected by Warner's portrait:

                      ... thou liest now
Alone in some *deep dungeon*'s earless den,
O *miserable Chieftain*! where and when

> Wilt thou find patience? Yet die not; do thou
> Wear rather in thy bonds a cheerful brow:
> *Though fallen* Thyself, never to rise again,
> Live, and take comfort . . .
> . . . thou hast great allies;
> Thy friends are exultations, agonies,
> And love, and Man's *unconquerable mind*.
> ('To Toussaint L'Ouverture', ll. 3–9, 12–14)[98]

That final phrase is a borrowing from Gray's 'The Progress of Poesy' – 'Th'unconquerable Mind, and Freedom's holy flame' – but the italicized phrases strongly suggest that another of Toussaint's literary 'allies' here is (once again) the chained and defeated 'miserable chieftain' Satan, lying in Hell's 'dungeon horrible', who seeks to rouse Beelzebub ('If thou beest he; but O how fallen!') with talk of his 'fixed mind' (I, 97) and 'unconquerable will' (I, 106). Milton's description of his own 'defeated' republican self in the invocation to Book VII of *Paradise Lost* – 'though fallen on evil days, / On evil days though fallen' (ll. 25–6) – adds to the resonance of Wordsworth's sonnet. Warner, as we have seen, was to invoke the satanic archetype in the description of his meeting with Kosciusko included in the *Literary Recollections*. He may well have communicated to Wordsworth in 1798 his sense of the fraught aptness of the Miltonic model, and it is possible that a memory of the conversation informs Wordsworth's own picture in 'To Toussaint L'Ouverture', written four years later, of another 'fallen General'.

At Bath in July 1798, the story Warner is likely to have related would have fallen also on the attentive ears of a soldier. Present at the meals at Losh's with Warner and Wordsworth was Warner's friend, William Johnson, who was to accompany Warner, Richard Cruttwell and his brother Clement on a second walk through Wales in August and September 1798, an account of which Warner published in 1799. As Warner states in his fascinating portrait of Johnson in the *Literary Recollections*, he had 'in early youth deeply imbibed the French revolutionary principles', enlisted with the National Guard and borne a commission in the French army, serving for a time under General Dumourier (vilified by the French as a traitor after he defected to the Allies in April 1793). Warner describes Johnson as

> efficient, not only as an officer, but as a *vocalist*; for, frequently, when his soldiers were exhausted with a march . . . he would mount on an

ammunition waggon, or piece of ordnance; thunder out some of their national airs, with all his deep enthusiasm, and exciting animation; and, in a short time, dissipate their tedium or gloom, and revive all their feelings of ardour and recklessness. (Warner, *Recollections*, II, 141–2)

Like Wordsworth and David Williams, however, he was to suffer political disillusionment:

Awakened by the unprincipled ambition of the rulers; and the sanguinary spirit of the more vulgar instruments, in this marvellous scene of moral and political disorganisation; he turned from it in disgust; quitted the army; retired, with his father and family, from Bourdeaux [*sic*]; came to Bath; and remained in that city, till the peace of Amiens enabled the party to return to their concerns in France. (Warner, *Recollections*, II, 141)

Warner's account is close to David Williams's description of his own experience of moral anarchy: 'I withdrew from the political arena . . . from despair occasioned by the ignorance and impetuosity of those reformers . . . From this chaos of good and evil, or of principles and passions, I withdrew.' The *Recollections* then proceed to relate a story whose appearance in *A Second Walk Through Wales* in 1799 would have been a dangerous thing. Wales again becomes, in the words of Paul Wright, 'a mirror of, and substitute for' revolutionary France:

Often, among the rocks of the valleys, and on the summits of the mountains of Wales, did we prevail upon our accomplished songster, to give us the sublime *Marseillois* Hymn, and the Ca Ira; and felt a *stirring within us*, which well accounted for the effect produced on the mad *sans culottes*, by the vocal powers of Mr Johnson. (II, 142)

This Briton who had played an active rôle in the armies of the French republic would have been an evocative presence, a second self, for Wordsworth at Bath – a man of action, like Kosciusko, whose career was a reminder of Wordsworth's erstwhile commitment to the revolution, of his desire to be actively involved ('Yet would I willingly have taken up / A service at [that] time for cause so great, / However dangerous') and also of his own subsequent moral and political disillusionment. Johnson would also have evoked in Wordsworth's mind the figure of another revolutionary soldier and important

Wordsworthian model, Michel Beaupuy,[99] by whom he had been profoundly influenced in 1792 at Blois. The name of Beaupuy would surely have been invoked; perhaps Johnson at Bath was prevailed upon, as he would be in a few weeks' time during Warner's second tour of Wales, to sing 'the sublime *Marseillois* Hymn, and the Ca Ira'.[100]

Interestingly, on the outskirts of Cardigan during that second walk, Warner and Johnson were 'with huzzas and halloos' taken to be French prisoners by a 'troop of women and children'; 'an idea naturally enough suggested', Warner explains, by the presence of their guide – a member of the local volunteers corps, in uniform, carrying a fowling-gun – and by 'the order of our march, our thread-bare apparel, and the news that had arrived on the preceding day of the French troops in Ireland having surrended to Lord Cornwallis'. He proceeds to list the various identities which the 'vagrant' pedestrian tourist had to negotiate at a tense time following the recent French 'invasion' of Pembrokeshire and the final bloody throes of the French-assisted Irish Rebellion: 'We thought that fancy had already exhausted herself in forming imaginary *characters* for us, and never apprehended we should have to add to the respectable list, (which comprised foot-pads, gaol-birds, militia-men, and acquitted felons) the reputation of being *Sans Culottes*' (*A Second Walk Through Wales*, 334). In view of his reputation as a democratic sympathizer, and of the company he was keeping in Wales – Johnson the ex-French army officer and commander of '*Sans Culottes*' – Warner's tone ('apprehended' seems nervously balanced between fancy and felony) surely hides deeper anxieties concerning his radical identity and that of his friend Johnson.

In concert with Warner's description of Kosciusko at Bath, Johnson, who had turned his back on a revolution that had produced the September Massacres and Robespierre's Terror, might also have stirred in Wordsworth memories of the blighted royalist soldier, bent on 'un-doing what was done', whom he had known at Blois in 1792 and whose portrait, written in 1804, was to appear in *The Prelude*, Book IX:

> One, reckoning by years,
> Was in the prime of manhood, and erewhile
> He had sate lord in many tender hearts,
> Though heedless of such honours now, and changed:
> His temper was quite mastered by the times,
> And they had blighted him, had eat away
> The beauty of his person, doing wrong

> Alike to body and to mind. His port,
> Which once had been erect and open, now
> Was stooping and contracted, and a face
> By nature lovely in itself, expressed,
> As much as any that was ever seen,
> A ravage out of season, made by thoughts
> Unhealthy and vexatious. At the hour,
> The most important of each day, in which
> The public news was read, the fever came,
> A punctual visitant, to shake this man,
> Disarmed his voice and fanned his yellow cheek
> Into a thousand colours. While he read,
> Or mused, his sword was haunted by his touch
> Continually, like an uneasy place
> In his own body . . .
>   (*The Prelude* (1805), IX, 143–64)

This soldier, whose haunting touch seems to prefigure his wounding ('like an uneasy place / In his own body'), is devastatingly 'changed' ('O how fallen! how changed / From him, who in the happy realms of light'); his beauty eaten away, he again evokes the 'archangel ruined' (*PL*, I, 593) whose brightness was 'obscured' by terrible conflict. The echo of 'The Discharged Soldier' in the final lines quoted above – 'From his lips meanwhile / There issued murmuring sounds as if of pain / Or of uneasy thought' – together with the Miltonic resonance, connects this fallen royalist angel with a group of broken soldiers who made a deep impact on Wordsworth in the years 1798–1804. I have been arguing that Kosciusko, whom Warner could not have failed to speak of at Bath in 1798, should also be seen as part of that group, and as a subtle presence in Wordsworth's poetry of that period.

    As a powerful symbol of vanquished liberty; a means of getting a purchase on past and present political identities, actual and *manqué*; a focus for the political dialogues and ideological battles of the 1790s and a rallying point of shared allegiances; an important catalyst in the development of a stringent poetic vision sensitive to suffering; and a figure who was both a graphic incarnation of the contemporary struggle against tyranny and an emblematic presence, elevated to the status of myth – a '*kind* of man' in Byron's words – Kosciusko was for Warner, Coleridge, Thelwall, Keats, Wordsworth and their contemporaries another presence not to be put by.

4
Models of Bardic Jacobinism and Gratitude: Edward Williams

My old acquaintance (those, I mean, who were elders when I was a young man) are dropping on all sides. One very remarkable one is just gone to his rest after a pilgrimage of fourscore years. Edward Williams, the Welsh bard, whom, under his Welsh name of Iolo, some lines in Madoc were intended to describe and gratify. He was the most eccentric man I ever knew, in whose eccentricity there was no affectation, and in whose conduct there was nothing morally wrong. Poor fellow! with a wild heart and a warm head, he had the simplicity of a child and the tenderness of a woman, and more knowledge of the traditions and antiquities of his own country than it is to be feared will ever be possessed by any one after him. I could tell you some odd anecdotes of him which ought not to be lost. (Southey to Henry Taylor, 24 January 1827)[1]

My fourth instructive model for the 1790s has already raised his 'warm head' in the first two chapters. He was a phenomenon of the age – an eccentric genius whose impact on the radical culture of the 1790s has so far received scant attention. Drawing on a large body of unpublished manuscript material, the present chapter offers a new account of this figure's position in the radical debates of the decade, focusing on his construction of an elaborate, pseudo-antiquarian Bardic discourse as a vehicle for his jacobin sympathies. His studious fashioning of himself as the modern incarnation and repository of what he propagated as the liberal ideology of ancient Bardism made him an object of fascination – and indeed, pity and abuse – in a culture profoundly aware of the political valency of his programme. Hitherto, no critic has offered a full account of the status in 1790s metropolitan radicalism of one who was, as Robert Southey put it in 1802, 'brimfull of genius and jacobinism'.[2] The second half of the chapter reveals the significant part he played in the formative ideological battles – already mentioned in Chapter 3 – between Coleridge and Wordsworth on the one hand and William Godwin on the other. In order to appreciate the significance of this figure as a material exemplum of the poets' anti-Godwinian positions and as a compelling second self during the 1790s, the exact nature of what might be termed his 'Bardic Jacobinism' and his contribution to the cultural politics of the age need to be interrogated.

Profile of a Jacobin Bard in London, 1791–1795

This colourful model of Romantic identity is the polymath Edward Williams (1747–1826), known as 'Iolo Morganwg' and 'The Bard of Liberty': stonemason, poet, scholar, antiquary, historian, opium-addict,[3] Unitarian, forger, radical, anti-slavery campaigner and inventor of the philosophy, rites and arcana of Bardism. The list almost brings the young Coleridge to mind. Indeed, Coleridge and Williams knew each other; they probably met through their mutual friend John Prior Estlin, the Unitarian minister of Bristol,[4] or through other Bristol Unitarians. A central figure of the Welsh cultural renaissance of the late eighteenth century, Williams was also part of English jacobin circles in London in the early years of the 1790s, and was known to all the major radicals in the metropolis and beyond. He was also the friend of Southey, Paine, Priestley (whom he saw off to America[5]), Thelwall, Horne Tooke, David Williams, Mrs Barbauld, George Dyer, Gilbert Wakefield and Talleyrand (whom he met at the house of David Williams) and Welsh radicals such as John Jones (Jac Glan-y-Gors), William Owen (-Pughe), Owen Jones ('Owain Myfyr') and Thomas Evans ('Tomos Glyn Cothi').[6]

Born at Pennon in the parish of Llancarfan, Glamorgan, Williams first appeared before the English public in November 1789, when a biographical piece appeared in *The Gentleman's Magazine*, together with his 'Ode, Imitated from the Gododin [sic] of Aneurin Gwawdrydd, a Welsh Bard that flourished about the Year 550'.[7] The account is signed 'J.D.', but it is certain the author is Williams himself. Williams skilfully constructs himself here as an object worthy of the English literary establishment's attention:

> The pieces you herewith receive were written by *Edward Williams*, of Flimston, near Cowbridge. – He is absolutely self-taught, and was never at school . . . About the age of twenty he was admitted a *Bard* in the ancient manner; a custom still retained in Glamorgan, but, I believe, in no other part of Wales . . . Besides Edward Williams, there is, I believe, now remaining only one regular bard in Glamorgan, or in the world: this is the Rev. Mr *Edward Evans*, of *Aberdare*, a Dissenting Minister. These two persons are the only legitimate descendants of the so-long-celebrated *Ancient British Bards* . . . the few that remain of the successors of the *Ancient Bards* pretend to mysteries in their art entirely unknown to what they call the modern book-taught poets. *Edward Williams* is now about forty years of age, and lives by the humble occupation of *a journeyman mason*. He is remarkably sober and temperate, very seldom drinks any strong liquors, and, if he sometimes tastes them, it is in very small quantities, and was never seen in liquor. His food is almost entirely vegetables; and he is a professed Pythagorean with respect to his opinion of animal food. He has other singularities: none of them, however, to my knowledge, of a vicious cast . . . *Edward Williams* lives the life of a hermit, is very little known, and knows very few; is never seen in any kind of company . . . He is naturally reserved, very bashful, and has been very unfortunate in his little concerns through life hitherto; yet he is chearfully [*sic*] contented with his lot, diffident to a fault, and too inoffensive to thrive in such a world as we live in. He is however respected by some gentlemen of learning and genius. – He is never seen walking without a book in his hand . . . He has acquired considerable reputation in his trade.

It is a masterful piece of self-promotion, appealing to the age's primitivist, antiquarian and literary tastes. The self-portrait is certainly not a wholly dramatic fiction, but the various personae Williams fashions for himself here are clearly designed to pique the interest of London's literary and intellectual circles in cult figures and fashions. He appears here as the autodidact; the descendant of the Welsh bards and the guardian of their mysteries (which gives the lie to Gray); the humble, rustic, industrious, abstemious, vegetarian artisan, brimful of genius; and the unworldly, bookish solitary. His radicalism was to be a unique product of these prototypical identities.

Although other aspects of Williams's life and achievement, such as his consummate skill as a forger of poetic and antiquarian material,[8] have been documented and disentangled by the monumental scholarship of G. J. Williams,[9] his radical activities and contacts in London

Edward Williams ('Iolo Morganwg'), frontispiece illustration to Elijah Waring's *Recollections and Anecdotes of Edward Williams* (1850), 'etched by Robert Cruickshank from a memoriter drawing by EW' (*by permission of the National Library of Wales, Aberystwyth*).

from 1791 to 1795 have received little attention. The massive body of correspondence and manuscripts in the National Library of Wales, Aberystwyth, offers a fascinating portrait of Williams as a Welsh jacobin in London and of the city's political climate in the 1790s. In the following profile, Williams's idiosyncratic punctuation is retained throughout.

Williams arrived in London in 1791 (he had also spent some time there in the early 1770s working as a stonemason) with the aim of marketing himself as a poet and scholar in English literary circles and securing the patronage and subscriptions that would enable him to see his *Poems, Lyric and Pastoral* (1794) through the press. At the same time, he immersed himself in contemporary radical culture, befriending radical writers and publishers such as the Unitarian Joseph Johnson, who offered advice on various projects and introduced him to radical and literary contacts.[10] Williams's letters of the period, especially those to his long-suffering and distressed wife Peggy (who was struggling to care for a cottage full of children in delicate health back in Glamorgan) and to the Revd John Walters, Cowbridge, rail furiously against what Williams calls 'Church and Kingism' – systems of political and religious imposture anathema to his Christian–Unitarian radicalism. A letter of 21 January 1794 informs Walters that he will not publish his projected pamphlet, *Kingcraft versus Christianity*, until he is safely in America, and in a statement reminiscent of Blake's famous note to Bishop Watson's *Apology for the Bible* – 'To defend the Bible in this year 1798 would cost a man his life'[11] – Williams told Walters that 'the man who would now preach up the scriptural doctrine of Government, would, notwithstanding our pretended tolleration [sic] be as infallibly consigned to the stake and faggot at this day as ever *Cranmer, Hooper*, and others were'.[12] In a letter of 19 February 1795, Williams remarked to his wife that 'all Systems of *Church and Kingism*, are, as if with might and main *preaching Christianity out of the World*'.[13] Even in his more playful and ironic moods, the man who claimed descent from the king-killer Cromwell (a troubling radical avatar)[14] was levelling barbs at his *bête noire* of institutionalized oppression; one fragment has him posing as 'Morgan ap Howel, ap Shenkin, ap Griffith . . . ap Owen Glendower, of the uninterrupted line of Cadwalader King of Wales and England and Scotland, and Ireland, and the plains of Shinor, and the Tower of Babel. Antiquary to the Swinish Multitude', author of 'Royal antiquities or anecdotes of Kingism and Kingcrafft' [sic].[15] The cultural and political identity he was forging for himself was a colourful product of such radical pedigrees. The mnemonic device of the Welsh Triads, so many of which he was to forge during the 1790s, was also enlisted by Williams in the service of Bardic Jacobin rhetoric, as Southey records: 'His toast was, "The three securities of liberty. All Kings in hell; the door locked; the key lost".'[16]

In 1793, Williams informed his wife that he had completed 'a little pamphlet' (which never appeared) entitled *War Incompatible with the Spirit of Christianity – an Essay by an Ancient British Bard*.[17] Williams at this time had many contacts in Bristol, and it is tempting to suppose that the title of Richard Warner's published sermon of 1804, mentioned in the previous chapter – *War Inconsistent with Christianity* (which, as Erdman has surmised, made a deep impression on Blake) – owes something to Williams's pamphlet. With Warner himself, then, Williams can be seen as a radical presence behind Albion's friend, 'Bath, healing city', in Blake's *Jerusalem*. A remarkable letter to the Revd Hugh Jones, Lewisham, of 4 June 1794 deserves to be quoted at length here since it affords a dramatic portrait of Williams's experiences in London and a valuable insight into the nature of his radical stance in the early 1790s. The date is followed by 'alias Dagon-massday' – a reference to the pagan idol of the Philistines which serves as an indictment of Britain's religious and political idolatry:

> I thank you for the favour of your subscription to my Poems . . . The *Poet*, especially the *Bard according to the rights and institutes of the Bards of the Island of Britain*, is only benignly mad, by thinking that it will avail him anything to preach up his fundamental principle of *peace* to a *King-ridden* world. The monarchical madness instigates to fury, and carries fire and sword, the most woful distress and destruction into every part of the world that is inhabited by *Man*. it voraciously feeds on human blood, and it dares to attempt to *cajole* the *Almighty* into these measures . . . All the whores and thieves of London are assembled about the fellow called *Reeves* and his *fiddlers* and *faddlers* in a mighty band, *bawling* and *squawking*, like the Songs of *caterwauling God-Save-the-King! – Church and King for ever!* they press everyone that passes by into this infernal service, crying to him *blast your eyes cry church and king, Church and King, damn your soul*! I *jabber'd Welsh*, squeaked out *Shursh sans King*, in as broken a manner as I could, and passed for a *Dutchman* with all but a *Welshman* or two, who laughed at me . . . I was amongst this *king-ridden* mob in real danger of my Life. they were egged on by *Parsons* in abundance. I was afraid that the butchers who were parading the streets

with their marrow bones and cleavers would have split my skull with one of them . . . I am no enemy to Kings – and am a friend to every Church that retains some appearance of Christianity, and is not degenerated into the *rank Idolatry* of *Church-and-Kingism*. I honor the minister (and not the less for his being termed *priest*) of every Sect and party in Religion, who appears to have a true sense of piety . . . who never with parsonic shears fleeces the sheep of his fold, never uses them as mules or jack-asses. A riding priest, who is often ridden by a king, is a heavy burden indeed, and what was never laid on man by him who said that his yoke and burden was light.

> If on my back bestrides a Priest,
> And on that Priest a King,
> I'm lost in vice, become a beast,
> A slave, a worthless thing.
>
> I with such pravities of soul
> Should not with man remain,
> But sent to rage where tygers howl
> On Afric's burning plain.

I am fully perswaded [*sic*] and even convinced to demonstration, that all the evils that now deluge the *nominally-Christian World* are the unavoidable effects of *Church-and-Kingical* hypocrisy, Priestcraft, and imposition – *blasphemously* called *religion*, but productive of all the bad effects of open, rank, and professed *Atheism* . . . Let *Churchism* and *Kingism* be founded on their genuine and primeval principles, of true religion, of piety towards *God*, Benevolence and Justice towards man, on the real *Rights of God and Man* and I shall not much object to the *modes* and *externalities* of either . . . I care not what title the Chief Magistrate may bear, whether it be King, Protector, President, or it may be emperor for aught I care, whether (for I can grant much to the bauble-adoring mind, and ever-childish ideas of kings) he be crowned or uncrowned. In short I care nothing for mere words and modes that are themselves *nothing*, or merely *indifferent*. I only wish to see *principles*, and not empty *sounds* and *forms* govern . . . *Church and King* at present is only a recreation of the Great Image which was formerly by monarchs and Priests commanded to be worship'd in the plains of Dura, and all that will not worship it are cast into the fiery furnace, and I freely confess that I am prepared for this, await it daily, am willing, and anxiously long to undergo the fate of Shadrach M[eshach] and

Abednego. truth Justice and the Rights of Man will never be restored to this depraved Kingdom but from the sufferings of those who dare assert the cause of that external rectitude that is now so successfully trampled upon. in this I am anxious to act a feeble part, the utmost that I am able not by acting the part (like kings) of a murder, but by dint of pacific reasoning. but where is now the king that will hear reason? any reason but that on which they founded the present suspension of the habeas corpus act, the banishment of those who assert the claims of truth, the imprisonment of others who utter the language of rationality. I long to suffer in the cause . . . let them heat the furnace ever so high, I can stand fire of every description but that which preys on the Conscience.[18]

Williams, then, like Thelwall, who was regularly threatened with loyalist violence, had terrifying first-hand experience of the truth plainly stated in Thelwall's *Appeal to Popular Opinion against Kidnapping and Murder* (1796) – that '"God Save the King" . . . has been made the war-hoop [*sic*] of tumult and civil commotion'.[19] Williams's contempt in this letter for the 'mere words' by which Government and the Established Church sustain themselves – 'In short I care nothing for mere words and modes that are themselves *nothing*, or merely *indifferent*. I only wish to see *principles*, and not empty *sounds* and *forms* govern' – was to be reiterated by Coleridge, in startlingly similar language, four years later in 'Fears in Solitude', significantly in the context of his indictment of a belligerent, blasphemous and atheistic England:

> all our dainty terms for fratricide,
> Terms which we trundle smoothly o'er our tongues
> Like *mere abstractions, empty sounds* to which
> We join no feeling and attach no *form* . . .
> (FiS, 6; my emphasis)

Coleridge would certainly have discussed the state of the nation with Williams, and perhaps these lines resonate with a reminiscence of such a conversation. Williams's references towards the end of the letter, as he plainly states his willingness to become a martyr in the cause of liberty, bring into focus the plight of the 'Edinburgh martyrs' Thomas Muir and Thomas Fysshe Palmer, recently transported to Botany Bay, and of Hardy, Horne Tooke, Thelwall and the other defendants of the 1794 Treason Trials.[20] One should take seriously Williams's longing to be counted amongst their ranks as an offering on the altar of the radical cause. As Williams makes clear in a letter of 19 February 1795 to Peggy,[21] he was present at the trial of Horne Tooke, 'an eye and an ear Witness to *Pitt's Perjury*' (a reference to what Coleridge described in his 'Letter to Edward Long Fox' as Pitt's 'epileptic memory' during his examination as a witness).[22] To celebrate the acquittal in late 1794 of Hardy, Horne Tooke and Thelwall, it was Williams who was asked to compose a song – *Trial by Jury, The Grand Palladium of British Liberty* – which he sang at the Crown and Anchor Tavern on 4 February 1795. Williams, frequenter of the meetings of the Society for Constitutional Information and the London Constitutional Society,[23] informed his wife on 12 February 1795: 'I wrote a Song some time ago which the Constitutional Society printed'.

> Come hither! ye *Spies* and *Informers of State*!
>   With Consciences offer'd for sale;
> Come hither! and all your atchievements [*sic*] relate!
>   Whilst Ridicule joys in the tale!
> Or will ye, disgrac'd, to your PERJURER throng,
>   Nor *Memory* wish to possess;
> Then haste! gnash your fangs! whilst we call for the song
>   Of Triumph's exulting excess![24]

A week later Williams must have horrified Peggy when he told her that he had been advised not to publish his 'History of the Druids' 'till we see Peace return', at which time he will print his book in France: 'stare not and wonder as much as you please, but I have it in serious contemplation to take you and the Children to Paris'.[25] Williams sent a copy of his *Poems, Lyric and Pastoral* to Thomas Palmer in Botany Bay, who on 12 September 1795 wrote a gracious and moving letter from his exile thanking the Welsh Bard:

> I received your letter yesterday, and was much flattered by the obliging present of your poems, but still more for the good opinion you are pleased to entertain of me. The approbation of the intelligent and worthy is the brightest reward I can receive next to that of my own mind. Superior poetry is my delight and from the little I have seen I hope that yours will afford it. Mr Muir took away the book last night and sat up till five reading it. I have received a letter from my friend Mr Dyer a brother poet also, from no one else at present but from his letter

TRIAL BY JURY,
The Grand Palladium of BRITISH LIBERTY.

A SONG,

SUNG AT THE CROWN AND ANCHOR, FEB. 4, 1795,

In CELEBRATION of the Late TRIALS for HIGH TREASON,
and TRIUMPHANT ACQUITTALS of

THOMAS HARDY, JOHN HORNE TOOKE,
AND
JOHN THELWALL;

AND IN HONOUR OF THEIR COUNSEL

THOMAS ERSKINE, AND VICARY GIBBS.

By EDWARD WILLIAMS,
Author of POEMS, LYRIC and PASTORAL, lately published.

HERE, Brothers, we meet in th' abundance of joy,
Prepar'd with our festival strain,
The storms, tho' severe, did but little annoy,
Their thunders exploded in vain:
See how firmly the mountain sustains ev'ry shock,
Tho' lightenings fly, raging 'round,
And INNOCENCE, like an immoveable rock,
Is ever invincible found.

Come hither! ye *Spies* and *Informers of State!* †
With Consciences offer'd for sale;
Come hither! and all your atchievements relate!
Whilst Ridicule joys in the tale!
Or will ye, disgrac'd, to your PERJURER throng,
Nor *Memory* wish to possess;
Then haste! gnash your fangs! whilst we call for the song
Of Triumph's exulting excess!

Th' ASSERTORS OF TRUTH that were trampl'd awhile,
That *Villainy* fiercely pursued,
Claim the song of our gladness—true Sons of our Isle,
With virtues gigantic endued.
What joy to the world! these to MAN and his CAUSE,
The JURIES OF BRITAIN restor'd:
Our JURIES—our themes of eternal Applause!
Let their names be for ever ador'd.

Boast, BRITAIN, thy JURIES! thy glory! thy plan! †
They treat the *stern Tyrant* with scorn!
O! bid them descend, the best Guardians of Man,
To millions of ages unborn:
Far and wide as the light, of true FREEDOM the soul,
Be thy BLEST INSTITUTION proclaim'd;
With ERSKINE, with GIBBS, on Eternity's roll,
In the language of Glory be nam'd.

† The Principle of Trial by Jury originated in Britain.

Edward Williams, *Trial by Jury, The Grand Palladium of British Liberty. A Song* (1795) and yours I will hope that I am not forgotten. Did you know with what sensibility we read letters from Old England sixteen thousand miles distance. I am sure our friends would think nothing of the trouble.[26]

A copy was also dispatched to Gilbert Wakefield, who, in a letter to Williams, pronounced himself 'much obliged & honoured by Mr Williams' present of his poems' and announced that he would call on Williams 'with one of his pamphlets in his pocket'.[27] For these radical figures, *Poems, Lyric and Pastoral*, discussed below, was a talisman of political fellowship and token of ideological support.

As well as frequenting the radical societies of the metropolis, Williams was closely involved during the early 1790s with the London Gwyneddigion Society, whose avowed aim was 'Liberty in Church and State'[28] and whose members included noted Welsh radicals such as John Jones, Thomas Roberts, Llwynrhudol – author of the radical pamphlet *Cwyn yn erbyn Gorthrymder* (A Complaint against Oppression, 1798[29]) – William Owen Pughe and Owain Myfyr (into whose 1789 edition of the poetry of Dafydd ap Gwilym Williams had inserted a number of brilliant forgeries). From 1789 onwards, a series of seminal *eisteddfodau* – formalized and radically charged reinstitutions of ancient bardic competitions – were organized in Wales under the patronage of the London Gwyneddigion. The prescribed title for the strict-metre *awdl* and the essay in the St Asaph *eisteddfod* of 1790 – 'Liberty' – reflected the radical bias of its members, and Walter Davies ('Gwallter Mechain'), the winner of the essay competition that year, received a silver medal designed by Dupré, official engraver of the French Republic.[30]

Such contacts meant that the forces of reaction regarded Williams as a subversive presence whose movements had to be scrutinized. Williams's letters regularly complain of his being watched and intimidated by the 'captain commandant of the spy-gang',[31] John Reeves (founder in 1792 of the Association for Preserving Liberty and Property Against Republicans and Levellers), and his army of spies and informers – 'vermin working out of reach', as Wordsworth was to describe them in Book X of *The Prelude*. A letter to Peggy of 27 August 1794 shows Williams beset by Reeves and a jealous Edward Jones, harpist to the Prince of Wales:

one of my reasons for staying at Hackney was to be out of the mobbing and kidnapping part of the Town for there are some Blackguards, and amongst them *one Reeves, Jones the Harper*, and others that would injure me if possible and are daily laying snares for me. but they are not cunning enough. these *very loyal sons of Bitches* have nothing in view but self interest . . . *Reeves* is angry with me for the *compliment* that I paid him in the first page of my preface – Jones is as angry with me because I would not give *him* the materials that I have for the History of the Bards . . . he became mad, he thought he should be able to get me into *Newgate, The Tower, Botany Bay* . . . and for that reason went to the fellow called *Reeves*, to *magistrates*; to every person and place where he thought he should succeed endeavouring to lay informations against [me] for what he called *Sedition Treason,* &cc.[32]

Indeed, from early 1794, the letters repeatedly testify to the seizure and examination of his papers. Williams became increasingly vigilant: 'my papers are often wantonly examined but nothing is to be found. the danger is over for I am now on my guard', he wrote to Peggy; 'there are a set of wretches employed by Government to go about daily to examine the papers of *suspected persons*, of whom I am one'. He goes on to tell her that he is writing the letter 'in a field . . . least [sic] the bloodhound should come in whilst I am writing' and warns her against frank and open communication with him: 'be cautious what you say in your letters, and say but what is barely necessary . . . I will go to M^r. William Owens [sic] . . . out of the informer's way.'[33] Another letter, declaring that his papers had been searched by the Privy Council, is a conflation of real concern for his own safety and that of his papers and bravado in the face of State surveillance:

> they confessed that I was too *prudent* for them. they are satisfied they say that I have seditious papers somewhere. I told them that I should be obliged to them for finding them out. – I will put you, said one, in Custody of the Messengers. – do so said I, and after you have done so, ask the laws of the land for what . . . and away I came – I must send my papers away soon, for I must secure them.[34]

Though some of the details supplied by Williams's friend and biographer Elijah Waring cannot be accepted unquestioningly, his statement that 'In consequence of some unfounded information against him, [Williams's] papers were seized by an order from Government, and conveyed to Whitehall, and he was summoned to present himself before Mr. Pitt . . . as a person suspected of disaffection to the State' accords with the details vouchsafed in the letters. Waring records that after a deliberate examination of the curious varieties contained in the Bard's budget of manuscripts, Pitt dismissed him with some kind admonitory observations, and concluded with 'Now, Mr. Williams, you may carry home all your papers, and make yourself perfectly easy'. This style of dismissal did not, however, meet the Bard's ideas of propriety. He told the Premier that as his papers had been brought thither without his consent, he should expect to have them conveyed back again, by the same authority which took them away. The requirement was deemed a reasonable one, and an official was ordered to attend him with the papers to his quarters.[35]

This was in 1794. Throughout that year, Williams was sending parcels of books west to the relative safety of Wales and Bristol. To John Walters he wrote on 9 January 1794: 'A parcel of my books will be down in Wales very soon. somethings that I have written have had the honour of being reviewed by the *Grand Jury of Middlesex*, poor Devils!'[36] To his wife on 13 September he boldly stated:

> when [Edward] Jones made the second attempt [to ruin me] I sent my box and papers to Bristol, to M^r. Lloyd, as I was not sure but that they would be a second time turned over by *Scoundrel Pit* [*sic*] and his brother bears. but it was necessary for me to stay here myself to make a proper defence. to absent myself would give *Reeves* and the rascally Magistrates a good pretence to prosecute me for a Libel, or Sedition.[37]

Such experiences ensured that Williams became known in radical circles as a representative figure of persecution, if not prosecution, by the State.

His was a Christianized radicalism in many ways akin to that of Coleridge, who felt compelled in the 1790s to denounce the 'atheistic' radicalism of such theorists as Godwin. Indeed, Coleridge's Unitarian radicalism, as I want to suggest in the second part of this chapter, should be viewed in the context of his friendship with this eloquent and compelling second self. Although Williams shared much common political ground with Paine (whom he knew), he objected violently, as did Coleridge and Williams's friend Wakefield, to Paine's deist attack on Christianity in *The Age of Reason* (1794), and immediately set about preparing an answer. As Unitarians,[38] both Williams and Coleridge recognized Jesus as the model reformer; for Williams, Jesus was the model *sansculotte*, who offered a template for those French sympathizers of the 1790s who saw politics and religion as inseparable and deprecated the bloody turn the revolution had taken:

> I am as much a republican as Tom Paine and more of a leveler [sic] because I am so on the principles of Jesus Christ, a Sanculotte [sic] indeed in whom there is no guile. I wish the french as much success in their present struggle as he does, perhaps more; but I will venture to say that a manly fortitude regulated by the precepts of the Prince of Peace would have produced more favourable effects than *all* their horridly sanguinary proceedings.[39]

In one letter to his wife, Williams reports the purchase of £2 worth of books which he needed to consult before drafting his riposte to Paine's 'Atheistical work'.[40] By February 1795, he had decided that the time was not right for him to put his 'answer to Paines Age of Reason to the Press, tho'' it has been approved of by the most respectable literary gentlemen in London' – wisely so, since he claims to 'defend Christianity by arguments that will enrage Government ten thousand times more than any thing that *Paine* has wrote against it'.[41] The reply to Paine never appeared, but fragments of it have survived; they represent an attempt to meet the 'would-be-thought-of Philosophical' Paine 'on his own ground'.[42] Another of Williams's fascinating religious and political manifestos shows him to be quite capable of calling Paine 'Iscariot' as readily as Coleridge could address Pitt as 'O calumniated Judas Iscariot!' in *Conciones ad Populum*.[43] It serves as a salutary reminder of the presence of competing ideologies *within* the radical movement of the day:

> I find my old Friend *Tom Paine*, who has been labouring hard to destroy, in this attempted subversion of Christianity, to deprive a very great number of human beings of the best comforts, the most solid consolations that this life afforded them; he has thus acted a very malevolent part, and is no longer worthy to be called by the truly noble title of *Citizen Paine*. He has here acted the part of Judas. look at his rights of Man, his Common Sense, &c. in those he salutes the Christian Religion with *Hail Master* and a *Kiss*. we poor fools thought it the Kiss of Friendship, of Love, of Charity. how have we been mistaken? But to view the rank villainy of this second Iscariot . . . Whilst I thus endeavour to repulse *Iscariot Paine* let it not be insinuated that I am slyly veering about, that I am changing my political opinions, which have

long been known, for which I have to my infinite Joy and satisfaction been abused and injured in person and property. I am still an honest Republican. I am whatever the foul slanderous mouths of the believers in the *Gospel according to S^t. Burke* (which seems to be the Creed of Church-and-Kingism.) may be pleased to call me. Democrate [sic], Leveler [sic], Jacobin, Sanculotte [sic], or any thing that may be manufactured from the cream that swims on the surface of their malevolence, or from the black dregs at bottom. I glory in all these titles.[44]

The trajectory of Williams's political beliefs during the 1790s broadly follows that of David Williams, Coleridge and Wordsworth. His radicalism certainly cooled towards the end of the 1790s in response to bloody internecine strife in France, French expansionist aggression in Europe and the threat of a French invasion of Britain. In a letter of March 1798 from Flimston, Glamorgan, to a Miss Barker (in which Williams, with a good sense of his audience, describes himself as being 'considerably assertive of the *Rights of Ladies*' even if his 'ideas go not the length of Mary *Wolstoncraft's*' [sic]), he rejects the badge of 'jacobin' and calls himself a 'reformist', pronouncing himself, like his friend David Williams, distrustful of political 'innovation'. He was soon to write a poem to the Glamorganshire Volunteers.[45] But it should be noted that Williams denies the title 'jacobin' in this letter in order to level a charge of treason against the ministers themselves, just as Coleridge had done in 1795 in *The Plot Discovered* (subtitled 'An Address to the People against Ministerial Treason'):

> Miss *Blanch Lewis* informs you that I am a *terrible Jacobin*, a terrible accusation indeed. Jacobin, Madam, is a nickname that those who have an interest in the present *just and necessary war*, as it it *blasphemously* called, give to all that disapprove of it . . . My political sentiments have [been] greatly, and what is worse, wilfully, misrepresented. I am it is true a *Reformist*, but not what may be termed a *Jacobin* . . . Whether in itself it is best that the sovereign should be hereditary or elective is a question upon which I am not decided in cases (as it was not long ago in America) where a new Constitution is to be formed, and it is a matter of free choice, but where either the one or the other has been long established, I think it best to let it remain so, and better than, by contending with deep-rooted prepossessions, to risk the very great dangers of *innovation*, and that for a merely imaginary advantage . . . A pure House of Commons, rendered so by a judicious reform, would

supply all that of Democracy is valuable in Legislation . . . I think madame that you will find no *Jacobinism* in what I have said if by the term you mean the infernally sanguine Spirit that has too much prevailed in *France*. if by it any thing else is intended I should wish to know what that may be. I should then know whether I am or am not a *Jacobin* . . . *Will Pitt, Harry Dundas* and their *understrappers* are the only real *Jacobins* that I know in this [land?]. they have introduced the *Terrorism* by which *Marat & Robespiere* [sic] [ruled?] for a while in *France*.[46]

The letter is pitched towards an indictment of William Pitt and his ministers. Williams sees Pitt as an imitator of the tyranny of Robespierre, just as Thelwall in *The Tribune* had characterized the Premier as a pale imitation of the energetic 'Incorruptible',[47] and just as Wordsworth was to denounce Pitt and his government in Book X of *The Prelude* as childish and perverse mimics:

> They who ruled the state,
> Though with such awful proof before their eyes
> That he who would sow death, reaps death, or worse,
> And can reap nothing better, childlike longed
> To imitate – not wise enough to avoid.
> (*The Prelude* (1805), X, 647–51)

In early 1795, Williams was involved in a bizarre incident which again brought him into contact with the authorities. Both Williams, in an undated letter, and Waring's biography relate the story. Writing to a certain 'Madam', Williams tells how the vicar of Reculver had informed him of a 'strange account . . . of several conversations with angels' given to him by the millenarian prophet Richard Brothers. 'I suspected instantly that all this originated with a *wag* or rather a *villain* of a *ventriloquist*', Williams remarks; 'I have now and then been successful in tracing out difficulties. I have set my wits at work, and traced the delusion up to a French *ventriloquist* who has imposed upon many others in Town.' Williams states that after Brothers was arrested on 4 March 1795, he, 'out of compassion', 'gave some account in a letter to M^r. Pitt':

> the next day I received a letter from M^r. Carthew, M^r. Pit's [sic] Secretary requesting my attendance in Downing Street. This letter I carefully keep. I attended, and told him what I knew. in a day or two

after wards I found that a (packed beyond a doubt) Jury had found the poor fellow a Lunatic. M^r. Kinaird the druggist of Holborn, where I often buy my *laudanum* was one of the Jury. I sought and soon found an opportunity of asking M^r. Kinaird whether any thing of this delusion of ventriloquacity had been . . . mentioned. I was told 'not at all' . . . the poor man is imprisoned in a madhouse . . . I strongly suspect from some anecdotes that I have gathered that french ventriloquists are at present practissing [*sic*] the same delusions . . . it is of importance to detect all delusion, but this is not the minister's object. he wants a victim wherewith to strike terror.[48]

Williams's account is confirmed by the presence in his papers of a letter of 11 March 1795 from 'J. Carthew, Downing Street' to Williams at 'No 1, Star Court, Chancery Lane': 'Mr Carthew will be glad if Mr William's [*sic*] will call upon him here, whenever it may be convenient to him, in consequence of a Letter which Mr Pitt has received from him respecting Mr Brother's [*sic*]'.[49] (Waring's claim that Williams actually met with Pitt on this occasion, and that Pitt 'complimented [Williams] on the sagacity of his discovery, which involved consequences that might probably be of real importance to the State' before regaling him with a lavish meal, is probably the Bard's own embellishment.[50])

Williams knew the dissenting minister William Winterbotham (1763–1829), who was convicted in 1793 for preaching sedition from the pulpit of How's Lane chapel, Plymouth – the only man to be imprisoned during Pitt's 'reign of terror' for that crime, as Ralph A. Manogue reminds us.[51] He spent the years 1793–7 in Newgate, where Southey visited him (and, as Winterbotham later claimed, gave him the manuscript of the infamous *Wat Tyler*, which in 1817 came back to haunt the then reactionary laureate[52]). Williams also famously visited Winterbotham in Newgate, and the visit is one of the more celebrated anecdotes surrounding the radical Bard. The incident, and the 'Newgate Stanzas' that were inspired by it, are recorded by Williams himself:

> None are admitted to see the state Prisoners in Newgate without writing in a book, kept for that purpose, their names and places of abode. *Edward Williams* the *Welsh Bard*, going there some time ago to see the Rev^d M^r. Winterbotham, wrote, in addition to his name, *Bard of Liberty*, as he had done several times before; but this being now noticed,

he was refused admission, in words '*we admit no Bards of Liberty here*'. on this occasion he wrote the following verses in imitation of *Horace* Ode. 22, Book I . . .

> 1.
> Dear Liberty! thy sacred name
> O! let me to the world proclaim!
>   Thy daring ardor [*sic*] sing!
> Known as thy son, nor *Knaves* of state
> Nor *spies* I fear, nor Placeman's hate,
>   Nor mobs of *Church and King*.
> 2.
> Of late when at the close of day
> To Newgate's cells I bent my way
>   Where Truth is held in thrall,
> I wrote, that all might plainly see,
> My name the *bard of Liberty*,
>   And terror seized on all.[53]

His self-appointed emblematic status as 'The Bard of Liberty' was a persona that wed jacobin ideology to august Bardic – that is, public – duty. Author of relatively sober liberty songs in Welsh such as 'Breiniau Dyn' (The Rights of Man) and 'Gwawr Borau Rhyddid' (The Dawn of Liberty), he would also dash off inflammatory portraits of his jacobin self:

> There is a Man in Cowbridge Town
>   A confirmed Sanculotte [*sic*],
> He would kill all clergy is well known
>   And he wants to cut the Kings throat . . .
> He's [*sic*] name is Edward Williams,
>   a Poet and a poor Mason,
> Democracy into his guts ran,
>   Without either rule or reason.[54]

Priest- and king-killer, jacobin descendant of Oliver Cromwell (a chip off the old block), poet and indigent Welsh artisan: this piece is a good example of Williams's construction of a vivid, multi-faceted identity in the 1790s, as is his major production of this period, the two-volume *Poems, Lyric and Pastoral*.

'Kingflogging Notes' and The Politics of Dedication:
Poems, Lyric and Pastoral

Published by J. Nichols and sold by Joseph Johnson, *Poems, Lyric and Pastoral* was favourably reviewed in the London press, as Williams repeatedly reported to his wife.[55] Williams presented a copy to Coleridge, probably around 1795–6, which bears Coleridge's annotation.[56] The list of subscribers ostentatiously displayed at the head of the first volume is an index of the extent and pedigree of Williams's radical acquaintances and contacts; it includes John Aikin, Mrs Barbauld, Brissot, Horne Tooke, Joseph Johnson, John Oswald, Paine, Price, Priestley, Samuel Rogers, George Washington, Wilberforce and a host of other radical luminaries. 'I trust that none will be offended at me for printing the names of my most distinguished friends in *Italics*', Williams remarks.[57] Each one of the above names except Washington and Brissot is italicized – with Wilberforce, whom Williams certainly knew, and whose anti-slavery campaigns he supported,[58] appearing imposingly capitalized as 'HUMANITY'S WILBERFORCE'. But *Poems, Lyric and Pastoral* was also to be Williams's passport into polite society, not just into radical circles, and another glance at the list of subscribers reveals Williams's links with titled nobility and with literary and public figures such as Boswell, the Bowdlers, Bowles, Charles and Fanny Burney, William Cowper, Sir William Jones the orientalist, Hannah More, Thomas Pennant, Mrs Piozzi, Anna Seward (proudly recorded as a member of Williams's assembly of bards with the title 'Ofyddes ym mraint Beirdd Ynys Prydain' – An Ovate according to the immunities and customs of the Bards of the Isle of Britain[59]), Horace Walpole and the apostate bishop, Richard Watson of Llandaff.[60]

Informed throughout, especially in the more unorthodox second volume, by Williams's Bardic paraphernalia of antiquarian and pseudo-antiquarian notes, expositions of 'THE *Patriarchal Religion* of ANCIENT BRITAIN' and the '*British Bardic* Mythology', and 'An account of, and extracts from, the Welsh-Bardic Triades',[61] Williams's collection of 'lyric pastorals', adaptations of medieval Welsh poetry, songs, satires and odes appears strikingly politicized from the outset.[62] The first page of the autobiographical preface announces that his desire to track down the 'Welsh' Madogian Indians (he was one of the prime movers of the decade's 'Madoc fever') was not the only reason for his planned flight to asylum in America:[63]

I had, and still have, an intention of going to America, partly to fly from the numerous injuries I have received from the boasted laws of this land, that are not, whatever one REEVES, or his brother *Bear-monger,* of Holborn-Hill, may say, made equally for the poor as for the rich . . . I have some *general,* but no *personal* satire; there is too much *Priestcraft* amongst every sect; too much *Kingcraft* in all, even *Republican,* Governments; yet there are many *good Priests;* and, I believe, a brace of *good Kings,* may be found; at least I will venture on *One* [Our Welsh Bard probably means the KING OF KINGS. *Printer's Devil*]. I have always, with an *Ancient Briton's warm pride,* preserved the freedom of my thoughts, and the independence of my mind: these shall not be subjected to any thing but my own conscience. Wherever I meet with *scoundrelism,* though captained by ever so GREAT A NAME, my pen shall have all the liberty of my sentiments . . . I have declared myself the friend of *Peace, Benevolence, Liberty,* and the transcendently lovely *Christian Religion* . . . Who knows but that in the bright constellation of stars of the first magnitude, that now illumine the Horizon of Truth, I may be one of the feeblest; at least I would not for the world be a *cloud* in it . . .[64]

The final sentence is a possible source for the title of *Seren Tan Gwmmwl* (The Cloud-hidden Star), by Williams's friend and fellow London-Welsh radical, John Jones. Draft prefaces amongst Williams's papers go further than the published preface in asserting more explicitly his devotion to 'equality' and the Rights of Man.[65] Like the private letters, Williams's politicized pastorals, Bardic odes, and notes in *Poems, Lyric and Pastoral* rail against priest- and kingcraft ('Where *Kings,* that *fiends incarnate* reign'; 'the head-bitten brood of vanity'; 'That bauble called a crown!'; 'War and conquest are, generally speaking, the *aim* and *ambition* of monarchs in all ages; to them the slaughtering of 40 or 50,000 subjects . . . is a thing of no moment'[66]). His 'Ode on converting a Sword into a Pruning Hook. Recited on Primrose Hill, at a Meeting of ANCIENT BRITISH BARDS . . . Sept. 22, 1793',[67] together with his 'Ode on the Mythology of the Ancient British Bards . . . Recited on Primrose Hill . . . on the Summer Solstice of 1792', are powerful, if general and inflated, indictments of royal ambition, tyranny and violence, against which Williams sets the pacific philosophy and political liberty of Bardism.[68] A separate advertisement to the latter poem, not included in the published volume, denounces 'royal Butchery' by visualizing on 'the field of slaughter' the 'aged father on his crutches, or the blind mother led along in search of a beloved son . . . and in her arms the pretty little orphan anxiously calling on a father that never answers. The king looks on . . . oh! how glorious!'⁶⁹

It has gone unnoticed that Williams's 'Ode on converting a Sword into a Pruning Hook' is unmistakably an influence on the first epode of Coleridge's 'Ode on the Departing Year', which, as shown in Chapter 3, was part of a political dialogue between Coleridge and Thelwall. Significantly, Coleridge's ode was composed in December 1796 – around the time he received the gift of *Poems, Lyric and Pastoral* from Williams. Williams's ode is a picture of imperialist aggression – he has in mind the 'fiendish' conqueress Catherine the Great – finally brought to account. Lines and phrases which were to be echoed by Coleridge are identified in bold:

> Fell weapon, that in ruthless hand
> Of warrior fierce, or despot king,
> Hast long career'd o'er ev'ry land . . .
> . . .
> I bear thee now to rural shades,
> Where nought of Hell-born War invades;
> Where **plum'd** AMBITION feels her little soul . . .
>
> **I saw the *Tyrant*** on her throne,
> With **wrathful eyes** and venom'd breath,
> Enjoy the world's unceasing groan,
> **And boast, unsham'd,** her fields of death;
> When through the skies her banners wav'd,
> When, ***drunk with blood***, her legions rav'd . . .
> . . .
> **I saw the *Victor's* dreadful day**,
> He, through the world, in regal robe,
> Tore to renown his gory way;
> With carnage *zon'd* th'affrighted globe:
> Whilst from huge towns involv'd in flame
> The *Monster* claim'd immortal fame,
> What **lamentable shrieks** arose,
> In all th'excess of direst woes!
> Loud was the *Sycophant's* applauding voice:
> Together throng'd the sceptered band,
> Hymn'd by the **Fiends** of ev'ry land:
> How mourn'd my soul to hear the tale
> Of sad Humanity's unpity'd wail!

> And each *Imperial dome* with horrid shouts rejoice!
> But hear from HEAV'N the dread command,
> It gives to speed that awful hour,
> When from OPPRESSION's trembling hand
> Must fall th'*insulting rod of pow'r*;
> Long vers'd in mysteries of war,
> She scyth'd her **huge triumphant car;**
> Her lance with look infuriate hurl'd . . .
> . . .
> Now brought before th'*eternal throne*,
> Where *Truth* prevails, all hearts are *known*,
> **She, self-condemn'd, with horrid call,**
> **Bids on her head the rocks and mountains fall . . .**
>
> (*PLP*, II, 160–5)

The radical rhetoric of this 'Bardic' poem, publicly performed 'in the eye of the light'[70] on Primrose Hill in 1793, evidently provides Coleridge in 'Ode on the Departing Year' (see Chapter 3, p. 115, above) with a template for his own picture of imperialist tyranny and of the demise in November 1796 of Catherine the Great. Williams's 'plum'd AMBITION', together with the lines 'I saw the *Tyrant* on her throne' and 'I saw the *Victor's* dreadful day' are echoed in Coleridge's 'I mark'd Ambition in his war-array' and his 'mailed Monarch'; Williams's references to the tyrant's 'wrathful eyes', her 'unsham'd' boasting over her infernal handiwork, and her legions, 'drunk with blood', are collapsed into Coleridge's 'Th'insatiate Hag shall gloat with drunken eye!'; and Williams's 'huge triumphant car' (he explains he has the 'war-chariots of the *Ancient Britons*' in mind) appears at the beginning of Coleridge's epode as the tyrant's groaning 'chariot'. Coleridge can also be seen to pick up on Williams's 'fiends' and 'shrieks', and 'Ode on the Departing Year' fulfils the prophecies of 'Ode on converting a Sword into a Pruning Hook' by celebrating the death of the Empress, which Williams's poem had graphically envisaged. Coleridge ends his ode by 'recentring' himself, 'Cleans'd from the fears and anguish that bedim / God's Image, Sister of the Seraphim', just as Williams's ends with 'the scalding tears' being 'wip'd away' and with the song of 'seraphic lyres'. Williams's ode – formally articulated as part of a ceremony at whose heart lay the anti-monarchical and pacific discourse of Bardism – can now be seen as a crucial element in that fascinating radical dialogue between 'Ode on the Departing Year' and Thelwall's *Tribune* analysed in Chapter 3.

The radical flavour of the *Poems* caused his more reactionary contemporaries obvious unease. Writing to Williams on 18 October 1805 on Literary Fund business, William Thomas Fitzgerald thanked him for the gift of his *Poems*, but took issue with the political valency of the volume, and informed him that he had been compelled to doctor Williams's application to the Fund since his 'P:S: would tend to injure [him] in the opinion of the Majority of those Gentlemen who might otherwise be conciliated':

> I take the liberty of saying that I very much prefer your *Poetry* to your *Prose* – the first, as far as I have read, entitles you to a high degree of praise, and proves you to be of the true Family of the Bards; but the last, I am sorry to observe, contains opinions both political & religious that are directly in opposition to mine . . . As you mention an intention of publishing a second Edition of your Poems, permit me to give you a hint, which I do from the most benevolent motives, tho' I have not the pleasure of your Acquaintance & most probably shall never see your face – it is to omit many of your *Notes* which have a political tendency, and to leave out or totally alter the page of your Preface . . . I think, in our own days we have had sufficient experience of the Danger of *Political Theorists* when we contemplate the bloody Annals of France; who after all her political and religious struggles! after wading thro' Oceans of Blood! has submitted at last to the Iron Despotism of an *Atheistical Foreigner*.[71]

In the light of what Williams himself referred to as his '*Kingflogging* Notes', his dedication of *Poems, Lyric and Pastoral* 'By permission, and with the respect of gratitude' to 'His Royal Highness George Prince of Wales, By His Most Humble Servant' comes as a surprise. His relationship with the Prince was a profoundly ambiguous one. On 5 May 1792, Williams informed his wife that 'I have had permission to dedicate to the *Prince of Wales*. this is a bit of vanity that I am quite ashamed of, though I must comply out of respect to those who obtained it for me',[72] and in a letter of 21 January 1794 to John Walters, he remarks:

> Some of my books will be soon at Cowbridge. the Rev^d. Dr. *Knox* assures me that they stand a fair chance of being reviewed by *Archy Macblunder* and his *Pack'd Furies*; (and yet they are dedicated to the *Prince of Wales*.) should this be the case, my fortune is made, but such

good luck never yet attended me. yet it was not with any such views that I wrote my *Kingflogging* Notes. it was a weak endeavour to abet the cause of truth, Justice, and humanity, a cause to which I long to be a martyr. The Notes on my Ode on converting a sword into a pruning hook, and those on the modern *War-song* of *British Savages*, are the most obnoxious, but unluckily, I fear not sufficiently so; too general, no particular, application. 'tis too late to repent, or alter for the better. I hope however they will make some noise from the circumstance (which some have called impudence) of their being dedicated to the Prince. should this be the case my book will sell, and a new edition, and another, and a fourth, &c. *Tom Paine* ran in six months through more than twenty editions. but I am not *Tom Paine* yet, and for the sake of my little Children to whom a father will, for a little while, be better than money, I will not endeavour to be so till I am in America.[73]

The 'War Song of British Savages' referred to here (*PLP*, II, 132–5) is a pointed recasting of 'God Save the King' as a pacifist song of peace and prophecy for the next reign.[74] Williams's cultivation of the Prince's patronage during the 1790s coincides with that of his friend David Williams. It is evident from his draft letters and dedications to the Prince that, in part at least, Williams wished to view his relationship with him in the context of a historical paradigm: that of the social bond between the medieval bard and his patron-prince – specifically Dafydd ap Gwilym and his noble patron, Ifor Hael, 'Ifor the Generous' (a figure whom Williams did much to popularize in Wales, and the subject of a poem, discussed below, in Williams's collection):

> I am one of the very few that are now remaining of the Welsh Bards of the genuine succession. Those songsters of Nature were formerly highly patronized by the Princes of Wales. One, probably the very last of them, presumes now with humility to solicit a little of that patronage.[75]

Significantly, Waring's account of the interview Williams claimed he had with Pitt regarding Richard Brothers represents an interesting politicization of the Ifor Hael–Dafydd ap Gwilym relationship:

> Our imagination has lately depicted [Williams], magnificently seated in the Prime Minister's apartment, after a conversation of the most

gracious freedom, partaking of an elegant refection, and served by a respectful attendant from a salver of massive plate, with a libation worthy of Ivor the Liberal to his favourite Dafydd ap Gwilym.[76]

On 20 June 1794, Williams wrote an irreverently familiar letter to the Prince (addressing him simply as 'George') informing him of the *gorsedd* (Bardic assembly or moot) to be held on Primrose Hill the next day.[77] In 1795, he composed an epithalamium on the Prince's marriage, which he presented to the Prince dressed in a stonemason's apron with a trowel in his hand.[78]

As might be expected, however, other draft dedications to the Prince reveal the politics of dedication to be more a complex affair. The medieval poet-patron nexus, transposed by Waring and by Williams himself to the context of the 1790s, was for the Welsh Bard of Liberty an ideologically fraught model. One manuscript dedication is addressed to 'M^r. Nobody': 'Whether you are all head, all heart, or all arms or legs concerns me not at present. whether it be one or the other, or all, or neither, is equally the same to me. you sir are No Body.'[79] Another states that 'when I was informed that you had dismissed M^r. Erskine from your service for making such a defence for M^r. Paine as the Laws of this Realm . . . admitted and even required, I began to look at the stilts whereon I was going to mount myself.[80] Yet another tracks the politics of patronage to its deadly source behind royal thrones:

> my dedication sir is not according to the modes of fashion, but its detestable name I hate and treat with the most sovereign contempt. Fashion that deadly stream that springing from under a throne, spreads o'er the land a black deluge of corruptions, having . . . its periodical overflowings in Birth-days and Levees.[81]

Williams's *political* opposition to what the Prince represented (George's Whig sympathies notwithstanding) only partly explains this manuscript frankness. As remembrancer to his nation, he looked back longingly to the cultural and political conditions which had allowed Wales's great medieval tradition of praise poetry to emerge from the central relation between the Welsh *Cynfeirdd* and *Gogynfeirdd* poets and their *native* princes and noblemen. With *Poems, Lyric and Pastoral,* Williams had fashioned himself as a 1790s reincarnation of that august tradition – but with a difference. At the psychological and emotional root of the comments quoted above is also a cultural and nationalist unease.

Bardic Jacobinism: Williams and the *Gorsedd*

One might say of Williams, as Blake said of himself, that he created a system to avoid being enslaved by another man's – or another nation's. Williams's involvement with the *gorsedd* and his popularization of the philosophy and theology of Bardism, which was clearly a vehicle for jacobin propaganda, represent the core of his radical identity at this time. Williams's Bardic forgeries constitute one of the prime examples of the period of the politicization of pseudo-antiquarian discourse. On 21 June 1792 – the summer solstice – Williams convened on Primrose Hill, London, the first of his *gorseddau*,[82] whose ceremonies and druidic philosophy he claimed were of great antiquity but which were in fact the product of his own fertile invention. An account of the second meeting of 22 September 1792 appeared in the *Morning Chronicle* and also in *The Gentleman's Magazine*, accompanied by Williams's anti-slave-trade 'Apostrophe to Liberty'.[83] Williams immediately set about establishing the institution of the *gorsedd* in Wales, and in 1819, it was grafted onto the *eisteddfod*, where it is enshrined to this day. For a country deprived centuries earlier of the pomp and ceremony of its native cultural and political institutions, the *gorsedd* was to become a powerful signifier of nationhood and cultural difference over the next two hundred years.

It is Williams who lies behind much of the sketch of the Bardic 'system' that prefaces *The Heroic Elegies and Other Pieces of Llywarç Hen, Prince of the Cumbrian Britons* (1793).[84] This volume – a translation of a ninth–tenth-century Welsh poetic cycle – was edited by the friend of Williams and Southey, William Owen Pughe, but, as Pughe declares,

> It is [Edward Williams] who has given a taste for Bardism to several, which is likely to be the means of reviving the institution; and it is from his communications and assistance, that I have been enabled to give this account of the Bards.[85]

The iconic institution of Bardism and the expositions of the Bardic codes contained in such works as the *Heroic Elegies* and *Poems, Lyric and Pastoral* were marshalled by Williams in the service of a politicized agenda that located the ideals of liberty, equality and peace as the cornerstones of a surviving body of a specifically Welsh (and Glamorgan-based) Bardic philosophy of which such figures as

Williams and Pughe appear as incarnations and guardians.[86] The radical principles of Bardism were emphatically the product of jacobin sympathies, as is evident from the dissertation on Bardism in the *Heroic Elegies*:

> To the period above-mentioned we must attribute the Institution of BARDISM,[87] amongst the *Cynmry*, a system embracing all the leading principles which tend to spread liberty, peace and happiness amongst mankind . . .
> What may be considered as the foundation of the Order was the doctrine of *Universal Peace*, and *Good Will* . . .
> The next important object of the bardic Institution, was the free investigation of all matters contributing to the attainment of truth and wisdom, grounded upon the aphorism – 'COELIAW DIM, A ÇOELIAW POB PETH.' – *To believe nothing, and to believe every thing*; that is, to believe every thing supported by reason and proof, and nothing without. In addition to that the Bard was to be bold in the cause of Truth; for his motto was – 'Y GWIR YN ERBYN Y BYD'. – *The Truth in opposition to the World*.
> Another maxim of the order was, the perfect equality of its members, and of three branches, whereof it consisted, one with another. Each order was held in a peculiarity of estimation, though neither of them were entitled to superiority, nor any one deemed more intrinsically excellent than the other . . .
> The publicity of their actions was also a leading consideration amongst the bards; for all their meetings or *Gorseddau*, were held in the open air, on a conspicuous place, whilst the sun was above the horizon; as they were to perform every thing *in the eye of the light, and in the face of the sun* . . .
> I am tempted to recapitulate the leading articles in the system . . . whereby it will be seen what a surprising coincidence there is between it and the principles of a modern sect that is respected through the world.[88]
> PEACE. – There is a necessity of restoring, establishing, and preserving peace toward the happiness of mankind; therefore the Bards give an example by refraining from bearing arms, and from all things that tend to form one party in opposition to another. The Bard amid the storms of the moral world must assume the serenity of the unclouded blue sky.
> EQUALITY. – Superiority of individual power is what none but God can possibly be intitled to; for the power that gave existence to all is the only power that has a claim of right to rule over all. A man cannot

assume authority over another; for if he may over one, by the same reason he may rule over a million, or over a world. All men are necessarily equal: the FOUR ELEMENTS in their natural state, or every thing not manufactured by art, is the common property of all.[89]

The 'leading articles' of Bardism, inscribed in Williams's quasi-masonic *gorsedd* and its Bardic elite, amount to a template – indeed, a constitution – for a utopian republic established on the principles of social equality, common property, public accountability and a bold, freethinking search after 'Truth'. Indeed, as Gwyn A. Williams reminds us: 'When Iolo devised a plan for a Welsh liberty settlement in the USA, it was to be run by just such a *gorsedd*'.[90] Williams's *gorsedd*, governed by the 'whimsical compound'[91] (Waring's phrase) of his Bardic theology (which owes much to his Unitarianism, and, as various commentators have emphasized, to his good friend David Williams's Margaret Street *Liturgy on the Universal Principles of Religion and Morality*[92]), together with his projected *History of the Bards*, embodied a radical conception of an ideal political, religious, and poetic institution that was to be the blueprint for 'the recreation of [the Welsh Bards'] libertarian world'.[93]

A further remarkable instance of the politicized public agenda of Williams's *gorsedd* and of the Bardic theology as outlined in the *Heroic Elegies* appeared in the *Monthly Magazine* for August 1798. Writing under the pseudonym 'Meirion', William Owen Pughe (who during 1796–7 had been engaged in a dialogue with Southey on Welsh antiquarian matters in the same periodical[94]), provided a translation of the supposed 'form, by which great criminals were excommunicated and put out of the protection of the laws, by the bardic circles, convened in the three classes of *Bards*, *Druids*, and *Ovates*'. He claimed that the ceremonial formulation that followed 'was made during the agitation of the question respecting the Slave-Trade, by a few persons, who held a meeting near London, for the sake of keeping up their venerated system of bardism' – evidently one of Williams's *gorseddau*, held at a time when petitions and bills for the abolition of slavery were introduced almost annually (and unsuccessfully) in both Houses.[95] The ceremony obviously represents radical Bardism's bold excommunication of Britain's predatory, imperialist government:

The complaint of the *people*, and the *prince*; the complaint of the *world*; the complaint of the *bards of the island of Britain*; participating in the

grievances of the *black inhabitants of Africa*, who being ignorant and helpless, are therefore entitled to the rights and privileges of brothers; and to protection against all assaults. But men, who know, and ought to have done better, have with *war and depredation* assailed these poor people; have captured them; have torn them forcibly from their country; from their dearest relatives; and, instead of affording to them the protection due to brothers, have enslaved them . . . so that they are unable to escape from the *circle of necessity and evil* . . . Their oppressors have been reprehended; but they have not repented; nor will they desist from their *oppressions and depredations*; for this reason it is *lamentably necessary*, though a matter of great *reluctance* for us, to *wage the assault of war against the unmerciful oppressors*!
HE THAT KILLS MUST BE KILLED[96]

Pughe then states that three bards raised a sword from the 'stone of covenant'; one of them unsheathed it, and holding it aloft, pronounced '*The sword is naked against . . . men attached* to *anarchy and devastation*'.[97] In 'Fears in Solitude', Coleridge was likewise to prophesy the imminent retribution of 'all-avenging Providence', visited on an unrepentant, imperialist Britain:

> Ev'n so, my countrymen! have we gone forth
> And borne to distant tribes slavery and pangs,
> And, deadlier far, our vices, whose deep taint
> With slow perdition murders the whole man,
> His body and his soul!
> . . .
> Secure from actual warfare, we have lov'd
> To swell the war-whoop, passionate for war!
> . . .
>   Therefore evil days
> Are coming on us, O my countrymen!
>   (*FiS*, 3, 5, 6–7)

While Coleridge can merely warn his countrymen of the coming judgement, Williams's *gorsedd* takes matters into its own hands, damning the state in a public ceremony. At a time when British radicalism could conceive of tribunals only as unjust State bodies before which one had to plead 'with a voice / Labouring, a brain confounded' (*The Prelude* (1805), X, 377–8), the *gorsedd* in this ceremony constitutes itself as a legislative and executive body before which the State itself now appears as the defendant. Bardism becomes the just antithesis of a despotic State.

The patronage which Williams had secured in London based on his *Poems, Lyric and Pastoral* did not, however, prove sufficiently promising and lucrative for him to remain in London and establish a permanent domestic base there. Answering his wife's earnest calls to rejoin a family struggling with poverty (his favourite daughter Lilly had died during his absence), he returned to Glamorgan in 1795 and set up a grocer's, and subsequently a bookshop, in Cowbridge.[98] On 10 May 1798, Thelwall wrote to Williams from Llyswen, lamenting the fact that they had missed each other when Thelwall passed through Cowbridge on his 'Pedestrian Excursion' the previous summer and inviting him to stay at Llyswen. His recent decision to visit Williams, he explained, had been rendered imprudent by 'the prejudices with which [he knew himself] to be watched' – 'lest picturesque curiosity, & visits of friendship should be construed into High Treason' (Appendix, Letter No. 5). After his return to Cowbridge, Williams devoted his energies to producing a vast body of Bardic material, posing as its supposed 'editor'. Drawn up in London, one of Williams's lists of projects due to appear 'as soon as possible' contains the following: 'Dissertations on the Rights of Man', 'Christianity *versus* Kingcraft', 'A new and equitable plan for the Abolition of Slavery in the West Indies', 'The History of the *Ancient British Bards*' and 'A search after Political Truth'.[99] Referring to these enterprises, Gwyneth Lewis has argued that after the mid-1790s Williams 'felt unable to pursue this aspect of his literary career overtly' and that 'Whereas his projected *History of the Ancient British Bards* was fifth on this early list of projects, after the mid 1790s it became the only literary undertaking which seemed viable'. But Lewis further remarks that in *The History of the Ancient British Bards*, the institution of the *gorsedd* and the forged poems, laws and Bardic Triads to which he now devoted his talents, Williams found

> a medium which would enable him to explore every single one of the issues outlined in his abandoned list of projected publications – the rights of man, the primacy of patriarchal religion over all church establishments, the importance of bardism as a model for civil government, and the suitability of the critical precepts of bardism as a model for modern writing. Iolo withdrew from the literary and political arena

of London, therefore, to prepare an extensive critique of the system which, he felt, had denied him free speech and patronage.[100]

Lewis continues: 'Whereas Macpherson, Chatterton, and Ireland had each taken advantage of the strategy of composing in the poetic personae of earlier writers, Iolo formulated a theory of forgery which encompassed the ancient British bards' duties as poets, priests, and politicians.'[101] Bardism, then, provided an all-encompassing model that allowed Williams, under the cover of historical and antiquarian research, to comment on the contemporary political system.

For writers such as Southey, Williams was a storehouse of such historical and arcane knowledge. *Madoc* (1805) pays tribute to him thus:

> Iolo, old Iolo, he who knows
> The virtue of all herbs of mount or vale,
> Or greenwood shade, or quiet brooklet's bed;
> Whatever lore of science, or of song,
> Sages and Bards of old have handed down.
> (p. 79)

Many of the copious antiquarian notes to Southey's poem were either gleaned from Williams's *Poems, Lyric and Pastoral* and from works by Williams and Pughe (*The Heroic Elegies, The Cambrian Register, The Cambrian Biography*), or provided personally by them. Southey openly thanked both in *Madoc*:

> Mr Owen's very curious introduction to his translation of Llywarc Hen has supplied me with materials for the account of the *Gorsedd*, introduced in the poem. That it might be as accurate as possible, he himself and Edward Williams the Bard did me the favour of examining it. To their knowledge . . . and to the liberality and friendliness with which they have ever been willing to assist me therewith, I am greatly and variously indebted.[102]

On 25 August 1805, Southey gave Joseph Cottle advice regarding the latter's *Fall of Cambria*:

> You will do well to introduce lyrical pieces where the subject requires them. I am doing the same in Madoc, converting the odes of Cyveilioc

and Caradoc and the song of Hoel into lyrical measures . . . Edward Williams if you write to him will gladly tell you all that either history or tradition has preserved concerning the event you have chosen.[103]

Others were not so convinced. In *The Mythology and Rites of the British Druids* (1809), Edward 'Celtic' Davies expressed his doubts regarding the historicity of Bardic doctrine as put forward by Williams and Pughe in the *Heroic Elegies* and drew attention to the debt Williams's Bardic philosophy owed to the revolutionary spirit of the age:

> I do not recollect to have seen this doctrine, in its full extent, promulgated by any code, before a certain period of the French Revolution, when the *meek* Republicans of Gaul, and their modest partizans in other countries, joined the *indefeasible right of equality* with the *inviolable duty of peace*, and impressed them upon the orderly subjects of every state; whilst they themselves were preparing for every species of injury to civil society. But whencesoever this fallacious principle took its rise, it certainly did not belong to the *Druids*, or to the *Bards*, without great limitation.[104]

Davies recognized that the section on Bardism was 'a *made Dish*, cooked up from obscure scraps of the ancient Bards, and the Cabala of the modern ones; a superficial acquaintance with the Metempsychosis; and these ingredients spiced with an immoderate quantity of wild Invention'.[105] Referring to Williams in a letter of 6 June 1828 to Walter Davies, Peter Bailey Williams also saw Williams's institution as the product of a revolutionary decade:

> I know he did not adhere to the truth and would invent anything that would suit his purpose; – witness the Preface or Introduction to Llywarch Hên during the French Revolution, and his endeavours to prove that the Druids were all equal – that there was no superiority of Rank amongst them, contrary to all History; – and all this in order to favour the wild Scheme or System of Liberty and Equality then so prevalent. *Glan y Gors* [John Jones] and *Iolo* were violent Republicans; – Witness Seren tan Gwmwl &c; – their enmity to Tithes, and their abuse of the Clergy.[106]

In his review of David Williams's *History of Monmouthshire* in the *Cambrian Register*, Theophilus Jones characterizes Edward Williams's 'attempts to revive the religious, but ridiculous mummeries of ancient druids' as 'Exhibitions to make the vulgar stare, and the worshipful magistrates tremble for the fate of the nation', and goes on to ridicule one of Williams's *gorseddau*, held in 1797 on the Garth mountain in Glamorgan, which was actually suppressed by the Glamorgan Yeomanry:

> a silly attempt [was] lately made in Glamorganshire, to hold something like a poetic session upon a hill, preceded, by a ridiculous advertisement or hand bill, which the magistrates, knowing the harlequin of the farce to be of democratic principles, apprehended might endanger the peace of the kingdom; they therefore very properly prevented his rising in the world, least [sic] when he got to the summit he might beckon to Buonaparte, and bring him over the British channel; to the top of the Garth.[107]

The reference to Williams's 'rising in the world' cleverly plays on the elevation of Williams's *gorsedd* on the Garth and on his social pretensions as revealed in *Poems, Lyric and Pastoral*. A peevish Jones dismisses the meeting as absurd, but his account is dramatic proof that the *gorsedd* was taken seriously by the authorities as a jacobin threat and as a dangerous paradigm for reform.

Coleridge's 'Answer to Godwin': Gratitude, Pride, Filial Affection and the Slighting of Edward Williams

Having profiled Williams's construction of a radical Bardic self and politicized Bardic system in the 1790s, I now want to focus on his impact on Coleridge and Wordsworth in the context of the poets' formative negotiations with William Godwin and the philosophy of *Political Justice*. Kathleen Coburn has remarked that 'Williams perhaps had more influence on the early romantics, especially Coleridge and Southey, than has been recognized',[108] and it is this influence that will be revealed in detail here. I see Williams's dramatic personal confrontation with Godwin, together with the radical tenets of his Bardic philosophy, as important elements in Coleridge's Christian–radical stance on the central issues of gratitude, filial and domestic affection and pride at a time when Coleridge was contemplating his 'answer to Godwin' – a formal rebuttal of the 'absurdities and wickedness of

[Godwin's] System',[109] grounded in the opposition of Jesus to Godwin.[110] I also regard Williams as an influential model of Romantic identity in two poems from the *Lyrical Ballads* in which Wordsworth offers a critique of Godwinian intellectualism and of Godwin's position on gratitude. I therefore conceive of Williams's 'presence' in the works of Coleridge and Wordsworth in terms of cultural influence, as against the modes of inscription or haunting profiled in previous chapters. My discussion of David Williams's intellectual influence on 'Tintern Abbey', however, was similarly conceived, and represents an interesting point of reference in this chapter. A letter written by Coleridge to Thelwall on 13 May 1796 provides a springboard into the debate.

A few weeks after first writing to John Thelwall with an overture of friendship ('Pursuing the same end by the same means we ought not to be strangers to each other'[111]), Coleridge wrote to his new correspondent to defend himself against Thelwall's charge that he had treated 'systems & opinions with the furious prejudices of the conventicle, & the illiberal dogmatism of the Cynic'[112] and to take issue with the atheistic 'New Philosophy'. Lecturing Thelwall on morality and religion, Coleridge went on to single out William Godwin's 'system' for censure and reprove his manners:

> Godwin, whose very heart is cankered by the love of singularity & who feels no disinclination to wound by abrupt harshness, pleads for absolute Sincerity, because such a system gives him a frequent opportunity of indulging his misanthropy. – Poor Williams, the Welch bard – (a very meek man) brought the tear into my Eye by a simple narration of the manner in which Godwin had insulted him, under the pretence of Reproof – & Thomas Walker of Manchester told me, that his Indignation & Contempt were never more powerfully excited than by an unfeeling and insolent Speech of the said Godwin to the poor Welch Bard.[113]

Thomas Walker (1749–1817) was a leading Manchester reformer who in 1790 had founded the Manchester Constitutional Society and in 1792 had been prosecuted unsuccessfully (with Erskine defending) for treasonable conspiracy. What, then, were the grounds of that 'insolent Speech of the said Godwin to the poor Welch Bard'? The evidence suggests that it was a confrontation of personalities and ideologies in which Coleridge felt deeply involved.

Discussing 'Gratitude and Ingratitude' in his *Lectures on Education* (1789), David Williams had declared that gratitude

> is an effect of beneficence so natural, that the obligations of it in children, are generally acknowledged; and filial ingratitude deemed infamous . . . though the duty be natural, clear, and readily acknowledged: no vice is so much complained of in life; no misfortune so frequently lamented in families, as ingratitude.[114]

Illustrating the immutable dictates of reason and justice in the celebrated 'fire clause' of his *Political Justice* (1793), William Godwin took a contrary view, presenting his readers with a scenario that was soon to become infamous. If Archbishop Fénelon and his chambermaid – who might be one's wife, mother or benefactor – were caught in a flaming building and the life of only one of them could be saved, one is under a moral obligation, Godwin argues, to save the author of the 'immortal Telemachus', since 'The life of Fenelon would still be more valuable than that of the chambermaid; and justice, pure, unadulterated justice, would still have preferred that which was most valuable'. Going on to consider the claims of filial gratitude, Godwin plays the ventriloquist – ' "But my mother endured for me the pains of child bearing, and nourished me in the helplessness of infancy" ' – only to dismiss that filial cry with the comment: 'When she first subjected herself to the necessity of these cares, she was probably influenced by no particular motives of benevolence to her future offspring'. 'What magic is there in the pronoun "my" ', he declares, 'to overturn the decisions of everlasting truth? My wife or my mother may be a fool or a prostitute, malicious, lying, or dishonest. If they be, of what consequence is it that they are mine?'[115] Soon after the third edition of *Political Justice* had gone to press in 1798, Godwin saw fit to soften his stance on the domestic affections,[116] but here, a cold appraisal of utilitarian worth is to outweigh filial affection. Popularizing Godwin's philosophy in the political lectures of *The Tribune*,[117] Thelwall, despite his reference to the 'odium' which Godwin's position on gratitude 'has drawn upon his head', was himself to characterize gratitude in terms of a heinous moral synecdoche that sabotaged justice:

> I am not afraid, however, of popularising those ideas which I believe to be true, because the persons who first propagated them have

encountered reproach . . . If gratitude . . . has a tendency to draw the human mind from the consideration of the whole, and to fix it, from a principle of self love, upon a few individuals, then I shall be obliged to conclude that gratitude is no virtue, but that, on the contrary, it is an enemy to that great fountain of all virtue – Justice! . . . It is mistaking a part for the whole, and confining our exertions to a few particular individuals, merely because they have done more for us than we were entitled to, and thereby neglecting that great scale of justice . . . On the other hand lies some worthless individual whom nature may have made my relation, who may have heaped, in profligacy and idle intoxication, perhaps, unmerited favours upon my head: I have the power of serving one: Who does gratitude call upon me to serve?[118]

In the light of this, Coburn is surely right in suggesting that Godwin's humiliation of Williams was related in some way to the bard's strong attachment to his mother:

Williams's mother died when he was twenty-three, and the personal anecdotes given in his introduction to his poems reveal a particularly close relation to her. One may reasonably conjecture that Godwin's contempt for Williams may have had something to do with the strength of that filial affection of which Godwin at this time disapproved, which disapproval in turn met with sharp criticism from Coleridge.[119]

Ann Williams, née Matthew (1713–70), was a remarkable woman of noble south Walian stock who, as Williams states in a draft version of the preface to *Poems, Lyric and Pastoral*, had been 'educated in a manner that was rather disadvantageous to a woman of no fortune. she had all the qualifications but Wealth that could be required in the Wife of a Peer of the Realm, but it was her lot to marry a mason'.[120] He further claimed that she belonged to a family of Glamorgan poets. She was a crucially formative influence on the young Williams, introducing her son to English literature, arithmetic and music. 'Let the Reader pardon my filial partiality', Williams remarks,

and allow me to say that she was a woman of uncommon mental abilities. her taste in polite literature was uncommonly [sic], but unperceived by those amongst whom it was her destiny to pass thro' life. She had a dignity of mind which kept aloof from many. this was by many who knew no better called pride, vanity, or anything envious ignorance could conceive . . . [She] amongst other things had no despicable knowledge of surgery and Physic.[121]

The preface to *Poems, Lyric and Pastoral* made public the strength of Williams's affection for, and gratitude to, his mother:

> My mother . . . was the daughter of a gentleman who had wasted a pretty fortune: she had been well educated; she taught me to read in a volume of *Songs*, intituled *The Vocal Miscellany* . . . My mother sang agreeably, and I understood that she learned her songs from this book, which made me so very desirous of learning it. This I did in a short time, and hence, I doubt not, my original turn for poetry . . . In 1770, my best of mothers died; I was then, though twenty-three years of age, as ignorant of the world almost as a new-born child . . . I returned every night to my mother's fire-side, where I talked or read with her; if ever I walked out, it was by myself in unfrequented places, woods, the sea-shore, &c. for I was very pensive, melancholy, and very *stupid*, as all but my mother thought . . . After my mother's death I could no longer be happy at home, where she was *never more to be seen*. I rambled for some time over a great part of England and Wales . . .[122]

Much of this portrait of a 'pensive, melancholy' youth embarking on a vagrant life after the death of his mother is a fiction designed to appeal to potential patrons and literary editors, and as his biographer has warned, should not be accepted unquestioningly. As G. J. Williams goes on to remark, however:

> There is no doubt that there is exaggeration here, and that [Williams] set out to give a wholly misleading impression when speaking of his youth, but everything suggests that we can accept his portrait of this mother . . . That portion of genius that made Iolo Morganwg one of the marvels of the Welsh nation was part of the inheritance he had received from his mother. (GJW, 94; my translation)

Williams's *Poems* also contains a candid 'Sonnet, written in 1790, To the Memory of my Mother, who died Aug. 20, 1770':

> Since first I mourn'd thee number'd with the dead,
> I've known distress in ev'ry woful form,
> Through twice ten years – and o'er my batter'd head
> With fellest rage has blown the wint'ry storm.

> Oh, my *lost mother!* – still I weep for thee –
> Safe in thy care I pass'd through feeble youth;
> Unschool'd beside, I, tutor'd at thy knee,
> Caught from thy lips the sacred lore of truth . . .
> (*PLP*, II, 97)

'How irreparable was the loss of her to me!', Williams wrote; 'my grief was extreme.'[123] A letter of 2 May 1795 to Peggy from London also strongly testifies to his grief at the death of his father, aged eighty, on 23 April – 'I would have given the world for a sight of him alive, and to have been with him in his last illness . . . I believe I shall die very soon of a broken heart.'[124] Paternal affection and grief also haunt the preface to *Poems, Lyric and Pastoral* as Williams, accounting for the delay in the appearance of the volume, records the death of his beloved Lilly during his absence in London:

> Every thing would have been very well now, and my Poems would soon have appeared; but for, what I had always dreaded, an account of the death of one of my *dear children, a favourite little girl*, with whom went more by far the joys of my life than can ever be recovered in this world . . . I forgive every thing to my enemies but their having been the means of detaining me from home when my *pretty little infant* was in the hour of death calling upon me.[125]

In letters of the period, Williams could also eloquently formulate the societal significance of such devotion. Writing to Miss Barker on 26 March 1798, Williams, in Coleridgean fashion, stressed the importance of domestic affections in the moral make-up of those exercising power over others:

> I would have every Legislator as well as his elector a married man. a legislator [should] be acquainted with all the feelings of humanity before he can possibly Judge as he [should of] human actions, before he can make just allowances for human frailties. [?] can he be acquainted with these feelings unless he has passed thro' the several stages of Husband, and Parent, wherein only the best and finest sensibilities of human nature become known to us, and without these sensibilities man is little better [than] a Devil. (witness Billy Pitt).[126]

The intensity of Williams's attachment as a son and father would indeed appear to be the grounds of Godwin's infamous reproof.

My point is that at a time (1794–7) when Coleridge was setting Godwin's atheism 'at Defiance',[127] formulating his own opposition to certain aspects of Godwinian ethics and contemplating a formal answer to him, the figure of the slighted Edward Williams would have both dramatically confirmed and helped to galvanize his opposition. In the third of his lectures on 'Revealed Religion', delivered at Bristol in May 1795, Coleridge had squarely confronted *Political Justice* on the issues of gratitude and the domestic affections to refute what he saw as simplistic and pernicious theories divorced from any knowledge – either observed, intuitively felt or physiologically proven ('See this *demonstrated* by Hartley', as he states in a footnote to 'Religious Musings') – of human nature:

> The filial and paternal affections discipline the heart and prepare it for that blessed state of perfection in which all our Passions are to be absorbed in the Love of God . . . Jesus knew our Nature – and that expands like the circles of a Lake – the Love of our Friends, parents, and neighbours lead[s] us to the love of our Country and to the love of all Mankind. The intensity of private attachment encourages, not prevents, universal philanthropy . . . I have dwelt more particularly on this part of Christ's character and doctrine because the Stoical morality which disclaims all the duties of Gratitude and domestic Affection has been lately revived in a book popular among the professed Friends of civil Freedom – a book which builds without foundation, proposes an end without establishing the means, and discovers a total ignorance of that obvious Fact in human nature that in virtue and in knowledge we must be infants and be nourished with milk in order that we may be men and eat strong meat. Of this work it may be truly said, that whatever is just in it, is more forcibly recommended in the Gospel and whatever is new is absurd. Severe Moralist! that teaches us that filial Love is a Folly, Gratitude criminal, Marriage Injustice, and a promiscuous intercourse of the Sexes our wisdom and our duty.[128]

Williams's experience at the hands of Godwin would have been a compelling exemplum of the dangerous moral effects of the latter's refusal to countenance 'obvious Fact[s] in human nature'. Shortly before the beginning of their correspondence, Coleridge had attacked Thelwall in an essay entitled 'Modern Patriotism', printed in *The Watchman* for 17 March 1796, which again articulates these objections:

> You have studied Mr Godwin's Essay on Political Justice; but to think filial affection folly, gratitude a crime . . . may class you among the despisers of vulgar prejudices, but cannot increase the probability that you are a PATRIOT. But you act up to your principles. – So much the worse! Your principles are villainous ones! I would not entrust my wife or sister to you – Think you, I would entrust my country?[129]

Coleridge's letter to Thelwall on Godwin's treatment of Williams, who was also known to Thelwall at this time, can be seen to be a reiteration – and triumphant vindication – of Coleridge's argument. Thelwall is presented with the case of a mutual acquaintance slighted by Godwinian theory as an instructive, monitory example of the 'absurdities and wickedness of [Godwin's] System' in action. Williams's experience embodied the opposition between the facts of man's emotional life as understood and sanctioned by Jesus and by Coleridge's philosopher-hero David Hartley and the cold categorical imperatives enjoined by Godwin. And it is obvious from Coleridge's *Notebooks* that Williams figured importantly in Coleridge's political and moral consciousness at this time as a poignant human focus of competing ethical and political ideologies. Adding, probably in late September 1802, to some notebook entries of 1798 on 'Infancy & Infants', Coleridge imagined Williams's devotion in religious terms – 'Poor Williams seeking his Mother, in love with her Picture – & having that vision of Beauty & filial affection, that the Virgin Mary may be supposed to give.' – and as an entry of November/ December 1799 makes clear, he planned to 'introduce poor Williams' into his projected 'poems on Infancy'.[130]

But Williams's valency as victim was not the only one he offered Coleridge in the latter's anti-Godwinian crusade. It is important to stress that Coleridge's pitying references to 'poor Williams' and 'the poor Welch Bard' (and Southey's references to him are often in the same mode) run the risk of obscuring the profound respect in which Williams was held as a radical and philosophical thinker. The eloquent jacobin Bard inspired far more than pity, however formative in Coleridge's intellectual development 'poor Williams', victim of Godwin's reprehensible 'sincerity', may have proved. Indeed, Williams's writings on Bardism seem to have played a significant rôle in Coleridge's thinking on the related issue of 'the Godwinian system of Pride' – another vice he saw as characterizing those 'Friends of civil Freedom' who were, like Godwin, inclined to atheism: 'We find in

Jesus nothing of that Pride which affects to inculcate benevolence while it does away every home-born Feeling, by which it is produced and nurtured'.[131] Coburn has perceptively suggested that Coleridge's anti-Godwinian strictures on Pride in a 1795–6 Notebook entry –

> Hymns to the Sun, the Moon, and the Elements – six hymns. – In one of them to introduce a dissection of Atheism – particularly the Godwinian System of Pride[.] Proud of what? An outcast of blind Nature ruled by a fatal Necessity – Slave of an ideot [sic] Nature![132]

– may have been influenced by Williams's remarks on the same topic in his 'outlines of Bardism, Druidism, or the Ancient British Philosophy' in *Poems, Lyric and Pastoral*:

> *Pride* is the utmost degree of human depravity; it supplies the motive for perpetrating every kind of wickedness, it aims at *Superiority* and *Power*, which none but GOD is, of *right*, entitled to . . . PRIDE is the destroyer (CYTHRAUL [devil, adversary]) of the works of the CREATOR, the subverter of all order, forces itself obtrusively into a station that was never allotted to it. All men are equal in the CREATOR's paternality, as his children . . . PRIDE casts down into the *lowest point of existence*.[133]

The poems and Bardic Triads in *Poems, Lyric and Pastoral* also rail repeatedly and vociferously against 'Pride's malignant ardour' and 'odious birth'.[134] Coleridge may also have known of the strictures on Pride in the 'Sketch of British Bardism' – heavily influenced by Williams – which prefaces William Owen Pughe's *Heroic Elegies*. Imbuing Williams's philosophy of Bardism with a contemporary political flavour, Pughe states that

> Pride is that passion by which man assumes more than the laws of nature allow him; for all men are equal, though differently stationed in the state of humanity for common good. Whoever assumes such a superiority is an usurper; and by this assumption of power, derived from pride, a man attaches himself to evil, in such a degree, that his soul passes at death into the meanest worm; or he falls into the lowest point of existence.[135]

I suggest, therefore, that Williams occupies an important place in Coleridge's rejection of certain aspects of Godwin's philosophy. The

Welshman's writing on Bardism was certainly grist to the mill in the debate with the author of *Political Justice*, and Williams himself was living proof of the moral bankruptcy of abstract Godwinian theory – another of those 'appropriate human centre[s]' around whom the ideological debates of the 1790s were played out.

Before analysing the way in which Wordsworth enlisted the example of Williams in his refutations of Godwin, I want to suggest that Williams – ironically in the context of the foregoing argument – was perceived by Godwin himself as a resonant icon. As already noted, Williams claimed descent from Cromwell, and this king-killing forebear represented a prototype for Williams's jacobin persona in the 1790s. Citing prototypes for Caleb Williams in Godwin's novel of 1794, Gary Kelly has suggested that 'the archetypal rebel' Cromwell may well be a disturbing presence in Caleb's surname, since Mark Noble's *Memoirs of the Protectoral-House of Cromwell* (1784), the 1787 edition of which was in Godwin's library, notes that Cromwell was registered as 'Oliver Cromwell, *alias* Williams' at his marriage.[136] Kelly goes on to suggest other seventeenth-century archetypes bearing the surname Williams who were 'victims of monarchic power [and of] "things as they were"'. Kelly also notes that the surname is Welsh, 'like that of Holcroft's Hugh Trevor and Richard Graves's Mr Powell [in *The Spiritual Quixote*]' and that 'all three "quixotes" display that excessive impetuosity which is supposed to afflict the Cambrian race'. It would seem, however, that a contemporary model, whose identity was a conflation of all the personae cited above and who was well-known to Godwin, also inhabits the novel as Caleb's second self and namesake. Fitting the bill on all counts is the self-proclaimed descendant of Cromwell and radical victim of State persecution and of 'things as they were' in the 1790s – the 'impetuous' Welshman, Edward Williams.

Wordsworth's 'Answer to Godwin': *Poems, Lyric and Pastoral* and 'A Poet's Epitaph'

Williams's *Poems* is reckoned among the books Wordsworth may have read.[137] It is indeed likely that Coleridge would have introduced Wordsworth, probably around 1797–8, to the English poems of a man such as Williams, many of whose acquaintances, including Godwin, were also known to Wordsworth. Coleridge is also likely to have related to Wordsworth the story of Williams's encounter with the author of *Political Justice* and the specific grounds of Godwin's insult. Moreover, it is certainly possible – probable, even – that Wordsworth and Williams actually met in the early 1790s at one of the gravitational centres of metropolitan radicalism – the bookshop of Joseph Johnson, who in 1793 had published Wordsworth's *An Evening Walk* and *Descriptive Sketches*.

One can go further, and posit the influence of one of Williams's pieces from *Poems, Lyric and Pastoral* on Wordsworth's 'A Poet's Epitaph', written in late 1798 and published in the *Lyrical Ballads* of 1800. Wordsworth's poem can be seen to enlist Williams's as part of a response to *Political Justice* and to Godwin's treatment of the Welsh Bard. In this respect, Williams's poem represents a more pointed and politicized analogue of 'A Poet's Epitaph' than Theocritus's Epigram XIX[138] and Burns's 'A Bard's Epitaph',[139] both of which have also been seen as models for Wordsworth's poem.

Williams had already contrasted himself with 'book-taught poets' in the autobiographical piece that appeared in *The Gentleman's Magazine* in November 1789, and 'The Learned Ignorants, A Song, written in 1772' included in his *Poems* elaborates on this:

> Ye book-poring pedants, by learning made fools,
> Whose skulls are well-stuff'd with the rubbish of schools,
> Ye boast your old *ballads* that classics ye call,
> Your *Homers*, your *Virgils*, your devil and all;
> True, you know *Greek* enough to make any dog sick,
> Nor less are ye skill'd in the cant of *Old Nick*;
> But, how does it happen? ye constantly prove
> Mere dunces indeed in the language of *Love*.

> A tatter'd *Oxonian* I t'other day met,
> One of those that make books (I was quite in a pet),
> He was filching from *Horace* old thoughts for a song,
> Where through the green wood I walk'd pensive along;
> He look'd wild around him, and ask'd with surprize,
> If Duns or Bumbailiffs occasion'd my sighs,
> But I sought my dear Phillis, and flew from the grove,
> Alas! the poor *Soph* knows but little of *Love*.

> Once forc'd from my charmer abruptly to part,
> Grief harrow'd my soul, drew the blood from my heart;

In my way an absurd astronomical ass
Bo-peep'd at the sky through a queer-fashion'd glass;
He saw my sad looks, and the briny tears run,
And suppos'd 'twas by staring, like him, at the Sun;
At the Sun! yes, you block-head, but not that above,
'Twas a brighter by far, the bright eyes of my *Love*.

One morning in May, as I walk'd by the rill
That tinkles along near the foot of yon hill,
Gay Spring bloom'd around, how serene the sweet air,
And, weeping, I wish'd my dear *Phillis* was there;
When a booby old *Botanist*, haunting the place,
Through a pair of broad spectacles star'd in my face;
This *eye-seed*, quoth he, will your anguish remove: —
'Twas a *weed-monger's* tale, that knew nothing of *Love*.

As saunt'ring last night in the pine-shaded walk,
Where often I'm bless'd with my charmer's dear talk;
I long'd to behold her, look'd anxious around,
But my fair-one, alas! was no where to be found;
A *Philosopher* ask'd, if I wept, sigh'd, and whin'd,
Like *Heraclitus* once, for the whims of mankind?
A *Philosopher* you! that's amazing, by Jove!
And ignorant thus of the nature of *Love*.

In a glade far-sequester'd, as lately retir'd,
I wept the sad absence of her I admir'd;
When a son of old *Galen* came hobbling that way,
And, like other dull sots, wanted something to say;
He ask'd me, observing my tears and my sighs,
If a *lachrymal fistula* flooded my eyes?
Alas, the poor *Doctor*! 'twas easy to prove
His heart never felt the keen *lancet* of *Love*.

As, weeping, I pass'd by the church t'other day,
In search of my Phillis who rambled that way;
I was taken to task by a preaching old *prig*,
'Twas a *double-chinn'd Priest*, in a full-bottom'd wig;
He of fasting and pray'r made a wonderful din,
And hop'd, he pretended, I wept for my sin;
But how can *he* claim those bless'd mansions above,
That's not of the faith and religion of *Love*?

> The billet from Phillis, her hand and her seal,
> Drew me out of the parlour my tears to conceal;
> When a grizzly old *Alchymist* meets me, and cries,
> 'You've been toiling in smoke, I perceive by your eyes',
> His *Philosopher's stone* turns a brick-bat to gold,
> Yet *Love's* nobler essence he ne'er could unfold;
> But I flew to my charmer, we met in the grove,
> And join'd soul to soul in th'endearments of *Love.*
>
> Hush, Pedants, be mute! you may think me quite rude,
> Because I dare thus on your studies intrude;
> But quit this dull farce, your poor college grimace,
> And study the charms of a *pretty girl's* face;
> The tender expressions of love-tutor'd eyes;
> And construe the language of heart-speaking sighs;
> Do this, and your learning to wisdom improve,
> And you'll own that true knowledge is nothing but *Love!*
> (*PLP*, I, 85–90)

Here is Wordsworth's poem:

> Art thou a Statesman, in the van
> Of public business train'd and bred?
> – First learn to love one living man;
> *Then* may'st thou think upon the dead.
>
> A Lawyer art thou? – draw not nigh;
> Go, carry to some other place
> The hardness of thy coward eye,
> The falshood of thy sallow face.[140]
>
> Art thou a man of purple cheer?
> A rosy man, right plump to see?
> Approach; yet Doctor, not too near:
> This grave no cushion is for thee.
>
> Art thou a man of gallant pride,
> A Soldier, and no man of chaff?
> Welcome! – but lay thy sword aside,
> And lean upon a Peasant's staff.

Physician art thou? One, all eyes,
Philosopher! a fingering slave,
One that would peep and botanize
Upon his mother's grave?

Wrapp'd closely in thy sensual fleece
O turn aside, and take, I pray,
That he below may rest in peace,
Thy pin-point of a soul away!

– A Moralist perchance appears;
Led, heaven knows how! to this poor sod,
And *He* has neither eyes nor ears;
Himself his world, and his own God;

One to whose smooth-rubb'd soul can cling
Nor form nor feeling great nor small,
A reasoning, self-sufficing thing,
An intellectual All in All!

Shut close the door! press down the latch:
Sleep in thy intellectual crust,
Nor lose ten tickings of thy watch,
Near this unprofitable dust.

But who is He, with modest looks,
And clad in homely russet brown?
He murmurs near the running brooks
A music sweeter than their own.

He is retired as noontide dew,
Or fountain in a noonday grove;
And you must love him, ere to you
He will seem worthy of your love.

The outward shews of sky and earth,
Of hill and valley he has view'd;
And impulses of deeper birth
Have come to him in solitude.

> In common things that round us lie
> Some random truths he can impart,
> The harvest of a quiet eye
> That broods and sleeps on his own heart.
>
> But he is weak, both man and boy,
> Hath been an idler in the land;
> Contented if he might enjoy
> The things which others understand.
>
> – Come hither in thy hour of strength,
> Come, weak as is a breaking wave!
> Here stretch thy body at full length;
> Or build thy house upon this grave. –
>
> (LB, 235–7)

The general similarity between the two pieces is apparent in the roll-call of stock middle-class professionals whose characteristics and capacity for imaginative response are measured (and found wanting) against those of a more feeling model. Moreover, there are compelling details common to both. Williams's astronomer who 'Bo-peep[s] at the sky' and his bespectacled botanist who recommends 'eye-seed' offer prototypes for Wordsworth's curiously conflated physician–philosopher–field-biologist – 'all eyes' – who 'would peep and botanize / Upon his mother's grave'.[141] Indeed, the focus in Williams's poem on eyes, vision and the lack of vision of pedantic 'porers' – 'the bright eyes of my *Love*', 'eye-seed', 'a *lachrymal fistula* flooded my eyes', '"You've been toiling in smoke, I perceive from your eyes"', 'love-tutor'd eyes' – is also apparent in Wordsworth's – 'thy coward eye', 'One all eyes', 'And he has neither eyes nor ears', 'The harvest of a quiet eye'. The astronomer of Williams's poem, though without his exact double in Wordsworth's, finds one in the 1802 additions to the Preface to *Lyrical Ballads*, in which Wordsworth has his own 'A Poet's Epitaph' in mind:

> Aristotle, I have been told, hath said, that Poetry is the most philosophical of all writing: it is so: its object is truth . . . not standing upon external testimony, but carried alive into the heart by passion . . . The Poet writes under one restriction only, namely, that of the necessity of giving immediate pleasure to a human Being possessed of that

information which may be expected of him, not as a lawyer, a physician, a mariner, an astronomer, or a natural philosopher, but as a Man.[142]

Williams's poetic persona who walks weeping 'by the rill / That tinkles along near the foot of yon hill', in 'a glade far-sequester'd, as lately retir'd' and 'in the grove' is a prototype of Wordsworth's rustic wanderer who is 'retired as noontide dew / Or fountain in a noonday grove' and who 'murmurs near the running brooks / A music sweeter than their own'. The ideal in Williams's piece is a simple soul amongst the glades that can 'construe the language of heart-speaking sighs'; in Wordsworth's, it is a similarly artless, meditative being receptive to the language of Nature – and, by implication, to such poems as 'A Poet's Epitaph'. In a discussion of Wordsworth's anxieties regarding readership and reception, Lucy Newlyn interprets his 'retired' rustic as 'unmistakably . . . a poet in the Wordsworthian mould' and as an ideal reader of the poem-epitaph onto whom Wordsworth projects 'both his own self-image, and (in a reflexive doubling of that image) his best hopes of being understood by his readers: "And you must love him, ere to you / He will seem worthy of your love"'.[143] It is a 'self-image' that Wordsworth, I argue, recognized in both Williams's person and his poetic persona – an act of recognition that construes Wordsworth himself, in Newlyn's terms, as the ideal reader of Williams's poem.

'The Learned Ignorants' sets up a clear opposition between the cold formality of classical and neo-classical poetry, written in a language unmotivated by Nature, and the simplicity of a language that acts as a window on, and a mode of communion with, Nature. The Wordsworth of the *Lyrical Ballads* would certainly have shared the views expressed in one of Williams's manuscript jottings: 'Language that brings our ideas nearest to nature is doubtless the best, and nothing can be more evident than that, in many instances, the learned languages lead us out of the round of nature'.[144] Indeed, the linguistic programme of the *Lyrical Ballads* as set out in the prefaces of 1800 and 1802 is perfectly in tune with one of Williams's Bardic formulations in *Poems, Lyric and Pastoral*. Wordsworth would have recognized in the following passage a conception of poetic 'naturalness' that was strikingly in tune with his own thinking at the time:

> A Poet in the character of a Shepherd, an occupation the most proper of all others to represent primeval simplicity and virtue, describes objects as they naturally present themselves to the senses, and affect

the mind; or utters sentiments that spring from the simple notions and inborn feelings of those that are unacquainted with the abstractions of philosophy, and the complex ideas derived from art . . . It would, perhaps, not be amiss if our modern *Critics* and *Poets* would take into consideration the following maxim of the *Welsh Bards*, from their *Poetic Triades* . . . the three primary and indispensable requisites of poetic genius are, An eye that can see Nature; A heart that can feel Nature; And a resolution that dares follow Nature. Quære? Have any of the great *Manufacturers* of Poets, from the days of *Aristotle* to the present time, ever said any thing more to the purpose? (*PLP*, I, 173–4; 175–6)

To emphasize its importance, Williams also printed the above Triad – his own – twice in the 'Account of, and Extracts from, the Welsh-Bardic Triades' in the second volume of the *Poems*.[145] The Welsh Bards appear here as theorists of a doctrine of radical linguistic 'simplicity' of which the Preface to the *Lyrical Ballads* was to become a celebrated expression. Williams's statements obviously prefigure – and I would argue, inform – Wordsworth's Preface, which famously argues that 'low and rustic life' was chosen as a subject since 'in that situation the essential passions of the heart . . . are less under restraint, and speak a plainer and more emphatic language', and that 'such a language . . . is a more permanent and a far more philosophical language than that which is frequently substituted for it by Poets'[146] (a claim that is in fact in accord with, not in opposition to, Williams's statement that the rustic poet is 'unacquainted with the abstractions of philosophy').

It is significant that Williams's poem 'On Love', which has obvious affinities with 'The Learned Ignorants' and which bears a striking similarity to Wordsworth's 'A Poet's Epitaph', once again contrasts moral and linguistic 'simplicity' and 'hypocrisy':

> Love, bold intruder, since my lay
> Derives a theme from thee,
> My bow'r approach; but drive away
> That fiend Hypocrisy:
> Come simple, as in days of yore,
> Untried in feats of art:
> Attend me thus, I'll own thy pow'r;
> Admit thee to my heart.
> (*PLP*, I, 136)

William Knight noted in 1896 that Wordsworth's portrait of an ideal, feeling soul in 'A Poet's Epitaph', 'clad in homely russet brown', is indebted to James Thomson's description of the Bard in *The Castle of Indolence* (1748):[147]

> He came, the bard, a little Druid wight,
> Of withered aspect; but his eye was keen,
> With sweetness mixed. *In russet brown bedight* . . .
> He crept along, unpromising of mien.
>   (Canto II, stanza xxxiii; my emphasis)

The echo of Thomson is unmistakable, but for the Wordsworth of 1798, this literary prototype would also have comprehended the living model of a contemporary Bard and 'Druid wight', Edward Williams – small, keen-eyed – whose persona in 'The Learned Ignorants' and other pieces in *Poems, Lyric and Pastoral* represents a model for Wordsworth's responsive rustic. Moreover, Wordsworth would have recognized in Williams a mirror of himself – an act of identification in which Edwin, the protagonist of James Beattie's poem *The Minstrel* (1771 and 1774 – a significant influence on both the young Wordsworth and the mature poet of *The Prelude*[148]), plays an interesting rôle as yet another model for the Romantic self. In a letter of 1793, Dorothy Wordsworth described Wordsworth as Edwin's second self – 'Beattie's "Minstrel" always reminds me of [Wordsworth] and indeed the whole character of Edwin resembles much what William was when I first knew him'[149] – while Mary Moorman has emphasized that the solitary Edwin, alive to Nature's wonders, was 'a poetic creation after [Wordsworth's] own image'.[150] Wordsworth would also have seen his own Edwinian image in the Edward Williams of *Poems, Lyric and Pastoral*: intriguingly, an anonymous reviewer of the volume in the *Critical Review* declares that 'Those who have read Beatie's [*sic*] Minstrel, will be struck with the similarity between young Edwin' and Williams the 'rustic poet'.[151] Such mirror images are a choice example of the way in which Romantic identity was fashioned in the 1790s in relation to both literary and living models.

Wordsworth's critique of intellectualism, directed in 'A Poet's Epitaph' specifically at the Moralist, is the main thrust of Williams's 'The Learned Ignorants' as a whole, which is levelled from the outset against all 'book-poring pedants, by learning made fools'.[152] Describing the atheistic Moralist (here, a moral philosopher) as 'A reasoning, self-sufficing thing, / An intellectual All in All!', Wordsworth surely has in mind the Godwin of *Political Justice* – the 'Moralist' who had famously insulted Williams and whose philosophy was predicated on reason and, in Wordsworth's phrase from *The Prelude*, the 'independent intellect'. As we have seen, Coleridge had characterized Godwin as a 'Severe Moralist' in his discussion of gratitude and filial affection at Bristol in 1795. Wordsworth himself had already written a powerful analysis of perverted Godwinian reason (and of pride, filial love and gratitude – 'a heavy burden to a proud soul') in *The Borderers*, and was to write devastatingly in *The Prelude* of the 'barren seas' of Godwinism which took him far from the 'arbours' of 'blessèd sentiment and fearless love' (significantly, 'blissful *gratitude* and fearless love' in the 1850 version).[153] Enlisting metaphors of sight and blindness to emphasize the moral and imaginative myopia of the Godwinians, Coleridge in the third of his Bristol lectures on 'Revealed Religion' called them the 'dim eyed Sons of Blasphemy',[154] and quoted Beattie's *Minstrel* to characterize Godwinian atheistical 'sensualists', blind to Nature as the language of God:

> The dark cold-hearted Sceptics creeping pore
> Through microscope of Metaphysic Lore;
> And much they grope for Truth but never hit[.]
> Their heavy powers, inadequate before[,]
> Their earthly Lusts make more and more unfit[,]
> Yet deem they Darkness Light, and their vain Blunders Wit.[155]

Likewise, Wordsworth in the fragment 'Not useless do I deem' – written for 'The Ruined Cottage' and envisaged at this time (1798) as part of *The Recluse* – asks:

> For was it meant
> That we should pore, and dwindle as we pore
> Forever dimly pore on things minute,
> On solitary objects, still beheld
> In disconnection, dead and spiritless;
> And still dividing, and dividing still,
> Break down all grandeur, still unsatisfied
> With our unnatural toil while littleness
> May yet become more little, waging thus

> An impious warfare with the very life
> Of our own souls?
>
> (*MoH*, 270–1; ll. 58–68)

In this context, Williams's poem, levelled against canting 'sophisters' who murder to dissect and against 'porers', blind to 'the language', 'the nature' and 'the religion of *Love*', would have struck Wordsworth and Coleridge as a piece to which they could readily ascribe a specifically anti-Godwinian agenda. Moreover, Wordsworth's line 'One that would peep and botanize / Upon his mother's grave' gains an added tragic *frisson* as it conjures up both the bereaved Williams at his mother's grave – Williams, tellingly, was well known as an accomplished botanist and herbalist[156] – and, troublingly, Godwin the 'Severe Moralist'.

Wordsworth's poem is cast as an epitaph (a form he was to theorize, of course[157]), and Williams's *Poems, Lyric and Pastoral*, as well as Burns's 'A Bard's Epitaph', may well be informing Wordsworth's poem on this score, too, since Williams, a stonemason, describes himself in the preface to the *Poems* as having 'learned the alphabet before I can well remember, by seeing my father inscribe grave-stones', adding 'it is of no importance to any one to know how many stones I hewed, or on how many grave-stones I have inscribed vile doggerel'.[158] In 'A Poet's Epitaph', Wordsworth aligns himself with the slighted Edward Williams by inscribing an epitaphic 'answer' to Godwin. Further, it is significant that another poem in Williams's collection carries the title 'Epitaph on a Poet' and contains the lines

> Escap'd from the familiar curse
> Of *threadbare coat* and *empty purse*,
> From rough *Bumbailiffs*, threat'ning *Duns*,
> From stupid *Pride's* detested sons . . .
>
> (*PLP*, I, 115)

– which are recapitulated in the couplet 'He look'd wild around him, and ask'd with surprize, / If Duns or Bumbailiffs occasion'd my sighs' in 'The Learned Ignorants'. My discussion, then, has identified *Poems, Lyric and Pastoral* as informing both Wordsworth's conception of a language of poetic sincerity in the *Lyrical Ballads* and the poetic inscription in 'A Poet's Epitaph' of his ideological quarrel with Godwin. In the final section of this chapter, I explore the way in which Edward Williams inhabits another poem from the *Lyrical Ballads* which dramatizes Wordsworth's response to Godwin's position on the contentious issue of gratitude – 'Simon Lee, the Old Huntsman'.

'Alas! the Gratitude of Men': *Poems, Lyric and Pastoral* and 'Simon Lee'

It should not be forgotten, of course, that a discourse of gratitude permeates the greatest poem in the *Lyrical Ballads*. 'Tintern Abbey' repeatedly records and celebrates *debts* – to Nature, to memory, to Dorothy – with its repeated references to 'gifts' and 'recompence'. If Wordsworth's sense of gratitude is diffused throughout 'Tintern Abbey', 'Simon Lee' is from the outset pitched (in a curiously bloody-minded way, one feels) towards an effusive expression of it. As Wordsworth explains in the Fenwick note, the poem narrates an actual encounter with an old servant of the Alfoxden estate in Somerset, Christopher Tricky.[159] The locus of the poem, however, is Wales: 'In the sweet shire of Cardigan, / Not far from pleasant Ivor-Hall'. Time's toll on Simon Lee's body is mirrored in the abandoned state of Ivor Hall: 'His master's dead, and no one now / Dwells in the hall of Ivor' (*LB*, 64–5; ll. 1–2, 21–2). In 'Simon Lee and Ivor Hall: A Possible Source', Peter Bement suggests that Wordsworth's decision to change the setting from Somerset to Cardiganshire 'may have been motivated by a desire to avoid giving offence at Alfoxden', and contends that

> the abandoned 'hall of Ivor' calls to mind the ruins, at Bassaleg, near Newport in Monmouthshire, of the palace of Ifor ap Llywelyn, known as *Ifor Hael* ('Ivor the Generous') . . . famous in Welsh literary and antiquarian circles as the supposed patron of the great medieval poet, Dafydd ap Gwilym.[160]

For Edward Williams, as we have seen, the relationship between Dafydd and Ifor Hael represented a model which he sought to resuscitate in the 1790s. Further, Bement argues that Wordsworth might have known of this historical 'hall of Ivor' from the famous series of *englynion* (strict-metre stanzas) entitled 'Llys Ifor Hael' (The Palace of Ifor Hael) by Evan Evans (1731–88) – the Cardiganshire-born poet, antiquarian, scholar and friend of Thomas Gray and

Thomas Percy known as 'Ieuan Brydydd Hir' (Evan the Tall Poet) or 'Ieuan Fardd' (Evan the Bard). The first of these *englynion* runs:

> Llys Ifor Hael! gwael yw'r gwedd, – yn garnau
> Mewn gwerni mae'n gorwedd;
> Drain ac ysgall mall a'i medd,
> Mieri, lle bu marwedd.[161]

Bement further argues that Wordsworth may have seen Evans's own translation of the poem or heard it discussed during a visit in 1791 or 1793 to Downing, Flintshire, home of Thomas Pennant, one of Evans's patrons:

> Amidst its alders Ivor's palace lies
> In heaps of ruins to my wondering eyes;
> Where greatness dwelt in pomp, now thistles reign,
> And prickly thorns assert their wide domain.
>
> No longer Bards inspired thy tables grace,
> Nor hospitable deeds adorn the place;
> No more the generous owner gives his gold
> To modest merit, as to Bards of old.
>
> In plaintive verse his Ivor, Gwilym moans,
> His patron lost, the pensive poet groans:
> What mighty loss, that Ivor's lofty hall
> Should now with screeching owls rehearse its fall![162]

But the important fact here is that Evan Evans was accompanied to the ruins of Ifor Hael's hall at Gwernyclepa (not Basaleg, as Bement has it[163]) in 1779 or 1780 by none other than Edward Williams. Indeed, Williams might even have led the threadbare curate of Basaleg to the ruins and inspired him to write his famous stanzas.[164] It was certainly Williams who from 1789 onwards was responsible for establishing the fame of Ifor Hael as an archetype of – and household name for – generosity.

Moreover, I suggest that Williams the man and his *Poems, Lyric and Pastoral* are part of the full resonance of 'Simon Lee' on the question of gratitude. Another possible source for 'Ivor Hall' in 'Simon Lee' is Williams's own poem 'To Ivor the Liberal, on being presented by him with a pair of gloves, from the Welsh of Dafydd ap Gwilym'.[165] The piece is dedicated to John Morgan of Tredegar, a descendant of Ifor Hael and one of the chief sponsors of David Williams's *History of Monmouthshire*, in which, significantly, an appendix drawn up by Edward Williams mentions Ifor Hael and quotes Evan Evans's poem.[166]

Williams's poem can be seen to provide Wordsworth not only with the phrase 'Ivor Hall' but also with an added anti-Godwin charge. The poem is a free rendering of Dafydd ap Gwilym's *cywydd* to Ifor Hael, 'Diolch am Fenig' (Thanksgiving for a pair of Gloves), and is prefaced by the following account of Ifor:

> IVOR the LIBERAL, in Welsh IFOR HAEL, was Lord of BASELEG, in the County of MONMOUTH. He lived about the middle of the fourteenth century, and was celebrated by the Bards of his age, and of all succeeding ages, for his unexampled liberality. He was the warm patron of DAFYDD AP GWILYM, the most renowned Bard of his time, whose works are to this day held in the highest estimation.

The first lines of the poem celebrate Ivor's welcoming hall and expansive benevolence. Williams patently modernizes and radicalizes him; this is a medieval Welsh lord with not a little of the George Dyer of the *Dissertation on the Theory and Practice of Benevolence* and the *Complaints of the Poor People of England* about him:

> THOU IVOR, darling of the Muse,
> Who through the world thy fame pursues;
> Proclaims thy worth in ev'ry clime,
> Whilst rapture fills her lay sublime;
> And feels her thrilling soul expand,
> Whilst foster'd by thy bounteous hand.
> Thy ample gate, thy ample hall,
> Are ever op'ning wide to all;
> And, warm'd in Heav'n, thy ampler mind
> Dilates in Love to all mankind.

'Jesus knew our Nature – and that expands like the circles of a Lake – the Love of our Friends, parents, and neighbours lead[s] us to the love of our Country and to the love of all Mankind', Coleridge was to state a year after this poem appeared. The discourse of praise and gratitude that lies at the heart of the Welsh poetic tradition then becomes the defining characteristic of Williams's piece:

> As, lately, sitting at thy board,
> Where ev'ry guest thy worth ador'd,
> With grateful warmth I tun'd my lays,
> And felt high transport in thy praise . . .
> Thy Bard, esteem'd the nobler guest,
> Was with distinguish'd bounty bless'd;
> The gifts of NUDD could not excel
> The gloves that to my portion fell;
> Surpassing MORDAF's boon of old,
> For both my gloves were cramm'd with gold;
> And RHYDDERCH's hand could not reward
> With nobler meeds his tuneful Bard . . .
> Great IVOR's friendship shall inspire
> His Bard with ARTHUR's martial fire
> His grateful Bard, that dares advance,
> Unarm'd, against that warrior's lance.[167]

It seems highly likely that Wordsworth's 'Ivor Hall' is the product of an English ear's processing of 'Ifor Hael' (correct pronunciation, [haIl]): an interesting act of 'translation' whereby generosity ('Hael') and the feeling it inspires – gratitude – can be seen to exist in Wordsworth's poem as a suggestive cross-cultural echo *from the outset* ('In the sweet shire of Cardigan, / Not far from pleasant *Ivor-Hall*'). But more significant than its having provided Wordsworth with 'Ivor Hall' is the part the poem plays in Wordsworth's critique of Godwin on gratitude.

It is worth quoting here another passage of Godwin's discussion of gratitude:

> My benefactor ought to be esteemed, not because he bestowed a benefit upon me, but because he bestowed it upon a human being. His desert will be in exact proportion to the degree, in which that human being was worthy of the distinction conferred. Thus every view of the subject brings us back to the consideration of my neighbour's moral worth and his importance to the general weal, as the only standard to determine the treatment to which he is entitled. Gratitude therefore, a principle which has so often been the theme of the moralist and the poet, is no part either of justice or virtue. By gratitude I understand a sentiment, which would lead me to prefer one man to another, from some other consideration than that of his superior usefulness or worth.
> (*An Enquiry concerning Political Justice*, I, 84)

Commentators such as Legouis, Hutchinson and Moorman have read the ending of 'Simon Lee' as a *specifically* anti-Godwin piece which sends 'Godwinian theories whistling down the wind'[168] by vindicating 'the instinctive character of the emotion of gratitude as against Godwin, who represented it as an unjust and degrading sentiment'.[169] Wordsworth's famous ending strikes at the root of Godwinian morality:

> I struck, and with a single blow
> The tangled root I sever'd,
> At which the poor old man so long
> And vainly had endeavour'd.
>
> The tears into his eyes were brought,
> And thanks and praises seemed to run
> So fast out of his heart, I thought
> They never would have done.
>
> – I've heard of hearts unkind, kind deeds
> With coldness still returning.
> Alas! the gratitude of men
> Has oftener left me mourning.
> (*LB*, 67; ll. 93–104)

Referring directly to 'Simon Lee', Legouis has commented that

> One who has read the judgment pronounced by Godwin upon gratitude . . . will be surprised to find his feelings stirred by grateful words; and his astonishment will be the greater, his emotion the stronger, if the gratitude expressed is out of all reasonable proportion to the service rendered.[170]

In this respect, the status of Williams's poem as an adaptation of a *cywydd* of gratitude is significant: Wordsworth's reference to 'Ivor Hall' in 'Simon Lee' and his relocation of the poem to Wales are part of a larger debt to Williams's poem and the tradition of which it is part – one which invests 'Simon Lee' with a superadded, and Welsh-inflected, critique of Godwin on gratitude. Of course, it was Williams's sense of filial gratitude that had initially aroused Godwin's ire, and it might not be fanciful to hear an echo of Coleridge's letter to

Thelwall – 'Poor Williams, the Welch bard – (a very meek man) brought the tear into my Eye by a simple narration of the manner in which Godwin had insulted him' (an account which Coleridge would doubtless have communicated to Wordsworth) – in Wordsworth's conclusion: 'The tears into his eyes were brought . . .' 'Simon Lee', then, becomes another of those sites of complex cultural confluence, another example of those reticular literary structures typical of the 1790s, which I have been considering in this book.

In this chapter, we have seen how Wordsworth and Coleridge enlisted Edward Williams as an instructive ally in the case against facile Godwinian theory. They found in this compelling Welshman of 'wild heart' and 'warm head' a radical and fellow poet whose Bardic persona, writings and personal experience – 'Felt in the blood, and felt along the heart ('Tintern Abbey', l. 29) – offered influential templates for their own poetical, political and moral identities in the 1790s.

5
Models of Fellowship and Fulfilment: Wordsworth, Coleridge, John Thelwall

John Thelwall has already been a palpable presence in the preceding examinations of the valency for the 1790s of my first four models. In Chapter 3, I outlined the 'symbiotic relationship' that developed between Coleridge and Thelwall in the 1790s as they responded in their poetry, political writings and letters to each other's works and ideological positions. Thelwall, as we have seen, visited Wordsworth and Coleridge in the West Country in July 1797, anxious to settle down near them. In late 1796 and early 1797, Coleridge had informed Thelwall of his own plan of devoting his time in a rural retreat to agriculture and literary pursuits and had sought to persuade Thelwall that such a life would suit the harried jacobin, too: 'Fifty £ you might, I doubt not, gain by reviewing; & furnishing miscellanies for the different magazines; you might safely speculate on twenty pound a year more from your compositions . . . & by severe economy, a little garden labour, & a pig stie, this would do.'[1] Coleridge's plan was obviously conceived in part as a fulfilment of his and Southey's Pantisocratic programme, whose projected location had initially been the Susquehanna Valley and, subsequently, Wales. At the end of 1796, Coleridge, who during the previous two years had been, in the words of E. P. Thompson, 'a sort of little Bristol Thelwall',[2] settled at the 'Susquehanna' of Stowey, and Wordsworth was soon to follow. As I have already outlined, however, Thelwall's longed-for retirement amongst the poets in the West Country did not materialize, and circumstances drove him into retreat at Llyswen, Brecknockshire, in late 1797. Roe contends that 'Coleridge and Poole . . . sacrificed Thelwall's residence in the neighbourhood for the company of Wordsworth and Dorothy'.[3]

My final chapter focuses on the productions of Thelwall's Welsh years of exile as the 'new Recluse' in the Wye Valley (1797–1800). A consideration of the politics of Thelwall's 'Pedestrian Excursion' of 1797 leads to an examination of the politics of identity in the 'Prefatory Memoir' to his *Poems, Chiefly Written in Retirement*. This provides a context for my analysis of Thelwall's 'Paternal Tears' sequence – ten blank verse elegies for his daughter, Maria, who died at Llyswen. I contend that these poems constitute a conscious intertextual dialogue – hitherto unnoticed by critics – with poems by Wordsworth and Coleridge through which the exiled Thelwall sought to register the gulf that now lay between them. As Thelwall had recently seen, Wordsworth and Coleridge were enjoying a life of 'philosophical amity' together in a fruitful, symbiotic relationship based on mutual admiration – an ideal 'society' from which he had been excluded. Through direct allusion, deliberate echo and parallelism, Thelwall invokes them as models and foils for his exiled self – paradigms of fulfilment against which he constructs himself as a tragic counterpart confronting, in the words of 'Tintern Abbey', 'solitude, [and] fear, [and] pain, [and] grief'. Reading Thelwall, we read the poems of his friends as in a distorting mirror. Absence is in fact implied presence; soliloquy is in fact dialogue. Rather than the inscription of presence in a single, culturally embedded image or a cryptic, historically ramifying reference as was the case with the hermit and Vortigern in 'Tintern Abbey', what we have here is the inscription of Wordsworth and Coleridge themselves in poems whose *immediate* context of signification is not the wider political culture or 'history' *per se*, but other poems. We will, of course, be making that further step from these 'other poems' to the culture out of which they were written, since Thelwall's elegies negotiate the wider cultural meanings of his friends' works. Thelwall's allusions would certainly have been registered by initiated readers – not least, of course, Wordsworth and Coleridge themselves. The elegies of 'Paternal Tears' can also be seen to offer a complex commentary on the canonized Romantic texts of his friends which serves to highlight their inner tensions and implied agendas.

Towards Retirement: Thelwall's 'Pedestrian Excursion'

The road to Llyswen needs first to be traced in order to establish the context out of which this dialogue with Coleridge and Wordsworth emerged. When Thelwall set off on his 'Pedestrian Excursion' through England and Wales in the summer of 1797 with his friend Wimpory – an account of which was published in the *Monthly Magazine* from August 1799 to November 1801 – he was already in retreat, his political voice effectively silenced by the repressive measures of Pitt's government and by the actual physical violence of government-sanctioned mobs. One motivation for the tour was to observe the state of the 'laborious classes' at a time of bad harvests and war, and the 'Pedestrian Excursion' focuses at every turn on their condition, conscientiously recording their wages and railing against the wretchedness of their existence and especially 'the monopolising calculation of the age': 'Every fact connected with the history and actual condition of the laborious classes had become important to a heart throbbing with anxiety for the welfare of the human race', Thelwall declares at the beginning of his account.[4] In this sense, the 'Pedestrian Excursion' obviously prefigures *Rural Rides*, by the man who was to succeed Thelwall as the new democratic tribune – William Cobbett.[5] But another motive propelled Thelwall westward. As he remarks in the 'Prefatory Memoir', he envisaged the 'Pedestrian Excursion' as 'a search for an elegible [*sic*] retreat' and the journey was pitched towards what he viewed at the time as a beacon of hope and solace – Coleridge in the West Country:

> On the Somerset shire coast, and not many miles from Bridgewater, the author has an invaluable friend, well known in the literary world, whom as yet he had never seen, but for whom, during the imperfect intercourse of a familiar and confidential correspondence, he had conceived all the affection of a brother. With his friend an opportunity of more immediate and intimate communication of sentiments had been long and mutually desired; and as the family of the journalist [Thelwall] was then in Derby, he was determined to take the opportunity, in his way from Somersetshire to that place, of visiting some of the picturesque and romantic scenery of Wales.[6]

There he was aimed. On his way westward, retirement was much on his mind. Near Bagshot, he and Wimpory

> formed Utopian plans of retirement and colonisations . . . [Our conversation] matured and methodised in our minds the project (which before had only floated across our brains in moments of weariness and

disgust) of retiring to some sequestered spot, and spending the remainder of our days in rustic industry and philosophical seclusion.[7]

The 'Pedestrian Excursion' is obviously no political tract. Given Thelwall's plans for retirement, it is no surprise that his tour often seems an exercise in depoliticization. It does not explicitly mention Thelwall's experiences at the hands of Pitt's government and its various agents, the violence offered him in the provinces in 1796–7 and the suppression of his political career. Thelwall was still a shadowed man, and the tour at one point offers a fascinating glimpse of him confronting the wariness, suspicion and fear of the populace: an 'old thresher' near Squires repels each question regarding 'the price of labour, or the condition of the labouring poor' with 'some *sly rub*, or *sagacious* hint', his 'arch gestures, and emphatic half-syllables' displaying 'the self-congratulating cunning of suspicion'.[8] Speaking of his conversation with an intelligent-looking, though intoxicated, 'common labourer', again near Squires, Thelwall laments that

> we could no way turn his conversation into the channel we desired. He talked of nothing but Parker and the delegates, of war and of politics. In short, he was too full of liquor and *temporary politics*, to furnish any information on the subject of *political oeconomy*.

The labourer was referring to the recent, month-long (10 May–13 June) naval mutiny at the Nore, led by Richard Parker (who had actually been hanged on board ship the day before this conversation took place). Michael Scrivener has remarked that

> Thelwall makes it seem that the labourer was interested in mere trivia . . . In actual context, talking about 'political economy' would have been intellectually escapist. Something else might be at work here, namely Thelwall's own strenuous desire to separate himself from political activism, at least in writing. There was much speculation at the time about the mutineers' possible revolutionary motives, so that it would not have been entirely impossible for Thelwall to have got re-imprisoned on some imagined link between himself and the naval mutinies. Additionally, in the final years of the London Corresponding Society's existence, from 1797 to 1799 when it was outlawed altogether, the group moved toward plotting violence with the United Irishmen. What better way to illustrate how utterly free he was from

anything resembling violent conspiracies against the government than to express boredom and lofty disdain for discussions with labourers about the naval mutinies?[9]

However, one does hear the voice of Thelwall the metropolitan intellectual, the political lecturer of Copenhagen Fields and Beaufort Buildings, from time to time during the tour. As Nicholas Roe and others have argued, the very act of walking would have been construed in the 1790s as an expression of radical sympathies; Jeffrey Robinson sees it as signifying 'the restlessness, negatively the uprootedness and political drivenness, more positively the *mobility*, of the radical mind'.[10] Indeed, Thelwall himself identified pedestrian vigour with radical mobility in *The Tribune*: 'I have been rambling, according to my wonted practice, in the true democratic way, on foot, from village to village',[11] and in the 'Pedestrian Excursion', the confirmed walker celebrated the White Hart at Basingstoke as an inn which

> the pedestrian may regard as a prize in the lottery. No swaggering postboy to jostle him from the fire, no powdered waiter to sneer at his dusty garb, no pursey landlady to measure him, with her eye, from head to foot, and inquire for his horses, or his carriage![12]

In this context, it is salutary to remember that framing John Thelwall's political career in the 1790s are two pedestrian tours: one marking the emergence of his political consciousness, the other the gagging of his political voice and the beginning of his 'intellectual proscription' in the Wye Valley. The first tour appeared as Thelwall's *Peripatetic; or, Sketches of the Heart, of Nature and Society; in a series of Politico-Sentimental Journals* of 1793 (identified as informing the scheme of Wordsworth's planned philosophical poem, *The Recluse*[13]), which adopts the narrative device of a series of pedestrian excursions in the neighbourhood of London, interlacing loco-descriptive prose 'chapters' with autobiographical incident, historical and antiquarian accounts, literary discussion, political commentary and poetical 'effusions' to comment on social conditions. In a passage from his 'Second Lecture on the Causes of the Present Dearness and Scarcity of Provisions' published in *The Tribune*, Thelwall states that the tour (early 1790s) that resulted in *The Peripatetic* disabused him of arcadian notions of 'rural felicity', gleaned through literature, by forcing him to confront real poverty and suffering, concluding that it was this 'touristic' experience that ultimately made him a radical: 'This made, I own, a deep impression on my mind; which, though it did not operate immediately, stimulated me to a train of enquiry, which could not fail of its ultimate effect.'[14] *The Peripatetic* itself plainly announces that 'the subject of our political abuses is so interwoven with the scenes of distress so perpetually recurring to the observer, that it were impossible to be silent in this respect'.[15] With the politicized prototype of that first tour in mind, one should be aware that to regard the 'Pedestrian Excursion' as a text that elides the political is radically to misread Thelwall, and to forget that potent political meanings may be inscribed in modes of writing other than the political tract. As Michael Scrivener rightly remarks in his review of Gregory Claeys's 1995 edition of Thelwall's political writings: '[Thelwall's] poetry, novels, scientific essays, literary criticism and so on are all saturated with explicit and implied political meanings . . . little is gained and much lost by segregating one set of texts from another'.[16] Indeed, Thelwall's 1797 tour shows jacobinism driven not only to ground, but also into other genres, compelled to appropriate other discourses such as the travel journal, picturesque theory and landscape description, historical writing, antiquarianism, art and literary criticism.

Thelwall's descriptions of the 'picturesque of nature', for example, are regularly located in the context of the social, economic and political forces to which the landscape bears witness. At so many points, conventional picturesque description is suddenly subverted as Thelwall's focus on the socio-political realities which condition the scene conspires to reveal the full 'meaning' of the prospect. In this respect, Thelwall's programme reminds us once again of David Williams's landscape vision in *The History of Monmouthshire*: 'hamlets, churches, houses, cottages and farms, are blended into one general and extensive scene, which is wonderfully picturesque. But the contemplation of these scenes, must be exchanged for the occurrences and events that have occupied them' (*Hist. of Mon.*, 9–10). For example, Thelwall declares of the parish of Shepperton:

> The affluence of nature, and the toil of man, conspire to produce one continued scene of fertility; while from every eminence the mansions of opulence overlook the prospect with exultation. But man, aggregate man, seems little benefited by this abundance. Cottages (none of which have the advantage of a cow) are very thinly scattered; and *little* farm houses are still more rare. The few peasants we met looked (as the

peasantry of England too generally do) careworn and toilworn; and the children seem to be brought up in the most oafish ignorance. In short, every thing has the appearance of that desolating monopoly which makes fertility itself a desert.[17]

What Thelwall offers in such passages is a kind of *paysage moralisé*. At Wilton House, the man who had sought to circumvent the restrictions imposed upon him by the Two Acts of 1795 by lecturing on abuses of power in ancient Rome performs a masterful jacobin *ekphrasis* on Wilton's collection of classical busts,[18] and having crossed the 'inextricable labyrinths' of Salisbury Plain, he inveighs against the confinement of young girls in the nunnery of Amesbury House, berating 'the criminality of the government that suffers such snares to be spread in the way of inexperienced youth' and declaring that

> Every individual ought to be at liberty to follow, without restraint or qualification, whatever religion or opinion he thinks fit . . . It is not toleration, to suffer designing priests to enchain the consciences of their deluded votaries with oaths that prohibit the progress of inquiry, and institutions that annihilate the free agency of reason, and interdict the feelings and utilities of nature . . . civilized society owes instruction . . . to all its offspring, as a compensation, for those natural rights which its necessary institutions have taken away.[19]

At Mere, he relishes the 'curiosity' of 'a publick-house sign' showing 'a sorry black dog, with a coronet round his neck, and a chain; over which is written, "The Old George!"'. Following hard on the heels of this vision of an enchained, mad king, Thelwall, in an ironic passage that the Byron of *The Vision of Judgement* would surely have enjoyed, offers an account of hearing at Maiden Bradley 'a Cornish song, giving the French and all Revolutionists to the devil, and exalting "George the Great", with all due veneration, to the skies' declaimed by a group of colliers ('not very angelic indeed in their appearance') who 'joined in the apotheosis with such Stentorian force of lungs, that I think it may be safely affirmed that never conqueror or mighty potentate had his praise more loudly celebrated'.[20]

The jacobin fire of the 1790s had not yet been entirely extinguished, then, and arriving at Frome in early July, he was immediately welcomed by radical sympathizers: 'To this place, and all its inhabitants, I was hitherto a perfect stranger. But I was not long permitted to remain so. My name soon transpired. It flew from house to house; and I found myself suddenly and unexpectedly in the midst of friends.'[21] At Bristol a few days later, he enjoyed 'a social (almost a public) breakfast' at which passages from Lucan's *Pharsalia* and Southey's *Joan of Arc* – both texts with contemporary radical resonances – were read out.[22] Thelwall, *persona non grata* in the eyes of the State, could still count on a warm welcome. A letter of 18 July 1797 to his wife Susan (Stella) from 'All fox den' (presented in full for the first time in the Appendix) offers a fascinating glimpse of his time at Frome, Bath and Bristol and contains details about his jacobin contacts and activities which could not be openly stated in the account published in the *Monthly Magazine*. He reveals to his wife that at Frome – 'a sad den of Jacobins' – he was persuaded to extend his stay by some who had been at his lectures in London and that he sold '5 or 6 £ worth of [his] publications' and had been encouraged to do the same at Bath and Bristol. Of his time at Bristol he states:

> I met with many friends in Bristol who were encreasing in greater & greater degree every hour I staid – i.e. in exact proportion as it became known that I was in town . . . In short at Bristol & Bath as at Froome I have met with some frie enthusiasm, & some solid friendships . . . (Appendix, p. 296)

Thelwall, so long the object of violent intimidation, must have been cheered by this reception, and must have looked forward to his imminent visit to Nether Stowey where he hoped another 'solid friendship' would soon be sealed. The final instalment of the 'Pedestrian Excursion' breaks off two days before he visited the poets; as it stands, however, the final paragraph is a fitting one, since in its sentiments and tone it prefigures certain passages in the 'Prefatory Memoir' to *Poems, Chiefly Written in Retirement* and, as we shall see, is rhetorically very similar indeed to many poems in that volume. The 'Pedestrian Excursion', in which one can still glimpse Thelwall the jacobin commentator, ends with a passage in which political involvement is emphatically set aside. Thelwall appears as the solitary, vagrant and broken jacobin longing for a life of retirement and obscurity:

> *Saturday* 15, my companion took his farewel [*sic*] of me, directing his course homeward in the Southampton stage; and shortly after I took my farewell of Bath, thenceforward to pursue my way with solitary step

– far from each endearing intercourse – seeking from without for the happiness that was not within, and exclaiming, every time that the smoke of the lone cottage from some sequestered dingle chanced to rise upon my view – 'When – when shall I be the peaceful lord of such a mansion, and repose me again in obscurity!'[23]

This passage finally appeared in the *Monthly Magazine* of November 1801. 'Seeking from without for the happiness that was not within': it might not be fanciful to claim that Coleridge – the man Thelwall was about to visit in July 1797 – echoes this passage in his 'Letter to Sara Hutchinson' at a moment of personal crisis a year after the appearance of Thelwall's account: 'I may not hope from outward Forms to win / The passion & the Life, whose Fountains are within!' (ll. 50–1).[24] It was to be a poignant allusion to the work of a man who in the summer of 1797 was facing his own crisis.

And so, on 17 July 1797, Thelwall reached Nether Stowey, the 'permanent shelter' Coleridge had just celebrated in his poem 'To the Rev. George Coleridge', to find Coleridge was at Alfoxden House, into which the Wordsworths had only just moved. Thelwall's letter of 18 July to Stella from Alfoxden informs her that

> Samuel was not at home (he was here) when I arrived last night – nor would Sara have been but that she had quitted this friendly retreat, to superintend the wash tub. I have spoiled the soap suds however. It was too late to come to this place last night, for it is 3 or 4 miles from Stowey. I slept therefore at Coleridges Cot; & this morning we rose by times, & came here time enough to call Samuel & his friend Wordsworth up to breakfast. (Appendix, p. 296)

In retrospect, Coleridge's absence from Stowey on 17 July was perhaps rather ominous. However, Thelwall's account to his wife of the 'delightful Society' at Alfoxden eloquently articulates the joy he experienced in this happy den of jacobins. E. P. Thompson has described Thelwall's ten-day stay with the poets in July as a 'spot of time', and it certainly retained 'A fructifying virtue' which 'nourished and invisibly repaired'[25] Thelwall's spirit for a while:

> But profit & everything else but my Stella & my Babes are now banished from my mind by the Enchanting retreat (the Academus of Stowey) from which I write this, & by the delightful Society of

Coleridge & of Wordsworth – the present Occupier of All fox Den. We have been having a delightful ramble to day among the plantations & along [word deleted] a wild romantic dell in these grounds thro which a foaming, murmuring, rushing torrent of water winds its long artless course – There have we sometime sitting on a tree – sometimes wading boot-top deep thro the stream ~~sometime~~ & again stretched on some mossy stone or root of a decayed tree, a [word deleted] literary & political triumvirate [word deleted] passed sentence on the productions and characters of the age – burst forth in poetical flights of enthusiasm – & philosophised our minds into a state of tranquility which the leaders of nations might envy and the residents of Cities can never know. (Appendix, p. 296)

He learned that Wordsworth had taken Alfoxden 'merely that he might enjoy the Society of Coleridge'. For the next ten days, he enjoyed the company of the poets in their rambles and conversations. It must have appeared an ideal society – a sequestered, energizing fellowship which promised emotional sustenance, safety and the prospect of literary collaboration. 'Delightful spot! O were my Stella here!' he exclaimed to his wife, significantly echoing Coleridge's 'Lines composed while climbing the left ascent of Brockley Coomb' – 'Enchanting spot! O were my SARA here!' – the echo dramatically foregrounding his desire to be permanently one of the 'triumvirate'.[26] 'During the whole of this ramble', he told Stella, 'I have had serious thoughts of a cottage – Do not be surprised if my next should inform you that I have taken one'; 'I have by no means forgotten Jack', he continued, referring to his brother-in-law John Vellum, 'Can he reconcile himself to a philosophical bread & small beer way of living?' As I shall show, recollections of this society of like-minded men, and of their poetry, were to haunt the disillusioned Thelwall at Llyswen.

When he left the poets on 27 July to continue his 'Pedestrian Excursion', he immediately articulated his longings in paradisal, Pantisocratic terms in his 'conversation' poem, 'Lines, written at Bridgewater . . . on the 27th of July 1797; during a long excursion, in quest of a peaceful retreat', which was to appear in *Poems, Chiefly Written in Retirement*. Coleridge, Wordsworth, Dorothy and Tom Poole are all explicitly mentioned:

> Ah! let me then, far from the strifeful scenes
> Of public life (where Reason's warning voice

> Is heard no longer, and the trump of Truth
> Who blows but wakes The Ruffian Crew of Power
> To deeds of maddest anarchy and blood)
> Ah! let me, far in some sequester'd dell,
> Build my low cot; most happy might it prove,
> My Samuel! near to thine, that I might oft
> Share thy sweet converse, best-belov'd of friends! –
> . . .
> Ah! 'twould be sweet, beneath the neighb'ring thatch,
> In philosophic amity to dwell . . .
> . . . and it would be sweet,
> With kindly interchange of mutual aid,
> To delve our little garden plots, the while
> Sweet converse flow'd, suspending oft the arm
> And half-driven spade, while, eager, one propounds,
> And listens one, weighing each pregnant word,
> And pondering fit reply, that may untwist
> The knotty point – perchance, of import high –
> Of Moral Truth, of Causes Infinite . . .
> . . . by our sides
> Thy Sara, and my Susan, and, perchance,
> Allfoxden's musing tenant, and the maid
> Of ardent eye, who, with fraternal love,
> Sweetens his solitude. With these should join
> Arcadian Pool, swain of a happier age . . .[27]
>
> (*Poems*, 129–31)

The inflated rhetoric is a measure of the strength of his attachment. John Rieder remarks that Thelwall's 'fantasy of a sympathetic community' here establishes retirement as 'a way of extricating [a] community of virtue, and along with it a mode of virtuous action, from the web of state violence'; it is 'a kind of afterimage left burning on Thelwall's eye after the curse of violence turns him away from revolutionary desire'.[28] As outlined in Chapter 2, however, permanent retirement in the West Country was to elude him forever. As Thelwall left 'the Bottoms of Glocestershire [*sic*]' on 12 August 1797, having been 'entertained by several families with great hospitality', he imagined himself in the future fondly remembering the welcome he had received from faithful friends, conscious at the same time, however, that there were others who had already ceased to acknowledge him:

> ... some there are – some few,
> Still warm and generous, by the changeling world
> Not yet debauch'd, nor to the yoke of fear
> Bending the abject neck: but who, erect
> In conscious principle, still dare to love
> The Man proscrib'd for loving human kind.
>
> (*Poems*, 139)

Coleridge would surely at this moment have been numbered among this faithful elect. (Indeed, one can be fairly certain from Coleridge's comments in a letter of 14 October 1797 that 'On leaving the Bottoms of Glocestershire' was one of two poems Coleridge had just received from his friend: 'I do not wonder that your poem procured you kisses & hospitality – It is indeed a very sweet one – and I have not only admired your genius more, but I have loved YOU better, since I have read it'.[29]) While Thelwall wandered in Wales, Coleridge had made an effort to secure a cottage for him '*any where* 5 or 6 miles round Stowey'.[30] But a matter of days after Thelwall wrote the poem quoted above, Coleridge on 21 August wrote to him, worried that his presence would result in 'tumult' and 'calumnies' similar to those which he claimed his own – and Wordsworth's – arrival in the area had occasioned. Indeed, Coleridge informed Thelwall that such 'tumult' might be intensified into 'riots & dangerous riots' if '*all three* together' were to settle near Stowey.[31] Coleridge's argument can be seen to emphasize the similarity between the members of the 'political triumvirate' – dangerous, tumult-inspiring radicals – only to distance Thelwall from that fellowship. Coleridge's fears were not wholly unfounded, of course – on 15 August, after Thelwall's departure from Stowey, local gossip, relayed to the Duke of Portland, was to bring James Walsh – the agent who had dogged Thelwall since 1792 and actually arrested him in 1794 – to investigate the activities of the 'mischiefuous [*sic*] gang of disaffected Englishmen' at Alfoxden.[32] But Coleridge doubtless had other concerns: his letter of 21 August marks the beginning of his anxious attempt to distance himself from his infamous radical friend and from his own jacobin past, and Thelwall would have realized that Coleridge was also jealously guarding his productive relationship with 'the only man, to whom *at all times* & in *all modes of excellence*' he felt himself 'inferior'[33] – 'The Giant Wordsworth'[34] – the fruits of which would soon constitute an *annus mirabilis* in their poetical careers. Devastatingly, on 16 September, Thomas

Poole drafted a letter – evidently in collaboration with Coleridge and Wordsworth – to Mrs St Albyn, the owner of Alfoxden House, distancing themselves from Thelwall.[35] Coleridge had indeed effectively sacrificed Thelwall for Wordsworth. It was an act that was to set Thelwall on the road to exile at Llyswen, where, in the 'Prefatory Memoir' and the 'Paternal Tears' sequence, he would clearly dramatize his own identity as that of a Wordsworth *manqué*.

A poignant postscript to Thelwall's thwarted attempt to settle in the vicinity of Nether Stowey and Alfoxden is provided by David Simpson's ingenious Marxist reading of Wordsworth's spring 1798 poem, 'Anecdote for Fathers', in which Thelwall's Welsh retreat figures as 'sweet Liswyn farm'. Simpson interprets the poem as a 'private drama that has less to do with educational debates than with personal anxieties about home and shelter, about money, and about public images and political identities'.[36] 'Liswyn farm', though of course a real place, has generally (and fairly) been taken by commentators to refer to Alfoxden; Simpson explains the 'renaming of Alfoxden as Liswyn' by a Wordsworth concerned about his tenure at Alfoxden House (an uneasy Mrs St Albyn had already terminated it) with reference to a hidden pun: 'There is a teasing homophone latent in the real name of Thelwall's home: "lease when?"'. Further, the 'renaming' 'implicates Thelwall himself in a residence at Alfoxden' in an act of displacement through which Wordsworth's democratic anxieties about living in the rather grand surroundings of Alfoxden House are offloaded onto Thelwall – 'By imagining radical John in a place with a broad and gilded vane, Wordsworth eases his mind that he is not the only democrat with a taste for grand houses' – and his guilty conscience regarding his having set Thelwall on the road to Llyswen is assuaged. 'It is as if Wordsworth casts himself as Thelwall', Simpson contends. What emerges from this discussion is a Thelwall who, as implied narrator of the poem, finally gets to live at Alfoxden – but only within the imaginative construct of an anxious, guilty lyric.

At Bay at Llyswen: The 'Prefatory Memoir' to *Poems, Chiefly Written in Retirement* (1801)

The section of the 'Prefatory Memoir' to *Poems, Chiefly Written in Retirement* which recounts Thelwall's residence at Llyswen (a portion of which was considered in Chapter 2) begins geographically, chronologically and rhetorically where the 'Pedestrian Excursion' left off. It not only dramatizes the political defeat and personal tragedy of an individual in frank, confessional terms, but also stands as an emotive portrait of what happened to the radical movement more generally after 1795. As autobiography charting the growth of a radical's (and poet's) mind in the 1790s, the Memoir as a whole can illuminatingly be read alongside the greatest autobiographical work of the period, which also traces the progress of its author's 'moral and political' opinions – Wordsworth's *Prelude*. But the Memoir and the poems it frames represent a darker version of Wordsworth's poem in which the differences and distance between Thelwall and 'Allfoxden's musing tenant' can be seen to be poignantly inscribed.

The agenda of the 'Prefatory Memoir' is essentially twofold. Thelwall's claim that 'It is not even attempted to vindicate the *public* conduct of the individual from the misrepresentations of party animosity: for political discussion would ill accord with the character and contents of the ensuing volume' is disingenuous in that the whole of the Memoir, and the highly rhetorical Llyswen section in particular, is a vindication of his political career and personal character cast ultimately, as Michael Scrivener remarks, as a 'sentimental performance – an appeal to the reader on the basis of feeling and sensibility'[37] and as a public manifesto that would act as a passport back into polite society. It is also an indictment of the tyranny and violence of an anti-jacobin regime represented as mercilessly hounding him and his family into exile.

This is no political apostasy, then, but Thelwall's retrospect certainly acknowledges, and faces up to, political defeat and personal loss. It is a tonally complex performance, however. Thelwall, given to posturing and dramatization, articulates that experience of defeat and disillusionment in language that is by turns stoic, accusatory, analytical, melodramatic and, at the end of the Memoir, highly ironic:

> For since he has proved so bad a politician as to plunge himself and his family in ruin, for the dissemination of a principle which he thought conducive to the happiness of mankind, it ought to be regarded as an argument *a priori* in favour of his poetical talent: that species of imprudence (a sort of failing so rare and so fatal in politics) having always been considered as the distinguishing characteristic of those whom Apollo and the Muse inspire.[38]

Thelwall is at pains to announce a change of career, and a much emphasized disjunction throughout the Memoir and the subsequent poems is that between past and present selves, radical and 'The new Recluse', politician (now silenced and defunct, Thelwall claims) and poet (the new identity he seeks to embrace): 'It is The Man, and not The Politician, that is here delineated, The disciple of the Muses; not The Lecturer and Leader of Popular Societies now no more.'[39] While Thelwall is being sincere here, he is aware that such a simple disjunction is hardly possible. The other major task of the Memoir, then, is to persuade his potential new audience to come to his poetry without any prejudice against his former self, and to appeal against that 'proscriptive species of criticism that will condemn the Poet from hostility to the politician'. An interesting parallel can be drawn here with Wordsworth's programme in the Preface to the *Lyrical Ballads*, in which the reader is asked to lay aside his poetical prejudices.[40] But another disjunction subtly inscribed in the poems in Thelwall's volume is that between his present self and the self he had dreamed of becoming at Nether Stowey and Alfoxden – in other words, between himself and the two poets who had let him down.

The Llyswen section of Thelwall's autobiography provides the immediate context in which Thelwall's dialogue with Wordsworth and Coleridge is to be interpreted. As we have seen, on first arriving in the Wye Valley in late 1797, Thelwall optimistically conceived of the place as an 'enchanted dormitory, where the agitations of political feeling might be cradled to forgetfulness, and the delicious day dreams of poesy might be renewed'.[41] Separation from his fellow poets might not have seemed too traumatic a loss in these early days, and his 'retirement' seems to have begun auspiciously. A letter of 3 March 1798 to Peter Crompton provides a fascinating glimpse of Thelwall enjoying the early period of his sojourn at Llyswen:

> In addition to the pleasures beauty of the Country & the improving health of our family, we have reason to be pleased with Llyswen on account of the respectful civility of all our neighbours. The rustic villagers pays us every mark of attention – Jack & I are regarded as a sort of Oracles, our votes are law at all the parish meetings, we receive & return visits with the farmers, & have had civil messages from some of the surrounding gentry. Tho' I am by this time pretty generally known, I have never in any single instance received the slightest insult since I came to settle in Wales; & among the more intelligent part of the people, the hat is off & the eye brightens whenever I pass by. (Appendix, p. 303)

Thelwall refers to the health enjoyed by his young daughter Maria – 'she bounds along in her trowsers in all the romping vivacity of independence' – and by his son Algernon Sidney, for whom Thelwall was building 'a rude hermitage (a sequestered summer study)' in a 'small romantic dingle' next to the Wye. 'This is the bright side of the picture', Thelwall adds, 'It has its shades, & those I shall not disguise', but at this stage, these were merely the financial concerns of the farmer. In the same letter, Thelwall drew a vibrant portrait of Coleridge at this moment which concludes with a reference to the silence Coleridge had observed since his last letter of 30 January informing Thelwall of his Wedgwood annuity:

> he cannot ~~frequently~~ preach very often ~~without~~ without ~~mounting~~ travelling from the pulpit to the Tower – Mount him but upon his darling hobby horse 'the republic of God's own making', & away he goes like hey go mad, spattering & splashing thro thick & thin & scatter~~s~~ing more <u>levelling</u> sedition, & constructive treason, than poor <u>Gilly</u>, or myself ever dreamt of. He promised to ~~answer~~ write to me again in a few days; but tho' I ans.rd. his letter directly, I have not heard from him ~~again~~ since. (Appendix, p. 301)

Coleridge was to visit Thelwall briefly at Llyswen in early August 1798 in the company of Wordsworth and Dorothy, but after Thelwall's removal to Brecknockshire, the stream of letters from Coleridge – some of the best he ever wrote – which had so influenced Thelwall from 1796 onwards, thinned. And the ideal of Pantisocratic retirement in Wales, accompanied by rustic labour and poetico-philosophical musing, was soon to be violated as Thelwall found himself shadowed and harassed even at his retreat. He tells how the local priest inveighed against the troublesome new arrival from the pulpit, and how the animosity of the Welsh populace was further excited by some of his idiosyncratic habits.[42] We have proof that he was 'obliged to take one of his brutal neighbours to Brecknock sessions, for ferociously assaulting him with a pick-axe',[43] and Thelwall further claims that he was at one point obliged to defend his house against attack. He was still corresponding with radical contacts, both locally and nationally, and local informants regularly relayed information about his movements to Pitt's ministers.[44] His post was intercepted and 'bandied about the country', as it had been throughout the 1790s (see Appendix, pp. 287–90 for palpable proof of this). Though he claims the locality benefited from his agricultural ingenuity, 'the inclement rage / Of an ungenial season' (*Poems*, 159), which the poems in his volume document, wreaked havoc on his land.[45] The final blow was dealt him when Maria died on 28 December 1799. The portrait in the 'Prefatory Memoir' of the place he had hoped would offer him the arcadian retirement he had briefly experienced in the West Country is shot through with references to the locals' 'ignorance and gross vulgarity', their 'animosity (national and political)', 'barbarous solitude', the cruelty of his landlord, his 'ill-starred experiment' and his 'hostile stars'. In an article published in the *Monthly Magazine* in July 1800, he even described the morals 'of the very sheep' as 'contaminated'.[46] At Hereford, shortly after emerging from his retreat at the end of 1800 to embark on a new career as a teacher of elocution, Thelwall received a letter of 17 December 1800 from Coleridge at Keswick – forwarded from Llyswen and possibly the first for nearly three years. In it, Coleridge stated that he would have plunged himself into financial ruin (something Thelwall had nearly experienced at Llyswen) had he written to Thelwall as often as he had tenderly thought of him and 'felt for [his] afflictions'. Coleridge went on: 'I am settled in this delightful county comfortably – Wordsworth lives 13 miles from me'.[47] The man who had suffered so much at Llyswen was here informed that the 'delightful society' he had briefly tasted and had wished to join at Stowey and Alfoxden had remained intact and had been transplanted to the Lakes.

Another important context for my discussion of Thelwall's poems is provided by a prominent theme in the 'Prefatory Memoir' – that of the politics of friendship. Speaking of the State harassment he experienced, Thelwall remarks that

> The channels of vital sustenance have been dried up: and Friendship (the last stay of the human heart) – even Friendship, itself (a few instances of generous perseverance alone excepted) wearied and intimidated with the hostilities to which it was exposed, has shrunk from its own convictions, and left him in comparative insulation.[48]

Thelwall surely has Coleridge, amongst others, in mind here – the man who had certainly 'shrunk from [his] own convictions' in his dealings with him.[49] A few friends, however, remained faithful and true, and Thelwall remarks that it was 'The assistance of a few friends' that enabled him to stock his 'little farm, of about five-and-thirty acres'. Letters of the period reveal that he was indeed relying financially on radical friends and acquaintances: on 25 October 1797, he wrote to Thomas Hardy, informing him that 'as this is a plan for my *permanent* establishment there may perhaps be some persons who would interest themselves about it', and asking whether Hardy could '*raise any wind* for [him] by loan or patriotic contribution'.[50] He thanked Dr Peter Crompton for a gift of £15 in his letter of 3 March 1798 (Appendix, p. 300), which also reveals that the Quaker William Rathbone had sent him £10.[51] Referring to the assistance that rescued him from financial ruin following the disastrous harvest of 1799, Thelwall pointedly refers later in the Memoir to 'the liberality of a few unshaken, tho distant, friends' and to 'the exertions of one, in particular' – either Hardy or Crompton – 'who, on a former occasion, had not been among the least conspicuous in the zeal of manliness and friendly interference'.[52] The opening poem in the 'Paternal Tears' sequence, addressed 'To J— G—' (either the shorthand writer Joseph Gurney or lawyer John Gurney), provides a useful point of departure for my analysis of Thelwall's poems. 'Effusion I' directly addresses an unshaken friend and acknowledges his support:

> AH! generous friend! who, with a patriot's zeal,
> Stood'st forth, undaunted, in oppression's hour,
> To shield this head devoted; and who still,
> With unrepenting kindness (most unlike
> The changeling multitude) essay'st to prop
> The reed thou sav'st unbroken – vain the hope!
> (*Poems*, 145)

But references to other, less 'undaunted' friends, of whom much had also been asked 'in oppression's hour', are also articulated in subtle, allusive ways in the poems that emerged from Thelwall's experience of exile and harassment.

The Effusions of 'Paternal Tears': The Politics of Allusion

In a study of the early poetry of Wordsworth and Coleridge and the letters of Charles Lamb, Lucy Newlyn has illuminatingly explored the 'sustained undercurrent of allusions and cross-references that creates its own pattern of meaning' – an allusive agenda that serves to focus similarities and differences between the three men 'that were felt to lie very deep'.⁵³ In her later, book-length analysis of the intertextual resonances of the poets' work, Newlyn comments that

> [The uses of allusion], whether conscious or unconscious, imply a private bond: with the initiated reader, who is allowed access to hidden meanings, and with the other writer, whose words are being quoted, appropriated, or misused. The writer whose work is alluded to can rarely be at the same time an initiated reader; but when this is the case allusion becomes dialogue . . . Hidden meanings, for those overhearing the dialogue, become accessible through familiarity with the speakers and their relationship, and with the texts themselves.⁵⁴

Paul Magnuson has also offered a detailed dialogic reading of 'The figures, turns, and transitions' of what he refers to as the single entity of 'the Coleridge–Wordsworth canon'.⁵⁵ 'Dialogue', Magnuson remarks, 'is the essential generative condition of their poetry', 'the enabling condition of their utterance'.⁵⁶ But the sustained dialogue which the poetry of the exiled John Thelwall conducts with a number of Wordsworth and Coleridge poems has gone unnoticed by critics. It is a dialogue that points up the radical difference between the erstwhile members of Alfoxden's poetical and political 'triumvirate' that was also 'felt to lie very deep'. To dialogize the sequence of elegies for his daughter which Thelwall wrote at Llyswen, to restore these poems to their original signifying context and to position Wordsworth and Coleridge as Thelwall's 'initiated readers' is to witness Thelwall's dialectic construction of himself as a harassed and exiled second self of the two poets. Identity is defined through allusion. On 10 May 1796, Thelwall thanked Coleridge for a sonnet in which he figured as 'the model for [Coleridge's] own radical identity'⁵⁷ ('First by thy example [taught] to glow / With patriot zeal'): 'I should be wanting in justice', Thelwall stated, 'if I did not take an early opportunity of acknowledging the very handsome favour for which I am indebted to your Muse'.⁵⁸ The dialogic reading I offer locates Thelwall's darker debt to Wordsworth's and Coleridge's 'Muse'.

Though haunted by memories of 'The Ruffian Crew of Power' and 'deeds of maddest anarchy and blood' – Pitt's, not Robespierre's – 'Lines, written at Bridgewater', which apostrophizes Coleridge and Wordsworth, is essentially a poem of hope for the future that looks forward to a 'Golden Age reviv'd' in the company of the poets and concludes with Thelwall's desire to 'taste the joys my soul best loves, / And find, once more, "that being is a bliss"' (*Poems*, 132). Hereafter, however, the poems in Thelwall's volume become increasingly distressed as they document his trajectory towards Llyswen and finally his tragic experiences there. As we have already seen in Chapter 2, Thelwall, quitting the West Country to pursue his 'Pedestrian Excursion' into Wales, casts himself in the rôle of the harried Wandering Jew in 'On leaving the Bottoms of Glocestershire'. The next poem but one, 'To the Infant Hampden', written 'during a sleepless night at Derby' in October 1797 as Thelwall prepared to remove his family to Llyswen, deepens this sense of persecution and proscription. At Llyswen in 1800, Thelwall in the 'Paternal Tears' sequence was self-consciously to respond to Coleridge's poems; that dialogue is in fact anticipated by Coleridge in 'Frost at Midnight' (written at Stowey in February 1798), which is clearly an 'answer' to Thelwall's 'To the Infant Hampden'. We know for certain that Coleridge had read a shorter manuscript version of 'To the Infant Hampden' by mid-October 1797 since he offers a critique of it in a letter to Thelwall of 14 October, which also refers to 'On leaving the Bottoms of Glocestershire'.[59]

What emerges initially from a comparison of the two poets' cradle-songs is a clear sense of the painful distance between Coleridge and Thelwall at this moment. Coleridge does seem to rewrite 'To the Infant Hampden' in positive terms, as if in grateful recognition that his fate is very different from Thelwall's. But, as Judith Thompson has emphasized in a subtle and detailed discussion, Coleridge's negotiation with 'To the Infant Hampden' is more complex.[60] In its dialogic context, 'Frost at Midnight' (many of whose images critics have found strangely troubling) becomes a far more vexed and politically aware poem in which Thelwall – a determining presence as the implied addressee – elicits from Coleridge an interrogation of the disturbing implications of domestic retirement.

In 'Frost at Midnight', Coleridge embraces his nocturnal solitude and highly sensitized wakefulness, whereas Thelwall's poem is the product of a 'sleepless night' during which the wished-for oblivion of rest is denied him. Though the infant Hampden sleeps on 'unheedful' of the 'autumnal blast' that 'rocks' Thelwall's cottage and of the 'persecuting rage' his father had recently experienced, Thelwall himself is acutely aware of literal and figurative tempests, just as the anxious, apocalyptic Yeats would be at the beginning of his own cradle-song, 'A Prayer for my Daughter' – 'Once more the storm is howling, and half hid / Under this cradle-hood and coverlid / My child sleeps on'. Coleridge's poem, however, is suffused by what seems to be a holy quietness – a 'strange / And extreme silentness' – as the frost performs its benedictory 'ministry', 'Unhelp'd by any wind'. As Coleridge returns in memory to his own childhood, this 'hush of nature' modulates into the music of the church bells of his 'sweet birthplace' – 'Most like articulate sounds of things to come' – which lulled him to sleep as a child. The music of Thelwall's poem is altogether more tempestuous as the 'rocking wind / Pipes, mournful, lengthening [his] nocturnal plaint / With troubled symphony' (lines that anticipate the distressed Coleridge of the 1802 'Letter to Sara Hutchinson'[61]). Thelwall develops the storm raging outside into a metaphor for his own persecution, enlisting the imagery of the Deluge to figure his tragedy:

> Visions (Ah! that they were but such indeed!)
> That show this world a wilderness of wrongs –
> A waste of troubled waters: whelming floods
> Of tyrannous injustice, canopy'd
> With clouds dark louring; whence the pelting storms
> Of cold unkindness the rough torrents swell,
> On every side resistless. There my Ark –
> The scanty remnant of my delug'd joys!
> Floats anchorless . . .
>
> (*Poems*, 141)

The fluttering film or 'stranger' in the grate at Stowey – 'the sole unquiet thing' – which Coleridge imagines is animated with 'dim sympathies with me, who live', becomes a 'companionable form', traditionally presaging the arrival (as Coleridge's note explains) of 'some absent friend'. As Newlyn has described it, the stranger is 'an echo of the self that initiates human response and leads towards imaginative sharing'.[62] The case is very different with the unquiet and 'unblest' Thelwall, who appears here as a solitary exile, vagrant stranger and victim of 'cold unkindness', whose 'tired foot', significantly '*Fluttering* on anxious pinion' (my emphasis) can find no place to rest. Coleridge's image of the 'stranger' which 'flutter'd on the grate' and 'Still flutters there', together with the coda of 'Frost at Midnight', in which Hartley is seen to 'stretch and flutter' joyfully from his mother's arms at the sight of the 'silent icicles', appear to mark a pointed engagement with the Thelwall of 'To the Infant Hampden':

an image of Thelwall's frustrated search for security – his sense of himself as an 'anxious', 'fluttering' stranger – seems transformed into one of domestic warmth, companionship and sympathy.[63]

In 'Frost at Midnight' and 'To the Infant Hampden', both fathers wish a destiny for their children that is to be very different from their own, and this again seems dramatically to distinguish Thelwall's fate from Coleridge's at this moment. Far from Nature's ministrations, the schoolboy Coleridge had experienced a kind of incarceration at Christ's Hospital, but young Hartley, as Coleridge announces with prophetic confidence, will experience a privileged, spiritual communion with Nature, the language of God:

> Dear babe, that sleepest cradled by my side . . .
> . . . it fills my heart
> With tender gladness, thus to look at thee,
> And think, that thou shalt learn far other lore,
> And in far other scenes! For I was rear'd
> In the great city, pent mid cloisters dim,
> And saw naught lovely but the sky and stars.
> But *thou*, my babe! shalt wander, like a breeze,
> By lakes and sandy shores, beneath the crags
> Of ancient mountain, and beneath the clouds,
> Which image in their bulk both lakes and shores
> And mountain crags: so shalt thou see and hear
> The lovely shapes and sounds intelligible
> Of that eternal language, which thy God
> Utters, who from eternity doth teach
> Himself in all, and all things in himself.
>
> (*FiS*, 21–2)

In a passage which Coleridge is clearly echoing here, Thelwall, in contrast, prays that Hampden, who carries the ominous burden of history and political martyrdom in his very name,[64] might escape visions of the *literal* incarceration and violent persecution to which his father was subjected:

> SWEET *Babe! that, on thy mother's guardian breast,*
> *Slumberest* . . .
> . . . sleep on;
> Sleep, and be happy! – 'Tis the sole relief
> This anxious mind can hope, from the dire pangs

> Of deep corroding wrong, *that thou, my babe!*
> And the sweet twain – the firstlings of my love!
> As yet are blest; and that my heart's best pride,
> Who, with maternal fondness, pillows thee
> Beside thy Life's warm fountain, is not quite
> Hopeless . . .
>   . . . Ah! sleep on! –
> As yet unconscious of The Patriot's name,
> Or of a patriot's sorrows – of the cares
> For which thy name-sire bled . . .
>   . . . Ill-omen'd babe!
> Conceiv'd in tempests, and in tempests born!
> *What destiny awaits thee?* – Reekless thou.
> Oh! blest inapprehension! – Let it last.
>   . . . Ah! sleep secure:
> And may thy dream of Life be ne'er disturb'd
> With visions such as mar thy father's peace . . .
>   (*Poems*, 141; my emphasis)[65]

Hartley, whose own 'name-sire' – Coleridge's hero-philosopher David Hartley – is a far less troubling second self, is proleptically constructed in 'Frost at Midnight' as a favoured being sensitive to the One Life in Nature, and as a means by which Coleridge himself can – if only vicariously – partake of the One Life. As Newlyn remarks: 'As in "This Lime-Tree Bower", perception and release are achieved by wishing them on to someone else'.[66] Hampden, however, is an 'Ill-omen'd babe', and his father cannot hope to escape, vicariously or otherwise, from persecution. Coleridge is 'thrilled' by the prospect of his son's future; Thelwall can experience only the pitiful, 'sole relief' enshrined in the hope – not conviction – that his son will escape harm. Coleridge is in Berkeleian mode here (David Hartley had of course recently been displaced in his philosophical affections by the Bishop of Cloyne), and the Nature that is to be enjoyed by young Hartley is seen as a divine sign-system through which the Godhead can be 'read'. In Thelwall's poem, Nature, as we have seen, is figured emphatically as the *curse* of the Old Testament God – deluging and louring. Moreover, for the atheist Thelwall, no beneficent, communicative God was to be glimpsed through Nature. In a later addition to 'Frost at Midnight', Coleridge's 'idling Spirit' interprets the 'puny flaps and freaks' of the film on the grate at Stowey 'By its own moods', 'every where / Echo or mirror seeking of itself'. Thelwall's poem, a few months only after its composition, seems to have found an utterly transformed 'mirror . . . of itself' in 'Frost at Midnight'.

As Thompson contends, however, Coleridge's poem should not be read as a quietist meditation undisturbed by pressing personal and political anxieties – a blithely positive reconfiguration of 'To the Infant Hampden' that would merely confirm Thelwall's sense of his own misfortune by celebrating everything Thelwall was not and did not have. Rather, it represents 'another installment' in Coleridge's 'continuing debate' with Thelwall 'about the forms and effects of political repression, the ideology of retirement and the relative values of private and public speaking, in which Thelwall acts as a foil for Coleridge's own beliefs and anxieties'.[67] The disturbed weather of Thelwall's poem alerts us to the disturbing and vexing – Coleridge's words – qualities of the 'strange / And extreme silentness' of 'Frost at Midnight'. Beneath the poem's 'deceptively tranquil surface', Thompson argues, Coleridge 'acknowledg[es] and counter[s] Thelwall's implied criticisms of him', hinting that the 'secret ministry' of frost – a suggestive phrase in the context of agent James Walsh's presence at Stowey and a culture of political distrust and fear – might in fact turn out to be 'an aguish killing frost that freezes honest hearts, minds and voices against . . . thoughts of freedom and expressions of patriotism', resulting in a 'wilful and misanthropic shutting out of society and its interests'.[68] The poem is thus 'as much about the dangers of domesticity and solitude as about its consolations'. In other words, Thompson sees Thelwall's 'To the Infant Hampden' as prompting in 'Frost at Midnight' in February 1798 a consideration of Coleridge's own situation, identity and radical past (and future?). The superficial contentment of 'Frost at Midnight' is balanced by an implied acknowledgement, engendered by its Thelwallian model, of the fragility of its portrait of domestic harmony and the wishfulness of its construction of Hartley as a surrogate self. But at the same time, 'Frost at Midnight' is undeniably affirmative and consolatory; it rewrites Thelwall's anguished appeal in positive terms, not to pain him but to comfort him. As Thompson states, Coleridge responds by 'sympathizing with the situation of the beleaguered reformer . . . offering consolation by developing his own religious answer to the materialist philosophy which Thelwall develops'.[69] Thompson's reading is a fine one that forces us to re-examine the political resonance of a Romantic lyric that seems untroubled by wider public pressures. However, her statement that 'there is . . . no evidence of further poetic exchange [between Coleridge and Thelwall] after 1798' is inaccurate. As we shall now see, there is in fact ample evidence of a continued dialogue in the elegies Thelwall wrote at Llyswen, though it is he who now plaintively responds to the poetry of Coleridge and Wordsworth.

'To the Infant Hampden' and another Derby poem of October 1797, 'Maria. A Fragment', ominously herald the sequence of elegies, written in 1800, for the much-loved daughter Thelwall lost at the end of 1799. Writing to Benjamin Robert Haydon in 1817, Wordsworth stated:

> Thelwall the Politician many years ago lost a Daughter about the Age of Scott's child. I knew her she was a charming creature. Thelwall's were the agonies of an unbeliever, and he expressed them vigorously in several copies of harmonious blank verse, a metre which he wrote well for he has a good ear. These effusions of anguish were published, but though they have great merit, one cannot read them but with much more pain than pleasure.[70]

And in response to a letter of 12 November 1838 from Henrietta Cecil Thelwall, Thelwall's second wife (see Appendix, pp. 327–9), Wordsworth wrote: 'I possess a small printed volume of his, containing specimens of an Epic Poem and several miscellaneous Pieces, in some of which he laments the death of a Daughter in strains that shew how grievously he suffered by that event'.[71] Even Francis Jeffrey in his sneering review of Thelwall's *Poems* in the *Edinburgh Review* acknowledged that 'There are some passages in the Lamentation for his Daughter's Death that are written with tenderness and effect'.[72] Maria was six years old, and her death 'of the croup' was a heavy blow which left Thelwall in 'anguish and frenzy', 'amid the horrors of solitude, in a state of mind which souls of the keenest sensibility can alone conceive'.[73] The 'Prefatory Memoir' and the obituary Thelwall wrote in the *Monthly Magazine* describe her as a child 'of most premature attractions',[74] 'whose premature expansion of mind, whose endearing manners and benevolent disposition had rendered her an object of affection in all the various circles of society in which (young as she was) the peculiar fortune of her parents had occasioned her to be known'.[75] In a letter of 10 March 1794 to his brother-in-law Jack Vellum, Thelwall had written: 'I assure you the child does not thrive the worse for not being christened. It is a bonny wench – very cheerful – very full of health, & will I hope some time or other be the happy mother of a fine hardy race of Republicans, & Sans Culottes' (Appendix, p. 290). But Maria was not to become the republican matron Thelwall imagined here, at a time when his troubles were just beginning. The loss of Maria, and the other tragedies experienced at Llyswen, turned Thelwall's mind back to his friendship with the poets in the halcyon days of July 1797, and to the subsequent disillusionment he had known when he was pushed out of the pale of love. The prospect of poetic collaboration with Wordsworth and Coleridge that had stirred him at Stowey and Alfoxden is, I argue, realized in the 'Paternal Tears' sequence in an ironic sense. Thelwall's conversation with the poets is a tragic version of the dialogue that produced the *Lyrical Ballads*, published a matter of weeks after the poets visited the 'inner émigré' at Llyswen in August 1798, and of the formative poetico-political conversations that Thelwall had conducted with Coleridge during the 1790s. Wordsworth and Coleridge figure as 'presences that disturb' in the effusions of 'Paternal Tears' in that their poems determine the contours of Thelwall's. To put it simply: Wordsworth and Coleridge are Thelwall's implied auditors; reading Thelwall's *Poems c.*20 April 1802,[76] they could not have failed to recognize him as their alter-ego.[77]

In 'Effusion I', headed 'To J— G—' and dated February 1800,[78] Thelwall thanks his distant friend for his continued kindness, but immediately turns to bewail his fate as exile and bereaved father:

> Me, from ill to ill,
> From woe to woe still urging, [Destiny's] fierce hate
> Pursues incessant, and has pierc'd, at last,
> With barbed shaft, that never shall be drawn
> The seat of vital feeling. Yes, 'tis here:
> Deep in my heart I feel it: the poor heart,
> That with convulsive wildness throbs, awhile,
> But soon shall throb no more. So deems, at least,
> Hope, that has now now refuge but despair –
> In soothing strain so whispers: *So the chords*
> *Of this frail being (sensitive too much*
> *To every touch of passion) sad, reply*
> *With dissonance responsive.* Yes they jar:
> *Each nerve and fibre feels the untuning touch*
> *Of most assur'd decay.*
>
> (*Poems*, 145–6; my emphasis)

It is inconceivable that Thelwall would not have been familiar with the *Lyrical Ballads* soon after its publication; the volume would clearly have been the subject of much discussion during the poets' visit to Llyswen in August 1798, a month before its appearance. Moreover, in January 1801, Coleridge wrote to Thelwall stating: 'By all means procure a sight of the 2nd Volume of the Lyrical Ballads, and of the second Edition of the first Volume – the Preface is invaluable'[79] – an injunction that suggests Thelwall already possessed the first edition. In the lines quoted above, Thelwall identifies a 'generating text'[80] in a poem by Coleridge in the *Lyrical Ballads* of 1798 – 'The Dungeon'. Confined in the 'steams and vapour' of the cell, the 'energies' of the prisoner in the first verse paragraph of Coleridge's poem become corrupt; the unwholesome space poisons and 'deform[s]' the spirit, and 'Each pore and natural outlet' is 'shrivell'd up' (a portrait which Thelwall had himself anticipated in his 'Ode II', published in *Poems Written In Close Confinement in the Tower and Newgate* (1795), which refers to 'the Prison's pent-up breeze' and 'The gale impure that round the sullen walls / Creeps noxious'[81]). The second movement of 'The Dungeon' offers an answer to Coleridge's question 'Is this the only cure?' by emphasizing how the rehabilitative ministrations of Nature will heal the prisoner ('Most innocent, perhaps – and what if guilty?') whom State institutions have themselves heinously corrupted:

> With other ministrations thou, O nature!
> Healest thy wandering and distempered child:
> Thou pourest on him thy soft influences,
> Thy sunny hues, fair forms, and breathing sweets,
> Thy melodies of woods, and winds, and waters,
> *Till he relent, and can no more endure*
> *To be a jarring and a dissonant thing,*
> Amid this general dance and minstrelsy;
> But, bursting into tears, wins back his way,
> His angry spirit healed and harmonized
> *By the benignant touch of love and beauty.*
> (LB, 797–8; ll. 20–30; my emphasis)

The companion-poem to 'The Dungeon' in the *Lyrical Ballads* – Wordsworth's 'The Convict' – likewise envisages the effects of a healing transplantation from 'the comfortless vault of disease' to Nature: 'My care, if the arm of the mighty were mine, / Would plant thee where yet thou might'st blossom again'. The man who had been one of the most famous prisoners of the decade, confined, as he relates in the 'Prefatory Memoir', for five months in the 'grated chambers' of the Tower and for seven weeks in the 'noxious dungeons' and *The Common Charnel House* of Newgate (this is spoken without metaphor)',[82] casts himself in 'To J— G—' as the lost counterpart of the healed convict of 'The Dungeon'. In tune with the healing spirit of Nature, the prisoner of Coleridge's poem 'can no more endure / To be a jarring and a dissonant thing' while the 'chords' of the ex-prisoner Thelwall's heart 'reply / With dissonance responsive. Yes they jar'. 'Each pore and natural outlet' is healed by the 'benignant touch of love and beauty' in 'The Dungeon', whereas 'Each nerve and fibre' in Thelwall's body conversely 'feels the untuning touch / Of most assur'd decay'. Indeed, the spiritual and biological 'sickness' of the unreconstructed prisoner in the first section of Coleridge's poem is further paralleled by Thelwall's description of his 'blood, / No more obedient to the order'd course / Of self-preserving Nature' which

> ... refluent oft
> Turns on her o'ercharged fountain; or, impelled
> By wildering Anguish, rushes to the brain,
> And whelms the sense in apoplectic whirl,
> That Nature's chain seems bursting.
>
> (*Poems*, 146)

'Ah! what to *him* avails the sentient power / To whom all sense is pain?' asks the distempered Thelwall, who, as if imagining himself in prison again (or in Bedlam), 'benighted, droops, appall'd / Amid the horrors of sepulchral gloom – / A conscious maniac'.

In constructing himself as the antithesis of the prisoner of Coleridge's 'The Dungeon', Thelwall is also poignantly invoking his own dungeon poem – 'The Cell', written in Newgate in 1794 – and contrasting present weakness with the resilience of a former self. On entering Newgate, Thelwall had been appalled by the conditions – 'so vile, so filthy, and so abhorrent to all feelings and senses of man'[83] – and immediately set about writing a sonnet, published the following year in *Poems Written In Close Confinement*. 'The Cell' is no lament, however; essentially, it is a poem about republican 'Virtue' and imaginative vision transcending State confinement. Though the horrific conditions of Newgate may 'appal' the 'trembling Ruffian', 'Whose thoughts no sweet resource supply', Thelwall in contrast, cheered by a sense of his republican probity, makes a heaven of hell by casting a 'retrospective view' over 'a race of well-spent years' and by looking 'inward to his heart' to see 'The objects that must ever please' in an imaginative act that defies State repression (*Poems Written in Close Confinement*, 9).[84] Thelwall's 'Maria. A Fragment', written in October 1797 before the move to Llyswen, though offering a more troubled delineation of the incarcerated Thelwall's emotional state, similarly recalls how 'the strong sense of duty' and 'the voice / Of patriots and of martyrs' were for him 'props' and 'consolations' that 'Could make [him] laugh to scorn the threats of power'.[85] The poem also fondly recalls the sustaining visits his wife and the young Maria paid him in prison. No such consoling visions allow the Thelwall of 'To J— G—' to escape from his 'despair', and the implication – generated intertextually through the echoes of Coleridge's poem and the concomitant invocation of Thelwall's own dungeon sonnet and his 'Maria. A Fragment' – is that the bereaved Thelwall of 1800 is more of a prisoner than the literally incarcerated radical of 1794. Though Thelwall in 'The Cell' draws a clear distinction between himself – of 'dauntless breast' and 'cheerful aspect' – and the 'trembling', 'appalled' prisoner, the allusiveness of 'To J— G—' figures Thelwall at Llyswen – 'benighted' and 'appalled' – as just such a hopeless soul.

Released from the 'dismal twilight' of his cell, Coleridge's prisoner finds himself responsive to Nature's 'fair forms', but for the 'apoplectic' Thelwall, Nature, irremediably blighted by a perpetual winter of the heart, can never offer rehabilitation but merely echo back Thelwall's own grief: 'all / That in the frame of Nature wont to joy / Sight, or the touch, or hearing, seems to blend / In funeral lamentation'. It is on this note that 'To J— G—' ends, transforming the Wye Valley and the wandering river (a companionable form for the vagrant, exiled Thelwall) into a landscape that, like Thelwall, replies 'With dissonance responsive':

> O, my babe!
> Maria! Oh, Maria! thy lov'd name,
> While Nature yet is vocal – while this heart
> To this sad tongue can dictate, thy lov'd name
> The rocks and conscious echoes shall repeat,
> And murmuring Vaga mourn no loss but thine.
> (*Poems*, 149)

Thelwall here might also be echoing the very different 'sweet inland murmur' of the Wye in Wordsworth's 'Tintern Abbey' (which Wordsworth surely would have recited at Llyswen in August 1798). Further, the poet who saw the Wye Valley as echoing back his own distemper would have responded as if to a version of himself in another poem in the *Lyrical Ballads* of 1798 – Coleridge's 'The Nightingale', addressed, significantly, to Wordsworth and Dorothy:

> 'Most musical, most melancholy' Bird!
> A melancholy Bird! O idle thought!
> In nature there is nothing melancholy.
> – But some night-wandering Man, whose heart was pierc'd
> With the remembrance of a grievous wrong,
> Or slow distemper or neglected love,
> (And so, poor Wretch! fill'd all things with himself
> And made all gentle sounds tell back the tale
> Of his own sorrows) he and such as he
> First nam'd these notes a melancholy strain . . .
> (*LB*, 794–5; ll. 13–22; my emphasis)

While the poems of Wordsworth and Coleridge are emotionally disabling for Thelwall, they are also imaginatively enabling in that they provide him with templates for what one must acknowledge to be a dramatic performance. While there is no doubting the sincerity of his grief – even Francis Jeffrey acknowledged that much – the 'Paternal Tears' poems are also part of the 'sentimental performance' identified by Scrivener as characterizing the framing 'Prefatory Memoir', designed as an appeal to the reader and as a passport back into society. They are enabling, then, in a wider sense. This, of course, raises the difficult issue of the use to which Thelwall's grief is put. In the context of the underlying agenda of the volume as a whole, are these poems to be viewed sceptically as less poignant than they first appear? There is certainly a sense in which the models offered by Wordsworth and Coleridge are being 'used' for a specific personal and economic purpose – that of rehabilitating Thelwall's image in the public sphere and literary marketplace. To recognize the poems as performances of this kind is to concede that Thelwall's implied auditors, in addition to the coterie audience of Wordsworth and Coleridge, are the potential patrons and customers of the post-proscription years whom these effusions are designed to cultivate.

Throughout this book, I have offered readings of 'Tintern Abbey' that excavate the poem's sites of disturbance to reveal moments at which its superficially placid surface is disturbed by haunting presences. Thelwall would certainly have been sensitive to some of these resonances (and his poems, as we shall see, serve to activate them), but generally, a sense of Wordsworth's emotional stability and fulfilment would have been uppermost in Thelwall's reading. In 'Effusion III. – On the Banks of the Wye. May 15, 1800', 'Effusion IV. During a severe Indisposition. May 18, 1800' and 'Effusion VI. On returning from a Journey to Merthyr Tydfil. June, 1800', Thelwall, I contend, self-consciously writes an inversion of 'Tintern Abbey', holding up a distorting mirror to the greatest poem in the *Lyrical Ballads*. The opening of Wordsworth's poem – 'Five years have passed; five summers, with the length / Of five long winters! and again I hear / These waters' – serves to mark the distance between his far more troubled self of 1793 and the more tranquil (though still haunted) visitor of 1798. The opening of Thelwall's third effusion, 'On the Banks of the Wye', reverses this:

> Along thy varying banks, sequester'd Wye,
> At eve, I wonder mournfully – full oft
> Thridding the tangled maze, or under shade
> Of hoary oaks, that over-hang thy stream,
> Courting congenial gloom: but not, as erst,
> Or with the Painter's, or the Poet's glance,
> Noting thy wild varieties.
>
> (*Poems*, 150)

This crepuscular beginning is in contrast to the first verse paragraph of 'Tintern Abbey', which offers a wide daytime perspective over the landscape. Like Wordsworth, whom this poem ventriloquizes, Thelwall points up the distance between his present and former self to emphasize that it is not the creative artist's communion with Nature that he now 'courts', but rather the 'congenial gloom' of grief and obscurity. The 'Poet's glance' is to be read not only as a reference to Thelwall himself, but also to Wordsworth and to the landscape description which opens 'Tintern Abbey'. Indeed, Thelwall next offers a portrait of the landscape of the Wye Valley that bears some resemblance to Wordsworth's –

> Rocks, and falls,
> And deep-worn pools reflective, and ye woods
> Wash'd by the eddying stream, and you, ye hills
> Of fearful height, in wild perspective heap'd,
> Closing the sinuous valley . . .

– only to set himself apart from the author of 'Tintern Abbey': 'what to me/ Are all your varied forms?' (Thelwall's engagement with his poetical prototype is actually hinted at as he continues: 'Ah! what the charm / Of beauteous or sublime? – the scenes that nurse / Romantic vision, or invite *the skill / Of imitative effort?*' (my emphasis).) While the 'forms of beauty', the 'little lines / Of sportive wood run wild' in 'Tintern Abbey' have not been to Wordsworth 'As is a landscape to a blind man's eye' and have vouchsafed, in memory, 'sensations sweet, / Felt in the blood, and felt along the heart, / And passing even into my purer mind / With tranquil restoration' (ll. 25, 28–31), Thelwall's blunt statement is 'No more / Thy haunts romantic charm'. Indeed, the emphasis on the eye and on sight in 'Tintern Abbey' is replicated by Thelwall only to emphasize that he is, in effect, Wordsworth's 'blind man':

> No more mine eyes
> (Dim with their griefs) from tint or varied line
> Receive accustom'd joyance . . .
>   . . .
>   Other forms
> Possess my weeping fancy: other thoughts,
> Rending the grief-swoln bosom, vail [*sic*] the eye
> In dim abstraction . . .
>   All that once,
> With grace or mingled harmony, could thrill
> Sight or the list'ning sense, unheeded meets
> The unconscious organ . . .
>   . . .
>   At sight
> Of such mute record, in afflictive trance,
> Groaning I pause . . .
>   (*Poems*, 150–1)

The 'shooting lights' of Dorothy's 'wild eyes' at the end of 'Tintern Abbey' are transformed into Thelwall's 'dim eyes, suffus'd', from which 'Tears stream afresh'. Once again, past and present experiences are contrasted:

> my troubled soul
> Here while I rove, is absent; nor remains
> Ought but the wandering shade of him who erst
> Trac'd your wild haunts delighted.

This second self is the Thelwall who began his exile at Llyswen responsive to Nature's 'wild haunts', but the shade of Wordsworth is here, too – the man whom Nature had helped preserve through his own political crisis. As Thelwall turns to the spot 'Where buds the white-thorn o'er the turfted grave' of Maria, memory – another stay of Wordsworth's soul and one of the 'gifts' 'Tintern Abbey' celebrates – can only, torturingly, remind him of 'some remember'd scene / Of sweet endearment' in which he had heard 'the voice / Of [his] lost darling' and where 'her form, / Disporting gaily, with attractive charm, / Full in my view has bounded'. Thelwall here recasts the image of the 'bounding roe' of 'Tintern Abbey' which, pertinently, Wordsworth had used to figure his flight to the Wye in 1793, 'more like a man / Flying from something that he dreads, than one / Who sought the thing he loved'. Thelwall, then, appears to transform one of those sites of disturbance in Wordsworth's poem into a positive image – that of Maria's lively, 'bounding' figure – but he does so in the context of memory and of loss, thus recognizing and preserving the tremor of anxiety in Wordsworth's lines. Finally, Wordsworth's address to Dorothy at the end of 'Tintern Abbey' in which he euphemistically imagines his death – 'If I should be where I no more can hear / Thy voice, nor catch from thy wild eyes these gleams / Of past existence' – would have seemed to Thelwall a mere rhetorical flourish in the context of his own real, not imagined, bereavement on the banks of the Wye. Not for Thelwall, then, the 'healing thoughts / Of tender joy' with which Wordsworth comforts Dorothy at the end of 'Tintern Abbey'.

As Thelwall's negotiation with the image of the bounding roe suggests, however, the 'effusions' also work to foreground the disturbing subtext of 'Tintern Abbey'. Thelwall's elegies are palimpsestically *already present* in Wordsworth's poem, and they can be seen to offer a 'reading' of 'Tintern Abbey' which emphasizes the similarities as well as the differences between the experiences of both men in the 1790s.

Thelwall is alive to the anxieties and ambiguities of Wordsworth's poem at the same time as he is (all too) conscious of its confident declarations regarding a post-revolutionary future. The 'Paternal Tears' sequence thus becomes part of the contextual fabric and full significance of 'Tintern Abbey'.

It is clear, then, that Thelwall's effusions are not private soliloquies but dialogic utterances that address public as well as personal issues. The echoes of Wordsworth continue in Effusions IV and VI, which deepen the resonance of Thelwall's version of 'Tintern Abbey'. In the first of these, 'Stretch'd on a bed of pain' at Llyswen in May 1800, Thelwall's nerves are assailed by 'a feverish langour'. But this is not his complaint:

> Yet not for this
> Heave I the frequent groan – nor not for this
> Course down my wasted cheeks the chanell'd tears . . .
> (*Poems*, 152; my emphasis)

'Effusion VI' recapitulates these lines:

> Over thy heights, Farinioch, I have climb'd,
> With lonely tread; and, from the blaze of noon,
> Till now that Hesper rises, borne the thirst
> And turmoil of the day. *Yet not for this*
> *Droop I despondent*, or, with faltering step,
> Pause on the threshold of my lonely cot,
> Checking the starting tear. *Not this I moan.*
> (*Poems*, 154; my emphasis)

It is of course the loss of Maria that plagues him in both instances. The reference to Milton's *Samson Agonistes* in 'blaze of noon' ('O dark, dark, dark, amid the blaze of noon') aligns Thelwall with the model of the blinded Samson at Gaza, and further emphasizes Thelwall's construction of himself as a type of Wordsworth's 'blind man'. Moreover, the echoes of 'Tintern Abbey' here are obvious:

> Not for this
> Faint I, nor mourn nor murmur: other gifts
> Have followed, for such loss, I would believe,
> Abundant recompence.
> (*LB*, 118; ll. 86–9)

In the context of Wordsworth's 'loss', 'other gifts' – the ability to hear 'The still, sad music of humanity' and the 'presence' that disturbs him 'with the joy of elevated thoughts' – have made amends. While Wordsworth's 'Not for this' means 'I do not mourn for this (since other gifts have followed)', Thelwall's 'Yet not for this' is to be interpreted as 'I do not mourn for *this*, but rather for *another* loss'. In Thelwall's poems, Wordsworth's 'loss' takes on the palpable, tragic meaning of an actual human death. In 'Effusion IV', another echo of Milton, this time via Coleridge's 'The Nightingale', further emphasizes that loss. No doubt recalling how the exercise of the State-defying, liberating imagination sustained him during his incarceration, Thelwall recalls that 'the pensive hour / Of silent solitude' was never oppressively 'lonesome' since

> ... the Muse,
> *On Contemplation's wing, would haply soar*
> Into the realms of Fancy; bodying forth
> Ideal excellence ...
> ... or, more blest,
> *With whisper'd voice, most musical,* would tell
> Of future hopes (how specious) – flattering boons
> That the paternal heart might well repay
> For all its years of anguish.
> (*Poems*, 152; my emphasis)

Thelwall's reference to Coleridge's poem, already quoted above ('"Most musical, most melancholy" Bird! / A melancholy Bird? O idle thought!'), which takes issue with Milton's line from 'Il Penseroso' to argue that it is the distempered human mind that invests the bird's song with its own sickness, recasts the 'melancholy' Nightingale as a 'winged' Muse that whispers of future happiness. (In doing so, Thelwall is also recasting his own 'Sonnet to the Nightingale' – an elegy for a 'departed friend', printed earlier in the volume – which portrays the nightingale's song as a melancholy accompaniment to 'the Wretch's groan'; *Poems*, 101.) Thelwall's reconfiguration seems therefore in tune with the spirit of Coleridge's transformation of the melancholy bird into the 'merry Nightingale / That crowds, and hurries, and precipitates / With fast thick warble his delicious notes' – a metamorphosis that leads on from Coleridge's claim (echoing his own 'Frost at Midnight') that 'My Friend, and my Friend's Sister! we have learnt / A different lore: we may not thus profane / Nature's sweet voices always full of love / And joyance!' And Thelwall, though 'feverish', is briefly in tune with Wordsworth here, too, as he recalls how he was comforted in times of persecution by thoughts of Maria's future: '*Ah! how oft* / In such sweet vision has my raptur'd soul / Dwelt on thy form, Maria! – *Ah! how oft* / Imag'd thy rip'ning years' (*Poems*, 152; my emphasis). The lines echo the passage from 'Tintern Abbey' in which Wordsworth registers his gratitude to the landscape of the Wye for sustaining him amid 'the fever of the world':

> . . . yet, oh! *how oft,*
> In darkness, and amid the many shapes
> Of joyless day-light; when the fretful stir
> Unprofitable, and the *fever of the world,*
> Have hung upon the beatings of my heart,
> *How oft,* in spirit, have I turned to thee
> O sylvan Wye! Thou wanderer through the woods,
> *How often* has my spirit turned to thee!
> (*LB*, 117–18; ll. 51–8; my emphasis)

But the memory of the Muse's 'most musical' whisperings of hope is soon displaced in Thelwall's poem, and an oppressive consciousness of loss returns to close 'Effusion IV':

> Ah! most blest
> When thoughts like these were present! Pain, and Woe,
> And persecuting Fortune, lost their power,
> And my torn heart was heal'd. – But, she is gone!
> The balm of life is gone!; and its sore ills
> Fester irremeable! Yet, not these I feel:
> Nought but thy loss is poignant – O! Maria! –
> My health! – my joy! – my fortune! – all entomb'd!
> (*Poems*, 153)

Haunting Thelwall's ending is an awareness of the 'father's tale' that concludes 'The Nightingale', in which a fond Coleridge offers a picture of Hartley's responsiveness to the natural world (nightingale, evening star, moon) and, as in 'Frost at Midnight', projects for him a blessed childhood.

The dark negotiation continues in 'Effusion VII. On STELLA's leaving me, to Visit some Friends, at Hereford, with a View to the

Restoration of her Health. Llys-Wen. June, 1800'. Here, Thelwall's model is Coleridge's 'This Lime-Tree Bower My Prison', first published in Southey's *Annual Anthology* in February 1800. I consider it unlikely that Thelwall secured a copy of the *Annual Anthology* before June 1800, but one can confidently state that he knew the poem even before he reached Llyswen. On 7 July 1797, Charles Lamb visited Coleridge at Stowey, leaving a week later. He narrowly missed Thelwall's arrival on 17 July, and on 19 or 26 July he wrote to Coleridge: 'Is the Patriot come yet? . . . I was looking out for John Thelwall all the way from Bridgewater, and had I met him, I think it would have moved almost me to tears [*sic*]'.[86] For the duration of Lamb's stay, as Coleridge explained in a letter of *c*.17 July 1797 to Southey, he had been incapacitated by 'a skillet of boiling milk' which Sara had 'accidentally emptied' on his foot – hence his 'confinement' in Poole's jasmine arbour which resulted in 'This Lime-Tree Bower My Prison', the early version of which he sent Southey in the letter referred to above.[87] Coleridge stated in this letter – possibly written on the very day Thelwall arrived at Stowey – that his injury still prevented him from undertaking 'all *walks* longer than a furlong'. When Thelwall met Coleridge on 18 July, Coleridge's lameness would have been obvious during their walks in the vicinity of Alfoxden House, and Thelwall would have inquired as to the cause (and doubtless Coleridge would have given a humorous response in the company of Sara). The poem that was the result of the injury and which had been sent to Southey during the past few days would surely have been broached and recited. Indeed, on 14 October 1797, illustrating his desire to experience 'something *one & indivisible* . . . the sense of sublimity or majesty' in a letter to Thelwall at Derby, Coleridge quoted the Berkeley-influenced lines on Lamb's vision of the spirit of God-in-Nature that lies at the heart of 'This Lime-Tree Bower'.[88]

Thelwall's seventh elegy begins with an unmistakable echo of Coleridge's opening ('Well – they are gone: and here must I remain, / Lam'd by the scathe of fire, lonely and faint, / This lime-tree bower my prison'[89]):

> WELL thou art gone – gone to the City's throng,
> My soul's sad partner! mid the generous cares
> And kind solicitudes of pitying friends
> To sooth thy bosom's anguish.
>
> (*Poems*, 156)

Both Coleridge and Thelwall have been left solitary and in pain by the departure of their loved ones. Coleridge's poem continues in despondent mood – 'They, meantime, / My friends, whom I may never meet again' (the Wordsworths had not yet secured nearby Alfoxden House) – as does Thelwall's: 'Me, the while, / Here shall heart-eating Solitude consume – / O'er saddest thoughts still brooding'. 'The 'City' to which Stella has departed in search of health is Hereford – technically a city, but hardly the metropolis. Thelwall would have remembered that Coleridge's poem is addressed to Charles Lamb, who had just arrived at Stowey *from* London, and that Coleridge had addressed him in the poem as 'My gentle-hearted CHARLES! thou, who hast pin'd / And hunger'd after Nature many a year / *In the great City pent*, winning thy way, / With sad yet bowed soul, thro' evil & pain / And strange calamity' (my emphasis); in the context of his Coleridgean prototype, Thelwall's choice of 'City' here is surely deliberate. Moreover, that 'strange calamity' recently experienced by Lamb – a reference to the terrible day in September 1796 when his sister Mary fatally stabbed their mother in a fit of insanity – reminds us that untimely death is at the heart of both Coleridge's and Thelwall's poem.

But 'This Lime-Tree Bower My Prison' is fundamentally about the mind transcending confinement, pain and loneliness in an imaginative identification with others. This act of imaginative projection culminates in Lamb's – and, vicariously, Coleridge's – spiritual experience of God diffused through Nature in the lines Coleridge was soon to send Thelwall (minus, significantly, the reference to 'my friend'):

> So my friend
> Struck with joy's deepest calm, and gazing round
> On the wide view, may gaze till all doth seem
> Less gross than bodily, a living Thing
> That acts upon the mind, and with such hues
> As cloathe the Almighty Spirit, when he makes
> Spirits perceive His presence!
>   (*CL*, I, 335)

As in 'Frost at Midnight', which was to echo 'This Lime-Tree Bower' ('pent 'mid cloisters dim'), the result of Coleridge's act of sympathetic identification is a sense of companionship – 'A Delight / Comes sudden on my heart, and I am glad / As I myself were there!' Thelwall's experience is once again very different. The title of Coleridge's poem would have reminded him of his own literal confinement in the 1790s (Coleridge's metaphorical use of 'prison' would surely have jarred), but also of how he had succeeded in *transcending* incarceration, as recorded in his Newgate poem, 'The Cell', and in his Derby poem of 1797, 'Maria. A Fragment'. No such exercise of the radical, sustaining imagination is now possible. The proud 'retrospective view' which the incarcerated radical casts over his public, political career in 'The Cell' becomes in the Llyswen poems the torturing 'retrospective view' of private grief. While Coleridge remains in his bower in imaginative fellowship with his absent friends, Thelwall sits brooding – aware of loss, not emotional rapport – in his 'sequester'd cot', likewise 'embower'd'. Lamb and the Wordsworths roam the Quantocks and are vouchsafed a vision of the divine in Nature; Thelwall in his elegy also wanders the hills, but does so on his way to a very different, industrial landscape which offers no vision of comfort:

> . . . afar
> (Call'd by life's busy turmoil) over heights
> Of Alpine dreariness, my feet shall climb,
> To the once-peaceful vale, where sinuous Taff,
> (Stunn'd by Vulcanian clamour) writhing, shifts
> His devious course, and seeks for peace in vain.
> As vainly I.
> . . .
> . . . nor Taff's remoter vale,
> Late, by magic of Vulcanian art,
> Grown populous – nor busy cares of Life –
> No – nor the Muse's song, in this sad heart
> Shall ever more its wonted calm renew.
> (*Poems*, 156)

Thelwall's journey to the Welsh Valleys was probably no mere topographical jaunt in search of tranquil restoration; he had political contacts in the industrial centres, and he was possibly attending a political gathering. Referring to the disturbances at Merthyr Tydfil in 1800, Samuel Homfray, an ironmaster, wrote to the Home Secretary on 1 October 1800:

> I have very little doubt but political Principles have in some degree influenced the Minds of the lower Class of People . . . When the cryer

proclaimed in the public Markett [sic] a Meeting of the Workmen of the four Works near Merthyr for taking into consideration the high price of Provision Mr Thelwall was at no very great distance.[90]

All this, then, is very far from the experiences recorded in 'This Lime-Tree Bower My Prison'. The description Coleridge offers towards the end of the poem of the bower in which he sits is marked by a minute observation of the beauties of Nature – 'I watch'd / The sunshine of each broad transparent Leaf / Broke by the shadows of the Leaf or Stem, / Which hung above it: and that Wall-nut Tree / Was richly ting'd: and a deep radiance lay / Full on the ancient ivy which usurps / Those fronting elms' – while Thelwall is dead to the ministrations of Llyswen's 'circling scenes romantical'. 'Henceforth, I shall know', Coleridge declares, 'That nature ne'er deserts the wise & pure' – a line that was to be echoed by Wordsworth in 'Tintern Abbey' – 'Knowing that Nature never did betray / The heart that loved her'. The lines would have reminded Thelwall in 1800 of other betrayals – by Pitt, by the French, and by friends. And while Coleridge knows that his friends will return to his bower, Thelwall is conscious that there is one being who will not return; a poem that began with Stella's temporary absence – 'WELL thou art gone' – rounds back on itself (a feature of Coleridge's conversation poems) to end with the permanent absence of Maria: 'She, alas! is gone'.

The dialogue comes to an end in 'Effusion X. Cerrig-Enion: (Enion's Tomb) on Pen-Heol-Enion, in Brecknockshire. August, 1800', which, I argue, represents a complex negotiation with Wordsworth's 'The Thorn', published in the *Lyrical Ballads* of 1798. The frontispiece to *Poems, Chiefly Written in Retirement* – Thelwall's own drawing – dramatically depicts the opening lines of 'Effusion X'. The image shows a grieving, hooded female figure, wearing a small cloak, sitting on a mound with her head in her hands near a small (oak?) tree and a standing stone traditionally associated with a local medieval Welsh lord, Einon Glyd (an actual feature of the landscape north-west of Llyswen recorded in Theophilus Jones's county history of 1809[91]):

> WHY, on the mouldering tomb of other Times,
> Sits my lorn wanderer, in the muffled robe,
> Vailing her pensive brow, and to the winds
> Giving, on such bleak height, the unshelter'd form
> Of feminine softness!
>
> (*Poems*, 161)

Models of Fellowship and Fulfilment

'Cerrig-Enion': frontispiece illustration to John Thelwall's *Poems, Chiefly Written in Retirement* (1801); drawing by Thelwall, engraved by Thomas Sutherland (*by permission of the National Library of Wales, Aberystwyth*).

It transpires that the female figure is Thelwall's wife, Stella. These lines, together with the frontispiece illustration, inescapably evoke the cloaked Martha Ray of 'The Thorn' – the grieving mother of a dead (murdered?) child – who sits 'on a mountain's highest ridge', exposed to 'every wind that blows', near a thorn, a pond and a mysterious 'hill of moss', uttering the famous refrain 'Oh misery! oh misery! / Oh woe is me! oh misery!' Thelwall's megalith and Wordsworth's ancient thorn tree are in fact very similar: the thorn is 'Like a rock or stone' in that 'It stands erect, and like a stone / With lichens it is overgrown' (*LB*, p. 77; ll. 10–11). And just as the thorn is 'hung with heavy tufts of moss, / A melancholy crop', and the supposed grave of Martha Ray's child – 'grotesquely prettified', in John F. Danby's phrase[92] – is marked by a 'heap of earth o'ergrown with moss', so crops of moss and bramble seem insidiously to be reclaiming the desolate landscape in which Stella grieves:

> . . . oft the enquiring eye
> (Seeking the ancient site of rampir'd wall,
> Or bourg, or populous city) meets, perchance,
> Nought but the brambled fosse, some moss-grown heap
> Of shapeless fragments.
> (*Poems*, 161–2)

As Wordsworth explained in the 1798 Advertisement to the *Lyrical Ballads* and at greater length in a note in the 1800 edition, 'The Thorn' is narrated by a garrulous persona prone to superstition who is identified as 'a Captain of a small trading vessel'. Like Thelwall, he is supposed to have 'retired . . . to some village or country town of which he was not a native' (*LB*, 350). On three occasions, the narrator, who seeks to resist sensational village gossip regarding Martha Ray but whose reliance on hearsay shows himself to be complicit in it, is quizzed by a puzzled interlocutor (the reader's second self) regarding her tragedy:

> 'Now wherefore thus, by day and night,
> In rain, in tempest, and in snow,
> Thus to the dreary mountain-top
> Does this poor woman go? . . .
> Oh wherefore? wherefore? tell me why
> Does she repeat that doleful cry?'
>
> I cannot tell; I wish I could . . .
> (*LB*, 79; ll. 78–81, 87–9)

The opening of 'Effusion X' can be seen to enlist Wordsworth's narratorial technique as Thelwall, confronted by the grieving female whom he later reveals to be his wife, first casts himself as a baffled stranger – the curious interlocutor of 'The Thorn', perhaps – who seeks to make sense of the solitary female's situation:

> Broods her thoughtful mind
> Some legendary fiction? or some tale
> Of Tragic record, pregnant with the woes
> Of virtue vainly brave? Or does she mourn
> Time's changeful progress, thro' these desolate Realms
> Too sadly mark'd?
> (*Poems*, 161)

In the context of the 'tale / of tragic record' narrated in 'The Thorn', in which the jilted, pregnant, mad Martha Ray seeks the solitude of the mountain, Thelwall's line 'pregnant with the woes' is suggestive. As Thelwall is of course aware, Stella's mind is preoccupied by none of the literary and antiquarian subjects – all potentially sensational – that are broached, rhetorically, in the lines quoted above. It is rather 'the pangs of home-felt sufferance' that afflict her – a grief which Thelwall, identifying himself now as husband and bereaved father, shares:

> Woes that bend
> Our hearts, united in one common grief,
> Down to the earth they sprung from!

Here, the parents' tragedy is modelled on Wordsworth's description of the mosses' assault on the thorn: 'this poor thorn they clasp it round / So close, you'd say that they were *bent* / With plain and manifest intent, / To *drag it to the ground*' (my emphasis). Musing on 'Enion's Tomb' (the standing stone is both thorn tree and grave), Stella's thoughts 'flee' to a second grave in the valley at Llyswen, 'where, underneath / The turf, unhonour'd, save by frequent tears, / . . . our lost Maria sleeps'. I suggest, then, that Thelwall's epitaphic poem boldly models Stella on Martha Ray, and identifies Thelwall himself with Wordsworth's narrator. Just as the narrator in 'The Thorn' stumbles on Martha having mistaken her for a 'jutting crag' during a storm – 'And, as I am a man, / Instead of jutting crag, I found / A woman seated on the ground' – so Thelwall discovers Stella, herself a jutting, crag-like form in the illustration. Given the gossip surrounding the death of her child –

> . . . some will say
> She hanged her baby on the tree,
> Some say she drowned it in the pond . . .
> (*LB*, 84; ll. 214–16)

– Martha is a disturbing second self for Thelwall's bereaved wife. But the identification of Martha and Stella on which 'Effusion X' and the frontispiece illustration insist serves to emphasize the status of both women as outcasts in an essentially hostile and superstitious society. At Llyswen, Thelwall and Stella had themselves become victims of gossip, distrust and, as the 'Prefatory Memoir' records, the dangerous fancies of superstition: '"there was one man at Llys-Wen that could conjure; and that did walk in the woods, by night, to talk with his evil spirits"' (*Poems*, p. xxxvii). While idle talk in 'The Thorn' is a means of characterizing the narrator and his community, Thelwall's poem stresses that gossip and superstition lead, as they did in his case at Llyswen, to hostility and physical violence. Thelwall further remarks that grief at the loss of Maria 'dull[s] the edge of curious observation'. In its dialogic context, the phrase 'curious observation' suggests not only the father's antiquarian curiosity at the 'historic' sepulchral site of 'Cerrig-Enion' but also the hostile, prying eyes of gossips whose credulous speculation merely confirms the status of Thelwall, Stella and Martha Ray as pariah-figures.

Passages of social commentary in 'Effusion X' such as the lines on the peasant's pitiful appropriation of 'prostrate palaces' – 'now rudely heap'd, / Without cement, or order, to enroof / The toil-worn peasant, shivering in the blast / That winnows through the walls' and the description of the 'rent fragments' of 'wretched hives / Forlorn, and tenantless' (*Poems*, 162) offer a glimpse of the economic conditions at the mercy of which we must assume Martha Ray, discarded by her lover, must also find herself in 'The Thorn'. 'Effusion X' thus alerts us to a wider social context which the kindly but myopic narrator of 'The Thorn' (his one reference to Martha Ray's 'hut' notwithstanding) does not cite and which his community's craving for gothic sensationalism obscures. In other words, Thelwall's poem acts as a commentary on Wordsworth's, supplementing a narrative that seems to elide socio-economic realities and indicting a patriarchal society that is quick to label Martha Ray an infanticide rather than succour her as a bereaved mother and victim of betrayal and abandonment. One might say that the bereaved John Thelwall offers himself to Wordsworth as an alternative, more socially aware narrator for 'The Thorn'. The reader is also implicated in this commentary which Thelwall's poem supplies. Lucy Newlyn has recently examined the 'subtly dialogic' agenda of 'The Thorn' which, by dramatizing 'two different perspectives' on Martha Ray's story — that of the village gossips and that of the more sceptical sea-captain — is designed to alert us to the 'hermeneutic responsibilities' of reading. (Curiously, Newlyn fails to mention the interlocutor's quizzing of the captain, quoted above, which makes for an internal trialogue.) Newlyn sees the absence of 'authorial closure' regarding the final 'truth' of Martha Ray's story as

> an elaborate practical application of Wordsworth's concern (voiced in the Preface to the *Lyrical Ballads*) with reforming the contemporary reader's appetite for Gothic narrative. It succeeds in exposing the sea-captain's unwilling participation in the story purveyed by the local gossips, just as it parodies our own incipient sensationalism as readers. By implication, Wordsworth's audience is thereby reminded of the extent to which it remains steeped in the superstitions it believes itself to have surmounted; and is invited to become more reflective by becoming more sceptical.[93]

Thelwall's own 'subtly dialogic' engagement with 'The Thorn' works in a similar fashion. It 'corrects' an appetite for the gothic and sensational in both 'The Thorn' and 'Effusion X' by broaching the possibility that Stella sits brooding on 'Some legendary fiction' or 'some tale / Of Tragic record' only to dismiss it and alert the reader to harsh economic realities and to the painful autobiographical truth ('home-felt sufferance') of the Thelwalls' very real bereavement. Danby sees the direct encounter in 'The Thorn' between the narrator and Martha Ray as a significant moment at which dangerous folk fantasy comes up against the hard and pitiful physical facts of Martha's human tragedy: 'Stock reactions one after another have been tentatively indicated, only to be re-submitted to the test of the reality they would embroider or evade.'[94] This is precisely the moment at which Thelwall's 'Effusion X' locates itself, precisely the realization it works to foster in the readers of *Poems, Chiefly Written in Retirement* and *Lyrical Ballads* alike. 'Effusion X' would have led contemporary readers to a more sceptical, sympathetic and socially aware reading of 'The Thorn' – one divested, to quote Danby, 'of irrelevancy, of the fanciful, the idly curious, the indolently compassionate, or the "literary"'.[95]

'Effusion X', therefore, supplements 'The Thorn' in interesting ways, but as we have now come to expect, it also seeks to define Thelwall's experience *against* Wordsworth's. And the issue at stake here is profoundly that of autobiographical truth. Thelwall's negotiation with 'The Thorn' emphasizes that although Wordsworth's poem is the product of actual observation ('Arose out of my observing, on the ridge of Quantock Hill, on a stormy day a thorn', as Wordsworth informed Isabella Fenwick[96]), it is also an imaginative construction ('Cannot I by some invention do as much to make this thorn permanently an impressive object as the storm has made it to my eyes at this moment'[97]) that relies on literary models such as William Taylor's translation of Bürger.[98] In contrast, his and Stella's grief – *their* refrain of 'Oh misery! oh misery! / Oh woe is me! oh misery!' – is actual, not imagined. Though marked by Thelwall's interest in antiquarian pursuits, 'Effusion X' stresses that it is emphatically *not* on 'Some legendary fiction', some balladic 'tale / Of Tragic record' or some sensational gothic narrative that Stella broods. 'The Thorn', however, complicates any sense of 'invention' being answered by actual tragic experience in that 'Martha Ray', as Wordsworth knew, was the name of young Basil Montagu's grandmother, murdered in 1779 by a disappointed lover. In the late summer of 1800, then, wretched Martha Ray offered a bereaved Thelwall and his wife a complex model of identity to negotiate.

Considering E. P. Thompson's discussion of the modes of writing that emerged in the 1790s out of a culture of political repression that drove democrats 'into small and personal survival groups', Nicholas Roe has spoken of how Coleridge in the 'conversation' poems sought to integrate the private, 'interior monologue' of the isolated self with a 'personal dialogue with one intimate friend' in his attempt to 'orient the otherwise solitary, alienated self within a particular community'.[99] However, as I have shown, Thelwall's poems, which exemplify both the monologic discourse of the solitary individual and, in the light of the allusions I have been examining, a subtle dialogic discourse, ultimately emphasize the *impossibility* of integration within a sustaining, 'particular community'. The 'Paternal Tears' sequence constitutes a dialogue through which Thelwall expressed the public and private disappointments of the last years of the eighteenth century.

By April 1801, as Thelwall emerged from his 'proscription', a great gulf had opened up between Coleridge and himself. Offering advice on the 'mode of publication' of *Poems, Chiefly Written in Retirement*, Coleridge, in ill health, stated in a letter of 23 April:

> we are so utterly unlike each other in our habits of thinking, and we have adopted such irreconcileably different opinions in Politics, Religion, & Metaphysics . . . that I fear – I fear – I do not know how to express myself – but such, I fear, is the chasm between us, that so far from being able to shake hands across it, we cannot even make our Words intelligible to each other.[100]

He went on: 'I am sure I need not request you not to mention my name in your memoirs . . . because the thing may be of some importance to my poor Wife & Children'. On reading Thelwall's *Poems* the following year, Coleridge would have realized that he was in fact a palpable presence in Thelwall's 'memoirs'.[101]

Postscript: Thelwall as Model – *The Excursion*

Finally, it is worth remembering that, as E. P. Thompson has argued, Thelwall himself – Llyswen's despondent 'Recluse' – was to emerge as a disturbing paradigm in Wordsworth's later poetry as 'the primary, most significant and most acutely felt model'[102] for the disillusioned Solitary of *The Excursion*. (Thelwall, of course, was to suspect Wordsworth of plagiarizing his *Peripatetic* in *The Excursion*, as Henry Crabb Robinson, who in October 1799 had visited Thelwall at Llyswen,[103] recorded in his diary for 12 February 1815: '[Thelwall] talked of "The Excursion" as containing finer verses than there are in Milton, and as being in versification most admirable; but then Wordsworth borrows without acknowledgement from Thelwall himself!'[104]) The character of the Solitary is certainly a composite, drawn, as Wordsworth explained to Isabella Fenwick, 'from several persons with whom I had been connected & who fell under my observation during frequent residences in London at the beginning of the French Revolution'[105] – Joseph Fawcett being 'the chief of these'. Thompson persuasively argues, however, that it is the exiled Thelwall, as Wordsworth encountered him at Llyswen in 1798, who more aptly corresponds to the Solitary as drawn in *The Excursion*. Thompson is right, of course, when he reminds us that another important model for the Solitary 'was Wordsworth himself – or Wordsworth's Jacobin *alter ego*', and he further contends that

> The Solitary is a way in which Wordsworth could put a part of himself outside himself, a self-disowning. But what is disowned is not only himself, it is also the possibility of rational affirmative political action – to remake institutions and laws, to challenge custom and Gothic forms. The very pretence of such an aspiration is now presented as an object of scorn . . . The Solitary, then, is the failure of Wordsworth's own Jacobinical *alter ego* objectified and manipulated.[106]

In other words, the Solitary is employed by Wordsworth as a means of exorcizing his former jacobin self. Although Thompson here over-emphasizes what he sees as the now reactionary Wordsworth's 'scornful' attitude towards the Solitary (Wordsworth's delineation of him, and of his silences, is far more complex and eloquent than Thompson suggests), a certain 'disowning' is certainly at work here. And along with Wordsworth's jacobin past, John Thelwall – a major, if not the primary, model for the Solitary – is once more 'disowned'. The poetic dialogue of 1800 between the poems of 'Paternal Tears' and those of Wordsworth and Coleridge points forward to the dialogues between the Solitary, the Wanderer, the Poet and the Pastor in *The Excursion* and stands as one of the most poignant 'conversations' of the age.

Epilogue

One of the main aims of this book has been to expand the Romantic canon by introducing into critical currency certain neglected figures who exercised a major influence on the culture of the age and played a significant rôle in forging and figuring Romantic writers' cultural and political identities. I hope the profiles I have offered of David Williams and Edward Williams in particular will serve to establish their importance in Romantic Studies and prompt further scrutiny of their contribution to the radical culture of the 1790s. As this book appears, a major international research project is under way at the University of Wales which will provide a comprehensive account of Edward Williams's achievements. The wide range of neglected texts and archival material – antiquarian, topographical, political as well as literary – cited throughout this study enhances our awareness of how a number of discourses and cultural voices determined the shape of canonical Romanticism.

The account I have given of the Welsh contexts of Romanticism is an attempt to read canonical works from a fresh perspective. As we have seen, repositioning such works in relation to hitherto marginalized figures, locations and narratives reveals a text's cultural and political alignments. An exploration of what has been regarded as marginal to Romanticism in fact leads us to the centre of such poems as 'Tintern Abbey'. Wales and the haunted, liminal space of the Wye Valley have emerged in *Presences that Disturb* as sites which fostered a disruptive but educative historical awareness. In the light of this, I would argue that closer attention to the historical and political associations of place should inform our interpretations of Romantic lyrics, landscape poems and tours, for example. The notion of the

Welsh landscape as a text bearing the traces of history or as a substitute for revolutionary France problematizes our conception of the 'touristic' pleasure Wales is supposed to have offered in the 1790s.

Identifying presence rather than pointing accusingly to absence; reading dialogically rather than in cultural isolation; and viewing Romantic writers as part of a discursive community rather than as sequestered individuals – these are some of the ways in which I have sought to contest the more reductive readings of recent New Historicist criticism. By cultivating an awareness of what Judith Thompson has called 'the intertextual genetics of Romanticism'[1] we will be better qualified to defend a writer from the imputation of running away from history or of sublimating socio-political realities.

I have been concerned throughout this book to reveal the interconnectedness of 1790s culture and tune into the dialogues canonical poems conduct with other literary works and with non-literary writing (and vice versa). The picture of a reticular culture of interchange and conversation that has emerged from this rehistoricization of canonical works naturally leads us to question received hierarchical notions of the priority of literary 'text' over background 'context' or 'source'. It also forces us to interrogate our conception of an author's individuality and 'separateness' within a given culture. While the canonical stature of Wordsworth is not in the least usurped or diminished by the account I have given of the cultural embeddedness of 'Tintern Abbey', for example, my analysis does seek to add to our understanding of the other authors, voices, experiences and cultures that go to the making of such paradigmatic works by which we define the period. As with texts and authors, so with cultural histories: Wales is not a marginal context or background for Romanticism but rather a vital, contributory force within it. And implicitly, Chapter 5 makes a case for the inclusion of Thelwall's poems in an expanded canon in which his Llyswen elegies figure as texts for which 'Tintern Abbey' and 'This Lime-Tree Bower my Prison' are the *contexts*. As Michael Scrivener remarks, letting such voices as Thelwall's into the canon 'expands and complicates the overall literary conversation'.[2] It is an act of democratization that salutarily defamiliarizes canonical texts in order to provide further insights into them.

Notes

Introduction

1. J. J. McGann, *The Romantic Ideology* (Chicago: University of Chicago Press, 1983), 82.
2. See Marjorie Levinson, *Wordsworth's Great Period Poems: Four Essays* (Cambridge: Cambridge University Press, 1986), 14–57.
3. Ibid., 11.
4. John Rieder, *Wordsworth's Counterrevolutionary Turn: Community, Virtue, and Vision in the 1790s* (Newark: University of Delaware Press, 1997), 220.
5. Paul Magnuson, *Reading Public Romanticism* (Princeton: Princeton University Press, 1998), 5.
6. Ibid.
7. Judith Thompson, 'An Autumnal Blast, a Killing Frost: Coleridge's Poetic Conversation with John Thelwall', *Studies in Romanticism* 36, 3 (Fall 1997), 453.

Chapter 1: Models of Solitude and Involvement

1. Levinson, *Wordsworth's Great Period Poems*, 11.
2. John Dixon Hunt, *The Figure in the Landscape: Poetry, Painting, and Gardening during the Eighteenth Century* (Baltimore and London: Johns Hopkins University Press, 1976), 8.
3. William Gilpin, *Observations on the River Wye, and Several Parts of South Wales, &c. Relative Chiefly to Picturesque Beauty* (London: R. Blamire, 1782), 32.
4. Mary Jacobus, '"Tintern Abbey" and Topographical Prose', *Notes & Queries* 216 (October 1971), 368.
5. Geoffrey Hartman, *The Unmediated Vision: An Interpretation of Wordsworth, Hopkins, Rilke, and Valéry* (New York: Harcourt, Brace & World, 1966), 33–4.
6. Richard J. Onorato, *The Character of the Poet: Wordsworth in The Prelude* (Princeton: Princeton University Press, 1971), 46–8.

7. Levinson, *Wordsworth's Great Period Poems*, 34 and 41.
8. Kenneth R. Johnston, 'The Politics of "Tintern Abbey"', *WC* 14, 1 (Winter 1983), 8.
9. Harold Bloom, *Poetry and Repression: Revisionism from Blake to Stevens* (New Haven and London: Yale University Press, 1976), 70–1 and 81.
10. Robert A. Brinkley, 'Vagrant and Hermit: Milton and the Politics of "Tintern Abbey"', *WC* 16, 3 (Summer 1985), 126.
11. Ibid., 126 and 128.
12. Nicholas Roe, *The Politics of Nature: Wordsworth and Some Contemporaries* (Basingstoke: Macmillan, 1990), 126.
13. Ibid., 122.
14. Ibid., 121.
15. Ibid., 126–7; *King Lear*, III. iv. 28–33.
16. G. M. Doble, *Lives of the Welsh Saints*, ed. D. Simon Evans (Cardiff: University of Wales Press, 1971), 224.
17. *LL*, 383.
18. See J. R. Watson, 'A Note on the Date in the Title of *Tintern Abbey*', *WC* 10, 4 (Autumn 1979), 379–80 and Nicholas Roe, *Wordsworth and Coleridge: The Radical Years* (Oxford: Clarendon Press, 1988), 272–3.
19. Heath, *Tintern Abbey* (no pagination) devotes a brief chapter to the 'Etymology of Tintern': 'In the Monasticon it is spelt Dindryn, – which, according to the definition of an intelligent friend, is an ancient British word, and signifies a *fortified place*'. The 'friend' does not account for the *teyrn* – 'king' – element owing most probably to the metathesis in the form with which he was familiar (Dindryn).
20. *LL*, 383–4.
21. See A. R. Utting, *Tewdric: Saint and Warrior King* (Mathern: Mathern PCC, 1988), 7 and E. T. Davies, *A History of the Parish of Mathern* (2nd edn; Mathern: Mathern PCC, 1990), 3. See also James Tyrrell, *The General History of England, as well Ecclesiastical as Civil* (3 vols; London: W. Rogers, 1696–1704), I, 149; and John Morris, *The Age of Arthur: A History of the British Isles from 350 to 650* (London: Weidenfeld & Nicolson, 1973), 229 and 515.
22. E. T. Davies, *History of Mathern*, 4.
23. James Baker, *A Picturesque Guide through Wales and the Marches* (Worcester: J. Tymbs, 1795), 15.
24. See Wu, *1770–1799*, 40.
25. William Coxe, *An Historical Tour in Monmouthshire* (2 vols; London: T. Cadell & W. Davies, 1801), I, 8. Tewdrig's bones have been seen twice – by Godwin in 1614, and again during restoration work in 1881.
26. Heath, *Tintern Abbey* (no pagination).
27. Leitch Ritchie, *The Wye and its Associations: A Picturesque Ramble* (London: Longman, Orme, Brown, Green and Longmans, 1841), 172.
28. Jacobus, '"Tintern Abbey"', 368.

29 *MM* 2 (1796), 864–7.
30 George Dyer, *Poetics: or, a Series of Poems, and Disquisitions on Poetry* (2 vols; London: J. Johnson, 1812), v. See my '"G.D." is George Dyer', *Notes & Queries* 241 (March 1996), 31.
31 *MM* 2 (1796), 866; see *Hist. of Mon.*, 9.
32 Jacobus, '"Tintern Abbey"', 369; *Hist. of Mon.*, 161.
33 *MM* 2 (1796), 468.
34 Ibid., 487. Interestingly, the Revd John Gardnor was the painter and clergyman who officiated at the wedding of William and Catherine Blake at St Mary's, Battersea, on 18 August 1782.
35 Losh's diary, quoted in Wu, *1770–1799*, 101. See *EY*, 186.
36 *MM* 1 (1796), 135–7 and 223–4.
37 *MM* 2 (1796), 647 and 732.
38 Ibid., 865.
39 Ibid., 866.
40 Ibid.
41 For a list of reviews of *The History of Monmouthshire*, see J. Dybikowski, *On Burning Ground: An Examination of the Ideas, Projects, and Life of David Williams* (Oxford: Voltaire Foundation, 1993), 318.
42 *Hist. of Mon.*, appendices, 95. *Hist. of Mon.*, 89, locates the battle *near*, rather than *at*, Tintern; see also Heath, *Tintern Abbey* (no pagination): 'The FORD at Tintern, – Pull Brochuail (now called Brockwear) . . . confirm[s] the fact that such a battle took place . . . There is also a spot, about a mile from Tintern, called Pont-y-Saison (the Saxon's bridge)'.
43 *Hist. of Mon.*, 75.
44 Appendices III (13–17); XIX (45–53); XXIII (60–70); XXXII (85–6); XLVII (120–1); and LXIII (153–5) were prepared by Edward Williams. For David Williams's (often aggrieved) letters to a desultory Edward Williams who had been asked to supply material for *The History of Monmouthshire* but who was dragging his feet, see NLW MS 21283E/547 (29 December 1795: 'It has been the pride & satisfaction of my life, never to have intercourse with Great Men, who affect the privilege of disregarding Promises, & leaving Letters & memorials &c unanswered[.] But I have unwillingly stumbled on one in you'). See also NLW MS 21283E/544; NLW MS 21283E/545; and NLW MS 21283E/546.
45 *Hist. of Mon.*, appendices, 65. For other references to Tewdrig, see appendices, 31–2, 66 and 68.
46 Ibid., appendices, 89.
47 Ibid., appendices, 36.
48 Coxe, *An Historical Tour*, I, 7.
49 For comprehensive (and first-class) accounts of David Williams's life and thought, see Dybikowski, *On Burning Ground*, and Whitney R. D. Jones, *David Williams: The Anvil and the Hammer* (Cardiff: University of Wales Press,

1986). See also my entry on Williams in the forthcoming *New Dictionary of National Biography*.

50 Williams printed Frederick the Great's and Voltaire's replies in his *Lectures on Education* (3 vols; London: J. Bell, 1789), III, 299 and 302–3. Voltaire wrote: 'Returning home from mineral waters [sic], I find the precious book you honour me with. I have perused it with the pleasure that a Resucrucian [sic] would enjoy in reading the work of an adept. It is a great comfort to me, at the age of eighty-two years, to see the tolerance openly teach'd in your country, and the God of all mankind no more pent up in a narrow tract of land. That noble truth was worthy of your pen and of your tongue. I am with all my heart one of your followers, and of your admirers'. In the summer of 1776, Thomas Bentley presented a copy of the *Liturgy* to Rousseau in Paris; see *Incidents*, 20–1 for Williams's account of Rousseau's reaction.

51 See Williams's assessment in NLW MS 10336E/43–5 (Dr T.W.Thomas MSS): 'Letters on Political Liberty – This work was translated in to French & much made use of by some of the Authors of the French Revolution . . . The Principles of Constitutional Liberty were further developed [sic] – in Lectures on Political Principles – & in Lessons to a Young Prince – They were *partly* reduced to practice in the French Constitution – but they do not appear to be yet fully understood. All the other Works, such as those of Burke, Paine, Mackintosh, Cartwright are polemic – they contend on *known* principles – but they make no advance in the *Science* –'. See also Whitney Jones, *David Williams*, 116.

52 Waring, 49.

53 Julia Wedgwood, *The Personal Life of Josiah Wedgwood the Potter*, ed. C. H. Herford (London: Macmillan & Co., 1915), 34.

54 In the slightly altered 'Lesson, on the mode of studying and profiting by Mr Burke's Reflections on the Revolution in France' which closes the fourth edition (1790) of his *Lessons to a Young Prince*, Williams describes Burke's 'anger', directed at the Revolution, as 'not the emotion of a great and good mind: it is that of Milton's fiend contemplating the innocence of our first parents, and the possible happiness of their race' (p. 159). One gets a flavour of Williams's tone from such passages as: 'Burke put on his magic spectacles, distinctly saw, the Austrians marching through Flanders, the Spaniards in the Pyrennees, the Savoyards and Swiss in the Alps, and German and English officers sneaking off singly and reluctantly from poverty in England to assist in the projected massacre and devastation. Burke grew frantic with joy: he snuffed the murky air, loaded with the exhalations of twenty millions of atheistic and patriotic carcases. "The incense is divine!" exclaimed the "holy" man – "My prophecies and revelations shall be honoured"; and lo – the Book was published' (pp. 114–15).

55 *Biographical Anecdotes*, II, 10–11; *Incidents*, 25.

56 Quoted in *Incidents*, 2.

57 To Roland on 26 October 1792 from Great Russell Street, Williams wrote: 'Sir, Mr Rinhard, Secretary of Legation, has delivered to me your Letter, enclosing the Decree of the late National Assembly, conferring on me the Rank of Citizen of France. Though I am fully sensible of the honor, & feel the whole force of the Motives which induced the Representatives of a Great Nation to confer it, I think no circumstances relating to myself, could heighten the ardor of those wishes & hopes which have long possessed my mind, reflecting the construction & establishment of a French Constitution, involving probably the interests & happiness of human nature. It is not wonderful the first attempt should not have fully succeeded, but it developed principles & views, which alarmed Despotism, & the Instruments of Despotism throughout the world. All the Friends of that regulated humane & comprehensive justice, which is the ultimate object of political knowledge, have their eyes intensely fixed on the national Convention of France. The conspiracy of European Tyrants is defeated; the obstructions of hereditary Royalty & Aristocracy are removed; & France is distinguished by the first opportunity, afforded to Philosophy, of applying the principles of reason & virtue to the construction of a political Constitution. I take this occasion with pleasure, to express to you Sir, the high opinion I have conceived of your principles, from your public conduct; & the esteem with which I am your fellow-citizen & friend'; see H. P. Richards, *David Williams* (Cowbridge: D. Brown & Sons, 1980), 23.
58 See *Incidents*, 27.
59 The review, published in the *Analytical Review* 4 (1789), 410–24, is ascribed to Wollstonecraft by Butler and Todd in *The Works of Mary Wollstonecraft* (7 vols; London: Pickering, 1989), VII, 141–52.
60 *Incidents*, 27.
61 See J. M. Thompson, *English Witnesses of the French Revolution* (Oxford: Basil Blackwell, 1938), 254. See also J. G. Millingen, *Recollections of Republican France, from 1790 to 1801* (London: Henry Colburn, 1848), 240.
62 See *Incidents*, 28.
63 See Whitney Jones, *David Williams*, 125–35.
64 *Incidents*, 29.
65 Ibid., 28.
66 *Biographical Anecdotes*, II, 19.
67 *Incidents*, 29.
68 David Williams, 'The Missions of David Williams and James Tilly Matthews to England (1793)', *English Historical Review* 53 (1938), 651–68.
69 *Incidents*, 31.
70 See *Incidents*, 35–6: 'The Girondins not only wandered among abstractions, but they advised and superintended insurrectionary movements, and acted the parts of demagogues, in opposition to their original principles and destructive of their ultimate views . . . They were destined to be elective and occasional,

they became administrative and permanent, and it was by such usurpations that the Jacobins became tyrants of France'; and *Biographical Anecdotes*, II, 20: 'As a politician, [Brissot's] heart was better director than his head: he wanted knowledge of mankind'. These comments should be read alongside the similar assessments of Brissot and the Girondins by Coleridge in *Lectures 1795*, 34–5, and by Madame Roland in her *Appeal to Impartial Posterity* (London: J. Johnson, 1795), Part I, 52–6: 'excellent reasoners all, learned philosophers in theory; but totally ignorant of the art of leading men, and consequently of swaying an assembly'.

71 *Incidents*, 24 and 37.
72 Williams's note here refers the reader to his *Letters on Political Liberty* (1782).
73 *Incidents*, 32.
74 For this phrase, see also Thomas Holcroft, *A Letter to the Right Honourable William Windham* (London: H. D. Symonds, 1795), passim; John Thelwall, *Peaceful Discussion, and not Tumultuary Violence the Means of Redressing National Grievances* (London, 1795), 21; Coleridge to Thelwall on 19 November 1796 (*CL* I, 259): 'you, virtuous High-Treasonist, & your friends, the other Aquitted Felons!'; *Lectures 1795*, 288; and *Watchman*, 61.
75 *Incidents*, 120.
76 *The Letters of Joseph Ritson; edited chiefly from originals in the possession of his nephew* (2 vols; London: W. Pickering, 1833), II, 101.
77 See Wu, *1770–1799*, 118 and *EY*, 166.
78 Madame Roland, *Appeal*, Part II, 42–3.
79 Roe, *Radical Years*, 66–9.
80 *Prose Works*, I, 32.
81 Robert Southey, *Letters from England*, ed. J. Simmonds (Gloucester: Alan Sutton, 1984), 400.
82 Henri Grégoire, *Histoire des sectes religieuses* (6 vols; Paris: Baudouin Frères, 1828–45), I, 359–63. See Dybikowski, *On Burning Ground*, 111–12 and Whitney Jones, *David Williams*, 49–50. See also François Aulard, *Études et Leçons sur la Révolution Française*, 2nd series, IV, *La Séparation de l'Église et de l'État* (Paris, 1898), 147–8, and the same author's *Le Culte de la Raison et le Culte de l'Être Suprême* (Paris, 1892), 210, 330 and 345–7. The *Manuel* drafted for the followers of Theophilanthropy closely resembled Williams's own Liturgy.
83 *Anti-Jacobin Review and Magazine*, 1, folding plate opposite p. 115 (July 1798). For a detailed discussion of the cartoon, see the *Catalogue of Political and Personal Satires Preserved in the Department of Prints and Drawings in the British Museum*, ed. Mary Dorothy George and Frederic George Stephens (11 vols; London: Trustees of the British Museum, 1870–1954), 7 (*1793–1800*), 468–72.
84 Winifred Courtney in *Young Charles Lamb 1775–1802* (London: Macmillan, 1982), 193; Paul Betz in *Romantic Archaeologies* (Baltimore: Albin O. Kuhn Library & Gallery, 1995), 13; and, surprisingly, E. P. Thompson in 'Hunting

the Jacobin Fox', *Past and Present* 142 (1994), 110, all wrongly identify the snake as Helen Maria Williams.
85 For Oswald, see D. V. Erdman, *Commerce des Lumières: John Oswald and the British in Paris, 1790–1793* (Columbia: University of Missouri Press, 1986).
86 Quoted by Dybikowski, *On Burning Ground*, 161n.
87 In the National Library of Wales, Aberystwyth (MS 10333E/49), is an order in Oswald's hand for £10 drawn on and accepted by Williams, dated Paris, 19 April 1792.
88 David Erdman, 'The Man that was Not Napoleon', *WC* 12, 1 (Winter 1981), 92–6.
89 *EY*, 71.
90 Roe, *Radical Years*, 43.
91 *Times Literary Supplement* (29 January 1931), 79.
92 *Barron Field's Memoirs of Wordsworth*, ed. Geoffrey Little (Sydney: Sydney University Press, 1975), 26.
93 Christopher Wordsworth, *Memoirs of William Wordsworth* (2 vols; London: E. Moxon, 1851), I, 77, states that Wordsworth would have 'fallen victim among the Brissotins, with whom he was connected' had he remained longer in Paris.
94 As Roe remarks (*Radical Years*, 81–2), although the address to the National Convention drawn up by expatriate radicals at White's Hotel in Paris on 18 November 1792 was not signed by Wordsworth, he may very well have been present. J. G. Alger, writing in 1902 but citing no sources (*Paris in 1789–1794* (London: George Allen, 1902), 328), states, intriguingly, that Williams was also in Paris at the time but kept away from the gathering at White's Hotel because of its jacobinical nature.
95 In his *Early Life of Samuel Rogers* (London: Smith, Elder & Co., 1887), P. W. Clayden remarked of Rogers's visit to Paris in early 1791 (with an ironic reference, no doubt, to Rogers's poem *The Pleasures of Memory*, published the following year): 'Rogers looked back on this visit to Paris . . . with a feeling of horror. He often spoke of the men he had then seen, but he did not refresh his memory by references in his diary, which he seems to have put aside and almost forgotten. To read it would have been indeed to walk among ruins and tombs. He always recollected with a shudder that most of the men he met were, at the very time he was talking to them and sharing their glowing anticipations, standing, as it were, with one foot in the grave' (160). Doubtless Wordsworth would have remembered Brissot with exactly the same shudder.
96 On 24 November 1792, the French agent Noël told Le Brun that Williams would 'contribute by his enlightenment to the edifice of happiness and prosperity which the Convention is about to erect'; see Williams, 'The Missions', 654.
97 See *The Philosopher* (London: T. Becket, 1771), II, 49; *A Letter to the Body of Protestant Dissenters* (London: J. Almon & J. Wilkie, 1777), 4; *A Plan of*

       Association (London: G. Kearsly, 1780), 26–7; and *Letters on Political Liberty* (London: T. Evans, 1782), 17 and 29.
98 *Critical Review* 20 (1810), 13.
99 Williams's visit seems to have been a 'semi-official fact-finding mission' (*Incidents*, 81); see the Memoir (with a silhouette) in *GM* 85, ii (1816), 89: 'During the peace of Amiens Mr Williams again visited Paris, and is supposed to have been intrusted with some confidential mission from the Government of his own Country, his remarkable figure having previously been noticed entering the houses of several of the higher members of the then Administration'. Interestingly, Whitney Jones, *David Williams*, 158, discussing the change in Williams's social and political ideology, quotes Browning's 'The Lost Leader', which laments Wordsworth's own 'apostasy': 'It would be harsh to speak of a handful of silver or yet of a ribbon to put in his hair'.
100 'The Literary Fund', *Anti-Jacobin Review and Magazine* 3 (1799), 100–1.
101 W. H. Reid, *The Rise and Dissolution of the Infidel Societies in this Metropolis* (London: J. Hatchard, 1800), 25 and 90.
102 *MM* 10 (September 1800), 127–30. There is good reason to ascribe this article to Thelwall on internal evidence. Thelwall responds to what he regards as Reid's calumnies, deprecating the 'interference of the magistrate with the worship of Theists'.
103 Bodleian Library, Oxford, Abinger-Shelley Papers, Abinger dep., e. 202. See also C. Kegan Paul, *William Godwin: His Friends and Contemporaries* (2 vols; London: H. S. King, 1876), I, 71.
104 Bodleian Library, Oxford, Abinger-Shelley Papers, Abinger dep., e. 200.
105 Thomas Holcroft, *The Life of Thomas Holcroft, written by himself*, ed. E. Colby (2 vols; London: Constable & Co, 1925), I, 198.
106 Dyer, *An Inquiry into the Nature of Subscription to the Thirty-Nine Articles* (2nd edition; London: J. Johnson, 1792), 234, 268, 275 and 282.
107 Dyer, *The Complaints of the Poor People of England* (2nd edition; London: J. Ridgway & H. D. Symonds, 1793), p. 25; *Memoirs of the Life and Writings of Robert Robinson* (London: G. G. & J. Robinson, 1796), p. 232.
108 *HCR*, I, 4. Dyer cited the *Lectures* again in *The Reflector*, I (1811) and in his *Four Letters on the English Constitution* (4th edition; London: Longman, Hurst, Rees, Orme and Brown, 1818), 16–17 and 53.
109 See Wu, *1770–1799*, 50.
110 Dyer, *A Dissertation on the Theory and Practice of Benevolence* (London: G. Kearsley, 1795), 63–6. In *MM* 1 (February 1796), 8–9, Dyer published an article, signed 'A Friend to the Literary Fund', advertising the Fund. See also his note in the next issue, *MM* 1 (March 1796), 112.
111 Lamb punningly addressed Frend as 'Friend of the friendless, friend of all mankind, / To thy wide friendships I have not been blind; / But looking at them nearly, in the end / I love thee most that thou art Dyer's friend'; quoted

in Dudley Wright, 'Charles Lamb and George Dyer', *English Review* 39 (September 1924), 397.
112 Lamb, *Letters*, II, 30.
113 See NLW MS 21283E/542 (David Williams to Edward Williams, 22 December 1794); NLW MS 21283E/543 (DW to EW, 7 April 1795: 'I wish to see you, & to let you have your Money'); NLW MS 21283E/544 (DW to EW, 13 May 1795: 'You & I do business like Poets. You should let me have a letter to produce to the Committee of the Literary Fund – thanking the Committee for the Ten Guineas you have received through my hands').
114 NLW MS 21280E/135; no date, but clearly April or May 1799.
115 NLW MS 21280E/136. Dyer proceeds in this letter to mention such radical luminaries as Frend and Priestley. For further letters from Dyer to EW, see NLW MS 21280E/137–40.
116 For Coleridge's letter thanking the Fund, see *CL*, I, 220. The Fund was to assist Coleridge once again in February 1816 with a gift of £30.
117 See George Whalley, 'The Bristol Library Borrowings of Southey and Coleridge', *The Library*, 5th Series, 4 (1949–50), 123, and Ralph J. Coffman, *Coleridge's Library: A Bibliography of Books Owned or Read by Samuel Taylor Coleridge* (Boston: G. K. Hall, 1987), 233.
118 David Williams, *A Treatise on Education* (London: T. Payne et al., 1774), 90. Very much aware of how impractical his own education had been, Williams as an educational theorist and admirer of Comenius was a pioneer of a pedagogic method based on *things* rather than *words*; he strongly deprecated mechanical rote-learning. Coleridge, who on 1 November 1796 was to announce that 'Bishop Taylor, Old Baxter, David Hartley & the Bishop of Cloyne are *my men*' (*CL*, I, 245), would also doubtless have been drawn to Williams's *Treatise* because of its Hartleyan flavour.
119 See Warren E. Gibbs, 'An Unpublished Letter from John Thelwall to S. T. Coleridge', *Modern Language Review* 25 (January 1930), 89.
120 See Dorothy's letter of 19 March 1797 to Mrs John Marshall; *EY*, 180.
121 Dyer, *Poems* (London: Longman & Rees, 1801), 140 and 142.
122 For Dyer's presence in 'Tintern Abbey', see Roe, *Politics*, 29–35.
123 Roe, *Radical Years*, 192–3.
124 *Claims of Literature* (London: W. Miller, 1802), 77.
125 See Whalley, 'Bristol Library Borrowings', 129.
126 NLW MS 21286E/1032. Williams's unorthodox punctuation has been retained.
127 *English Review* 27 (1796), 332.
128 *Analytical Review* 24 (1796), 124–30.
129 *Cambrian Register* 2 (1799 [for the year 1796]), 458. See also David Williams, 'A Bibliography of the Printed Works of David Williams (1738–1816)', *National Library of Wales Journal* 10 (1957–8), 134.
130 *Hist. of Mon.*, 72.

[131] NLW MS 21286E/1032.
[132] *Hist. of Mon.*, 150.
[133] *British Critic* 8 (1796), 269.
[134] *Hist. of Mon.*, 48.
[135] See George Soule, '"Spots of Earth" in *The Excursion*', *Charles Lamb Bulletin* NS 85 (January 1994), 19–24.
[136] See *Prose Works*, II, 63–4: 'standing by the side of a smooth Sea, on a Summer's day . . . I have been rouzed from this reverie by a consciousness, suddenly flashing upon me, of the anxieties, the perturbations, and, in many instances, the vices and rancorous dispositions, by which the hearts of those who lie under so smooth a surface and so fair an outside must have been agitated. The image of an unruffled Sea has remained; but my fancy has penetrated into the depths of that Sea – with accompanying thoughts of Shipwreck, of the destruction of the Mariner's hopes, the bones of drowned Men heaped together, monsters of the deep, and all the hideous and confusing sights which Clarence saw in his Dream!'
[137] *Peripatetic*, II, 4–5.
[138] 'To J. H. Reynolds, Esq.', l. 97.
[139] By 1798, Wordsworth would have been familiar with a poem in which a hermit offers practical instruction to a future poet – James Beattie's *The Minstrel* (1771 and 1774) – a work that influenced both *Descriptive Sketches*, ll. 492–511, and the Climbing of Snowdon episode in *The Prelude*. In the second Canto, the hermit instructs Edwin in history, philosophy, law, science and government.
[140] See Alan Liu, *Wordsworth: The Sense of History* (Stanford, CA: Stanford University Press 1989), 3–31.
[141] The foregoing analysis adds to the resonance of the title for Wordsworth. For other presences in the title, see Kenneth Johnston, *Wordsworth and 'The Recluse'* (New Haven and London: Yale University Press, 1984), 13.
[142] In this letter of *c.*10 September 1799, Coleridge urges Wordsworth to buckle down to *The Recluse*.
[143] See Wu, *1770–1799*, 32.
[144] See Nicholas Roe's references to the 'antiphonal relation' of 'Tintern Abbey' to 'Fears in Solitude' in Roe, *Radical Years*, 268 and 272. Paul Magnuson points out the similar circular structure of 'Tintern Abbey' and Coleridge's 'Frost at Midnight' in *Coleridge and Wordsworth: A Lyrical Dialogue* (Princeton: Princeton University Press, 1988), 165–6.
[145] See John Rieder's differently inflected discussion of the 'topography' of Coleridge's poems and 'Tintern Abbey' in *Wordsworth's Counterrevolutionary Turn*, 199–200.
[146] I quote the poem as it appeared in Coleridge's *Poems . . . To which are now added Poems by Charles Lamb and Charles Lloyd* (Bristol: J. Cottle and London: G. G. & J. Robinson, 1797), 100–4.

147 I quote the poem as it first appeared in the quarto volume, *Fears in Solitude . . . To which are added, France, An Ode; and Frost at Midnight* (London: J. Johnson, 1798), 1–12.
148 Magnuson, *Lyrical Dialogue*, 152.
149 Roe, *Politics*, 31.
150 Ibid., 32.

Chapter 2: Models of Betrayal and Flight

1 Roe, *Radical Years*, 272.
2 The phrase is Whitney Jones's in a discussion of David Williams's response to war with revolutionary France; Whitney Jones, *David Williams*, 137.
3 Roe, *Radical Years*, 272.
4 Ibid., 269.
5 Ibid., 271–2.
6 *The Salisbury Plain Poems*, ed. Stephen Gill (Ithaca, NY, and London: Cornell University Press, 1975), 215–17
7 *The Prelude* (1805), XII, 312–53. See also ll. 91–9, 172–98 and 424–32 of Wordsworth's 'Salisbury Plain'.
8 See *The Pedlar, Tintern Abbey, and The Two-Part Prelude*, ed. Jonathan Wordsworth (Cambridge: Cambridge University Press, 1985), 36n., and *The Prelude: The Four Texts*, ed. Jonathan Wordsworth (Harmondsworth: Penguin, 1995), 653.
9 Mary Moorman, *William Wordsworth: A Biography; The Early Years, 1770–1803* (Oxford: Oxford University Press, 1957), 233.
10 Onorato, *Character of the Poet*, 51.
11 Bloom, *Poetry and Repression*, 80.
12 See Nennius's *History of the Britons*, ed. A. W. Wade-Evans (London: SPCK, 1938) and Geoffrey of Monmouth's *The History of the Kings of Britain*, tr. Lewis Thorpe (Harmondsworth: Penguin, 1966).
13 For the historical Vortigern, see D. P. Kirby, 'Vortigern', *Bulletin of the Board of Celtic Studies* 23 (1968), 37–59; D. N. Dumville, 'Sub-Roman Britain: History and Legend', *History* 62 (1977), 173–92; and Hector Munro Chadwick, 'Vortigern', *Studies in Early British History* (Cambridge: Cambridge University Press, 1954), 21–46.
14 It is possible that the legend of the Long Knives was taken from early Saxon tradition, since a similar story is to be found in Widukind's chronicle of the Saxons in Germany. It is from Widukind that the story entered German legend. The Roehm purge by Hitler in 1934 is known as 'The Night of the Long Knives'.

15. Such was the currency of the Treason of the Long Knives myth in nineteenth-century Wales that when in 1854 R. J. Derfel published his satirical play *Brad y Llyfrau Gleision* (The Treason of the Blue Books) in response to the objectionable reports of three government commissioners on the state of Welsh education and morals, he could rely on his public understanding the historical reference in the title.
16. Aaron Thompson, *The British History, translated into English from the Latin of Jeffrey of Monmouth* (London: J. Bower, 1718), 229–31.
17. Other versions of the tale locate his death elsewhere in Wales. Nennius has him burnt to death in his citadel on the river Teifi in modern-day Carmarthenshire; Thomas Pennant in his *Tour in Wales* (1778 and 1781) makes a case in favour of 'Nant y Gwrtheyrn, or Vortigern's Valley' in north Wales as the final refuge of the 'royal fugitive'; and William Warrington in his *History of Wales* (1786) locates the fired castle in modern-day Powys 'on the river Wye in *Arwystly*'.
18. As J. S. P. Tatlock points out in *The Legendary History of Britain: Geoffrey of Monmouth's* Historia Regum Britanniae *and its Early Vernacular Versions* (Berkeley: University of California Press, 1950), 72, *Cloartius* is a manuscript error for *Doartius*; Wace's French translation of Geoffrey's *Historia* has *Doar, Doare, Droac*.
19. Jacobus, '"Tintern Abbey"', 368.
20. Warner, *Walk*, 224. For Doward, see also Heath (1796), no pagination, and Samuel Ireland, *Picturesque Views on the River Wye* (London: R. Faulder & T. Egerton 1797), 98–9. Warner's *Walk*, 122–3, also mentions the Snowdon area's associations with Vortigern.
21. Daniel Defoe, *A Tour through the Whole Island of Great Britain*, ed. G. D. H. Cole and D. C. Browning (2 vols; London: J. M. Dent, 1974), II, 54.
22. *A History of the County of Brecknock* (2 vols; Brecknock: W. & G. North, 1805 and 1809), I, 281.
23. See Prys Morgan, 'From Long Knives to Blue Books', in R. R. Davies et al., eds., *Welsh Society and Nationhood: Historical Essays Presented to Glanmor Williams* (Cardiff: University of Wales Press, 1984), 199–215. Morgan refers to versions of the story occurring in the Welsh Triads, the work of the medieval Welsh poets, a seventeenth-century ballad by Matthew Owen, William Owen's *Y Drych Bradwriaethol, sef Hanes Brad y Cyllill Hirion* (The Treacherous Mirror, viz. The History of the Treason of the Long Knives, 1825), Edward Roberts's verse drama of 1853, *Brad y Cyllill Hirion*, and R. J. Derfel's *Brad y Llyfrau Gleision*, 1854 (see note 15). In 1822 the Cambrian Society of Gwent offered a medal for an essay on 'The Credibility of the Massacre of the British Nobles at Stonehenge'.
24. See Oliver Goldsmith, *An History of England* (2 vols; London: J. Newbery, 1764), I, 32–4; Duncan Wu, 'The Wordsworth Family Library at Cockermouth: Towards a Reconstruction', *The Library* 14 (1992), 132; and Wu, *1800–1815*, 94.

25 See Francis Celoria, 'Chatterton, Wordsworth and Stonhenge', *Notes and Queries* 221 (March 1976), 103–4.
26 *Hist. of Mon.*, 80; see also Jacobus, '"Tintern Abbey"', 368–9.
27 See *Poly-Olbion*, Song X, in *A Complete Edition of the Poets of Great Britain*, ed. Robert Anderson (14 vols; London: J. & A. Arch, 1792–5), III, 349; Wu, *1770–1799*, 4; and Wu, *1800–1815*, 76.
28 See Wu, *1800–1815*, 90. The other avowed source is Milton's *History of Britain* (1670), in which the Vortigern story is also related: see Wu, *1800–1815*, 147–8.
29 *Selections from the Letters of Robert Southey*, ed. John Wood Warter (4 vols; London: Longman et al., 1856), II, 27.
30 See *MM* 2 (September 1796), 618, and *NLRS* I, 115. Kenneth Curry in NLRS fails to identify 'Meirion'. He is William Owen, later William Owen Pughe, lexicographer, antiquarian and zealous factotum of Joanna Southcott from *c.*1803 until her death in 1814. His *Heroic Elegies and other Pieces of Llywarç Hen* (1793) is discussed in Chapter 4. See my article, 'Pwy yw "Meirion" y *Monthly Magazine*?' (Who is the *Monthly Magazine*'s 'Meirion'?), *Llên Cymru* 21 (July 1998), 182–8, which discusses the contributions of Robert Southey and William Owen Pughe to the *Monthly Magazine*, and the dialogue between them.
31 Losh's diary, quoted in Wu, *1770–1799*, 101. See also *EY*, 186.
32 Heath (1799), 124.
33 Ibid., 126–7.
34 Ibid., 129.
35 Heath (1803); no pagination.
36 Nennius, *History*, 70.
37 *The Prelude* (1805), XII, 153–6.
38 See Heath (1796), no pagination: 'I shall take the liberty to introduce some beautiful POETRY, from a volume of Poems, written by Mr. COLERIDGE of BRISTOL [*Poems on Various Subjects*, 1796], whose acquaintance I think it an happiness to share . . . The Reader will find the whole of the Collection deserving his highest approbation'.
39 *The Prelude* (1850), IV, 359.
40 See Phil Carradice, *The Last Invasion: The Story of the French Landing in Wales* (Pontypool: Village Publishing, 1992).
41 See also *Ecclesiastical Sketches*, Part I, x ('Struggle of the Britons against the Barbarians') and xi ('Saxon Conquest'), *PW*, III, 346–7.
42 Linda Colley, *Britons: Forging the Nation*, 1797–1837 (London: Vintage, 1996), 5.
43 Paul Wright, 'Vile Saxons and Ancient Britons: Wordsworth, the Ambivalent Welsh Tourist', in Katie Gramich and Andrew Hiscock, eds., *Dangerous Diversity: The Changing Faces of Wales* (Cardiff: University of Wales Press, 1998), 64–80.

44 Alan Liu, 'Wordsworth and Subversion, 1793–1804: Trying Cultural Criticism', *Yale Journal of Criticism* 2, 2 (1989), 70 and 81–2.
45 In Book XXII, ll. 500–2, Eleanor de Montfort contrasts the characters of Warwick and Talbot: 'He bore me from a man, / Mid Gloster's towers, his blackest antitype, / Talbot, inglorious name'.
46 *LY* ii, 77–9.
47 See the note to Milton's *History of Britain* (1670) in *The Complete Prose Works of John Milton*, ed. Don M. Wolfe et al. (8 vols; New Haven: Yale University Press, 1953–82), V, i. 141n. See also Ireland, *Confessions*, 134–5: 'A considerable time after the production of this play, some believer in the papers desired Mr. [Samuel] Ireland to refer to Milton's works; wherein it appears that he has mentioned the story of Vortigern and Rowena, with some others, as very appropriate for the drama'.
48 On *Vortigern* and the Ireland forgeries, see Derk Bodde, *Shakspeare and the Ireland Forgeries* (Cambridge, MA: Harvard University Press, 1930); Zoltán Haraszti, *The Shakespeare Forgeries of William Henry Ireland: The Story of a Famous Literary Fraud* (Boston: Boston Public Library, 1934); John Mair, *The Fourth Forger: William Ireland and the Shakespeare Papers* (London: Cobden-Sanderson, 1938); Bernard Grebanier, *The Great Shakespeare Forgery: A New Look at the Career of William Henry Ireland* (London: Heinemann, 1966); and Jeffrey Kahan, *Reforging Shakespeare: The Story of a Theatrical Scandal* (Bethlehem and London: Lehigh University Press, 1998).
49 Ritson, *Letters*, II, 141.
50 Ireland, *Vortigern*, p. iv.
51 See Mair, *Fourth Forger*, 143–6.
52 See Kahan, *Reforging*, 163–5.
53 Ireland, *Confessions*, 132–3.
54 See Kahan, *Reforging*, 126.
55 Ireland, *Confessions*, 161.
56 See *MM* 1 (February 1796), 43; *MM* 1 (April 1796), 231–2; and *MM* 2 (July 1796), 488.
57 Ireland, *Vortigern*, p. vi.
58 Ireland, *Confessions*, 157 and 158.
59 Ibid., 156. For an account of the performance, see Kahan, *Reforging*, 178–87.
60 Ireland, *Vortigern*, 50–1.
61 The play was resurrected from the theatre's 'lasting night', however, in October 1997, when Joe Harmston's production was staged at Bridewell. Jeremy Kingston's review in *The Times* of 27 October 1997 was generally favourable, and bore the witty title 'Ham wrote Shakespeare, not Bacon' (p. 19).
62 See *Watchman*, 92–8, 218 and 278–80. It is interesting to note that soon after the debacle at Drury Lane, Ireland absconded from his father's house and spent the summer of 1796 wandering in Wales before visiting Chatterton's

sister in Bristol. See Haraszti, *Shakespeare Forgeries*, 20: 'Having left his father's house, young Ireland, within a week, took a wife to himself. Together they wandered through Wales and Gloucestershire, trying to eke out a living somewhere'; Grebanier, *Great Shakespeare Forgery*, 258–9: 'Without notice, William Henry's threatened exile into Wales became a fact. Out of concern for him [John] Byng arranged with some friends, the Winders of Vaynor Park, Montgomeryshire, that William Henry be welcomed as a guest; the idea was that the young man might find it attractive enough to desire settling down on their farm'; and Mair, *Fourth Forger*, 214.

63 Lamb, *Letters*, I, 4.
64 Ibid., I, 40, 57 and 65. In December 1796 Coleridge sent a copy to John Thelwall (*CL*, I, 286).
65 *A Memoir of the Life and Writings of the Late William Taylor of Norwich*, ed. J. W. Robberds (2 vols; London: John Murray, 1843), I, 260.
66 *MM* 10 (January 1801), 643–60.
67 See Coleridge, *Essays on His Times*, ed. D. V. Erdman (3 vols; Princeton, NJ: Princeton University Press, 1978), III, 162–3, and Wu, *1700–1799*, 158. Wu suggests here that the book Stuart sent Coleridge in early 1798 was Ireland's *Vortigern*; it was in fact, as mentioned above, the Dudleys' *Passages*.
68 See *The Correspondence of Edmund Burke*, ed. Thomas W. Copeland et al. (10 vols; Cambridge: Cambridge University Press, 1958–78), VI, 181–2.
69 Peter Martin, *Edmond Malone, Shakespearean Scholar: A Literary Biography* (Cambridge: Cambridge University Press, 1995), 136–7.
70 Ibid., 200.
71 Edmond Malone, *An Inquiry into the Authenticity of Certain Miscellaneous Papers* (London: T. Cadell, 1796), 148 and 151.
72 Quoted in Kahan, *Reforging*, 215.
73 Ireland, *Vortigern*, 9.
74 Ibid., 30.
75 Mair, *Fourth Forger*, 234. Bodde, *Shakspeare*, 32, refers to 'certain ideas on God, liberty, and humanitarianism' in *Vortigern* that are 'quite in keeping with [Ireland's] own era of the French Revolution, but completely foreign to Shakspere's own dramas'.
76 *Vortigern* also incorporates unmistakable allusions to *Macbeth*, *Richard III*, *Antony and Cleopatra*, *Henry V* and *Cymbeline*; see Bodde, *Shakspeare*, 34–6 and 48–55.
77 See R. T. Jenkins and Helen M. Ramage, *A History of the Honourable Society of Cymmrodorion* (London: Honourable Society of Cymmrodorion, 1951), 91–137 and passim.
78 See *Y Geirgrawn* (1796), 16–21, 58–62, 76–8, 90–4, 144–6, 236–9, 238–42 and 243–6.
79 *Toriad y Dydd* (London, 1797), 23. For Jones, see J. J. Evans, *Dylanwad y Chwyldro Ffrengig ar Lenyddiaeth Cymru* (The Influence of the French

Revolution on Welsh Literature; Liverpool: Hugh Evans & Sons, 1928), 148–59; David Davies, *The Influence of the French Revolution on Welsh Life and Literature* (Carmarthen: W. Morgan Evans & Son, 1926), 53–5 and 170–90; Myddleton Pennant Jones, 'John Jones of Glan-y-Gors', *Transactions of the Honourable Society of Cymmrodorion* (1911), 60–94; 'Llyfrbryf' (Isaac Foulkes), 'John Jones o Lanygors', *Y Geninen* (January 1883), 275–81; Bob Owen, 'Jac Glanygors a'r Milisia' (Jac Glanygors and the Militia), *Y Genhinen* (Winter 1952), 1–7; Saunders Lewis, 'Jack Glan y Gors', *Welsh Outlook* 6 (September 1919), 238–9; and E. Gwynn Matthews, *Jac Glan-y-Gors a'r Baganiaeth Newydd* (Jac Glan-y-Gors and the New Paganism; National Eisteddfod of Wales: Llys yr Eisteddfod Genedlaethol, 1995).

80 *Seren Tan Gwmmwl* (London: Vaughan Griffiths, 1795), 3 and 11; my translation.
81 *Lectures 1795*, 301. Cf Coleridge on 'Commanding Genius' in his *Lay Sermons*, ed. R. J. White (Princeton: Princeton University Press, 1972), 65–6: 'This is the character which Milton has so philosophically as well as sublimely embodied in the Satan of Paradise Lost. Alas! too often has it been embodied in *real* life! Too often has it given a dark and savage grandeur to the historic page! . . . Hope in which there is no Chearfulness; Stedfastness within and immovable Resolve, with outward Restlessness and whirling Activity; Violence with Guile; Temerity with Cunning; and, as the result of all, Interminableness of Object with perfect Indifference of Means . . . these are the Marks, that have characterized the Masters of Mischief, the Liberticides, and mighty Hunters of Mankind, from NIMROD to NAPOLEON.'
82 For discussions of the antiquarian and primitivist vision of the 1790s that reanimated and invented the Welsh past in the service of a politically radical cultural renaissance emanating from the fertile imaginations of such figures as Edward Williams and the radical intelligentsia of the London Welsh societies, see, for example, Prys Morgan, *The Eighteenth-Century Renaissance* (Llandybïe: Christopher Davies, 1981), passim; Prys Morgan, 'From a Death to a View: The Hunt for the Welsh Past in the Romantic Period', in E. Hobsbawm and T. Ranger, eds., *The Invention of Tradition* (Cambridge: Cambridge University Press, 1983), 43–100; Gwyn A. Williams, 'Druids and Democrats: Organic Intellectuals and the First Welsh Nation', in *The Welsh in their History* (London: Croom Helm, 1982), 31–64; and the same author's 'Romanticism in Wales', in Roy Porter and Mikulás Teich, eds., *Romanticism in National Context* (Cambridge: Cambridge University Press, 1988), 9–36.
83 Roe, *Politics*, 130.
84 Ibid., 133.
85 *Poems*, pp. xxxiv–xxxv.
86 *Table Talk*, I, 180–1.
87 *CL*, I, 344; Coleridge to Thelwall, 21 August 1797.
88 Ibid., 343.

[89] *Poems*, 149: 'And murmuring Vaga mourn no loss but thine' and p. 159: 'I range thy lonely haunts, / Sequester'd Vaga'. See also Heath (1799), 60: 'THE WYE is called, in Welch, GWY [*Goo-ee*] from *CAU*, i.e. *shut up*, it being very much impeded in its course by the hills. From GWY comes the Latin name for it, VAGA, which if understood in its proper signification, i.e. *wandering*, is certainly a name very well appropriated'.

[90] See Geoffrey Little, '"Tintern Abbey" and Llyswen Farm', *WC* 8, 1 (Winter, 1977), 80–2, which (unconvincingly) raises the possibility of an earlier (May 1798) visit by Wordsworth to Llyswen.

[91] *Poems*, p. xxxiii.

[92] Mary Wollstonecraft, *Mary* and *The Wrongs of Woman*, ed. Gary Kelly (Oxford: Oxford University Press, 1976), 80 and 178. See also pp. 173 ('To avoid all danger of detection – I use the appropriate word, my child, for I was hunted out like a felon'); 194 ('Such was her state of mind when the dogs of law were let loose on her'); and 196 ('After leaving, what the law considers as my home, I was hunted like a criminal from place to place').

[93] For Thelwall and *The Champion*, and his involvement in Westminster politics during the volatile years 1819–21, see Michael Scrivener, 'John Thelwall and the Press', in Stephen C. Behrendt, ed., *Romanticism, Radicalism and the Press* (Detroit: Wayne State University Press, 1997), 120–36; and Scrivener, 'John Thelwall's Political Ambivalence: Reform and Revolution', in Michael T. Davis, ed., *Radicalism and Revolution in Britain, 1775–1848: Essays in Honour of Malcolm I. Thomis* (Basingstoke: Macmillan, 2000), 69–83.

[94] *The Champion* (6 June 1819), 351–2. Thelwall responds here to a printed attack accusing him of deserting the Liberal cause in the period 1800–19.

[95] *Life*, p. x.

[96] *CL*, I, 341–2.

[97] *Poems*, 126–63. This notion of being 'hunted' out of society like an animal is the structuring concept of E. P. Thompson's seminal 'Jacobin Fox' essay; witness the subtitles: 'View Halloo!' (p. 94); 'Gone to Ground' (p. 111); 'The Kill' (p. 123).

[98] *Poems*, pp. xxxvi and xxxviii.

[99] Ibid., p. xxxvii.

[100] See the account in *MM* 9 (April 1800), 228.

[101] See *Peripatetic*, II, 5–7.

[102] *The Politics of English Jacobinism: Writings of John Thelwall*, ed. Gregory Claeys (University Park, PA: Pennsylvania State University Press, 1995), 494–5.

[103] See Williams's note to his 'Ode on the Mythology of the Ancient British Bards . . . recited on Primrose Hill at a Meeting of British Bards, on the Summer Solstice of 1792' in *Poems, Lyric and Pastoral* (1794), II, 195: 'How truly ridiculous to an Ancient British Mythologist, appear the BARD OF GRAY with its savage Scandinavian Mythology'.

[104] *Poems*, p. xxxix.

105 *CL*, II, 724.
106 *Life*, 1.
107 *Caleb Williams*, ed. Maurice Hindle (Harmondsworth: Penguin, 1988), 287.
108 Ibid., 314. Laura Denison, the person in Wales whose estimation of him Caleb most anxiously cherishes, is the daughter of another political exile driven westwards to Wales – 'a Neapolitan nobleman who . . . had been banished his country upon suspicion of religious and political heresy, and his estates confiscated. With this only child, like Prospero in the Tempest, he had withdrawn himself to one of the most obscure and uncultivated regions of the world (p. 300).'
109 See Roe, *Politics*, 130–4.
110 Baker, *Picturesque Guide*, 20–1.
111 See Matthew Lewis's *The Monk*; Shelley's *Queen Mab*, *Hellas*, and 'The Wandering Jew's Soliloquy'; Byron's *Cain*, and De Quincey's *Suspiria de Profundis*. See also Eino Railo, *The Haunted Castle: A Study of the Elements of English Romanticism* (London: G. Routledge & Sons, 1927), 194–243.
112 The legend is primarily a Continental one, of course. For the British journeys of the Wandering Jew (which, according to folk-tales, extended into Glamorganshire and Pembrokeshire), see G. K. Anderson, 'Popular Survivals of the Wandering Jew in England', in Galit Hasan-Rokem and Alan Dundes, eds., *The Wandering Jew: Essays in the Interpretation of a Christian Legend* (Bloomington, IN: Indiana University Press, 1986), 76–104. The Wandering Jew was even spotted in America (ibid., 105–18). See also chapter 4, 'Wandering Jew, Vagabond Jews', in Frank Felsenstein, *Anti-Semitic Stereotypes: A Paradigm of Otherness in English Popular Culture, 1660–1830* (Baltimore and London: Johns Hopkins University Press, 1995).
113 Eric Rothstein, 'Allusion and Analogy in the Romance of Caleb Williams', *Toronto University Quarterly* 37 (1967–8), 28.
114 *Notebooks*, I (Text and Notes), #45.
115 *Table Talk*, I, 273–4. Henry Nelson Coleridge wrote in the *Quarterly Review* in 1834: 'It was a sad mistake in the able artist – Mr. Scott, we believe – who in his engravings has made the ancient mariner an old decrepit man. That is not the true image; no! he should have been a growthless, decayless being, impassive to time or season, a silent cloud – the wandering Jew'.
116 Judith Thompson, 'An Autumnal Blast', 432.
117 Cf the messianist Henry Francis Offley's *Richard Brothers, Neither a Madman nor an Impostor* (London, 1795), 8–9: 'Certainly the Jews almost ever since the destruction of their kingdom by Titus Vespasian, have been without a fix'd abode, and have been scattered all over the earth, neglecting the Lord their God – and I believe there is not a kingdom in the known world but there are Jews to be found in it; *yet among those Nations shall they find no ease* and truly may it be said that their *feet find no rest*, for every where these unfortunate people are derided, insulted and abused.'

118 See Wu, *1800–1815*, 220.
119 See *The Fall of Cambria*, I, 21–2, 38–9, 136–40 (a medieval version of the 'Treason of the Long Knives') and II, 242.

Chapter 3: Models of Defeat and 'Horrid Sufferance'

1 *Dictionary of National Biography*.
2 *The Anti-Jacobin Review and Magazine* 10 (December 1801), 355.
3 Edmund Burke, *Reflections on the Revolution in France*, ed. C. C. O'Brien (Harmondsworth: Penguin, 1986), 96–7.
4 In 1806, Warner was to dedicate another sermon – on 'National Blessings' – to Fox, appending to it a 'severe character' of Pitt, who had died that same year.
5 *The Poems of William Blake*, ed. W. H. Stevenson and David Erdman (London: Longman, 1971), 706; *J.* 39 [44], 43–4; 40 [45], 1–2.
6 See David Erdman, *Blake: Prophet against Empire* (3rd edition; Princeton: Princeton University Press, 1977), 476–8.
7 A Welsh writer signing himself 'Hirlas' punningly brings together Warner the priest and Warner the tourist in a humorous piece which appeared in *Bye-Gones* (9 June 1875), 253:

> Norway rats, in days of yore,
> To Cambria swarm'd for plunder:
> So Saxon Tourists by the score,
> Hasten'd to Wales to blunder!
> . . .
> *Warner* wander'd midst the flocks,
> And left his own erratic;
> *Aikin* next defin'd the rocks,
> Neptunian or Volcanic.

8 Warner, *Recollections*, II, 136.
9 Ibid., II, 132.
10 *GM* 67, ii (July 1797), 609. Kosciusko had sailed up the Thames the previous day, disembarking at Gravesend. He lodged at the Tabloners Hotel near Leicester Square.
11 See Miecislaus Haiman, *Kosciuszko in the American Revolution* (New York: Kosciuzsko Foundation, 1975 edition); Francis Casimir Kajencki, *Thaddeus Kosciuszko: Military Engineer of the American Revolution* (El Paso, TX: Southwest Polonia Press, 1998); and James S. Pula, *Thaddeus Kosciuszko: The Purest Son of Liberty* (New York: Hippocrene Books, 1999).
12 Quoted in Norman Davies, *God's Playground: A History of Poland* (2 vols; Oxford: Clarendon Press, 1981), I, 541.

13   GM 88, i (April 1818), 371, the year after his death, describes him thus: '[Kosciusko] had not only defended his Country against a press of foreign usurpation, but had refused wealth from the late Emperor Paul, and twice rejected the throne of Poland from Napoleon Buonaparte. Rather than receive a pension from the enemy of his country or be the crowned satellite of any Emperor upon earth, he retired to a miserable village in France, and fed himself on bread and water by the labour of his hands. If this be not honest patriotism, where is it to be found?'

14   GM 67, ii (July 1797), 609.

15   Miecislaus Haiman, *Kosciuszko: Leader and Exile* (New York: Polish Institute of Arts & Sciences in America, 1977 edition), 32–3.

16   *Examiner* (12 January 1817), 18.

17   Warner, *Recollections*, II, 133–4.

18   Ibid., II, 134.

19   Ibid., II, 135–6.

20   Southey, *Letters from England*, 481–2.

21   'Such is Joseph Gerald! Withering in the sickly and tainted gales of a prison, his healthful soul looks down from the citadel of his integrity on his impotent persecutors. I saw him in the foul and naked room of a jail – his cheek was sallow with confinement – his body was emaciated; yet his eye spoke the invincible purposes of his soul, and he still sounded with rapture the successes of Freemen, forgetful of his own lingering martyrdom!' (*Lectures 1795*, 41).

22   See Chloe Hamilton, 'A Portrait of General Kosciusko by Benjamin West', *Allen Memorial Art Museum Bulletin* 9 (1952), 87 and 89.

23   For West's portrait, see Helmut von Erffa and Walter Staley, *The Paintings of Benjamin West* (New Haven, CT: Yale University Press, 1986), 133 and 525–6 (No. 650); and for Cosway's, see Stephen Lloyd, *Richard and Maria Cosway: Regency Artists of Taste and Fashion* (Edinburgh: Scottish National Portrait Gallery, 1995), 122 (No. 100).

24   von Erffa and Staley, *Paintings of Benjamin West*, 130.

25   *Examiner* (3 July 1814), 428.

26   Thomas McLean, ' "When hope bade the world farewell": Responses to the 1794 Kosciuszko Uprising', *WC* 29, 3 (Summer 1998), 180, 183.

27   In *Milton and the English Revolution* (London: Faber, 1977), 36, Christopher Hill speaks of 'the view of Blake, Shelley, Belinsky – all romantic radicals, we note – that Satan is the hero of *Paradise Lost*, or that he is the first Whig'.

28   'Why did [Satan] rebel against his maker?' Godwin asks in *Political Justice*. 'It was, as he himself informs us, because he saw no sufficient reason for that extreme inequality of rank and power which the creator assumed'. In his *Lectures on the English Poets* (1818), Hazlitt wrote: 'Satan is the most heroic subject that ever was chosen for a poem . . . He was the greatest power that was ever overthrown, with the strongest will left to resist or endure'; both quoted in Lucy

Newlyn, *Paradise Lost and the Romantic Reader* (Oxford: Clarendon Press, 1993), 39.

29 Ibid., 81. Newlyn (pp. 81–2) then appositely quotes De Quincey on the operation of Milton's similes – 'Each image, from reciprocal contradiction, brightens and vivifies the other. The two images act, and react, by strong repulsion and antagonism' – and Wordsworth in the Preface to his *Poems* of 1815 on his own simile of the sea-beast in 'Resolution and Independence' – 'two objects unite and coalesce in just comparison'. Both comments capture the multi-valency of Warner's Miltonic model in his description of Kosciusko.

30 Keats, *Letters*, II, 207–8.

31 See Warner, *Recollections*, II, 133.

32 See the 'Introduction' to Heath (1799): 'Whether it be owing to the unsettled state of affairs on the Continent, which renders travelling, if not unsafe, at least disagreeable, – or to that well-founded curiosity, which excites the Man of Observation to survey its attractions, – certain it is that *Monmouthshire* has, in the course of the last four or five years, been honoured with a very large share of Public Notice'.

33 Edwin Stein in *Wordsworth's Art of Allusion* (University Park, PA: Pennsylvania State University, 1988), 177–8 suggests that ll. 7–8 and 23–4 of 'Lines written in Early Spring' and ll. 101–4 of 'Simon Lee' are indebted to ll. 55–6 of Burns's 'Man was made to Mourn': 'Man's inhumanity to man / Makes countless thousands mourn'. The passage in Book XI of *Paradise Lost* from which I quote above might lie behind Burns and Wordsworth:

> O what are these,
> Death's ministers, not men, who thus deal death
> Inhumanly to men, and multiply
> Ten thousand fold the sin of him who slew
> His brother; for of whom such massacre
> Make they but of their bethren, men of men?
> (*PL*, XI, 675–80)

34 Warner, *Walk*, 2–3. This focus on ancient British liberty was a feature of the more historically (and politically) minded Welsh tours of the period.

35 The piece appears as 'Ode to Liberty' in *Tribune*, II, 147–8.

36 George Dyer, *Poems* (London: J. Johnson, 1792), 38.

37 *The Poems of Anna Laetita Barbauld*, ed. William McCarthy and Elizabeth Kraft (Athens, GA: University of Georgia Press, 1994), 127–8.

38 *CL*, I, 86.

39 The sonnet appeared on 16 December 1794, and Coleridge sent it in a letter to Southey the following day: see *CL*, I, 140. It was reprinted in *Poems* (1796). The other 'Eminent Contemporaries' whom Coleridge addressed in

sonnets published in the *Morning Chronicle* between 1 December 1794 and 29 January 1795 included Burke, Pitt, Priestley, Erskine and Sheridan.

40   *CL*, IV, 830.
41   *CL*, I, 138–9.
42   *CL*, I, 102.
43   *Tribune*, III, 95.
44   Roe, *Radical Years*, 14 and 116.
45   *Lectures 1795*, 7.
46   *Watchman*, 367–9. See also Coleridge's 'Lines on Observing a Blossom on the First of February, 1796', first published in *The Watchman*: 'shall I liken thee / To some sweet girl of too, too rapid growth / Nipp'd by Consumption mid untimely charms? / Or to Bristowa's Bard, the wond'rous boy! / . . . Or with indignant grief / Shall I compare thee to poor POLAND's hopes, / Bright flower of hope kill'd in the opening bud! / Farewell, sweet blossom! better fate be thine / And mock my boding!' (*Watchman*, 202–3).
47   Lamb, *Letters*, I, 112. Lamb *had* seen a hero – one who, like Kosciusko, had recently set sail for Philadelphia – and had boasted about it to boot in a letter of 31 May 1796: 'Coleridge, in reading your R. Musings I felt a transient superiority over you, I *have* seen priestly [*sic*] . . . I love and honour him almost profanely' (Lamb, *Letters*, I, 12). Priestley had left for Philadelphia (via New York) in April 1794.
48   See Nicholas Roe, 'Coleridge and John Thelwall: The Road to Nether Stowey', in Richard Gravil and Molly Lefebure, eds., *The Coleridge Connection* (Basingstoke: Macmillan, 1990), 65: 'Coleridge and Thelwall were evidently familiar with each other's creative writing from the outset, but in 1795 their dialogue developed more immediately out of the political and philosophic issues of the day'. For the symbiosis outlined above, see Roe, 'Nether Stowey', passim, and Roe, *Radical Years*, 148–9 and 207–8. See also Burton R. Pollin and Redmond Burke, 'John Thelwall's Marginalia in a Copy of Coleridge's *Biographia Literaria*', *Bulletin of the New York Public Library* 74 (1970), 73–94.
49   Samuel Whitchurch was a follower of the millenarian prophet Richard Brothers and author of *Another Witness! or further testimony in favour of Richard Brothers* (1795). The volume from which Thelwall took this poem is *Elegy on the Death of Mr Thomas Tuppen; with some other Poetical Pieces* (London, 1795).
50   *Tribune*, II, 279–80.
51   See Nicholas Roe, 'Imagining Robespierre', *Coleridge's Imagination: Essays in Memory of Pete Laver* (Cambridge: Cambridge University Press, 1985), 164–8.
52   *Tribune*, II, 25–6.
53   Ibid., II, 76, 77–8.
54   First published as a quarto pamphlet in late December 1796; a shorter version entitled 'Ode for the last day of the year, 1796' appeared in the *Cambridge Intelligencer* on 31 December. The above text is quoted from the 1797 *Poems*, 7–9.

Notes 265

55 The portraits of Suvorov in the above works should be read alongside Byron's merciless treatment of him as Commander of the Russian Forces at the siege of Ismail – 'Hero, buffoon, half-demon and half-dirt' – in Cantos VII and VIII of *Don Juan*.

56 See *The Complete Poetical Works of Thomas Campbell*, ed. J. Logie Robertson (London: Oxford University Press, 1907), 13–14 and 219.

57 See *The Poetical Works of Leigh Hunt*, ed. H. S. Milford (London: Oxford University Press, 1923), 239.

58 See John Kandl, 'Private Lyrics in the Public Sphere: Leigh Hunt's *Examiner* and the Construction of a Public "John Keats"', *Keats–Shelley Journal* 44 (1995), 84–101 and Morris Dickstein, 'Keats and Politics', *Studies in Romanticism* 25 (Summer 1986), 175–81.

59 *Examiner* (12 January 1817), 18.

60 Kandl, 'Private Lyrics', 96.

61 Thomas McLean, '"Transformed, Not Inly Altered": Kosciuszko and Poland in Post-Waterloo Britain', *Keats–Shelley Journal* 50 (2001), 69 and 75, and *Examiner* (3 July 1814), 429.

62 McLean, '"Transformed"', 77.

63 See *Examiner* (6 September 1816), 571–3.

64 *Examiner* (12 January 1817), 17.

65 Charles and Mary Cowden Clarke, *Recollections of Writers* (London: Sampson Low & Co., 1878), 134.

66 It deserves to be mentioned that the fleeting ('Fled is that music') 'high requiem' and 'plaintive anthem' of the nightingale, which result in the poet's being 'tolled' back to a world of pain, also establish a *contrast* between the Keats of 1819 and the Kosciusko of Keats's 1816/17 *Examiner* sonnet, in which the Pole's name is heard in the 'glorious pealing' of a 'loud hymn' of 'everlasting tone'.

67 Keats's last known letter from Rome speaks affectingly of the mature poet's awareness of life's 'contrasts': 'I have been well, healthy, alert &c, walking with [Fanny Brawne] – and now – the knowledge of contrast, *feeling for light and shade*, all that information (primitive sense) necessary for a poem are great enemies to the recovery of the stomach' (Keats, *Letters*, II, 360; my emphasis). See also his annotations to *Paradise Lost* in Keats, *Poems*, 520.

68 Keats, *Letters*, I, 281.

69 Ibid.

70 Ibid.

71 Bransby Blake Cooper, *The Life of Sir Astley Cooper* (2 vols; London: John W. Parker, 1843), I, 244.

72 Ibid., I, 244 and 250. For Cooper's friendship with Thelwall and with the surgeon and democrat Henry Cline (a defence witness at Thelwall's trial), and for Cooper's place in the radical and medico-political culture of the early 1790s, see ibid., I, 95–7, 211–12, 218–24, 236–7, 239–40, 243–4 and 250–2;

Nicholas Roe, '"Atmospheric Air Itself": Medical Science, Politics and Poetry in Thelwall, Coleridge and Wordsworth', in Richard Cronin, ed., *1798: The Year of the Lyrical Ballads* (Basingstoke: Macmillan, 1998), 185–202; Nicholas Roe, *John Keats and the Culture of Dissent* (Oxford: Clarendon Press, 1997), 173–81; and *Life*, 80.

73 *The Lectures of Sir Astley Cooper . . . on the Principles and Practice of Surgery with Additional Notes and Cases by Frederick Tyrrell* (3 vols; London: Thomas & George Underwood, 1824–7), III, 262. For Keats and Cooper, see Donald C. Goellnicht, *The Poet-Physician: Keats and Medical Science* (Pittsburgh, PA: University of Pittsburgh Press, 1984), 12–47 and Roe, *Culture of Dissent*, 169–73.

74 *John Keats's Anatomical and Physiological Note Book*, ed. M. B. Forman (Oxford: Oxford University Press, 1934), 55.

75 See *Byron's Letters and Journals*, ed. Leslie A. Marchand (13 vols; London: John Murray, 1973–94), VIII, 40, and XI, 44 and 84.

76 *The Age of Bronze*, ll. 158–68; *Don Juan*, Canto X, ll. 465–72.

77 *Letters of Walter Savage Landor, Private and Public*, ed. Stephen Wheeler (London: Duckworth & Co., 1899), 196.

78 James T. Fields, *Biographical Notes and Personal Sketches with Unpublished Fragments and Tributes from Men and Women of Letters* (London: Sampson Low et al., 1881), 71.

79 'I have inscribed them to you, in few lines', Landor wrote to Wordsworth, and in a letter of 20 April 1822, Wordsworth responded: 'I am happy to hear of any intended Publication of yours and shall be proud to receive any public testimony of your esteem' (*LY* i, 123). The dedication has not survived, however. For Wordsworth's reaction to the *Imaginary Conversations*, see his letter to Landor of 11 December 1824 (*LY* i, 291).

80 *Imaginary Conversations of Literary Men and Statesmen* (3 vols; London: Taylor & Hessey, 1824), I, 336. The dialogue was expanded in the 2nd edition of 1826, in which Landor added a Latin 'inscription for Kosciusko'. Hazlitt, reviewing Landor's volumes in the *Edinburgh Review* in March 1824, was unimpressed by this particular dialogue: 'The dialogue between Kosciusko and Poniatowski (a subject capable of better things) is remarkable for nothing but a mawkish philanthropy, and a problematical defence of General Pichegru for betraying the Republic and leaguing with the Bourbons'; see *The Complete Works of William Hazlitt*, ed. P. P. Howe (21 vols; London: J. M. Dent, 1930–4), XVI, 259.

81 *The Fall of Robespierre* (Cambridge: W. H. Lunn and J. & J. Merrill, 1794), 12. Coleridge was also to echo these lines in 'Ode on the Departing Year', quoted above: 'Whose shrieks, whose screams were vain to stir / Loud-laughing, red-eyed Massacre!'.

82 *The Collection of Autograph Letters and Historical Documents formed by Alfred Morrison. The Blessington Papers*, ed. Alfred Morrison (2nd series, 1882–93;

London, 1895), 111. Landor goes on: 'I declare to you upon oath that I firmly believe myself superior to any duke, prince, king, emperor, or pope existing, as the best of these fellows is superior to the most sluggish and mangy turnspit in his dominions.'

83 *The Complete Works of Walter Savage Landor*, ed. Thomas Earle Welby and Stephen Wheeler (16 vols; London: Chapman & Hall, 1927–36), XV, 239.

84 *Prose Works*, I, 341.

85 Losh wrote in his diary on the 8th: 'Miss Wordsworth and Wordsworth . . . at Dinner Do. Tea & Supper'; and on the 9th: 'The Wordsworth's [sic] all night and at Breakfast. Walk with them'; quoted in Roe, *Radical Years*, 270. See also *EY*, 222n.

86 See Mark Reed, *Wordsworth: The Chronology of the Early Years, 1770–1799* (Cambridge, MA: Harvard University Press, 1967), 139n and Robert Woof and Stephen Hebron, *Towards Tintern Abbey* (Grasmere: The Wordsworth Trust, 1998), 84.

87 Roe, *Radical Years*, 270.

88 Roe, *Politics*, 128.

89 E. P. Thompson, 'Disenchantment or Default? A Lay Sermon', in C. C. O'Brien and W. D. Vanech, eds., *Power and Consciousness* (London and New York: University of London Press, 1969), 168–9.

90 See *MM* 5 (May 1798), 343–6 and *MM* 6 (July 1798), 20–1.

91 In 1801, Warner repaid the visit, calling in on 'the intellectual and philosophical Wordsworth' and meeting for the first time 'the soaring and radiant Coleridge': 'One of the most agreeable occurrences of the "Northern Tour" to myself and companion, was our introduction to Mr Coleridge; and his delightful society for three or four days, amid the romantic scenery of the lakes of Cumberland. It is quite possible that this highly-gifted man, may have long forgotten our ramble over those healthy mountains, and through those smiling valleys, in which his soul once delighted; – our call at the peaceful retreat of Wordsworth, – and our visit to Buttermere, and its ill-fated maiden: but, "the wear and tear" of thirty years, have not obliterated from *my* memory, these and other incidents of our temporary intercourse: impressed upon it, as they were, by the charms of his conversation; the flashings of his genius; the simplicity of his manners; and the ardour of his benevolence' (Warner, *Recollections*, II, 153–4 and note).

92 See Jacobus, '"Tintern Abbey"', 368, and Warner, *Walk*, 226.

93 Warner, *Walk*, 225, my emphasis; Jacobus, '"Tintern Abbey"', 368.

94 Jacobus, '"Tintern Abbey"', 368.

95 Warner, *Walk*, 224.

96 Ll. 43–50, 51–65, 68–71 and 87–99 of the text printed in Beth Darlington, 'Two Early Texts: *A Night-Piece* and *The Discharged Soldier*', in Jonathan Wordsworth, ed., *Bicentenary Wordsworth Studies* (Ithaca, NY and London: Cornell University Press, 1970), 434–5.

97 Roe, *Radical Years*, 143–4.
98 I quote the poem as first published in the *Morning Post* on 2 February 1803; my emphasis.
99 For Wordsworth on Beaupuy, see *The Prelude* (1805), IX, 294–543.
100 See Warner's account of Johnson's vocal skills on the summit of Craig-gwyn, Merionethshire, in *A Second Walk through Wales, in August and September 1798* (Bristol: R. Cruttwell, 1799), 182: 'A fine echo also lent its magical effects to make the spot more interesting, and regaled us highly by repeatedly reverberating the silver tone of J[ohnso]n's melodious voice.' Cf. also Elizabeth Sandford's account of a gathering at Stowey on 9 October 1797 comprising Wordsworth, Coleridge, Tom Poole and Poole's cousin, Penelope: 'Once Tom Poole, being there with his friends, begged Penelope to sing "Come, ever smiling Liberty!" (*Judas Maccabeus*) for Coleridge and Wordsworth. Many years afterwards she related the circumstances to her daughter, and told how she persistently selected another song. "I *could* not sing it", she said; "I knew what they meant with *their* liberty"'; *Thomas Poole and his Friends* (new edition; Over Stowey: Friarn Press, 1996), 135.

Chapter 4: Models of Bardic Jacobinism and Gratitude

1 *Life and Correspondence of Robert Southey*, ed. C. C. Southey (6 vols; London: Longman et al., 1849–50), V, 285.
2 Southey to Charles Danvers, 10 May 1802; *NLRS*, I, 276.
3 The poem given pride of place at the beginning of the first volume of Williams's collection, *Poems, Lyric and Pastoral* (1794), is, significantly, 'To Laudanum'. Cf. his friend David Samwell's lines: 'If magic Numbers ever won / The ear of Opium's eldest son, / Then may we hope Morganwg's Bard / Will claim thy somnolent regard, / Thy visions mild and soothing Pow'r / When pain assails the midnight hour'.
4 For Williams's acquaintance with Estlin, who 'held the bard in high esteem', see Waring, 134–5. In 1814, Williams published a Welsh translation of Estlin's *General Instructions in the Doctrines and Duties of Religion*.
5 Waring records that 'The Bard attended him to the place of embarkation, and was one of the last persons the Doctor conversed with upon British ground. Priestly's [*sic*] system of theology found in Edward Williams a partial, though not an implicit disciple; his science a warm and studious admirer; but his persecution on account of his opinions, rendered him an object of especial interest and sympathy, to this warm-hearted and free-spirited Welshman' (p. 134). For Williams's acquaintance with English men of letters, see Herbert G. Wright, 'The Relations of the Welsh Bard Iolo Morganwg with Dr. Johnson, Cowper and Southey', *Review of English Studies* 8 (1932), 129–38; *NLRS*, II, 436; and Waring, 86–94.

6   Williams had also been growled at by Dr Johnson: see Waring, 27–8.
7   *GM*, 59, ii (November 1789), 976–7 and 1035–6.
8   Interestingly, a letter of 9 August 1792 to his wife reveals that Williams lodged in London almost next door to the house in which that other famous eighteenth-century forger had committed suicide: 'I wish I was able to come home just to see you, and return. if the little ones are alive, take care of them. I should not have been in this world now but from the hope of still being of some help to them. it was from this street, and within a door or two, that poor *Chatterton* was obliged to force his way out of this good-for-nothing world' (NLW MS 21285E/811). See also NLW MS 21285E/812 for his next letter of 27 October 1792: 'I have but one hope left now, which is that I shall soon die, for it is impossible for me to be relieved any other way . . . Poor *Chatterton* who lived and died almost the next door to where I am found means, like myself, to keep his distresses unknown.'
9   See the following volumes by G. J. Williams: *Iolo Morganwg a Chywyddau'r Ychwanegiad* (Iolo Morganwg and the *Cywyddau* of the Appendix; Cardiff: University of Wales Press, 1926); *Traddodiad Llenyddol Morgannwg* (The Literary Tradition of Glamorgan; Cardiff: University of Wales Press, 1948); and his unfinished biography of Williams, *Iolo Morganwg* (Cardiff: University of Wales Press, 1956). See also Prys Morgan, *Iolo Morganwg* (Cardiff: University of Wales Press, 1975); Ceri W. Lewis, *Iolo Morganwg* (Caernarfon: Gwasg Pantycelyn, 1995); and Geraint H. Jenkins, *Facts, Fantasy and Fiction: The Historical Vision of Iolo Morganwg* (Aberystwyth: Centre for Advanced Welsh and Celtic Studies, 1997).
10 See Williams's letter of 30 October 1793 to his wife: 'I shall first translate the *Bardic Triads*. I have done a little of that and left it as a specimen of the work at some of the capital booksellers . . . I was yesterday at Mr Johnson St. Paul's Churchyard and he told me that Dr. Geddes, Dr. Aikin, and others of the first abilities spoke well of it' (NLW MS 21285E/822). See also his letter of 21 January 1794 to John Walters, in which he states that he knows Joseph Johnson well (NLW MS 21285E/826).
11 Blake, *Complete Writings*, ed. Geoffrey Keynes (Oxford: Oxford University Press, 1992), 383.
12 NLW MS 21285E/826.
13 NLW MS 21285E/850.
14 Cromwell was descended from the Williams family from Whitchurch and Llanisien, Glamorgan. See GJW, 83–5; Williams's undated letter to 'Miss [Hannah?] More', NLW MS 21286E/1023: 'I have . . . much of the enterprising spirit of my famous, or rather infamous, uncle *Oliver Cromwel* [*sic*], for I am of the family'; and his 'Hints for the History of my Life' (NLW MS 21387E/2): 'my Parents of respectable families my father's a collateral branch of the family from whom Oliver Cromwel was descended'.
15 NLW MS 21400C/32.

16 *SCPB*, IV, 364.
17 30 October 1793 (NLW MS 21285E/822).
18 NLW MS 21285E/838.
19 *An Appeal to Popular Opinion against Kidnapping and Murder* (London: J. S. Jordan, 1796), 48.
20 To John Walters on 9 January 1794, Williams wrote: 'to be serious matters have been carried too far. the public have been too sorely iritated [sic], too grossly insulted. The most violent *Aristocrate* [sic] that ever I knew on reading lately, where I was present, the acc^t. of the Kings signing the warrant for transporting *Palmer* & *Muir* to Botany Bay threw of [sic] his hat and wig and exclaimed *by G— he has signed his own Death Warrant*. the most violent sticklers for the *Constitution unreformed*, are offended at this proceeding' (NLW MS 21285E/824).
21 NLW MS 21285E/850.
22 *Lectures 1795*, 330. See also pp. 263 and note, 298, and *Watchman*, 41 and note.
23 Preserved amongst Williams's papers (NLW MS 21401E/35) are the minutes of a meeting of the SCI held on 18 May 1792.
24 The letter continues: 'I send you one [MS torn] last paper. let me know whether you had it. the [MS torn] them to News ment [sic] to be sent in Newspapers to all parts of the Kingdom' (NLW MS 21285E/848). What seems to be another hand has written below: 'the Cambrian Bard Mr Williams had he not too eager [sic] to sacrifice to the grim idol Democracy might have circulated this through England with general approbation.'
25 NLW MS 21285E/850; 19 February 1795.
26 NLW MS 21282E/376.
27 NLW MS 21283E/510; no date. Waring, 50, records that Taliesin Williams, Edward Williams's son, informed him that 'he never saw his father weep, except at the death of his own daughter, a grandchild, and that of Gilbert Wakefield'.
28 See NLW MS 1806E/665 for a letter of 31 October 1789 from the co-founder of the Society, Owain Myfyr, to Walter Davies: 'Rhydddid [sic] mewn Gwlad ac Eglwys yw amcan y Gymdeithas h. yw fod Dyn yn rhydd mewn perthynas iw Grefydd i ddilyn ei gydwybod ac nid yn ddarostyngedig iw dywys ai gaethiwo gan arall' (The aim of the Society is Freedom in State and Church – that is, that man is free in relation to his religion to be led by his conscience and not humbly to be led and imprisoned by another).
29 Roberts's work – with Jones's *Seren Tan Gwmmwl*, one of the most famous Welsh radical pamphlets of the decade – criticizes the Established Church, the tithe system, Methodists, lawyers and the *hunglwyf* (sleeping-sickness) of the Welsh, hampered by their belief in predestination.
30 For an account of these *eisteddfodau*, see G. J. Williams, 'Eisteddfodau'r Gwyneddigion', *Y Llenor* 14 (1935), 11–22 and 15 (1936), 88–96.
31 Coleridge's phrase in *Lectures 1795*, 303.

32   NLW 21285E/841.
33   NLW MS 21285E/843; no date. See also his letter to Peggy of 23 May 1794: 'I will write again tomorrow and will send you a *fictitious* Letter, which you must write to me word for word and letter to letter according to the copy . . . I know my reasons. they are the strongest that can be imagined, but you know nothing of them' (NLW MS 21285E/836).
34   NLW MS 21285E/837; no date.
35   Waring, 104–5.
36   NLW MS 21285E/824. Just as Thelwall was to resort to lecturing on abuses of power in ancient Rome after the Two Bills became law in December 1795, so Williams goes on in this letter to inform Walters that he will avail himself of the cover of more oblique political parables: 'it would have been well for Archy Mac Blunder [Reeves] and his Bear leaders if he had not been the means of acquainting *daring writers* that any one might write for the Kingdom of *Eutopia* [sic], whatever he pleased, provided he applied nothing to the Gov^t. of England: this is *very good*, and I shall soon avail myself of this information. *truth* and its *arguments* will have no less effect in *Utopian politics* than in *Tom Paines* [sic] pamphlets'.
37   NLW MS 21285E/842.
38   Williams was the principal founder in 1801–2 of the Welsh Unitarian Society of South Wales, and it was he who drew up its rules and constitution. In 1812 appeared a volume of his Unitarian hymns, *Salmau yr Eglwys yn yr Anialwch* (The Psalms of the Church in the Wilderness), with a second volume published posthumously in 1834. In a letter of 26 March 1798 to Miss Barker, Williams protested: 'In Religion I profess myself a *Unitarian Christian* . . . *Parsons* who ought to and actually do, know better malevolently attach most unfair ideas to the word *Unitarian.* sedition, Rebellion, Regicide, and I know not what. an *Unitarian*, say the Parsons, is one that denies his God, a disciple of Tom Paine. this is absolute villainy' (NLW MS 21285E/862). To David Williams on 8 January 1811, Williams declared: 'I am possibly the most thorough paced Unitarian that has yet declared himself. *One* God in my Theology – *One* primary original principle of matter of which all other secondary principles are only so many different modifications and resolveable into their original state' (NLW MS 21285E/886). In a letter of 29 April 1822 to a Mr Christie, Williams describes himself as 'The oldest Unitarian in Wales, and I believe the only one now living of M^r. Lindsey's first Congregation in Essex Street' (NLW MS 21286E/988).
39   No date; NLW MS 21396E/35.
40   No date, but 1794; NLW MS 21285E/837.
41   To Peggy, 19 February 1795; NLW MS 21285E/850.
42   See NLW MS 21396E/21–2, 33 and 35.
43   *Lectures 1795*, 64.
44   NLW MS 21392F/9.

45   NLW MS 21392F/35–8.
46   NLW MS 21285E/862.
47   See *Tribune*, I, 254.
48   NLW MS 21286E/1025.
49   NLW MS 21280E/49.
50   See Waring, 83–6.
51   Ralph A. Manogue, 'The Plight of James Ridgway, London Bookseller and Publisher, and the Newgate Radicals, 1792–7', *WC* 27, 3 (Summer 1996), 161.
52   See ibid., 161–2, and the same author's 'Southey and William Winterbotham: New Light on an Old Quarrel', *Charles Lamb Bulletin* NS 38 (April 1982), 110.
53   Undated manuscript; NLW MS 21401E/33. This manuscript is incomplete; another stanza refers to John Reeves: 'No jail I dread, no venal court, / And where belorded fools resort, / I scare them with a frown: / John Reeves and all his gang defeat, / And if a tyrant King I meet, / Clench fist and knock him down'; see *Gwaith Iolo Morganwg* (The Works of Iolo Morganwg), ed. Thomas Christopher Evans (Llanuwchllyn: Ab Owen, 1913), 44–6. See also Waring's account, pp. 47–8: '"Mr Bard of Liberty, you are to understand that the only liberty allowed you here, will be to walk out the way you came in." "O, very well, Mr Gaoler, by all means; and I wish no Bard of Liberty may ever meet with worse treatment, than being told to walk out of a prison." This smart and amusing colloquy is given verbatim from the Bard's lips.'
54   NLW MS 21424E/2; the date is probably 1795.
55   See the reviews in the *Analytical Review* 18 (February 1794), 196–200 and the *Critical Review* 11 (June 1794), 168–75. The latter comments: 'We are here presented with the poems of a genuine Welsh bard, an original genius, who derives his poetical descent from Taliessin, and his inspiration from nature, for his situation in life is no higher than that of a working stone-mason . . . A flowing and easy melody in a variety of measures; images and manners truly pastoral; enlarged ideas and glowing sentiments of liberty, civil and religious . . . which for sublimity of conception and loftiness of sentiment, may bear a comparison with some of the most esteemed in the language.' For Williams's letters to his wife reporting such praise, see NLW MS 21285E/825, 835, 847–8 and 850.
56   Coleridge's copy is now at the Victoria University Library, Toronto. On the fly-leaf preceding the title-pages of volumes I and II, Williams has written 'From the Author'. The title-page of volume I shows 'STC'. Referring to the seventh of Williams's 'Poetical Triades' ('The three principal considerations of Poetical description: what is obvious; what instantly engages the affections; and what is strikingly characteristic'), Coleridge has written on the final printed page of volume II (p. 256): '‡ I suppose, rather what p we ~~frequently~~ recollect / to have frequently seen in nature, though / not in the descriptions of it'. On the following page appears a list drawn up by Coleridge: 'The Harp

/ The Crwth / The Bow of twisted twigs / The Hirlas – a wild bull's horn / Rodris shield / Rodericus filius Geni Regis / The Leek'. See also Coffman, *Coleridge's Library*, 233 and H. O. Dendurent, 'The Coleridge Collection in Victoria University Library, Toronto', *WC* 5, 4 (Autumn 1974), 261.

57   *PLP*, I, xiv. See also NLW MS 21392F/66.

58   Williams often rebuked his brothers, Miles, John and Thomas, who had emigrated to Jamaica, for profiting from 'that most horrid traffick in human blood' (NLW MS 21387E/8). For Williams on the slave-trade and his refusal to accept an annuity and an inheritance from his brothers, see GJW, 233; Clare Taylor, 'Edward Williams ("Iolo Morganwg") and his Brothers: A Jamaican Inheritance', *Transactions of the Honourable Society of Cymmrodorion* (1980), 35–43; and Waring, 58–63 and 107–8: 'In the year 1797 he opened a shop in Cowbridge, where he sold books, stationery, and groceries: among the latter he introduced East Indian sugar, because it was the produce of free labour, and he wished to promote every measure that could tend to discourage the slave trade and its atrocities. This commodity was thus announced by a paper exhibited in his window, "*East India Sweets, uncontaminated with human gore*"'.

59   For this translation, see the 'Sketch of British Bardism' by Williams and William Owen Pughe in *Heroic Elegies*, p. xlii.

60   J. Kyrle Fletcher's 'Iolo Morganwg's List of Subscribers', *Journal of the Welsh Bibliographical Society* 6 (July 1943), 39–41 wildly identifies Jean-Jacques Rousseau, Samuel Richardson the novelist and Edward Gibbon the historian as among the subscribers.

61   *PLP*, II, 160–8, 193–216 and 217–56.

62   For an excellent discussion of *Poems, Lyric and Pastoral* and its place in the Welsh and English poetic tradition, see Gwyneth Lewis's unpublished University of Oxford doctoral thesis, 'Eighteenth-century Literary Forgeries, with Special Reference to the Work of Iolo Morganwg' (MS DPhil c. 8975, 1991), 167–202.

63   *PLP*, II, 186 contains his 'Sonnet, To Hope, On resolving to emigrate to America'.

64   *PLP*, I, pp. xi and xix–xx. Williams refers to Reeves a second time in *PLP*, II, 37n.: '[The Hottentot] dresses his hair well with any kind of grease, and then powders it, *à la mode de Londres*, with fine pulverised *cow-dung*, just in the same manner as the *Cockneys* use pomatum and powder; with this difference, that the *Hottentot* never imports, like MR. REEVES, any *bears* from *Russia*, but contents himself with the fat of his own *hog*'.

65   See, for example, NLW MS 21387E/9.

66   See *PLP*, I, 144–5 and 206; II, 106, 109 and 143.

67   Attempting to assuage Peggy's fears regarding his radical enterprises, Williams wrote to her on 6 April 1793: 'I shall send you a printed sheet soon that contains the severest thing that ever I wrote against government, and then you

will be able to judge whether I attempt to raise disturbances or not. – it is an *Ode on converting a sword into [a] pruning hook*' (NLW MS 21285E/817).
68 See *PLP*, II, 160–8 and 203–16.
69 NLW MS 21392F/5.
70 See *Heroic Elegies*, p. xxvii.
71 NLW MS 21281E/187.
72 NLW MS 21285E/808.
73 NLW MS 21285E/826.
74 A note appended to the poem runs: 'At OXFORD, a *bedoctored Song-wright*, divesting [the song] of its original pacific sentiments, pinned an additional stanza (like a dish-clout) to its tail, full of, doubtless very proper, severity against poor TOM PAINE. – *Alas! poor Song!*'
75 NLW MS 21392F/89; see also NLW MS 21392F/88. Letters of May and November 1794 to his wife show that Williams was summoned a number of times to Carlton House (NLW MS 21285E/836 and 845–6).
76 Waring, 103–4.
77 NLW MS 21285E/839.
78 See NLW MS 21285E/851 for his letter of 15 April 1795 to his wife on the subject, and NLW MS 21392F/67. See also Waring, 114.
79 NLW MS 21392F/94.
80 NLW MS 21392F/91.
81 NLW MS 21283E/601a. Some of his other papers show Williams having fun with irreverent dedications and identities: his fictional work, 'A push at the pillars of Priestcraft. By Samson Sancullotte [*sic*]', is dedicated to 'M^r. Sir John Ketch Esqr. . . . Lord Viscount Newgate, and Duke of Tyburn' (NLW MS 21400C/28a). See also NLW MS 21400C/28 and 28b.
82 For contemporary documents relating to the founding of the *gorsedd*, see Thomas Shankland, 'Hanes Dechreuad "Gorsedd Beirdd Ynys Prydain"' (The History of the Founding of 'The *Gorsedd* of the Bards of the Island of Britain'), *Y Llenor* 3 (1924), 94–102; William Ll. Davies, 'David Samwell (1751–1798)', *Transactions of the Honourable Society of Cymmrodorion* (1926–7), 98–102; and the second instalment of Tecwyn Ellis's essay, 'Bardd y Brenin, Iolo Morganwg a Derwyddiaeth' (The King's Bard, Iolo Morganwg and Druidism), *National Library of Wales Journal* 13 (1963–4), 224–34.
83 *GM* 62, ii (1792), 956–7. The *Morning Chronicle* piece is reproduced in William Ll. Davies, 'David Samwell', 99–101.
84 The title-page shows 1792, but some time during the first six months of 1793 is a more likely date. For the evidence supporting this assumption, see Glenda Carr, *William Owen Pughe* (Cardiff: University of Wales Press, 1983), 54.
85 *Heroic Elegies*, p. lxii. Williams generously repaid the compliment at the head of his section on the Bardic Triads in *PLP*, II, 233: 'Of all modern bardic historians, not one has given us a single word of truth, or any thing like good

sense, but Mr. W. OWEN, prefixed to his lately published translation from the *Welsh* of the Poetical Works of *Llywarch Hên*'.

86 For discussions of this radical appropriation and invention of the past, see Chapter 2, note 83.

87 Pughe's note runs: 'By this is meant what is generally conceived amongst the *English* of the term *Druidism*, which is a mistake, by giving the appellation of a particular branch to the whole of the order; for as a matter of convenience an appropriate set of Bards were distinguished by the name *Derwyddon*, or *Druids*, to give notoriety and discriminate visibility to the religious functionaries.'

88 Pughe's note adds: 'The society of *Friends*, or the people called *Quakers*'.

89 *Heroic Elegies*, pp. xxiv–xxvii and liv–lv.

90 Gwyn A. Williams, *The Search for Beulah Land* (New York: Holmes & Meier Publishers, 1980), 33.

91 Waring, 34.

92 See W. Philip Williams, 'David Williams', *Welsh Outlook* 13 (1926), 90; David Williams, 'A Priest of Nature', *Welsh Review* 5 (1946), 41; and Williams, *Beulah Land*, 17.

93 Williams, *Beulah Land*, 33.

94 For the identification of Pughe, and a full account of the dialogue, see my article cited in Chapter 2, note 30.

95 Major petition campaigns against the slave trade were organized in 1788 and 1792; during the latter campaign, 519 petitions, involving as many as 400,000 people, were signed. See J. R. Oldfield, *Popular Politics and British Anti-Slavery: The Mobilisation of Public Opinion against the Slave Trade* (Manchester: Manchester University Press, 1995).

96 *MM* 6 (August 1798), 93–4.

97 For the Bardic beliefs behind the ceremony, see *Heroic Elegies*, pp. xxix–xxx, xlvii–xlviii, li–lii and lv–lix.

98 Southey records that in Williams's bookshop, 'the Reflections on the French Revolution were entered as the Gospel according to St. Burke; and a collection of Jacobinical pamphlets as Directions for Duck-milking, a title which made all the Welsh farmers send for [it]'. He goes on to tell how the spy David Curtis, after being sold a book bearing the title *The Rights of Man* and gleefully declaring 'This shall go to Billy Pitt', opened it to exclaim 'Damn the rascal – the Bible, by God!' (*SCPB*, IV, 364). See also Waring's version, 108–9.

99 NLW MS 21400C/9.

100 Lewis, 'Eighteenth-Century Literary Forgeries', 202.

101 Ibid., 208. Williams's *History*, which was advertised in the *Cambrian Register* 2 (1796), viin. and in *Hist. of Mon.*, appendix III, 13, never appeared.

102 *Madoc* (London: Longman, Hurst, Rees & Orme, 1805), 486. For references in *Madoc* to *Poems, Lyric and Pastoral*, see 461–2, 487 and 498.

103 *NLRS*, I, 394.

104 *The Mythology and Rites of the British Druids* (London: J. Booth, 1809), 60.

105 Quoted in Trevor Herbert and Gareth Elwyn Jones, eds., *The Remaking of Wales in the Eighteenth Century* (Cardiff: University of Wales Press, 1988), 162.
106 NLW MS 1885B/44–5.
107 *Cambrian Register* 2 (1799 [for the year 1796]), 464–5.
108 *Notebooks*, I (Notes), #605.
109 For Coleridge's critiques of Godwin in his correspondence, see *CL*, I, 86, 102, 115, 138, 213, 247, 253, 267–8 and 293. For a valuable discussion of Coleridge and Godwin, see *Lectures 1795*, pp. lxvii–lxxx.
110 See Nicola Trott, 'The Coleridge Circle and the "Answer to Godwin"', *Review of English Studies* NS 41 (May 1990), 212–29.
111 *CL*, I, 204 (late April 1796).
112 Thelwall's letter to Coleridge in which he made this charge is lost; Coleridge quotes it in *CL*, I, 212.
113 *CL*, I, 214.
114 *Lectures on Education* (3 vols; London: J. Bell, 1789), II, 166.
115 William Godwin, *An Enquiry concerning Political Justice* (2 vols; London: G. G. & J. Robinson, 1793), I, 83.
116 See an entry of 1798 in Godwin's notebook quoted in Kegan Paul, *William Godwin*, I, 294–5; a passage added to the 2nd edition of Godwin's *Memoirs of the Author of a Vindication of the Rights of Woman*, ed. Richard Holmes (Harmondsworth: Penguin, 1987), 274–5; and the preface to Godwin's *St Leon* (4 vols; London: G. G. & J. Robinson, 1799).
117 See B. Sprague Allen, 'William Godwin's Influence upon John Thelwall', *Publications of the Modern Language Association of America* 37 (1922), 662–82.
118 See *Tribune*, I, 229–36.
119 *Notebooks*, I (Notes), #605.
120 Quoted in GJW, 91.
121 Ibid., 92–3.
122 *PLP*, I, pp. xv–xvi.
123 GJW, 165.
124 NLW MS 21285E/852.
125 *PLP*, I, p. xiv.
126 NLW MS 21285E/862.
127 See *CL*, I, 102.
128 *Lectures 1795*, 162–4.
129 *Watchman*, 98–9; see also pp. 194–8. In a letter of 10 May 1796 to Coleridge in which he offers a consideration of Coleridge's *Poems on Various Subjects*, Thelwall got his own back, ironically quoting 'Modern Patriotism' in the middle of his literary criticism: '[Effusions] 26, 27 & 28 breathe the very soul of love & fancy. Such warmth with such delicacy I think I have never met with before. If I were *jealous of honour* [sic] *of a wife, a sister, or a daughter*, I should fear such verses, more than *speculative opinions* I have heard of'; see Gibbs, 'Unpublished Letter', 86–7.

130 *Notebooks*, I (Text), #330 (15) and I (Text and Notes), #605.
131 *Lectures 1795*, 162. See also pp. 96, 156–7 and 164.
132 See *Notebooks*, I (Text and Notes), #174 (16). See also Coleridge to Josiah Wade, 27 January 1796, on Erasmus Darwin's atheism: 'He bantered me on the subject of religion . . . *all at once he makes up his mind* on such important subjects, as whether we be the outcasts of a blind idiot called Nature, or the children of an all-wise and infinitely good God' (*CL*, I, 177).
133 *PLP*, II, 200–1.
134 See, for example, *PLP*, I, 106 and 115; II, 179–80, 190, 197, 204, 215, 244, 250 and 251.
135 *Heroic Elegies*, p. lvii.
136 See Gary Kelly, *The English Jacobin Novel, 1780–1805* (Oxford: Clarendon Press, 1976), 204–5.
137 Wu, *1770–1799*, 161.
138 See T. E. Casson, 'Wordsworth and Theocritus', *Times Literary Supplement* (11 September 1937), 656.
139 See Russell Noyes, 'Wordsworth and Burns', *Publications of the Modern Language Association of America* 59 (1944), 817 and 820, and Stephen Parrish, *The Art of the Lyrical Ballads* (Cambridge, MA: Harvard University Press, 1973), 176–7. See also *EY*, 255–6.
140 This stanza was quoted by Thelwall (with 'harshness' instead of 'hardness') on the title-page of his *Reply to the Calumnies, Misrepresentations, and Literary Forgeries, contained in the Anonymous Observations on his Letter to the Editor of the Edinburgh Review* (Glasgow, 1804), which was motivated by Francis Jeffrey's sneering review in the *Edinburgh Review* (April 1803) of Thelwall's *Poems, Chiefly Written in Retirement*.
141 Commenting on the strange conflation of professions in Wordsworth's stanza, James H. Averill has suggested that Wordsworth is thinking of a particular 'physician-philosopher' – Erasmus Darwin; see Averill, 'Wordsworth and "Natural Science": The Poetry of 1798', *Journal of English and Germanic Philology* 77 (1978), 245–6.
142 *Prose Works*, I, 139.
143 Lucy Newlyn, *Reading, Writing, and Romanticism: The Anxiety of Reception* (Oxford: Clarendon Press, 2000), 126.
144 NLW MS 21419E/24.
145 *PLP*, II, 218 and 255.
146 *Prose Works*, I, 124.
147 See *The Poetical Works of William Wordsworth*, ed. William Knight (8 vols; London: Macmillan, 1896), II, 77.
148 See Jonathan Wordsworth, *William Wordsworth: The Borders of Vision* (Oxford: Clarendon Press, 1982), 310–12.
149 *EY*, 100–1.
150 See Moorman, *William Wordsworth*, 60–1.

151 *Critical Review* 11 (June 1794), 169.
152 See *PLP*, II, 102: '*Rustic* is often more usefully intelligent than *scholastic* philosophy', and cf. Wordsworth's passage on the Infant Prodigy in *The Prelude* (1805), V, 290–349 which, like 'The Learned Ignorants' and 'A Poet's Epitaph', contrasts wisdom and sensitivity (learned from contact with Nature and from human relations) with mere knowledge.
153 See *Borderers* (1797–1799), III. v. 24–33; *The Prelude* (1805), X, 818–29; and *The Prelude* (1805), XI, 42–73.
154 *Lectures 1795*, 165.
155 Ibid., 158–9.
156 See GJW, 329–32, 336 and 455.
157 Interesting in the light of the above discussion is Wordsworth's statement in the first of the *Essays upon Epitaphs*: 'But the writer of an epitaph is not an anatomist, who dissects the internal frame of mind'; *Prose Works*, II, 57.
158 *PLP*, I, pp. xv, xvii. For Williams as stonemason, see GJW, 344–67. Many of the monuments and graves Williams designed and inscribed survive, and among his papers are numerous designs for monuments and memorial inscriptions – see, for example, NLW MS 21417E/1–37 and 21418E/1–22. 21418E/2 contains drafts of his father's tombstone inscription.
159 *Fenwick Notes*, 37.
160 *WC* 13, 1 (Winter 1982), 35–6.
161 *Gwaith y Parchedig Evan Evans*, ed. D. Silvan Evans (Caernarfon: H. Humphreys, 1876), 51.
162 Ibid., 52.
163 The ruins at Gwernyclepa lie in the woods a mile or so from the present village of Basaleg. Basaleg was also the name of one of Ifor Hael's other halls in the area (a third was called Y Wenallt), but nothing remained of it in the later eighteenth century. See also *PLP*, I, 196–7 and *Barddoniaeth Dafydd ab Gwilym*, ed. Owen Jones and William Owen (London: H. Baldwin, 1789), pp. vi–vii.
164 See GJW, 378. Williams returned to Gwernyclepa in 1813. In a letter to his son he wrote: 'I made some sketches, which when finished you shall see. I had been there once before with the Revd. Evan Evans . . . but he had no patience then to stay and trace all the ruins and vestiges of this interesting ruin' (GJW, 378n.).
165 For a complementary discussion of 'To Ivor the Liberal' and 'Simon Lee', see David Simpson, *Wordsworth's Historical Imagination: The Poetry of Displacement* (New York and London: Methuen, 1987), 151–5; Simpson's emphasis is very different from my own.
166 *Hist. of Mon.*, appendix LXIII, 153–5: 'Ifor Hael . . . the Generous Lord of Maeselag, the Wenallt and Gwern-y-Cleppa . . . [His] House, at Maeselag [*sic*], has disappeared years ago. Gwern-y-Cleppa has been a heap of ruins a century at least; the paths where the Muse loved to tread are now the haunts of the moping owl, as the Rev. Evan Evans, in Dissertatio de Bardis, said of this place . . . Gwenallt still remains a large fair building, in the manner of the age of Ifor Hael.'

167 *PLP*, I, 193–5.
168 Moorman, *William Wordsworth*, 383.
169 *Lyrical Ballads, 1798*, ed. Thomas Hutchinson (3rd edition; London: Duckworth, 1920), 234. See also Émile Legouis, *The Early Life of William Wordsworth 1770–1798*, tr. J.W. Matthews (New York: Russell & Russell, 1965), 309–10.
170 Legouis, *Early Life*, 309.

Chapter 5: Models of Fellowship and Fulfilment

1 *CL*, I, 305; see also *CL*, I, 276–7.
2 Thompson, 'Disenchantment', 159.
3 Roe, 'Nether Stowey', 76.
4 *MM* 8 (August 1799), 532.
5 See Michael Scrivener, 'Jacobin Romanticism: John Thelwall's "Wye" Essay and "Pedestrian Excursion"', in Peter J. Kitson, ed., *Placing and Displacing Romanticism* (Aldershot: Ashgate, 2001), 82–3: 'The sociological observations predate Cobbett's by several decades and in some respects are superior to Cobbett's: Thelwall dramatizes himself far less, generates far fewer simplistic myths about an imaginary past, provides more information about the lives of the rural poor, and does not scapegoat Jews and Quakers'.
6 *MM* 8 (August 1799), 532.
7 *MM* 8 (September 1799), 618.
8 *MM* 8 (September 1799), 619.
9 Scrivener, 'Jacobin Romanticism', 85.
10 Quoted in Roe, *Politics*, 128; see also 127–9.
11 *Tribune*, II, 16–17. For Thelwall on the isolation of 'people of rank', who travel 'inclosed in a vehicle of modern luxury, called a coach or a post-chaise', and are therefore isolated from true contact with the rural people, see *Tribune*, II, 328–9, and cf. Coleridge's poem 'Perspiration: A Travelling Eclogue' in a letter to Southey of 6 July 1794, the day after he had set off in the company of Joseph Hucks on his own pedestrian excursion of Wales: 'The Dust flies smothering, as on clatt'ring Wheels/ Loath'd Aristocracy careers along' (*CL*, I, 84).
12 *MM* 8 (November 1799), 783.
13 For *The Peripatetic* and *The Recluse*, see Judson Stanley Lyon, *The Excursion: A Study* (New Haven, CT: Yale University Press, 1950), 35–7.
14 *Tribune*, II, 33.
15 *Peripatetic*, I, viii.
16 *Romanticism*, 3, 1 (1997), 137–8.
17 *MM* 8 (September 1799), 617.
18 *MM* 9 (February 1800), 16–19.
19 *MM* 9 (April 1800), 229.

20 *MM* 12 (September 1801), 106.
21 *MM* 12 (October 1801), 198.
22 *MM* 12 (November 1801), 307. The *Pharsalia* records the war between Caesar and Pompey. It displays a notable sympathy with the latter, the opponent of Caesar's autocratic authority, and its contemporary radical resonance would have been obvious to the assembled company. Southey's epic *Joan of Arc*, to which Coleridge contributed, deals – again with an obvious contemporary application – with the French fight for liberty against the English. See Coleridge's letter to Thelwall of 19 November 1796: 'Of course, you have read the Joan of Arc. Homer is the Poet for the warrior – Milton for the Religionist – Tasso for Women – Robert Southey for the Patriot' (*CL*, I, 258).
23 *MM* 12 (November 1801), 308.
24 See Scrivener, 'Jacobin Romanticism', 80.
25 *The Prelude* (1799), I, 290 and 294.
26 In a letter to Coleridge of 10 May 1796 commenting on Coleridge's *Poems* of 1796, Thelwall remarked: 'The ascent of Brockley comb is truly enchanting. The lively and varied powers of description were never more successfully exerted'; see Gibbs, 'Unpublished Letter', 86.
27 With the Pantisocratic scheme in mind, Southey wrote to H. W. Bedford on 22 August 1794: 'When Coleridge and I are sawing down a tree we shall discuss metaphysics; criticise poetry when hunting a buffalo, and write sonnets whilst following the plough' (*NLRS*, I, 72).
28 Rieder, *Wordsworth's Counterrevolutionary Turn*, 196 and 198.
29 *CL*, I, 351.
30 See Coleridge's letter to John Chubb, *CL*, I, 342–3.
31 *CL*, I, 343–4.
32 Walsh to John King, quoted in Roe, *Radical Years*, 258.
33 *CL*, I, 334: a letter to Southey – whom Wordsworth, of course, had displaced in Coleridge's affections.
34 *CL*, I, 391.
35 See Sandford, *Thomas Poole*, 133–4, and Roe, 'Nether Stowey', 76.
36 'Public Virtues, Private Vices: Reading Between the Lines of Wordsworth's "Anecdote for Fathers"', in David Simpson, ed., *Subject to History: Ideology, Class, Gender* (Ithaca, NY, and London: Cornell University Press, 1991), 175.
37 Michael Scrivener, 'The Rhetoric and Context of John Thelwall's "Memoir"', in G. A. Rosso and Daniel P. Watkins, eds., *Spirits of Fire: English Romantic Writers and Contemporary Historical Methods* (Rutherford, NJ: Farleigh Dickinson University Press, 1990), 123.
38 *Poems*, p. xliv.
39 *Poems*, p. i.
40 Thelwall's appeal is a politicized, personalized version of the call at the end of the Preface: 'I have one request to make of my Reader, which is, that in judging these Poems he would decide by his own feelings genuinely, and not

by reflection upon what will probably be the judgment of others . . . I have therefore to request that the Reader would abide independently by his own feelings, and that if he finds himself affected he would not suffer such conjectures to interfere with his pleasure' (*Prose Works*, I, 154).

41 *Poems*, p. xxxvi. At the end of October 1797, he told Thomas Hardy that his small farm at Llyswen was 'as desirable a literary retreat as Fancy could have suggested' (quoted in Thompson, 'Jacobin Fox', 111). On 24 May 1798, he wrote again to Hardy from Llyswen: 'As for the French Directory and its faction, nothing appears to be further from their design than to leave one atom of liberty either to their own or to any nation . . . But what have we to do with Directories or politics? Peaceful shades of Llyswen! shelter me beneath your luxuriant foliage: lull me to forgetfulness, ye murmuring waters of the Wye. Let me be part farmer and fisherman. But no more politics – no more politics in this bad world!'; quoted in J. Holland Rose, *William Pitt and the Great War* (London: G. Bell, 1911), 352n.

42 *Poems*, pp. xxxvi–xxxvii.

43 The ferocious Welsh warrior was a Roos Davies. Davies was fined sixpence and bound over to keep the peace for two years, 'The Defendant having pleaded guilty and the prosecutor inclining to be lenient' (quoted in Thompson, 'Jacobin Fox', 117 and n.). Jeering at Thelwall's experience at the hands of violent anti-jacobin thugs in the provinces during his lecture tour of 1796–7, Francis Jeffrey in his *Observations on Mr Thelwall's Letter to the Editor of the Edinburgh Review* (Edinburgh, 1804), 15–16, refers to Davies as 'a rustic royalist'. In his *Reply to the Calumnies, Misrepresentations, and Literary Forgeries, Contained in the Anonymous Observations on His Letter to the Editor of the Edinburgh Review* (Glasgow, 1804), 26 (his reply to Jeffrey's work quoted above), Thelwall stated that Davies's assault had its origins in a dispute about a watercourse, whereas the implication in the 'Prefatory Memoir' is that the attack was politically motivated.

44 Roderick Gwynne wrote to the Duke of Portland on 25 April 1798: '[Thelwall] is intimately acquainted with a man in Brecon, who is a member of a Club notorious for their seditious sentiments; and he constantly writes and receives from twelve to twenty letters daily; his correspondents are supposed to be members of the Corresponding Society', and on 30 April 1798 Edward Edwards reported: 'He lives in the Parish of Llyswen about seven miles distant from this Town, and writes and receives . . . a vast number of Letters by every post. But what does not a little add to my Suspicions about him is this, that he goes once a Fortnight to a Society of Jacobins at the Crown and Sceptre in the City of Hereford' (probably the remains of the Hereford Philanthropic Society); see P. J. Corfield and Chris Evans, 'John Thelwall in Wales: New Documentary Evidence', *Bulletin of the Institute of Historical Research* 59 (1986), 236.

45 For Thelwall's graphic accounts of the inclemencies and 'inundations' he faced at Llyswen, see his articles 'The Phenomena of the Wye, during the Winter of 1797–8', *MM* 5 (May 1798), 343–6 and *MM* 6 (July 1798), 20–1.

On 20 September 1799, Thelwall wrote to Thomas Hardy stating that he was 'almost harassed & tormented to death by the perverseness of the season' (quoted in Thompson, 'Jacobin Fox', 120).

46 *MM* 9 (July 1800), 532.
47 See *CL*, I, 655–6.
48 *Poems*, p. xxxiv.
49 I disagree, therefore, with Kelvin Everest, who argues that Thelwall is referring to Coleridge here as an example of the 'generous perseverance' he encountered; see Kelvin Everest, *Coleridge's Secret Ministry: The Context of the Conversation Poems, 1795–1798* (Hassocks, Sussex: Harvester Press, 1979), 127.
50 Quoted in Thompson, 'Jacobin Fox', 111–12.
51 Coleridge wrote to Thelwall at Llyswen on 30 January 1798 stating: 'I wrote back to Dr B.[eddoes] that I believed you would probably accomplish your plan by the assistance of your friends; but that if you had occasion for his *individual* assistance, I would inform him as soon as I heard from you' (*CL*, I, 382).
52 *Poems*, p. xli.
53 '"In City Pent": Echo and Allusion in Wordsworth, Coleridge and Lamb, 1797–1801', *Review of English Studies* NS 32 (November 1981), 408.
54 Lucy Newlyn, *Coleridge, Wordsworth, and the Language of Allusion* (Oxford: Clarendon Press, 1986), p. vii.
55 Magnuson, *Lyrical Dialogue*, 318 and 18.
56 Ibid., pp. x and 32.
57 Roe, 'Nether Stowey', 68.
58 Gibbs, 'Unpublished Letter', 85.
59 See *CL*, I, 351. Though 'much pleased' with the poem, Coleridge took Thelwall to task for 'pedantry' and other 'inaccuracies' of expression and for using '*corporealizing*' epithets to describe Stella ('thy mother's downy breast').
60 Judith Thompson, 'An Autumnal Blast', 427–56.
61 Cf. ll. 186–207 of the 'Letter to Sara Hutchinson' and ll. 96–117 of 'Dejection: An Ode'. Cf. also the letter a convalescing Coleridge sent Thomas Poole on 1 February 1801, nine days after writing to Thelwall: 'O my dear dear Friend! That you were with me by the fireside of my Study here, that I might talk it over with you to the Tune of this Night Wind that pipes it's thin doleful climbing sinking Notes like a child that has lost it's way and is crying aloud, half in grief and half in the hope to be heard by it's Mother' (*CL*, II, 669).
62 Newlyn, '"In City Pent"', 410.
63 There are other echoes of Thelwall in 'Frost at Midnight': lines 10–11 – 'Sea, hill, and wood, / This populous village! Sea, and hill, and wood' – are indebted to Thelwall's lines in 'On leaving the Bottoms of Glocestershire' (sent in manuscript to Coleridge with 'To the Infant Hampden'): 'For I must leave ye, pleasant haunts! Brakes, bourns, / And populous hill, and dale, and pendant woods'.
64 See *Poems*, 143: ''Twas for mankind I suffer'd – for the cause / For which a Hampden fought, a Sidney bled'.

65 It has not been noted that Wordsworth the bereaved father was to echo Thelwall's reference to his wife here – 'my heart's best pride' – in his description of his daughter Catherine, 'long after her death' (*Fenwick Notes*, 21), in 'Surprised by Joy': 'Knowing my heart's best treasure was no more'.
66 Newlyn, ' "In City Pent" ', 411.
67 Judith Thompson, 'An Autumnal Blast', 429.
68 Ibid., 438 and 434.
69 Ibid., 435–6.
70 *MY* ii, 361.
71 *LY* iii, 641.
72 *Edinburgh Review* 2 (April 1803), 202.
73 *Poems*, p. xlii.
74 Ibid., p. xli.
75 *MM* 9 (February 1800), 94.
76 See Wu, *1800–1815*, 220.
77 Writing to Thelwall, soon after he had emerged from his exile, to offer advice on the publication of the *Poems*, Coleridge commented: 'Paternal Tears instead of Poems on that particular subject is a quaint &, at the same time, trite conceit. To call a poem *a Tear* is quite Italian – Milton was young enough to be your Son when he used the phrase "melodious Tear" ' (*CL*, II, 723).
78 Coleridge had included a copy of his *Poems on Various Subjects* in his first letter to Thelwall of late April 1796 (*CL*, I, 204–5), and in a letter of 10 May, Thelwall described the sequence of 'effusions' in Coleridge's volume as having 'considerable merit' (Gibbs, 'Unpublished Letter', 86). Thelwall might therefore be taking his cue from Coleridge's volume in describing his own anguished poems as 'effusions'.
79 *CL*, II, 668.
80 Magnuson, *Lyrical Dialogue*, 170.
81 *Poems Written in Close Confinement in the Tower and Newgate, under a Charge of High Treason* (London, 1795), 19.
82 *Poems*, pp. xxviii–xxix.
83 See *Life*, 224–5.
84 For another discussion of the poem, see Roe, *Politics*, 81–2.
85 *Poems*, 143.
86 Lamb, *Letters* I, 117.
87 See *CL*, I, 334–6
88 *CL*, I, 349–50. This is the letter that also offers an assessment of Thelwall's 'On leaving the Bottoms of Glocestershire' and 'To the Infant Hampden'.
89 I cite the text as sent to Southey in *CL*, I, 334–6.
90 See Corfield and Evans, 'John Thelwall in Wales', 236–8.
91 Jones, *History of Brecknock*, II, 317 (Llandefalle parish): 'on the northern confines of this parish is a lane running nearly east and west called Heol Einon, but more generally Penheol Einon, on the side of which, near a gate leading to Crickadarn, is a stone of about four feet high which some have

supposed to be sepulchral; it may be so . . . I deliver my opinion that it was a boundary, and marked the extremity or termination of Einon's property . . . This of course leads to an enquiry who this Einon was who gave name to the place; and here there can be little or no doubt that Einon Glyd, commonly called lord of Elvel, was the person . . .'

92 John F. Danby, *The Simple Wordsworth: Studies in the Poems, 1797–1807* (London: Routledge & Kegan Paul, 1960), 61.
93 See Newlyn, *Reading*, 113–15.
94 Danby, *The Simple Wordsworth*, 69.
95 Ibid.
96 *Fenwick Notes*, 14.
97 Ibid.
98 See *LB*, 352.
99 Roe, *Culture of Dissent*, 113. See also Thompson, 'Disenchantment', 162.
100 *CL*, II, 723.
101 The gulf between Thelwall and the poets seems to have been bridged somewhat by November 1803, when all three met again: Thelwall, travelling north to deliver lectures on elocution, records the meeting in a hitherto unpublished letter to Stella (Appendix, pp. 315–19) that betrays no rancour or bitterness towards them.
102 Thompson, 'Jacobin Fox', 134.
103 See the letter from Crabb Robinson to Dorothy (11 October 1841) in *The Correspondence of Henry Crabb Robinson with the Wordsworth Circle*, ed. Edith J. Morley (2 vols; Oxford: Clarendon Press, 1927), I, 443: 'By the bye I have always forgotten to ask, but a thousand times intended it, whether the Lyswyn farm thus insiduously [sic] set up in opposition to Kilve be or not the farm in which John Thelwal [sic] lived in Wales & where I spent a week with him anno 1799 – I should like to know'. Mary Wordsworth answered him on 14 October 1841: 'Your letter is very interesting especially as we travelled over so much of the same ground ourselves – and shall have so much to say about it when we meet – You are right in your conjecture about Lyswyn farm' (*LY* iv, 249).
104 *Diary, Reminiscences and Correspondence of Henry Crabb Robinson*, ed. Thomas Sadler (3 vols; London: Macmillan & Co., 1869), I, 473.
105 *Fenwick Notes*, 80.
106 Thompson, 'Jacobin Fox', 137.

Epilogue

1 Judith Thompson, 'An Autumnal Blast', 429.
2 See Scrivener, 'Jacobin Romanticism', 90.

Appendix

'YOURS, A TRUE SANS CULOTTE' – LETTERS OF JOHN THELWALL AND HENRIETTA CECIL THELWALL, 1794–1838

None of the important personal documents presented here has ever been published in full. Brief, isolated passages from some have been quoted (details are given below), but they have often suffered from being wrongly transcribed. The edited texts presented here have been fully and faithfully transcribed from manuscripts held by the institutions listed at the head of each letter.[1]

Each letter is prefaced by an introduction discussing its context and salient features, while the annotation fills out this information with a more detailed commentary. What follows is a strictly *verbatim* transcription from the manuscripts that reproduces orthographical peculiarities and inconsistencies, unwitting repetitions, syntactical/ grammatical oversights, and so on. I have therefore dispensed with [*sic*]. When a word has been crossed out by Thelwall and is still legible, it is reproduced struckthrough; when a word has been deleted and is no longer legible, [word(s) deleted] is used; and when Thelwall's script cannot be made out owing to the state of the manuscript, [MS illegible] is employed.

---

[1] Two other important surviving Thelwall letters, use of which has been made in this book, were edited in 1930 (see Gibbs, 'Unpublished Letter') and in 1986 (see Corfield and Evans, 'John Thelwall in Wales'). A portion of another, to Thomas Hardy, dated 24 May 1798, appeared in Rose, *William Pitt*, 352n. Extracts from an important body of Thelwall letters to Thomas Hardy were published by the poet Edgell Rickword in the *Times Literary Supplement* on 19 June 1953 (p. 402) and subsequently by E. P. Thompson in 'Jacobin Fox'; the fate of both the originals and Thompson's transcripts is unknown. For a discussion of the state of the Thelwall manuscripts before Thompson's death in 1993, see Thompson, 'Jacobin Fox', 139–40.

1

John Thelwall to John Vellum, 10 March 1794[1]
Source: Public Record Office, T.S. 11/ 951/ 3495

As well as the letter from Thelwall to his brother-in-law transcribed below, the PRO files contain a fair copy in which the transcriber has in places misread Thelwall's script and has been unable to decipher the original where the seal has been broken. Another hand has written 'Mr Thelwall's Letter' on the original. This points to the fact that the copy is a government transcription; indeed, the letter formed part of the prosecution dossier at Thelwall's trial for High Treason in 1794. All this is hardly surprising given its contents: Thelwall rails against the 'despicable aristocratic banditti' who were intercepting his letters and confiscating Jack's papers. It is a document that provides a fascinating background to Thelwall's account in the 'Prefatory Memoir' to *Poems, Chiefly Written in Retirement* of the outrages committed against them both (see *Poems*, p. xxxvi). Pitt appears here as 'the arch insolent hypocrite', locked in what Thelwall rightly represents as a personal battle with his jacobin antagonist. Thelwall also gives Jack an account of the defiant political lectures he had been giving; two months after this, he was in State custody. His statement towards the end of the letter that he is willing to die for the cause of liberty is stirring and sincere (one is reminded of Edward Williams's similar remarks in his letters), and he signs off, with a touch of humour, as the proud atheist and begetter of a long line of jacobins. The injunction in the postscript placed at the head of the letter stands as a fitting motto for the hounded jacobins of the 1790s.

---

[1] Two sentences from this letter are quoted in Thompson, 'Disenchantment', 155, and the final sentence is cited in Thompson, 'Jacobin Fox', 112.

[Addressee: M^r. John Vellum/Oakham/Ruts]
2 Maze Pond. 10th March 1794.

[Postscript written above letter]
Seal your Letters first with a wafer, & then some good wax over it. You might as well stick your letters together with your spittle as use the wax you generally have. It all rubs off in powder as soon as it is cold. Get good wax! get <u>good</u> wax! When rogues & robbers are in authority every man ought to keep a good lock upon his door.

Dear Jack

Immediately after the receipt of your Sisters Letter which came thro' the hands of Miss C. I wrote an ans.^r. directed to her, but which it seems by yours of about a fortnight since you have never received. If I had leizure to attend to these insignificant rascals (your Combs, & your Berrys, & your postmasters,[2] who give themselves such insolent airs about me, it is not all their <u>estates</u> sold together should shelter them from the resentment due to their <u>impudent</u> & <u>illegal</u> conduct, & indeed if they continue their trick of intercepting letters I will make myself so much leizure as to do the public justice against this despicable aristocratic banditti who violate the laws of f~~r~~ the land & the intercourses of friendship[3] under pretences of loyalty. This letter

---

[2] See the preface to Thelwall's political satire, *John Gilpin's Ghost* (London: T. Smith, 1795), pp. iii–iv (in which the lawyer Combes seizes Thelwall's mail): 'An extract from a speech delivered by me at a debating society, having been printed by [Daniel Isaac] Eaton, in his Politics for the People, under the title of *King Chanticleer, or the Fate of Tyranny*, that intrepid bookseller was, in consequence, a third time indicted for sedition, and, as the public well knows, was a third time acquitted. Shortly after which, I took an opportunity of sending . . . a small packet of books to a brother-in-law who resides at *Oakham*, the county-town of *Rutland*, containing, among other articles, some copies of this ludicrous story, and of the still more ludicrous indictment to which it had given birth. But a conspiracy to intercept my papers had been formed by the great men of *Oakham* (particularly Mr *John Combes*, attorney at law, and agent to Lord *Winchelsea*) . . . and these books, by some accident or other . . . fell into *Combes*'s hand . . . the house of my brother-in-law was broke open, and rifled of papers, books, letters, &c. and *lawyer Combes* was posted to *London* to acquaint the GREAT MAN in DOWNING-STREET with the wonderful discovery. These particulars gave rise to the following ballad, which was written before the late arrests for High Treason.'

[3] Cf. Coleridge in *Conciones ad Populum*: 'The beautiful fabric of Love the system of Spies and Informers has shaken to the very foundation. There have been multiplied among us "Men who carry tales to shed blood!"' (*Lectures 1795*, 60).

(which, as you will see, is franked by a member of parliament) I shall take care to have delivered, by ~~my~~ the young lad whom I have lately taken into my house as secretary, at the General Post office, & to have its delivery so witnessed that if it is stopped I shall be able to bring it home to the parties who will find themselves involved ~~in~~ thereby in consequences they are not prepared for.

You see, Citizen! I am not much frightened with the prospect of the <u>sale of Mr Berrys estate</u>: & you may tell him that if matters go on with me for a year or two as they have done for this two months past I may perhaps come down to the auction, and be a bidder. To be serious Jack – the Circumstances that appear so formidable to you excite in my mind nothing but contempt. I have much more formidable enemies to contend with than the Apothecary & Pettifogger of a little country town – the arch insolent hypocrite, the minister of this ~~Country~~ insulted & ruined Country[4] himself condescends to honour me with his hatred, with all his lawyers & bloodhounds at his heels – Yet these I despise – over the villainous artifices even of these I shall triumph. The fact is their's is the cause of oppression & falshood – mine of Liberty, Truth, & Virtue; & it is therefore the insignificant individual (whom however their hatred & opposition have rendered of some importance) is too strong for all their artifices. ~~With~~

With respect to my private affairs you will be happy to ~~find~~ hear that the popularity I have acquired by labouring in the Cause of mankind, after having been long the cause of much loss & disappointment to myself, is at length beginning to make me ample amends: that I am getting forward in the world very fast by the profit of the political Lectures that I am publickly giving in open defiance of all the attempts of the tools of Government to suppress them, & by the encreasing sale of my books & pamphlets. For the purpose of these said Lectures I have procured a house to be taken with a large room – will hold six hundred people, at the standing rent of £132 a year, into which I hope to move in about a fortnight or so;[5] when I will let you know the direction – at present all is mum. If any of the London papers come to your part of the world, especially the <u>Morning Post</u> or <u>Chronicle</u>, or even those blackguard papers the

---

[4] Cf. Coleridge on Pitt as an 'apostate' and a 'calumniated Judas Iscariot' in *Lectures 1795*, 38 and 64–5.

[5] Beaufort Buildings, Strand.

Times & True Briton, you will by reading them have a chance of hearing about me now & then either by my advertisem.^ts. or by the abuse or praise that is bestowed upon me: this may remove the necessity on my part of writing often to you: for which I have, indeed, very little time. As the Morning Post is probably too honest a paper to be permitted to be permitted to enter your aristocratic town, I send you a coppy of a paragraph which was inserted in that print on Saturday and which, I suppose will please you a little – It is thus 'M^r. Thelwall's Lectures, on the moral tendency of Spies & informers,[6] are better attended than the debates in Parliament. They are calculated to <u>enlighten</u>, not to <u>confuse</u> the <u>swinish multitude</u>.' which you will see is saying in pretty plain terms that I am doing as much good as the parliament is doing mischief.

Do not, however, imagine that my head is intoxicated with vanity. The cause I am embarked in is, indeed, so dear to my heart that I could I believe cheerfully sacrifice my life for it – for what is my life – or the life of any one man, to the liberty – the Virtue – the happiness of so many millions of people as are now kept down by the degrading oppressions of tyranny & <u>taxation</u> – & I cannot therefore but be warmed at the prospect of a popularity which enables me to be the more powerfully assistant in promoting the welfare of my fellow creatures.

A word about this same robbery which Mr Combs, & or some other persons [MS illegible] committed upon the property I sent to you. I gave it as my opinion in my letter which appears to have been intercepted that [we?] ought to commence an action against the magistrates & scoundrels concerned in both this robery, & the infamous & illegal transaction of seizing your papers; & I repeat to you again that if you have the spirit to do so, I will undertake to procure you an attorney to conduct the business, & a Counsil to plead it without <u>fee or reward</u>. This is a piece of justice you owe to yourself, & to the Country. You, however, are the best judge whether your situation will permit you to undertake it. The whole of the proceeding is so infamous & <u>disloyal</u>[7] – (that is to say against law –

---

[6] Published later in 1794.

[7] Coleridge viewed the authorities' actions similarly as treason: his Bristol lecture against the Gagging Acts, published in December 1795, is entitled *The Plot Discovered; or An Address to the People against Ministerial Treason.*

for <u>loyalty</u> in reality means attachment to the laws, not attachment to Kings & Ministers) – that even as laws are at this time administered, I am sure they can never justify themselves in any Court of Justice in the Kingdom: tho' God knows these places and their proceedings are corrupt enough at present!

Adieu! my Stella & our baby[8] are very well. I assure you the child does not thrive the worse for not being christened. It is a bonny wench – very cheerful – very full of health, & will I hope some time or other be the happy mother of a fine hardy race of Republicans, & Sans Culottes

Loves and Services to all

Yours

a true Sans Culotte

J. Thelwall

---

[8] Frances Maria Thelwall, who was a year old at this time; see Chapter 5.

2

John Thelwall to J. Wimpory, 15 February 1797[1]
Source: The Houghton Library, Harvard University,
Lobby VIII. 4. 22, fMS Eng. 947. 2 (19)

This letter to the man who was to be Thelwall's companion on his 'Pedestrian Excursion' later in the summer of 1797 was written before Thelwall embarked on a visit to Derby to lecture as part of his attempt to 'revive discussion' following the abandonment of his lectures at Beaufort Buildings. From June to September 1796, during a lecture tour of East Anglia, he had already encountered organized loyalist violence; a month after writing this letter, he was again forced to defend himself with a pistol against an antagonistic mob at Derby. Thelwall mentions the high praise bestowed on his *Rights of Nature* (1796) by 'a young man . . . one of the most extraordinary Geniuses & finest scholars of the age' – Coleridge – and once again ends a letter with a reference to the 'inquisitorial tyranny' of those in power.

[Addressee: J. Wimpory/Shoemaker/Gosport/Hants]

15 Feb 1797

Dear Wimporey,

I have not time to write you a long Letter, but I will not quit London without once more greeting my friends of Gosport & Portsmouth – & thanking them for their exertions to serve me –
 I aim for Derby – where I am going to Lecture – My invitations are from the first people in the place – I set off <u>on foot</u>, with a friend, perhaps two, on Friday morning – walk to Woooburn (40 miles) part with my company there – Mount a Coach roof to Leicester – there sleep one night – visit the Sans-Culottes, – & then proceed on Horseback to Derby – There's variety for you –
 And so ~~my~~ the patriots of your part of the Country do not like the second part of R^{ts} Nat,[2] as well as the fs.^{t}. I am sorry for it – for reasons

---

[1] A brief passage from this letter is quoted in Thompson, 'Jacobin Fox', 106.
[2] *The Rights of Nature against the Usurpation of Establishments* (1796).

much more important than those connected with my own personal interests. It is a proof that they are more fond of invective than principle – for the 2ᵈ- is as superior to the fsᵗ- as the noon tide sun to the twinkling of a stinking mackrel in the dark. It is the uniform opinion of all the literary men whose judgments I have been able to collect (& their opinion in this respect perfectly agrees with mine) that the fsᵗ- is a very ~~badly~~ indifferent pamphlet – but that the second is [words deleted] very superior to any thing I ever produced before – And one in particular – I mean Coleridge, who tho' a young man is one of the most extraordinary Geniuses & finest scholars of the age does not scruple to pronounce it 'the best pamphlet that has been written since the commencement of the war'.[3] That it will not be understood without more serious attention than the former is necessarily true, because there is a great deal more in it to understand – yet I would fain persuade myself that the language is simple enough, & the arrangements are ~~plain~~ plain enough to [word deleted] be intelligible to any capacity that will ~~give~~ bestow the requisite attention. My object is to be understood by all classes; & I am therefore much obliged to you for your remarks – Before I publish the 3ᵈ part (which I shall not till autumn)[4] I will give the whole a very serious reading that I may judge whether it it be practicable to give ~~it~~ a still more popular cast to the language, &c –

To Howard or Tracey I suspect I shall not have it in my power to write before I get to Derby – from thence if I can find leizure I will write to both – Assure them of my civic & fraternal respect. Tell Howard that I have certainly always esteemed him, & continue so to do as much as ever. If I had the pleasure of more frequent intercourse with him, I should discharge the duty of a friend by animadverting on some little eccentricities – But eccentricity is no vice of the heart; & flights of the head shake not my friendships. – I am as full of maggots as a cheshire cheese myself –

With respect to the question about the Melitia – I gave no direct ans.ʳ. because there is no sanctuary against the inquisitorial tyranny of

---

[3] See Coleridge's letters to Thelwall of 22 June 1796: 'Your answer to Burke [*The Rights of Nature*] is, I will not say, the best – for that would be no praise – it is certainly the only good one; & it is a very good one. In style, and *in reflectiveness* it is, I think, your chef d'oeuvre' (*CL*, I, 221) and 6 February 1797: 'Without [*sic*] the exception of these passages the pamphlet is the best, I have read, since the commencement of the war; warm, not fiery; well-reasoned without being dry; the periods harmonious yet avoiding metrical harmony; and the ornaments so disposed as to set off the features of truth without turning the attention on themselves' (*CL*, I, 307).

[4] This never appeared.

our present governors, & it is scarcely possible to give any opinion on such a subject, that may not, in the course of events, be made a matter of crimination against a man situated as I am – To your female Cit^{n} & to all friends remember me most cordially

J. Thelwall
15 Feb. 1797

3

John Thelwall to Susan Thelwall ('Stella'), 18 July 1797[1]
Source: The Pierpont Morgan Library, New York, MA 77 (17)

As discussed in Chapter 5, Thelwall, on his 'Pedestrian Excursion', arrived at Nether Stowey on 17 July 1797 only to discover that Coleridge was at Alfoxden. The next day, in the company of Sara Coleridge, Thelwall walked to Alfoxden to meet both Coleridge and Wordsworth for the first time. The first third of this letter represents an important co-text for the 'Pedestrian Excursion' in that it provides private details about Thelwall's jacobin contacts in Frome, Bath and Bristol which could not be openly related in the account of the 'Pedestrian Excursion' published in the *Monthly Magazine*. In other details, such as his reaction to the architecture of Bath and Bristol, it accords with that account.

The picture Thelwall draws of the time spent in philosophical and literary discussion with Wordsworth and Coleridge is in stark contrast to the violence recently offered him in the provinces. The letter is upbeat and forward-looking, but Thelwall was at this moment far down the road to 'rustic obscurity' – and tragedy – at Llyswen.

[Addressee: S. Thelwall/G.Daniel's/Derby]

All fox den 18 July 1797 –

Dear Stella,

I did not arrive at Stowey till late last Night – my journey having been procrastinated at Froome at Bath & Bristol by the importunities & kindnesses of Friends – My plan of travelling unknown I soon found unpracticable & therefore relinquished it for one which I found more profitable. I flattered myself, indeed, that as far as Froome I had

---

[1] Isolated passages from this letter have been quoted in Elizabeth Sandford, *Thomas Poole and his Friends* (2 vols; London: Macmillan, 1888, I, 232–3; new edition, Over Stowey: Friarn Press, 1996, 130); James Dykes Campbell, *Samuel Taylor Coleridge: A Narrative of the Events of his Life* (London: Macmillan, 1894), 72–3; Thompson, 'Jacobin Fox', 106–8; and Woof and Hebron, *Towards Tintern Abbey*, 80.

enjoyed all the advantages of obscurity: but I was mistaken for I have since found out that I was known at Salisbury & that my passing thro that City had become the town's talk. At Froome, indeed, all pretences of privacy were progressively abandoned. W. has a relation there upon whom ~~he~~ we called, & where we had determined to ~~pass~~ take up our nights quarters. Some of the people of that town (a sad den of Jacobins) had been at my Lectures – I was recognised and persuaded to stop first one, & then an.^{r}. night longer than I [word deleted] intended – In this stay I sold 5 or 6 £ worth of my publications; & was encouraged by this circumstance to try if I could not do the same at Bath & Bristol. At the former of these I had, however, some other inducements to pause. In short I was fascinated with the beauty taste & splendour of the town, whose buildings have certainly a fascination not to be conceived by those who have been used [word deleted] only to the huge pigsties[2] & dog kennels which in other parts of England are called towns & Cities. As soon as we caught the first glimpse of this City of Palaces, we turned aside from the high road that we might command a full view of it from the brow of a fine [word deleted] fertile hill, ~~up~~ cose by a splendid mansion called Prior Park. Here the whole scene rushed upon our vision & a delightful scene it was. The City itself [word deleted] entirely built of the most beautiful stone. The streets & buildings grand & regular, ~~the~~ stretching to right & left along a most beautiful vale & ascending a considerable way up the hills on the other side these were the first objects that struck the imagination; & when the eye fatigued with splendour (for the declining sun shed its full radiance upon this ~~grand~~ group of artificial Grandeur) turned to contemplate the sober green of Nature, the hills, & vales, & woods afforded the most enchanting variety, & would, indeed, even if the City, which forms the chief object were removed, constitute of themselves a scene not to be rivalled in most of the Counties of G^t. Britain. We were so ~~spellb~~ spell bound by this combination of the beauties of art & nature that we sat contemplating it for a couple of hours before we descended into the town; & I had resolved before that time to stop a day or two in Bath. To Bristol however we went next morn^g for our apparel – for there we had sent our trunk – & we were not fit to be seen in Bath. [Word deleted] On our fst. entrance into Bristol I was horribly disgusted both with the town & people: but my prejudices ag^t. the latter were soon worn away –

---

[2] In his account of the 'Pedestrian Excursion' (*MM* 12 (November 1801), 306), Thelwall exclaimed: '[Bath] only is worthy of being called a city! – all that we have seen before were but congregations of pig sties!'

& the Londonish filthiness & higgletly-piggletiness of the former was amply compensated by the sublimity & beauty of the surrounding Country – I met with many friends in Bristol who were encreasing in greater & greater degree every hour I staid – i.e. in exact proportion as it became known that I was in town; & when I returned to Bath, I found it necessary to promise to return thro Bristol in my way to Wales. In short at Bristol & Bath as at Froome I have met with some ~~frie~~ enthusiasm, & some solid friendships, & I have good reason to suppose that the most profittable, & perhaps the most useful thing I could do would be to make a considerable progress thro the Country. But profit & everything else but my Stella & my Babes are now banished from my mind by the Enchanting retreat (the Academus of Stowey) from which I write this, & by the delightful Society of Coleridge & of Wordsworth – the present Occupier of All fox Den. We have been having a delightful ramble to day among the plantations & along [word deleted] a wild romantic dell in these grounds thro which a foaming, murmuring, rushing torrent of water winds its long artless course – There have we sometime sitting on a tree – sometimes wading boot-top deep thro the stream ~~sometime~~ & again stretched on some mossy stone or root of a decayed tree, a [word deleted] literary & political triumvirate [word deleted] passed sentence on the productions and characters of the age – burst forth in poetical flights of enthusiasm – & philosophised our minds into a state of tranquility which the leaders of nations might envy and the residents of Cities can never know.

Samuel was not at home (he was here) when I arrived last night – nor would Sara have been but that she had quitted this friendly retreat, to superintend the wash tub. I have spoiled the soap suds however. It was too late to come to this place last night, for it is 3 or 4 miles from Stowey. I slept therefore at Coleridges Cot; & this morning we rose by times, & came here time enough to call Samuel & his friend Wordsworth up to breakfast. Faith we are a most philosophical party. A large house with grounds and plantations about it which Wordsw.th. has hired (I understand for a trifle) merely that he might enjoy the Society of Coleridge)) contains the enthusiastic group – consisting of C. & his Sara – W. & his Sister – & myself – without any servant male or female – An old woman who lives in an adjoining Cottage does what is requisiste for our simple wants – 'Delightful spot! O were my Stella here!'[3]

---

[3] As noted in Chapter 5, Thelwall here consciously echoes the final line of Coleridge's 'Lines composed while climbing the left ascent of Brockley Coomb, in the county of Somerset, May 1795': 'Enchanting spot! O were my SARA here!'

Wimporey quitted me at Bath – his business calling him back to Gosport. – How many days I may loose the world in this scene of enchantment I cannot yet say but certainly long enough to get an ans.ʳ. from you. Direct to Coleridges as heretofore only do not put my name on the letter – The initials will be enough.[4]

During the whole of this ramble I have had serious thoughts of a Cottage – Do not be surprised if my next should inform you that I have taken one. I have by no means forgotten Jack, & if there are any means by which we can live together upon fair terms of reciprocal justice I should much rejoice in it. Can he reconcile himself to a philosophical bread & small beer way of living? & can he apply himself to ~~const~~ manual labour & regular assiduity [MS illegible] conversation with him upon this subject –

Remember me most affectionately to the Cromptons.[5] I am sorry the Dʳ is away: it must much diminish your comforts. I believe however that I should not consult your permanent happiness nor the interest of our dear babes if I were to hurry back to Derby. If I can get a Cot with a piece of land & keep a Cow & some pigs – with garden &c. would Jack be satisfied with a life of mere rustic obscurity & [MS illegible] ould do?

---

[4] A necessary precaution in view of the fact that all three men were under surveillance at this time.

[5] For Dr Peter Crompton and his wife, see the introduction and notes to Letter No. 4, below.

4

John Thelwall to Dr Peter Crompton, 3 March 1798[1]
The Houghton Library, Harvard University,
Lobby VIII. 4. 22, fMS Eng. 947. 2 (21)

Ensconced now at Llyswen, Thelwall writes this – one of the most important of his surviving letters – to his 'patron' Dr Peter Crompton, a physician and brewer from Derby who had by this time moved to Elton House, Wavertree, near Liverpool. Crompton stood as the parliamentary candidate for Nottingham in 1796 and 1807.[2] Coleridge also knew both Crompton and his wife well at this time, and held both in high respect and affection;[3] in August 1796 at Derby, Crompton had asked Coleridge to open a private school (an offer he ultimately declined).[4] The letter proves that Thelwall was in touch with the Liverpool circle of jacobins and reformers that included Shepherd, Smith, Rathbone, Roscoe and Rushton (full details are given in the notes).

[1] Brief passages from this letter have been quoted in *The Letters of Samuel Taylor Coleridge*, ed. E. H. Coleridge (2 vols; London: Heinemann, 1895), I, 234–5; Thompson, 'Disenchantment', 162; Thompson, 'Jacobin Fox', 112–13, 114, 134 and 135; Woof and Hebron, *Towards Tintern Abbey*, 80 and 82; and Nicholas Roe, 'Coleridge and John Thelwall: Medical Science, Politics, and Poetry', *The Coleridge Bulletin* NS 3 (1994), 17–18 (reprinted in Roe, 'Atmospheric Air', 198–9).

[2] See Thelwall's anecdote in *The Rights of Nature*: 'During the late election at Nottingham . . . A poor manufacturer, who was past his best days, and to whom, therefore, it was of serious consequence to be dismissed from an established shop . . . was pressed by his employer, in very authoritative terms, to vote for . . . Mr. Smith. He hesitated: but the very sustenance of his family was at stake; and he yielded. Going up to the hustings, and having given his name, he was asked by the poll-clerk, for whom he voted? "Why, I have two votes; have I not?" – "You have." – "Well, then, I give one of them to Mr. Smith – but that's not mine: it's my master's! The other's my own, and I'll give that to Dr. Crompton – for he's the man for the people!" – "Thank you, my good friend", (exclaims the *courtly* candidate) – "thank you, for me. Let me have the pleasure of shaking hands with you". – "No, I'm d—d if I do", replied the voter; "I was obliged to vote for you, but I an't obliged to shake hands with you, neither. But I'll shake hands with you, Dr Crompton; for I gave it *you* from my heart!"' (Claeys, *The Politics of English Jacobinism*, 402–3).

[3] In a letter of 6 February 1797 to Thelwall, Coleridge described them thus: 'Mrs Crompton is an Angel; & Dr Crompton a truly honest & benevolent man, possessing some good sense & a large portion of *humour*. I never think of him without respect, & tenderness; never (for thank heaven!) I abominate Godwinism) without gratitude' (*CL*, I, 305–6).

[4] As Coleridge records, Crompton called on him in August 1796 in Derby 'and made the following offer. That if I would take a house in Derby, and open a day-school, confining my number to twelve, he would send his three children. That, till I had completed my number, he would allow me One hundred a year . . . The plan to commence in November. I agreed with the Doctor, he telling me, that if, in the mean time, any thing more advantageous offered itself, I was to consider myself at perfect liberty to accept it' (*CL*, I, 229).

Once again, Thelwall mentions Coleridge (the good fortune of his Wedgwood annuity in this case), testifying to the influence the younger man had had on him throughout their correspondence and during Thelwall's July visit to Stowey and Alfoxden. The statement 'If I could ever turn Christian again I would certainly be an Unitarian Quaker' betrays the influence not only of William Rathbone, as Thelwall states, but of Coleridge, too. Indeed, the description Thelwall gives of Coleridge's 'rapid genius' and seditious 'preaching' is one of the most insightful and colourful portraits of the radical Coleridge of the 1790s. A reference to the prosecution of Gilbert Wakefield heralds Thelwall's fascinating portrait of life at Llyswen, which should be compared with the darker picture painted in the 'Prefatory Memoir' to his *Poems*. It is the father who speaks here, offering a humorous glimpse of little Maria (who was to die the following year) 'bound[ing] along' in her republican 'trowsers', as if attacking a State citadel. His son Sidney's activities are observed carefully from a philosophical perspective characteristic of the age's interest (shared by Wordsworth, of course) in the education of children. As E. P. Thompson has observed, Wordsworth's memory of the 'rude hermitage . . . a sequestered summer study' which Thelwall says he is building in his Llyswen dingle and which Wordsworth saw during his visit of August 1798 seems to have found its way into *The Excursion* (see note 14, below). Thelwall then turns to emphasise the darker 'shades' of the family's existence at Llyswen, troubled by pecuniary and agricultural difficulties. Towards the end of the letter, he gives a valuable insight into his daily regimen and reading, and announces his decision to supplement his income by writing for the *Monthly Magazine* and completing his 'Memoirs' and novel, *The Daughter of Adoption* (1801).

[Addressee: Dr Crompton/Eton House/near/Liverpool]

Llyswen 3^d March 1798.

Dear Doctor,

Your letter of Jany the 5th with P.S. of Feb. 25 enclosing a 15£ Manchester bank came to hand this day for which accept the thanks of the heart – I suppose you know that the remittance mentioned by our friend Smith[5] was a £10 note from Raithbone.[6] It was accompanied by a most friendly letter which gave additional value to the gift itself. I pray you make to him my most cordial remembrances. As a father, I sympathise in the loss you inform me he has sustained; & as loving the man & respecting the dignity of his character I rejoice to hear that tho' 'he suffered much he conducted himself with fortitude'. He is one of the many Quakers who impress me with veneration for that sect. If I could ever turn Christian again I would certainly be an Unitarian Quaker.

I am surprised ~~you hav~~ you have not heard the particulars of Coleridge's good fortune. It is not a legacy but a gift. The circumstances are thus expressed by himself in a letter of the 30th Jan.^y. 'I received an invitation from Shrewsbury to be the Unitarian Minsiter, & at the same time an order for 100£ from Thomas & Josiah Wedgwood – I accepted the former, & returned the latter in a long letter explanatory of my motives, & went off to Shrewsbury, where they were on the point of electing me unanimously & with unusual marks of affection, when I received an offer from T & J. Wedgewood of an annuity of 150£ to be legally settled on me. Astonished, agitated, ~~& feeli~~ & feeling as I could not help feeling, I accepted the offer in the same worthy spirit, I hope, in which it was made; & this morning I have returned from Shrewsbury'.[7] This letter was written in a great hurry at Cottle's shop in Bristol, ~~where a friend~~ in answer to one which a friend of mine,[8] had left for him there in his way from Llyswen to

---

[5] Joseph Smith (1765–1815), trained at Warrington Academy, and was known as 'Thumping Smith' because of his animated political sermons.
[6] William Rathbone (1757–1809), nicknamed 'The Hoary Traitor' because of his grey locks and admiration for Napoleon.
[7] *CL*, I, 383. For Josiah Wedgwood's letter, and Coleridge's reply, see *CL*, I, 373–4.
[8] Wimpory.

Gosport; & you will perceive that it has a dash of the obscure not uncommon to the rapid genius of C. Whether he did or did not accept the cure of Unitarian Souls, it is difficult from this acc.^t. to make out – I suppose he did not – for I know his aversion to preaching God's holy word for hire, ~~&~~ which is seconded a little I suspect by his repugnance to all regular ~~& habit~~ routine & application – I also hope he did not – for I know he cannot ~~frequently~~ preach very often ~~without~~ without ~~mounting~~ travelling from the pulpit to the Tower – Mount him but upon his darling hobby horse 'the republic of God's own making', & away he goes like hey go mad, spattering & splashing thro thick & thin & scatter~~s~~ing more <u>levelling</u> sedition, & constructive treason, than poor Gilly,[9] or myself ever dreamt of.[10] He promised to ~~answer~~ write to me again in a few days; but tho' I ans.^rd. his letter directly, I have not heard from him ~~again~~ since.

I am sorry (for his wife's sake) to hear of the prosecution going on ag.^t. G. Wakefield's ans.^r. to that precious apostate the Bp. of Llandaff[11] – as for the man himself I rather rejoice in it. His glorious spirit will not bow beneath the rod of persecution, & the short-lived malice of his enemies is only the prelude to his triumph. I have not seen the Book – but I suppose it has plenty of Cayane. (The Assessed Taxes I believe are brass pins in the Gizzards of the Aristocrats – they wound & fester – To us they matter not much: 5^s/6^d P year is the whole of our advance in consequence of them – they of course will play up old Gooseberry with you – But why lay down your carriage? – You must pay for it these 3 years whether you drive it or not.

---

[9] Gilbert Wakefield; see note 11, below.
[10] Cf. Thelwall's ill-humoured annotation to Coleridge's claim in *Biographia Literaria* that his 'principles' in the 1790s were far removed from 'those of jacobinism or even of democracy': 'I have never gone the lengths . . . which the Pantisocratist went at any rate, nay I may say I never had the slightest tinge of that with which Mr C. was deep died [*sic*]: but that Mr C. was indeed far from Democracy, because he was far beyond it, I well remember – for he was a down right zealous leveller & indeed in one of the worst senses of the word he was a Jacobin, a man of blood – Does he forget the letters he wrote to me (& which I believe I yet have) acknowledging the justice of my castigation of him for the violence, and sanguinary tendency of some of his doctrines –'; see Pollin and Burke, 'John Thelwall's Marginalia', 81.
[11] Gilbert Wakefield was prosecuted for his *Reply* (1798) to Richard Watson's *Address to the People of Great Britain* of the same year. He was incarcerated in Dorchester jail from May 1799 to May 1801, and died a matter of months after his release. Richard Watson (the 'apostate') had initially welcomed the French Revolution and was a supporter of Reform during the early 1790s, but his political views became increasingly reactionary as the decade wore on.

With respect to ourselves & our concerns – We are all very well & highly delighted with our situation. Maria in particular grows a very stout and vigorous girl, much taller also than we expected. We have daily & hourly proofs of the advantages of the stile of dress we have adopted – for she bounds along in her trowsers in all the romping vivacity of independence, runs up the mount, clambers among the rocks, & by her perpetual activity takes health by storm as it were. Sidney[12] continues still the same fantastic unmanagable & unaccountable boy he was at Derby. I have a thousand <u>Shandean</u> notions about him – the peculiar form of his head, the remarkable cast of his features, & the thousand antic forms into which he is every now & then distorting them fill me with many a proud, & many an anxious thought. That he will be no ordinary lad I think myself certain – but whether he will be an uncommon genius or an uncommon villain [word deleted] time & a thousand thousand accidents which it is impossible either to foresee or control [words deleted] must decide. I resign him, not without anxiety, to the guidance of my deity <u>philosophical necessity</u>.[13] There is one disposition in him awakened by our situation which gives me great consolation. Across one end of our orchard flows a pretty little brook buddling & babbling ~~over many~~ thro a [word deleted] small romantic dingle to empty itself into the wye; in which with hobbyhorsical industry I have built a cascade of 8 or 9 feet height & am making a rude hermitage (a sequestered summer study) in the dingle beneath. The boy has found out this place & is as delighted with it as myself[14] – for he will sit whole hours listning to the rush of the water & 'pouring on the brook that bubbles by' – a perfect 'Il Penseroso' – his whole countenance harmonises to a most soothing melancholy. The old women say he will be drowned – I say he will be philosophised – His violent passions will acquire, as he grows up, the curb of meditation. I know, by experience,

---

[12] Algernon Sidney Thelwall.
[13] One of the touchstones of both Coleridge's and Godwin's philosophy in the 1790s.
[14] Identifying Thelwall as the primary model for the Solitary in Wordsworth's *Excursion*, E. P. Thompson suggests that this 'hobbyhorse' of Thelwall's found its way into Wordsworth's poem: 'Beside this description [above] . . . one might set several passages from the *Excursion*. Thus in Book II the Pedlar and the Poet come upon "a penthouse" erected among the rocks, with the help of a child's hands, where – horrors! – they found a copy of *Candide*, "dull product of a scoffer's pen". Even more striking are several passages in Book III descriptive of a "hidden nook" beneath rocks down which water descended, a nook which the Solitary described as his "Druid Cromlech", and in the vicinity of which a "fair-faced cottage-boy" is busy "mending the defects / Left in the fabric of a leaky dam" . . . Undoubtedly Thelwall will have led Wordsworth and Coleridge to his hobby-horse, and traces of the memory survived' (Thompson, 'Jacobin Fox', 134).

the power & influence of such habits; & my maxim is, that Seneca and Socrates preach well – but rocks & brooks & waterfalls much better.[15] Hampden continues to be a stout, thriving, &, considering the pigmy race he springs from, a gigantic child.[16]

In addition to the ~~pleasures~~ beauty of the Country & the improving health of our family, we have reason to be pleased with Llyswen on account of the respectful civility of all our neighbours. The rustic villagers pay~~s~~ us every mark of attention – Jack & I are regarded as a sort of Oracles, our votes are law at all ~~the~~ parish meetings, we receive & return visits with the farmers, & have had civil messages from some of the surrounding gentry. Tho' I am by this time pretty generally known, I have never in any single instance received the slightest insult since I came to settle in Wales; & among the more intelligent part of the people, the hat is off & the eye brightens whenever I pass by. This is the bright side of the picture – It has its shades, & those I shall not disguise. In consequence of several disappointments, & some expences I was not aware of, the supply we set out with fell considerably short, & we have been obliged to sell part of the crop &c. which I had calculated upon for covering the expences of manure & the 1st half years rent, for the purpose of making good our first payments; & we therefore look with some anxiety to the heavy demands of the month of May – for which we calculate our deficiency (all expences ~~included~~ of lime &c – &c – included) at about 30£ – for this I have no resource but that precarious one the pen. I am writing for the M. Mag – but a guinea or two P Month is all that can be expected from that quarter. Phillips[17] seems also disposed to treat either for the Novel or the Memoirs, or both. I am getting a specemin of the latter ready to send to him – & I am therefore at present almost as little of a farmer as when in Beauf. B^{gs}.[18] I rise sometimes at 6. never later than 7 – go immediately into my studdy (where I breakfast) & write till 11 or 12 –

---

[15] For a Christianized version of Thelwall's faith in a 'preaching' Nature, see Coleridge's letter of 10 March 1795 to George Dyer: 'It is melancholy to think, that the best of us are liable to be shaped & coloured by surrounding Objects – and a demonstrative proof, that Man was not made to live in Great Cities! . . . The pleasures, which we receive from rural beauties, are of little Consequence compared with the Moral Effect of these pleasures – beholding constantly the Best possible we at last become ourselves the best possible' (*CL*, I, 154).

[16] Hampden was the youngest child.

[17] Richard Phillips (1767–1840), bookseller and radical publisher, who in 1796 established the *Monthly Magazine*.

[18] The place in the Strand where Thelwall delivered his political lectures.

then if the weather is fine ride my hobby horse (i.e. work at my cascade & hermitage) till dinner, & frequently from dinner till tea – when the weather is bad I write & read till tea, & indeed till the Children are put to bed. At which time my wife & brother join me, & Tacitus or ~~Milton~~ Tristram Shandy[19] – Milton or John Phillips, together with our suppers & a little chit chat occupy our time till about ½ past 10 when we go to bed. How far my literary efforts are successful in removing our difficulties you shall hear [word deleted] ~~any other good or~~ as soon as I am able to speak with any confidence – as you shall also of any good or evil that may betide us. The precautions you hint about stock at the end of the three years are not necessary – the customs of the Country & the terms of my lease give the going off tennant time & every advantage for the gradual disposal of stock & crop – ~~There is something in Emb~~ Add to which I do not consider it as at all difficult to procure another farm, if we should not keep this, in these parts. There is something, at this time, in embrio – which I could have wished to be somewhat matured before I wrote to you. But it will be a week at least before I can have any ground whatever to form an opinion upon, & I do not think right to delay so long the acknowledgement of the rec.ᵗ. of your kind favour. I shall therefore only just hint that, notwithstanding all that I have said above, it is <u>not impossible</u> that we should immediately take an.ʳ. farm, now unoccupied in our neighbourhood, of about 100 acres on a lease of 21 years – to hold in conjunction with Llyswen.[20] If this project fails, in the first stage, it will not be worth while to give you any particulars – if it is likely to go on, you shall know the whole history shortly – Farewell for

---

[19] Cf. Thelwall's earlier reference to Sterne's work in this letter: 'I have a thousand <u>Shandean</u> notions about [Sidney]'.
[20] This project did not materialize.

the present – Stella & Jack join me in most affectionate greetings to yourself, M.rs. C. & our kind benefactor Miss C. My best remembrances to Rathbone, Smith, Shepherd, Roscow – & tho' last not least – that poor worthy fellow Rushton –[21]

> Yours
> most sincerely J. Thelwall

---

[21] Thelwall sends his regards to a group of Liverpool jacobins and reformers that includes Rathbone and Smith, noticed above; the Revd William Shepherd (1768–1847), dissenting minister, author and politician (see Letter No. 11, below); William Roscoe (1753–1831), lawyer, poet, abolitionist, admirer of Paine and Wollstonecraft and author of the irreverent squib *The Life, Death, and Wonderful Achievements of Edmund Burke* (1791); and Edward Rushton (1756–1814), the 'Miltonic' republican (as Shepherd describes him in the introduction to Rushton's *Poems* of 1824). The circle also included James Currie (1756–1805), physician and abolitionist, and John Yates (1755–1811), a Unitarian minister who also trained at Warrington Academy. For this important group, see R. B. Rose, 'The "Jacobins" of Liverpool, 1789–1793', *Liverpool Bulletin* 9 (1960–1), 35–49 and Ian Sellers, 'William Roscoe, the Roscoe Circle, and Radical Politics in Liverpool, 1787–1807', *Transactions of the Historical Society of Lancashire and Cheshire* 120 (1968), 45–62. Coleridge was familiar with them all: see his descriptions of Currie, Roscoe and Rathbone in his letter to Poole of 24 July 1800 (*CL*, I, 607), and also Daniel Sanjiv Roberts, 'Coleridge's Liverpool Connection: An Unpublished Letter from William Roscoe to John Edwards', *Notes and Queries* 244 (December 1999), 455–7.

5

John Thelwall to Edward Williams ('Iolo Morganwg'), 10 May 1798[1]
Source: The National Library of Wales MS 21283E/471

Thelwall's letter to 'The Welch Bard' refers to his 'Pedestrian Excursion' and laments the fact that they did not meet at Cowbridge the previous summer. The letter proves that Thelwall knew he was still being watched at Llyswen; fraternal visits and picturesque tours, he says, might therefore be deemed capital offences.

[Addressee: Williams/The Welch Bard/Cowbridge[2]]

Llys wen 10 May 1798 –

Dear Bard,

It has been matter of great mortification to me that when I passed through Cowbridge last Summer[3] I was not acquainted with the circumstance of your residing there = as the pleasure of meeting you would have been one of the most agreeable circumstances of my ramble. This misfortune it was my intention to have repaired this spring by visiting again the Glamorganshire Coast – the State of affairs, however, & the prejudices with which I know myself to be watched have made me deem it prudent to lay this intention aside, lest picturesque curiosity, & visits of friendship should be construed into High Treason.[4] I seiz however the Opportunity of a Call from a Swansea Traveller, to send you ~~a letter~~ this letter & inform you that I am at present situated in a pleasant Cottage is the rustic village above named in a delightful situation on the banks of the Wye in Brecknockshire, where I f have a little farm of 36 Acres; & where I shall be right happy to see you, if ever you can make it convenient to ramble so far & spend a week or ten days with me. I can furnish you a spare bed,

---

[1] A portion of this letter is quoted in Thompson, 'Jacobin Fox', 117.
[2] Williams had opened a grocer's shop, then a bookshop, at Cowbridge after his return from London in 1795.
[3] On his 'Pedestrian Excursion'.
[4] For this very real surveillance, see Chapter 5, above.

a rasher of bacon, a draught of small ale, & such other homely accomodations as suit a poet a philosopher & a democrat.

Yours
most true
J. Thelwall

Llyswen lies directly in the Road from Brecknock to ~~the~~ Builth – Lres directed to be left for me at the 3 Cocks in the Road to Hay are furthered with.^t. delay –

6

John Thelwall to George Dyer, 12 August 1801[1]
Source: The Carl H. Pforzheimer Collection of Shelley and his Circle, The New York Public Library, Astor, Lenox and Tilden Foundations, Misc 672

Thelwall writes to Dyer from Hereford, where he had established himself after leaving Llyswen, to thank him for a list of books on historical, poetical and antiquarian topics which Dyer had recently sent him and to ask for guidance and assistance in securing similar reading. The letter represents an important Thelwall 'bibliography' for the years in which he produced *Poems, Chiefly Written in Retirement*. And it is to that volume of 1801, which was about to appear, that Thelwall then turns, providing a valuable discussion of its publication history – a discussion that should be read alongside that given by Coleridge in his peevish letter to Thelwall of 23 April 1801 (*CL*, II, 722–4).

[Addressee: G. Dyer/Clifford's Inn/Fleet Street]

Hereford 12 Aug 1801

Dear Dyer[2] –

Your Letter, without date, come to hand on Sunday night. I thank you for your list of Books. Cottles Edda[3] was given me by the Author when I was in London two years & a half ago – & Ossian[4] also I have. Percy's Reliques[5] I have borrowed; & find them replete with every species of poetical instruction. Olaus Magnus[6] I picked up at Chester a few weeks ago; & Sheffer's Hist. of Lapland[7] (which is somewhat in point) I

---

[1] Thompson refers to this letter but does not quote from it in 'Jacobin Fox', 123n.
[2] In a letter of 24 August 1796 to Thomas Hardy, Thelwall had written: 'Civic remembrances to all good Democrats – to Friend [*sic*] in particular, & to that Walking Benevolence George Dyer' (*Times Literary Supplement* (19 June 1953), 402).
[3] *Icelandic Poetry, or, The Edda of Saesmund*, tr. A. S. Cottle (1797).
[4] Thelwall is referring to James Macpherson's 'Ossian' poems, *Fingal, an Ancient Epic Poem* (1762) and *Temora* (1763).
[5] *Reliques of Ancient English Poetry*, ed. Thomas Percy (1765).
[6] Olaus Magnus, *A Compendious History of the Goths, Swedes & Vandals, and other Northern Nations* (1658).
[7] Johannes Scheffer, *Histoire de la Laponie, sa description, l'origine, les moeurs*, tr. par L.P.A.L. (1678).

ransacked at the Worcester College Library – Mallet's Northern Antiq[8] – (the same I suppose as you call Percy's) the five pieces of Runic poetry,[9] & Sayers's Poems,[10] I received on Monday from London – Of Chronicles I have only Baker[11] & an abridg.ᵗ. of Stow,[12] & a fragment without title page from Brute to Harold – b. letter. If Hollingshead – or a Geoffrey of Monmouth in Eng[13] – (& once I had seen such a thing in a Catalogue) or any other of the famous old black letter Chroniclers should fall into your way at a reasonable rate, I should be obliged to you to snap him up for me. Walker's <u>Mem. of Irish Bards</u>[14] & <u>Campbells Mem. of Scottish Poetry</u>[15] I have sometimes seen in Catalogues but was never so lucky as to be time enough to procure them. If you could meet with them for me I should be right glad – as also of <u>Pontoppidan's Norway</u>[16] – <u>Pinkerton's Scottish Poems</u>[17] – There is also I believe a Book called Fragments of ~~English Poet~~ ancient Poetry[18] – or something like it which I am told is valuable. I am also much in need of Books that will make me copiously acquainted with the history (fabulous history of course I mean) during & previous to the early part of the 7th Century – & I should be very glad of any thing of that kind –

I thank you, also, for your offer ~~also~~ with respect to my poems. I beg, however, that you will not do anything in the promotion of my interests that can at all impede your own – for there is very little prospect of my being able to make any return. With this proviso I shall be obliged to you for such help as you can lend, for it seems it is upon private circulation that I must almost entirely depend. I have been

---

[8] Paul Henri Mallet, *Northern Antiquities: or, A description of the manners, customs, religion and laws of the ancient Danes, and other northern nations; with a translation of the Edda, and other pieces, from the Icelandic*. Translated [by Thomas Percy et al.] *from Introduction à l'histoire de Dannemarc* (1770).

[9] *Five Pieces of Runic Poetry translated from the Icelandic Language* [by Thomas Percy] (1763).

[10] Frank Sayers, *Poems* (1792).

[11] Sir Richard Baker, *A Chronicle of the Kings of England from the Time of the Roman Government unto the Raigne of . . . King Charles* (1643).

[12] John Stow, *The Chronicles of England, from Bute unto this present yeare* (1580).

[13] Aaron Thompson, *The British History, translated into English from the Latin of Jeffrey of Monmouth* (1718).

[14] Joseph Cooper Walker, *Historical Memoirs of the Irish Bards, interspersed with Anecdotes of the Music of Ireland* (1786).

[15] Alexander Campbell, *An Introduction to the History of Poetry in Scotland* (1798).

[16] Erik Pontoppidan, *The Natural History of Norway*, tr. Andreas Berthelson (1755).

[17] *Scottish Tragic Ballads*, ed. J. Pinkerton (1781).

[18] James Macpherson, *Fragments of Ancient Poetry, collected in the Highlands of Scotland, and translated from the Galic or Erse Language* (1760).

these three months importuning Phillips[19] for his advice how I should proceed; & this day only (now that my work is half finished) I have received a letter ~~by~~ from him by which it seems I have done every thing that I ought not to have done & left undone every thing that I ought to do – 'On no account print in Demy 8vo', says he, 'or ~~dem~~ on demy paper'. But I have already printed on Demy & in octavo – & according to him have 'damned my book, lost my money & disgusted myself' ——— All which is certainly damned comfortable. – 'You might calculate upon 250', he says, 'beyond those subscribers' – Comfortable again – I have calculated upon three times that Number – What a blessed thing advice is when it comes too late –

     Yours very sincerely J. Thelwall

September 2 – My dear friend – The distance between the date of the letter, & the Post will shew me to be either a very busy, or a very lazy man – if you conclude the latter, you will do me injustice – My book is just ready for delivery –

---

[19] See Letter No.4, note 17, above.

7

John Thelwall to Joseph Strutt, 20 December 1801[1]
Source: Birmingham City Reference Library (Archives),
Galton MSS, 507/1

This is another highly significant document since it affords a glimpse of Thelwall newly emerged from the years of proscription. At this time he was about to start the process of reintegrating himself back into society, embarking on what was to prove a successful new career as a lecturer on elocution and speech therapist[2] (at once a natural and ironic development for an erstwhile radical orator). 'Flying is certainly a more salubrious exercise than creeping – I was not formed to creep', he confidently asserts to Joseph Strutt, another of his patrons. Strutt, a Derby industrialist (1765–1844), was the son of Jedediah Strutt, cotton-spinner and partner of Arkwright. As Albert Goodwin remarks, Joseph, with Samuel Fox, William Ward and Erasmus Darwin, was one of the 'prime movers . . . in the formation of the Derby Society for Political Information' early in 1792'.[3] Coleridge also knew and admired both Strutt and his wife.[4] This is a different, metamorphosed (his own word) Thelwall now: an aspiring professional who wishes to assimilate himself to the fashions – and views – of polite society. Thelwall here is confident, energetic, mobile.

---

[1] A brief passage from this letter is quoted in Thompson, 'Jacobin Fox', 122.
[2] Cecil Thelwall in the *Life*, 14, notes that Thelwall, like Demosthenes, had overcome a stutter. For his contribution as a speech therapist and theorist, see the following articles: Denyse Rockey, 'The Logopaedic Thought of John Thelwall, 1764–1834: First British Speech Therapist', *British Journal of Disorders of Communication* 12 (October 1977), 83–95; Denyse Rockey, 'John Thelwall and the Origins of British Speech Therapy', *Medical History* 23 (1979), 156–75; Robin Thelwall, 'The Phonetic Theory of John Thelwall', in R. E. Asher and Eugenie J. A. Henderson, eds., *Towards a History of Phonetics* (Edinburgh: Edinburgh University Press, 1981), 186–203. In 1805, Thelwall founded an institute for speech training in Liverpool which he then moved to London.
[3] Albert Goodwin, *The Friends of Liberty: The English Democratic Movement in the Age of the French Revolution* (London: Hutchinson, 1979), 230.
[4] Coleridge described Strutt in a letter of 6 February 1797 to Thelwall as 'every way amiable' and his wife as 'a sweet-minded Woman, and one that you would be apt to recollect whenever you met or used the words lovely, handsome, beautiful' (*CL*, I, 306; see also I, 179).

[Addressee: Mr Jos.^h. Strutt/Derby/Derbysh.]

Leeds 20th Decr. 1801

Dear Sir

Your kind letter of 18 Octr. has been in my hands ever since the beginning of Nov.^r. & if I supposed you to be one of those to whom excuse of business would not be an ~~acceptable~~ admissible apology, I know not how I could frame one for my long delay of acknowledgement. But some intimation of my new and arduous engagements you have probably received thro the channel of your provincial newspaper; into which, as I understand, some paragraphs from the Sheffield Iris have been copied.[5] The enclosed will give you a more particular idea of the nature of my undertaking.[6] You will be pleased to hear, ~~that~~ in defiance of all the disadvantages I have to combat, & the prejudices & apprehensions still unwilling to be laid asleep, that the dawnings of the prospect are highly promising – that conciliation & new & eligible connections have marked my progress – that my exertions have been crowned with the most distinguished marks of approbation ~~by~~ from all persons of <u>all parties</u> – & that altho my emoluments have not yet been very large, the blossoms of reputation have come out so thick & fair, as (barring the blight of incalculable disaster) to promise in due time, a rich & abundant vintage. The most unpleasant part of the adventure is that it divorces me from my family – no one of whom has blessed my sight for three whole months. ~~That~~ If my plan succeeds, new arrangements must be made to remedy this inconvenience; &, indeed I have commissioned my wife to sell our house at Hereford (i.e. if she can get, as is expected, £100 more ~~for~~ than I gave for it) remove the family to the more central town of Birmingham, & join me, as soon as it can be ~~rende~~ rendered convenient, with our eldest boy: for ~~the~~ my career, which will probably not very soon be terminated. You would smile to see me in my metamorphose – for I am really quite transformed. Nothing of the plain out-of-fashioned singularity of the old republican remains, but in my heart – & there it is smothered in

---

[5] Thelwall refers to his new career as a lecturer on elocution. Thompson, 'Jacobin Fox', 123n., remarks: 'The earliest notice I have found of Thelwall's elocution lectures is in Sheffield: *Leeds Mercury*, 14 Nov. 1801'.

[6] The 'enclosed' (untraced) was probably a prospectus of a course of lectures on elocution.

silence, except when with a chosen few I can indulge my native energies.⁷ In dress, in manners &c. I assimilate myself with all possible diligence to the fashion of the times; assume ~~to myself~~ the pride & port of a man of some importance; & aspire to the reputation of every aristocratical accomplishment. In short as persecution would not suffer me to crawl upon the earth, I am trying what can be done by soaring into the clouds. Hitherto I like the experiment vastly. Flying is certainly a more salubrious exercise than creeping — I was not formed to creep. To aspire is my natural motion; & I will indulge it. I will live in the world like a man who has energies and intellect, or I will not live at all. It is cheering to see how the world has mended upon me ever since I took this resolution:

'For he can conquer who but thinks he can.'⁸

But whether ultimately victor or vanquished I shall ever remember with emotions of esteem & affection the succour which in former defeats your family & connections have afforded to their & your obliged & fervent friend

John Thelwall

---

[7] Cf. Thelwall's letter of 16 January 1798 to Thomas Hardy from Llyswen: 'In short the political lecturer of Beaufort Buildings is a mere peasant in Llyswen; and you would smile to see me in an old threadbare jacket, a pair of cloth pantaloons rudely patched, and a silk handkerchief' (Corfield and Evans, 'John Thelwall in Wales', 235–6).

[8] John Dryden's translation of Virgil's *Æneid*, V, 300: 'For they can conquer who believe they can.'

8

John Thelwall to Joseph Strutt, no date; fragment[1]
Source: Birmingham City Reference Library (Archives), Galton MSS, 507

Only a fragment of this letter has survived. Looking back at the tempestuous years 1794–1801, Thelwall writes to Strutt, probably around the same time as the above letter, and uses a metaphor frequently employed during the 1790s to figure the upheavals of revolution. This is another letter of gratitude for the succour given to him during his hour of need, and Thelwall, erstwhile devotee and popularizer of *Political Justice*, wryly acknowledges how alien that feeling is to the 'New Philosophy' – Godwinism.

> past – [MS damaged] ssists to strangle her –
> My most cordial wishes & grateful remembrances wait upon yourself your brothers[2] & all your family, &c – The Storm is past – but I do not forget the Mast I clung to in the hour of Wreck:– all which (as some have interpretted [word deleted]) is not consistent with the New Philosophy – but it is perfectly consistent with those feelings of nature & rectitude, which no philosophy could ever mean to eradicate.[3]
> The like Greetings wait on Dr Fox;[4] &, on the part of M^{rs} T, on Mrs Noble.
>
> Your
obliged friend
& hble Servt
John Thelwall

---

[1] A sentence from this letter is quoted in Thompson, 'Jacobin Fox', 115n.
[2] Strutt had two brothers, the most accomplished of whom was William, an inventor.
[3] Presumably a reference to Godwinism.
[4] For Samuel Fox, see introduction to Letter No. 7, above.

9

John Thelwall to Stella Thelwall, 29 and 30 November 1803[1]
Source: The Pierpont Morgan Library, New York, MA 77 (18)

In late November 1803, Thelwall travelled north to Edinburgh to deliver lectures on elocution, calling on the way on the Coleridges, the Wordsworths and the Southeys. Southey's letter of 19 November 1803 to Charles Danvers draws a sharp distinction between the hunted jacobin of the 1790s and the rejuvenated lecturer on elocution:

> Thelwall is in this neighbourhood, and we shall probably see him soon. He is thriving upon Lectures on Elocution, actually thriving. We live in an odd world. They were going to hang and murder him for every intelligible Jacobinism and now when he rigmarolls them with a farrago of what he does not understand himself it is Oh Rare John Thelwall, and they give him three and six pence a piece, but he is an honest fellow. I have a great respect for him, and never yet suffered an Aristocrat to wag his tongue against him in my presence without giving him a set down. (*NLRS*, I, 336)

On 22 November 1803, Coleridge wrote to Stella Thelwall, describing her husband as a hardy 'Land–Nautilus' who 'drives on in his own Shell' (*CL*, II, 1018). For the journey between Keswick and Penrith, Thelwall had the company of Hazlitt, and his account in this letter of his 'duetto' with 'the disputatious metaphysical Hazlet' is interlaced with observations on the scenery of the lakes that reveal, as does the 'Pedestrian Excursion', his passion for landscape and talent for topographical description. Indeed, once he has crossed the border into Scotland, he provides a brilliant portrait of the physical and emotional landscape that forms the backdrop to Wordsworth's *The Borderers* (which Wordsworth had read to Thelwall at Alfoxden in July 1797).

It is clear from Thelwall's ascerbic annotations to *Biographia Literaria* that the war with France and theology were among the topics he discussed with Coleridge and Southey during his visit (see note 7, below). Thelwall's unflattering portraits of Sara Coleridge, Edith Southey and Mary Lovell are outdone by the account he gives of a

---

[1] A brief passage from this letter is quoted in Thompson, 'Jacobin Fox', 125.

vain Southey's 'execrable voice', 'half way between a croak & a scream'. After Thelwall's departure for Edinburgh, Southey was to get his own back and accuse Thelwall himself of vanity in a facetious letter to John Rickman:

> We have had John Thelwall here on his way to Edinburgh. He is on a course of Lectures on Elocution. I know not which be the more amusing his marvellous ignorance, or his still more marvellous vanity. However my gentleman drives his own gig, gets money and is very happy, and as he is an honest-hearted fellow at the bottom, I am heartily glad that the world goes so well with him. Not but the man is the worse for the deterioration of his pursuits. They are now wholly self-centering, and unconnected with the exertion of any one virtue or with any one good hope. It would probably have been better for him in the next world had John been hanged in 1794 – but not believing in another world John is exceedingly well satisfied to have been left in this. (*NLRS*, I, 337–8)[2]

On 3 December, the *Caledonian Mercury* announced the commencement of Thelwall's elocution lectures in Edinburgh. According to Francis Jeffrey's biographer, Lord Cockburn, the first lecture was disrupted by 'the laughter of the audience, aggravated . . . by the personal unpopularity . . . of the lecturer' (quoted in *EY*, 431n.). In his *Letter to Francis Jeffray* (1804), and his *Reply to the Calumnies, Misrepresentations, and Literary Forgeries, Contained in the Anonymous Observations on his Letter to the Editor of the Edinburgh Review* (1804), Thelwall accused Jeffrey of 'having confederated with certain associates to obstruct the lecture, and with having carried this conspiracy into effect by concealing himself behind a screen, and making the necessary signals' (see *EY*, 421n.). The real culprit was William Erskine, Walter Scott's friend, who accounted Thelwall a traitor, though acquitted. Thelwall had reinvented himself, but was still subject to abuse. After leaving Edinburgh, he travelled to Glasgow to deliver further lectures. In a letter of 16 November 1838 to Henrietta Cecil Thelwall (quoted in the introduction to Letter No. 12, below), Wordsworth stated that he and Thelwall saw each other only once after the latter's November 1803 visit to the Lakes.

---

[2] Cf. other comments of Southey's, reported by Henry Crabb Robinson: 'Coleridge and Southey spoke of Thelwall, calling him merely John. Southey said he is a very good-hearted man, though a consummate coxcomb. Besides, we ought never to forget that he was once as near being hanged as possible. And there is great merit in that'; *HCR*, I, 42.

[Addressee: Mrs Thelwall/Kendal/Westmorland.]

Penrith. Tuesday 29th Nov. 1803

My dear Stella

I am very well – perfectly sound in every thing but resolution. That I have suffered to be shaken so much as to stay 24 hours at Keswick longer than I intended. The scenery of the Lakes – the Cataract of Lodore, the presence of of Southey, & the conversation of Coleridge you will think perhaps sufficient inducements. I dined with Wordsworth's wife & Sister, at Grasmere, & just as I was about to depart, he arrived, on his return from Keswick. The want of sufficient decision & certainty in your letter occasioned as to my time & arrangements had prevented either him from remaining with Coleridge, or Coleridge from coming on with him to Grasmere to meet me.[3] These circumstances of course occasioned me some delay, & I lost part of the beauty of the scenery during the latter part of the road from Grasmere to Keswick. It was nevertheless interesting – highly so –

Carlisle Wednesday Morning
From Keswick to Penrith (for the change of weather I understood would render the other road impassable) the younger Hazlet[4] (who, at present, resides at K) accompanied me. It was a glorious day for the picturesque – Mists, & cloud, & transition from shade to brilliancy – bright gleams & flitting tints for ever varying. An artist was therefore the very companion in the world most acceptable to one of my taste. We could sympathise in every thing: & our duetto was sometimes in a tolerably high key –

[3] For these arrangements, see Coleridge's letter of 22 November 1803 to Stella: 'I did not receive your Husband's Letter, &c till the day before yesterday, when Mr Clarkson delivered it to me / I was vexed at the delay – as Thelwall would naturally think my silence a proof of neglect & forgetfulness of past kindness' (*CL,* II, 1017–18), and his letter of 25 November 1803 to Thelwall: 'I received your Wife's kind & very interesting Letter; but was too ill to answer it by return of Post. I cannot without the most culpable Imprudence attempt to reach Kendal; especially, as I could not possibly arrive there time enough to spend any time at all with your Family – but I will go to Grasmere, & meet you there' (*CL,* II, 1019).

[4] Thelwall refers to William Hazlitt as 'the younger' since he knew Hazlitt's brother, John, who had been present at a gathering at Thelwall's house in 1794 to celebrate his acquittal.

crescendo con expressivo. The scenery of the Lakes, however, ~~but~~ except under such circumstances of season & weather, is not picturesque (in the luxuriancy of summer it must be very far from it indeed) – Its beauties and its glories are of a very different – ~~I~~ a much higher character – grandly varied – majestic – awful – luxuriously sublime.

 At Penrith I met with G. Braithwaite:[5] & by his advice & assistance made an effort to dispose of my horse; but failed: & the only fruit of the experiment was the loss of an hour, or hour & half which made me late here. The necessity of finishing and sending my letter was however removed; as he was to write to his family & promised to request them to inform you that I was in health & spirits. Coleridge had also promised to write but upon him I should not have relied.

<u>Long Town</u> – 11 o'Clock.
Still well & cheerful, full of deep cogitations; expatiating & expanding my philosophical principle of pulsation; & brooding with encreasing confidence and satisfaction on the ready assent which every literary & scientific character I meet with (you know the isolated exception) gives to the truth & to the value of ~~my discov~~ this my fundamental axiome! Coleridge & Southey, & even the disputatious metaphysical Hazlet are already among the number of my disciples. – By the way H— is a very improved young man. His mind has unfolded. He has become less disputatious & more conversable. Sara[6] ~~is~~ seems only improved by becoming less talkative – (i.e. less obvious) – Mrs Southey & Mrs Lovell are both her superior in person &c. but they are neither of them interesting. – Mrs S., tho handsomest, least so – Her only expression is vanity – & she seems a mere mute in the drama. Even S. himself towers above his [word deleted] fellow beings more by his vanity than his genius. – he <u>looks</u> like a man who has read more than he has thought – & who has fancy without energy & <u>when</u> he speaks, you perceive, even

---

[5] See Coleridge's letter to Thelwall, *CL*, II, 1020: 'Do you know G. Braithwaite, Junr – a Quaker of our friend, Clarkson's, Acquaintance?'
[6] Sara Coleridge.

in the very tuning of his most <u>execrable</u> voice which is half way between a croak & a scream, rather the formality of the reader than the ear of the conversationalist.[7]

Longholme 2 o'Clock
At length I am fairly in Scotland. One half of my last stage has been highly interesting – thro hanging woods; along the winding banks of a romantic river. Indeed the whole stage from Long-ford has been considerably pleasing – the river having been my companion almost the whole way – but it is only as you approach Scotland (!!!) that plantations begin to make their appearance cloathing & diversifying the Country. From Carlisle to the English boundary, what dreary nakedness! Neither [word deleted] woodland nor arable nor pasture – at least to any ~~appearance~~ degree of luxuriency or culture:– flat, barren & furze-grown – a wretched common = as if Desolation sat brooding in silent triumph over the gilty ~~spot~~ tract polluted with the blood of reiterated contention – the scene of Scottish & of english massacres. To night I shall sleep at Mosspall – tomorrow at Bankhouse – the night following at Edinboro. Let me hear from you as soon as possible. If Molly is not better, I conjure you by <u>the most sacred of all things</u> by my love & ~~by~~ my peace of mind, <u>buy a bed</u>, & have her removed. The necessity of this is the only impression that haunts my imagination – & the spirit can never be laid but by the assurance that it is done. If by so doing you should inconveniently exhaust your finances, let me know & they shall <u>immediately</u> be supplied. I had no leizure to feel this consideration while I was at home – but <u>feel</u> it now.

---

[7] In his annotations to Coleridge's *Biographia Literaria*, Thelwall, misremembering the date of his visit, wrote, next to Coleridge's statement 'To this hour I cannot find reason to approve of the first war either in its commencement or its conduct': 'Yet when I visited Southey & Coleridge in the spring of 1804, when C., it seems, was writing for the *second* war, S. expressly stated, & C. tacitly admitted that the second was only the *rump*, or necessary consequence of the first, & as the country had submitted to the first ‹so› they ought to be content with the latter' (Pollin and Burke, 'John Thelwall's Marginalia', 82). Next to Coleridge's 'Thus too, without any tautology we contend for the EXISTENCE of the Supreme Being; that is, for a reality correspondent to the idea', Thelwall wrote: 'Mr C. seems to have received some new light upon the signification of the syllable ex, since he talked to me at Keswick of his design of writing an elaborate demonstration of the truth of Christian revelation which should commence with a denial of the *e*xistence of God' (ibid., 88).

10

Henrietta Cecil Thelwall to the Revd William Shepherd, March 1835[1]
Source: Harris-Manchester College, Oxford: Shepherd Papers, Vol. VII, No. 79

Thelwall's first wife, Susan ('Stella') Vellum, died in 1816. Thelwall married Henrietta Cecil Boyle (known after the marriage as Cecil Thelwall), many years his junior, in 1817. Initially, she had come to Thelwall the 'elocutionary scientist' to be trained for the stage. The *Dictionary of National Biography* records that she was 'a woman of great social charm and some literary ability' who, in addition to a biography of her husband, wrote 'several little works for children'. She died in 1863, leaving one son, Weymouth Birkbeck Thelwall.

The Revd William Shepherd (1768–1847), to whom Thelwall sends his regards in Letter No. 4, above, was a dissenting minister, author and politician. He was educated at the dissenting academies at Daventry and Hackney and in 1791 became the minister of the Unitarian chapel at Gateacre, Liverpool. He was closely associated with the fortunes of a number of radicals in the 1790s: he was a friend of the Revd Jeremiah Joyce (also educated at Daventry), whom he visited in the Tower in May 1794 when Joyce was arrested, with Thelwall, Hardy, Horne Tooke and Holcroft, on a charge of High Treason. He was to adopt Hannah, Joyce's youngest daughter. In July 1797, he visited his friend, the Baptist minister William Winterbotham, in Newgate Prison (as, of course, did Edward Williams). When Gilbert Wakefield was sentenced to two years' imprisonment in Dorchester in 1799, Shepherd visited him there and took his son and eldest daughter under his protection. He was a prominent figure in the public life of Liverpool, and part of a circle of radical intellectuals; for this Liverpool group, see Letter No. 4, note 20, above. Shepherd's *Life of Poggio Bracciolini* appeared in 1802, and his *Systematic Education, or Elementary Instruction in the various Departments of Literature and Science*, co-written with Joyce, was published in 1815. Thomas De Quincey, who as a young man observed Shepherd in

---

[1] Thompson quotes two phrases from this letter in 'Jacobin Fox', 139.

1801–2 at the banker William Clarke's house in Everton, later framed a colourful portrait of him in which he states with amusement that 'the pale pink' of Shepherd's radicalism was at the turn of the century 'accounted deep, deep scarlet'.[2]

Writing after the death of her husband in a decade of revolutions, uprisings and demonstrations throughout Europe, Henrietta Cecil Thelwall asks Shepherd for his advice regarding the biography of Thelwall she was researching. She speaks frankly of the difficulties and insecurities she was experiencing in seeking to write a fitting memoir, which was ultimately to appear in 1837 as her *Life of John Thelwall*. The letter provides a valuable background to this first book-length biography of Thelwall, and it is interesting to scrutinize the bibliography she drew up in an attempt to familiarize herself with the historical and political context of the 1790s; these texts are identified in full in the notes. The letter also shows that there was to be a second, 'entirely literary' volume which never appeared. The author writes from Oving, where Thelwall's son Hampden was rector. It seems that the judge and writer Thomas Noon Talfourd (1795–1854) – who was to offer a sympathetic sketch of Thelwall in his *Final Memorials of Charles Lamb* (1848) – had a hand in dispatching the letter since his name appears beneath Shepherd's address.

---

[2] See *The Collected Writings of Thomas De Quincey*, ed. David Masson (14 vols; Edinburgh: A. and C. Black, 1889–90), II, 128–9: '[Drollery and buffoonery] could be furnished of an inferior quality by Mr Shepherd, who . . . had but little dignity in private life. I know not how far he might alter in these respects; but certainly, at the time (1801–2), he was decidedly, or could be, a buffoon, and seemed even ambitious of the title, by courting notice for his grotesque manner and coarse stories, more than was altogether compatible with the pretensions of a scholar and a clergyman. I must have leave to think that such a man could not have emerged from any great University, or from any but a sectarian training . . . With what coarseness and low buffoonery have I heard this Mr Shepherd in those days run down the bishops then upon the bench, but especially those of any public pretensions or reputation, as Horsley and Porteus, and, in connexion with them, the pious Hannah More! Her he could not endure. Of this gentleman, having said something disparaging, I am bound to go on and add, that I believe him to have been at least a truly upright man – talking often wildly, but incapable of doing a conscious wrong to any man, be his party what it might; and, in the midst of fun or even buffoonery, a real, and, upon occasion, a stern patriot. Mr Canning and others he opposed to the teeth upon the Liverpool hustings, and would take no bribe, as others did, from literary feelings of sympathy, or (which is so hard for an amiable mind to resist) from personal applications of courtesy and respect. Amusing it is to look back upon any political work of Mr Shepherd's, as upon his "Tour of France", published in 1815, and to know that the pale pink of his Radicalism was then accounted deep, deep scarlet'.

[Addressee: The Rev. W. Shepherd/Gatacre/N^r Liverpool]

Oving Rectory N^r Aylesbury
Bucks.
March.

Dear Sir.
Nearly a twelvemonth ago, you were so very kind as to say to my friend Dr Birkbeck,[3] that if I would write the Memoirs of my late dear and lamented Husband, you would read and correct my manuscript, and introduce him to politics; and also write a Preface.

Upon my question to Dr Birkbeck, whether he thought it necessary for me to have another interview with you upon this subject, he gave me to understand that he thought not, as you had sufficiently expressed your views and intentions to him: and that therefore I had better send you my M.S.S. as I should finish each Chapter. or Part. I mention this circumstance as my excuse for not acknowledging your kindness to the memory of my dear husband at that period; and fearfull of being intrusive, I have since not liked to trouble you, untill I could be able to send you, some portion of my work.

As I was to spend the last summer at Ld Weymouth's N^r Wincanton, I deferred the commencement of my undertaking untill I could settle myself in the retirement of the Country

I did not leave London for Somersetshire till the latter end of May; and then for about a month after my arrival I found it impossible to set myself down to my melancholy task.

At length I was enabled to devote three or four hours of each day, to the beginning of the Memoir; and like all inexperienced writers, I thought I had only to sit down and give vent to the feelings and impressions of my mind and my task would soon be completed – as I had drawn up an Outline from mere recollection, I thought I had little else to do, than fill up that Outline from recollection also, with occasional referrence to my documents

With this undefined arrangement, I took up my pen; but I had not got thro' many pages, when I found something more was wanting, and

---

[3] George Birkbeck (1776–1841), physician and pioneer of popular education. He was the founder of the London Mechanics' Institution, at which John Thelwall lectured towards the end of his life, and the co-founder of University College, London. Weymouth Birkbeck Thelwall, the son of Thelwall and Henrietta Cecil, was named after him.

that the person who could sit down to write such a Memoir as Thelwall's ought to be, should be well acquainted with the Times and History of the period about which he wrote and that so far from merely writing up to the political part of the life, the whole of the first part of the Memoir must of necessity be political.

The consciousness of my ignorance on these points, and the toil to go thro' to remedy that ignorance, brought me at once to a stop, and I was well nigh giving up the undertaking in despair – But my heart and my hopes were in the work, and as I had devoted myself to it, I determined not to let the first obstacles which presented themselves, divert me from my duty. I accordingly resigned the pen, and sat myself down to read: and as I have no guide <u>now</u> to direct my studies, who by pointing out the most eligible works to refer to for the information, I sought, and thus shorten my labour, I was obliged to avail myself of every book that came in my way, which seemed to have any referrence to the latter part of the last Century. These were the following.

	'Adolphus' Hist: of George 3rd' – – 3 Vols.[4]
'Margorot's Trial[5]	'Butler's, Reminicenses' – – – – 2 Vols[6]
Stockdale's d[itt]o Warren Hastings.[7]	'Cartwrights Memoirs' – – – – 2 „[8]
Gerrald's Convention.[9]	'Horne Tooke's Memoirs' – – 2 – „[10]

---

[4] John Adolphus, *The History of England, from the Accession of George III to the conclusion of Peace in the year one thousand seven hundred and eighty-three* (1802).

[5] *The Tryal of M. Margarot, delegate from London, to the British Convention, before the High Court of Justiciary, at Edinburgh, on the 13th and 14th of January 1794, for Sedition* (1794).

[6] Charles Butler, *Reminiscences of Charles Butler*, Esq (1822 and 1827).

[7] [Thomas Erskine], *The Whole Proceedings on the trial of an information exhibited . . . by the . . . Attorney General, against John Stockdale, for a libel on the House of Commons* (1790).

[8] Frances Dorothy Cartwright, *The Life and Correspondence of Major Cartwright* (1826). In The Carl H. Pforzheimer Collection of The New York Public Library (Misc 227) is a letter of 23 February 1829 from Dorothy Cartwright, the daughter of Major John Cartwright (1740–1824), the 'Father of Reform' and founder of the Society for Constitutional Information, in which she asks Thelwall for a portrait of himself for her own edition: 'I am sorry to say there is no probability of a second edition of my uncle's life, my wish therefore in collecting portraits of his friends is only to illustrate my own private copy – I have been at considerable expence, in having every page inlaid folio size, so as to admit prints of a larger size than I could otherwise have inserted & I flatter myself that my Brother's sons (and perhaps their sons' sons) may find it a very valuable addition to the family library. As I certainly should be sorry to [?] any of the prints you mention of yourself, I should be very glad to obtain a copy from one of the drawings & I think from what you say, that the unfinished crayon by Smith would be the best for the purpose.'

[9] Joseph Gerrald, *A Convention the only means of saving us from Ruin* (1793).

[10] Alexander Stephens, *Memoirs of John Horne Tooke* (1813).

Holcroft's – defence[11]	'Nichol's Recollections – – – 1 – „[12]
Martin's – d[itt]o.[13]	'Wraxalls Memoirs' no use 2 – „[14]
Horne Tooke versus C. Fox. trial.[15]	'Mant's Wars of England' last – 3 – „[16]
Burke's Observations State of Nation.'[17]	'Hardy's Memoirs' – – – 1–[18]
Universal Magazines 1792-3[19]	History of Two Acts – – – 1–[20]
Sundry Pamphlets of Societies &c	Thelwall's Tribune – – 3[21]
Political Lectures –[22]	„ – Sober Reflections – –1[23]

and a great variety of Manuscripts besides. I have here enumerated them, that you may know my Authorities, for what I may have asserted.

And now after having laboured thro' all these works, my difficulties became greater than ever, for it is certainly most true, that the more we enquire into, and endeavour to compass an object, the greater the progress we make, the more we have cause to lament our own ignorance and insufficiency This was just my situation, I had accumulated facts and ideas, but I was at a loss how to use them properly The fact is, I was, and <u>am</u> willing to confess, that the vastness of the subject and my conceptions was too great for my limited capabilities and inexperience: and I have undertaken a task, that requires the powerful pen of an able writer, and the eloquence of a Giant mind to do adequate justice to.

However notwithstanding my conscious inability I still determined to persevere, and tho' I knew I was incapable of doing what ought to be done, yet I thought it was my sacred duty to try my best, and if I

---

[11] Thomas Holcroft, *A Narrative of facts, relating to a prosecution for high treason . . . and the Defence the author had prepared, if he had been brought to trial* (1795).
[12] Either John Nichols, *Brief Memoirs of John Nichols* (1804) or Alexander Chalmers, *Memoir of John Nichols* (1827).
[13] *An Account of the Proceedings on a Charge of High Treason against John Martin* (1795).
[14] N. W. Wraxall, *Historical Memoirs of my Own Time* (1815).
[15] *Proceedings in an action for debt . . . between C. J. Fox . . . and John Horne Tooke* (1792).
[16] Untraced.
[17] Edmund Burke, *Observations on a late State of the Nation* (1769).
[18] Thomas Hardy, *Memoir of Thomas Hardy, founder of . . . the London Corresponding Society* (1832).
[19] *The Universal Magazine of Knowledge and Pleasure* (1747–1800).
[20] *The History of Two Acts* (1796).
[21] John Thelwall, *The Tribune* (1795–6).
[22] Presumably a collection of Thelwall's political lectures apart from *The Tribune*.
[23] John Thelwall, *Sober Reflections on the Seditious and Inflammatory Letter of . . . Edmund Burke, to a Noble Lord* (1796).

found in persevering that my mind misgave me as did my heart, then indeed, and not till then, I should have a right to yield.[24]

I once more sat down to my desk, resolved not to contemplate my undertaking as a whole, but to go on gradually with each ~~part~~ event and incident, 'till I should have finished what might amount to the first or nearly the first volume.[25]

This I have at length accomplished, but how, I will not attempt to say: I can only feel ashamed, that in spite of all the perplexities by which I have been surrounded, (sometimes even to the feeling that I really must resign the pen) the narative should appear so easy in detail

In the course of two or three days I shall take the liberty of forwarding the Manuscript to you, and shall then feel indeed, that it is in the fittest hands; and that the memory of my dear husband will at last have justice done him. I have <u>attempted</u> to divide it into Chapters, and have concluded this part with the 'Trials' of the year 94.[26] It makes in all ten Chapters but as I suppose two more, will conclude the Political part of the Life, perhaps you will advise me to add them too, to the first volume, when they are written.[27] This then would make the volume, a complete History, and if you thought proper, might be made to suit well with the <u>present time</u>:[28] if so, it might be very soon got ready for the Press.

---

24   The sentiments of the previous paragraphs are repeated in the preface to the *Life*, pp. x–xi: 'The task of making a proper selection from these documents, and of arranging the selected matter, so as to throw the fullest light upon the principles by which Mr Thelwall was guided in his public conduct, she found to be arduous . . . In these circumstances, she would probably have given up her undertaking in despair, had she not felt a confidence in the kind promise of the Rev. Dr. Shepherd, of Gatacre [sic], who had been the steady friend of Mr Thelwall, that he would revise her manuscript and amend it by the necessary corrections. Feeling thus assured that her facts and style would undergo severe and impartial criticism before it met the eye of the public, she was encouraged to persevere in her new, but deeply interesting task. For the valuable assistance of the above-named gentleman, she now returns her sincere thanks.'

25   'In two volumes' appears on the title-page of the *Life*, but only one volume of the biography appeared.

26   The published *Life* concludes with an account of the passing in 1795 of the Pitt and Grenville Acts – the 'gagging' legislation specifically designed to silence Thelwall.

27   The published work comprises fifteen chapters.

28   The first 'political' instalment of the *Life* would certainly 'suit well' with the 'present time': Europe had in 1830–1 witnessed revoutions in France and Belgium and revolt in Poland. In Britain, an armed insurrection at Merthyr Tydfil – the Merthyr Rising – took place in 1831. Agitation for Reform resulted the following year in the passing of the first Reform Bill. Out of dissatisfaction with that Bill, the New Poor Law of 1834 and desperate economic depression was born the Chartist movement of the late 1830s. The rejection by Parliament in 1839 of the Chartist Petition resulted in another rising in the same year at Newport in which twenty-two protesters were killed by troops.

As I am not aware, if it be your intention to write the preface,[29] what points you intend to write upon, I think it will not be quite amiss, to send you the notes I made during my reading, that as they form something of an abstract of the History of the two Factions, viz: the Whigs and Tories till 'the Coalition'[30] and the principal events of the Reign of George the 3$\underline{^{rd}}$ up to the year 1789. they may not be quite useless (if you have patience to wade thro them) in recalling to your mind some topics to be treated on. I had began to put them into the form of an Essay, but as I went on, I found, both my time and my opportunity, might be better employed and I gave it up.

The second volume will be I conceive entirely literary,[31] and certainly not less interesting than the first, and by giving a slight sketch of my Husband's elocutionary Science, in referrence to the prosody and Metre of ~~the~~ our language, may be made as instructive as it will be, I trust, amusing.

With many apologies for inflicting this very long letter on you I beg to subscribe myself

     Dear Sir
      Your obliged, and respectful
       Henrietta Cecil Thelwall.

As it is likely I shall be in town for a few days in about a week, and if so, I shall most probably be ~~at~~ with my dear friend Mrs Harvey, will you be so kind as to direct me under cover to Mr D. W. Harvey,[32] and if I be not there, he will frank your letter on to me, here.

---

[29] Shepherd did not ultimately contribute a preface to the *Life*.
[30] The Fox-North Coalition of 1783.
[31] An interesting insight into the continuation of the *Life*. See *Life*, p. xii: 'The present volume which contains what may be called the history of Mr Thelwall's political life, will in due time be followed by a second, containing an account of his domestic history and of his labours in the field of literature, and of the Science of Elocution'. The period to be covered by this second volume, which never appeared, includes the Llyswen years (late 1797–late 1800). As editor of *The Champion* (1819–21), Thelwall was to re-enter the political arena when Reform was again the order of the day; it seems from HCT's comment to Shepherd that this second lease of political life was to be passed over in the projected 'literary' volume of the *Life*.
[32] Daniel Whittle Harvey – attorney, politician, MP for Colchester (1818–20 and 1826–34) and Southwark (1835–40). He founded the *Sunday Times* newspaper in 1822 and in 1840 became Commissioner of the Metropolitan Police.

11

Henrietta Cecil Thelwall to William Wordsworth, 12 November 1838[1]
Source: Dove Cottage, Grasmere, MS A/Thelwall/1

A year after the publication of the first volume of her *Life* of Thelwall, Henrietta Cecil Thelwall writes to Wordsworth seeking information for the projected second volume (which never appeared) which was to cover Thelwall's years of proscription. Coleridge was dead and Wordsworth's 'dear ruin of a Sister' had recently slipped deeper into illness, and so there is a poignancy to the reference at the beginning of the letter to 'Tintern Abbey' and to Wordsworth's Llyswen visit of August 1798. Henrietta Cecil's statement that she does not 'wish to have any political reference to the acquaintance which then subsisted' between Wordsworth and Thelwall is an assurance that bespeaks Wordsworth's revered Establishment status. Indeed, despite the repeated use of the words 'friends', friendly' and 'friendship', the whole letter, and Wordsworth's reply of 16 November 1838, testify to the changes in political and personal allegiances that occurred over those forty years. Wordsworth writes:

> Circumstances were not favourable to much intercourse between your late Husband and myself: I became acquainted with him during a visit which he made to Mr Coleridge, who was then residing at Nether-Stowey; and I was not a little pleased with the natural eloquence of his conversation, and his enthusiastic attachment to Poetry. He was likewise very sensible to the beauty of Rural Nature . . . After the year 1798 I do not recollect having had any intercourse with Mr Thelwall, till he called upon me at Grasmere on his way to Edinburgh, whither he was going to give Lectures upon Elocution. This must have been some time between 1801 and 1807, and I once called upon *him* in London. After that time I think I never saw him, and I am not aware of there having been any communication between us by letter . . . You will see therefore, that it is not in my power to add any thing to your intended publication. Had Mr Coleridge been living, he probably could have thrown light upon that portion of your Husband's life, of

---

[1] A brief passage from this letter is quoted in Thompson, 'Jacobin Fox', 126.

which you have no personal knowledge. All I can say is, that I retained towards Mr T. a very friendly feeling, grounded upon what I had seen of him, and particularly upon a vivid recollection of some pleasant days which I passed in his company – during the visit to him above mentioned, when with the assistance of his Brother-in-law, and the wife to whom he was first united, and who was a truly aimiable [sic] woman, he lived as a Farmer (not I believe a very successful one) in South Wales.[2]

D Gaskell Esq. Lupset Hall
Wakefield
Nov: 12th 1838

Sir.

In again renewing the gratification I have formerly enjoyed in the perusal of your works, I have just finished your lines upon Tintern Abbey in 1798. This poem recalls to my mind that I have heard my late Husband speak of a visit which you and your respected sister Miss Wordsworth made him about that time at Lyswen in Wales. I think he also said Mr Southey and Mr Coleridge were of the party likewise?[3] Thelwall often spoke of the friendly intercourse, which at one time subsisted between you with much pleasure: and always spoke of you with great admiration and friendship.

Circumstances, Time, and Distance too frequently estrange long tried and friendly intercourse, but altho' correspondence might cease with Thelwall, his heart ever remained true to his friends, and as such, he was always pleased to consider you.

I must however apologize and explain the reason of my now taking the liberty of intruding upon you.

In the 2nd Vol: of the 'Life of Thelwall' at present in hand,[4] I have to speak of my husband's sojourn in what he always in after time, termed 'his exile' That is to say, the interregnum between his political and scientific careers: from 1796 to 1801.

As this was a period of his Life of which I have no personal

---

[2] *LY* iii, 639–40.
[3] In reply, Wordsworth wrote: 'Your impression is correct that I, in company with my Sister and Mr Coleridge, visited him at his pleasant abode on the banks of the Wye. Mr Southey was not of the party, as you suppose' (*LY* iii, 640).
[4] This volume never appeared.

knowledge, I am obliged to refer to those persons who were best acquainted with him at the time, for those reminiscences which may seem interesting and illustrative of his character and his mind. I do not know any that could be more truly so, than what you may furnish either by recollection or in whatever letters you may have preserved, if you feel inclined to favor me. Of course I do not wish to have any political reference to the acquaintance which then subsisted between you; but merely of that communion of kindred minds, which poetry and literature linked in the bonds of Friendship.

Your kind attention to this will confer a favour upon me: and with much respect I beg to remain Sir

Your Obedient Ser^t
H. C. Thelwall

P.S. Upon mentioning to Mrs Gaskell[5] of Thorn's House that I would trouble her son Mr Milns Gaskell to frank this, she has requested me to say that 'she desires to be very kindly remember'd to Miss Wordsworth'.[6]

I will feel greatly obliged to you if you will transmit any communication you may kindly feel disposed to make me under cover to the above named Gentleman at Thorne's House Wakefield and I beg again you will accept my apologies for troubling you.

---

[5] As Alan G. Hill points out in *LY* iii, 467n., this Mrs Gaskell was 'A new acquaintance of the Wordsworths. She was Mary (d. 1845), eldest daughter of Dr. Brandreth of Liverpool, and in 1807 had married Benjamin Gaskell (1781–1855) of Thornes Hall, nr. Wakefield, M.P. for Maldon, 1812–26. She was, according to Dibdin, "an intellectual Circe, and can charm a Whig into a Tory" . . . In 1840 she was instrumental in obtaining for W.W. the Wordsworth family aumbry from the Beaumont family . . . De Selincourt confused Mary Gaskell with her more famous namesake, Elizabeth Gaskell, the novelist.'

[6] The poet's daughter, Dora.

Bibliography

Manuscript Sources

Birmingham City Reference Library (Archives)
Correspondence of John Thelwall
Galton MSS, 507 and 507/1

Bodleian Library, Oxford
Abinger-Shelley Papers: Diary of William Godwin
Abinger dep., e. 200 and 202

British Library, London
Place Papers: Correspondence of John Thelwall
Add. MSS 37,949, ff. 291–2
Add. MSS 37,950, ff. 131–2

Dove Cottage, Grasmere
Correspondence of John Thelwall
MS A/Thelwall/1

Harris-Manchester College, Oxford
Shepherd Papers: Correspondence of Henrietta Cecil Thelwall
Vol. VII, No. 79

The Houghton Library, Harvard University
Correspondence of John Thelwall
Lobby VIII. 4. 2, fMS Eng. 947. 2 (19) and (21)

National Library of Wales, Aberystwyth
Dr T. W. Thomas MSS
NLW MS 10336E/43–5

Diary of William Owen Pughe
NLW MS 13248B

Edward Williams (Iolo Morganwg) MSS
Correspondence and miscellaneous papers of Edward Williams
NLW MS 10333E/49
NLW MS 1806E/665
NLW MS 1885B/44–5
NLW MS 21280E/49
NLW MS 21280E/135–40
NLW MS 21281E/187
NLW MS 21282E/376
NLW MS 21283E/471
NLW MS 21283E/510
NLW MS 21283E/542–9
NLW MS 21283E/552
NLW MS 21283E/560
NLW MS 21283E/572–5
NLW MS 21283E/577–80
NLW MS 21283E/583
NLW MS 21283E/586
NLW MS 21283E/601a
NLW MS 21285E/808
NLW MS 21285E/811–12
NLW MS 21285E/817
NLW MS 21285E/822
NLW MS 21285E/824–6
NLW MS 21285E/835–9
NLW MS 21285E/841–3
NLW MS 21285E/845–8
NLW MS 21285E/850–2
NLW MS 21285E/862
NLW MS 21285E/886
NLW MS 21286E/988
NLW MS 21286E/1023
NLW MS 21286E/1025
NLW MS 21286E/1032
NLW MS 21387E/2
NLW MS 21387E/9
NLW MS 21392F/5
NLW MS 21392F/9

NLW MS 21392F/35–8
NLW MS 21392F/66–7
NLW MS 21392F/88–9
NLW MS 21392F/91
NLW MS 21392F/94
NLW MS 21396E/21–2
NLW MS 21396E/33
NLW MS 21396E/35
NLW MS 21400C/9
NLW MS 21400C/28, 28a and 28b
NLW MS 21400C/32
NLW MS 21401E/33
NLW MS 21401E/35
NLW MS 21417E/1–37
NLW MS 21418E/1–22
NLW MS 21419E/24
NLW MS 21424E/2

The New York Public Library
The Carl H. Pforzheimer Collection: Correspondence of John Thelwall and Dorothy Cartwright
Misc 227 and 672

The Pierpont Morgan Library, New York
Printed advertisement for a course of lectures by John Thelwall on 'Reading, Recitation and Oratory', 1830
PML 7580
Correspondence of John Thelwall
MA 77 (17) and (18)

Public Record Office, London
Correspondence of John Thelwall
T.S. 11/951/3495

Victoria University Library, Toronto, Ontario
Coleridge's marginalia in a copy of Edward Williams's *Poems, Lyric and Pastoral* (1794)

Printed Sources

(a) Primary

Analytical Review

Anderson, Robert (ed.), *A Complete Edition of the Poets of Great Britain* (14 vols; London: J. and A. Arch, 1792–5).

Anon., *A Defence of the Constitution of England* (London: R. Baldwin, 1791).

——, *Orpheus, Priest of Nature and Prophet of Infidelity* (London: J. Stockdale, 1781).

——, *The Civil and Ecclesiastical Systems of England Defended and Fortified* (London: T. Longman, 1791).

——, *The History of Two Acts* (London: G. G. & J. Robinson, 1796).

Anti-Jacobin; or, Weekly Examiner

Anti-Jacobin Review and Magazine; or, Monthly Political and Literary Censor

Baker, James, *A Picturesque Guide through Wales and the Marches* (Worcester: J. Tymbs, 1795).

Barbauld, Anna Laetitia, *The Poems of Anna Laetita Barbauld*, ed. William McCarthy and Elizabeth Kraft (Athens, GA: University of Georgia Press, 1994).

Baxter, John, *A New and Impartial History of England* (London: H. D. Symonds, 1796).

Beattie, James, *The Minstrel, or The Progress of Genius* (London: E. & C. Dilly, 1779).

Blake, William, *Complete Writings*, ed. Geoffrey Keynes (Oxford: Oxford University Press, 1992).

——, *Poems*, ed. W. H. Stevenson and David Erdman (London: Longman, 1971).

British Critic

Burke, Edmund, *A Letter to a Noble Lord* (London: J. Owen, F. & C. Rivington, 1796).

——, *A Philosophical Inquiry into the Origin of our Ideas of the Sublime and Beautiful*, ed. Adam Phillips (Oxford: Oxford University Press, 1990).

——, *Reflections on the Revolution in France*, ed. C. C. O'Brien (Harmondsworth: Penguin, 1986).

——, *The Correspondence of Edmund Burke*, ed. Thomas W. Copeland et al. (10 vols; Cambridge: Cambridge University Press, 1958–78).

Butler, Marilyn, ed., *Burke, Paine, Godwin, and the Revolution Controversy* (Cambridge: Cambridge University Press, 1984).

Byng, John, *The Torrington Diaries, containing the tours through England and Wales of the Hon. John Byng*, ed. C. Bruyn Andrews (4 vols; London: Eyre & Spottiswoode, 1934–8).

Byron, George Gordon, *Byron's Letters and Journals*, ed. Leslie A. Marchand (13 vols; London: John Murray, 1973–94).

——, *The Complete Poetical Works*, ed. J. J. McGann (7 vols; Oxford: Clarendon Press, 1980–93).

Cambrian Register (1796–1818).

Campbell, James Dykes, *Samuel Taylor Coleridge: A Narrative of the Events of his Life* (London: Macmillan, 1894).

Campbell, Thomas, *The Complete Poetical Works*, ed. J. Logie Robertson (London: Oxford University Press, 1907).

Cartwright, Frances Dorothy, *The Life and Correspondence of Major Cartwright* (2 vols; London: Henry Colburn, 1826).

Clayden, P. W., *The Early Life of Samuel Rogers* (London: Smith, Elder & Co., 1887).

Cobbett, William, *Rural Rides*, ed. George Woodcock (Harmondsworth: Penguin, 1985).

Coffman, Ralph J., *Coleridge's Library: A Bibliography of Books Owned Or Read by Samuel Taylor Coleridge* (Boston: G. K. Hall, 1987).

Coleridge, Samuel Taylor, *Collected Letters*, ed. E. L. Griggs (6 vols; Oxford: Clarendon Press, 1956–71).

——, *Collected Works*, Bollingen Series 75 (Princeton: Princeton University Press): i. *Lectures 1795 on Politics and Religion*, ed. Lewis Patton and Peter Mann (1971); ii. *The Watchman*, ed. Lewis Patton (1970); iii. *Essays on his Times*, ed. D. V. Erdman (3 vols, 1978); vi. *Lay Sermons*, ed. R. J. White (1972); xiv. *Table Talk*, ed. Carl Woodring (2 vols, 1990); xvi. *Poetical Works*, ed. J. C. C. Mays (3 vols, 2001).

——, *Fears in Solitude . . . To which are added, France, An Ode; and Frost at Midnight* (London: J. Johnson, 1798).

——, *Poems on Various Subjects* (Bristol: J. Cottle and London: G. G. & J. Robinson, 1796).

——, *Poems . . . To which are now added Poems by Charles Lamb and Charles Lloyd* (Bristol: J. Cottle and London: G. G. & J. Robinson, 1797).

——, *The Complete Poetical Works*, ed. E. H. Coleridge (2 vols; Oxford: Clarendon Press, 1912).

——, *The Fall of Robespierre* (Cambridge: W. H. Lunn & J. & J. Merrill, 1794).

——, *The Notebooks of Samuel Taylor Coleridge*, ed. Kathleen Coburn (6 vols; New York: Routledge & Kegan Paul, 1957–73).

——, *The Letters of Samuel Taylor Coleridge*, ed. E. H. Coleridge (2 vols; London: Heinemann, 1895).

Cooper, Astley, *The Lectures of Sir Astley Cooper . . . on the Principles and Practice of Surgery with Additional Notes and Cases by Frederick Tyrrell* (3 vols; London: Thomas & George Underwood, 1824–7).

Cooper, Bransby Blake, *The Life of Sir Astley Cooper* (2 vols; London: John W. Parker, 1843).

Corfield, P. J. and Evans, Chris, 'John Thelwall in Wales: New Documentary Evidence', *Bulletin of the Institute of Historical Research* 59 (1986), 231–9.

Cottle, Joseph, *The Fall of Cambria* (2 vols; London: Longman, Hurst, Rees & Orme, 1808).

Cowden Clarke, Charles and Mary, *Recollections of Writers* (London: Sampson Low & Co., 1878).

Coxe, William, *An Historical Tour in Monmouthshire* (2 vols; London: T. Cadell & W. Davies, 1801).

Critical Review

Cylch-grawn Cynmraeg; neu, Drysorfa Gwybodaeth

Dafydd ap Gwilym, *Apocrypha*, ed. Helen Fulton (Llandysul: Gwasg Gomer, 1996).

——, *Barddoniaeth Dafydd ab Gwilym*, ed. William Owen Pughe and Owen Jones (London: H. Baldwin, 1789).

——, *Gwaith Dafydd ap Gwilym*, ed. Thomas Parry (Cardiff: University of Wales Press, 1952).

Davies, Edward, *The Mythology and Rites of the British Druids* (London: J. Booth, 1809).

Davies, William Ll., 'David Samwell's Poem "The Padouca Hunt"', *National Library of Wales Journal* 2 (1941–2), 142–52.

Defoe, Daniel, *A Tour Through The Whole Island of Great Britain*, ed. G. D. H. Cole and D. C. Browning (2 vols; London: J. M. Dent, 1974).

Dendurent, H. O., 'The Coleridge Collection in Victoria University Library, Toronto', *The Wordsworth Circle* 5, 4 (Autumn 1974), 225–86.

De Quincey, Thomas, *The Collected Writings of Thomas De Quincey*, ed. David Masson (14 vols; Edinburgh: A. & C. Black, 1889–90).

Derfel, R. J., *Brad y Llyfrau Gleision* (Rhuthyn: I. Clarke, 1854).

Dudley, Henry and Mary Bate, *Passages Selected by Distinguished Personages, on the Great Literary trial of Vortigern and Rowena; A Comi-Tragedy* (London: J. Ridgway, 1795–1807).

Dyer, George, *A Dissertation on the Theory and Practice of Benevolence* (London: G. Kearsley, 1795).

——, An *Inquiry into the Nature of Subscription to the Thirty-Nine Articles* (2nd edition; London: J. Johnson, 1792).

Dyer, George, *Four Letters on the English Constitution* (4th edition; London: Longman, Hurst, Rees, Orme & Brown, 1818).
——, *Memoirs of the Life and Writings of Robert Robinson* (London: G. G. & J. Robinson, 1796).
——, *Poems* (London: J. Johnson, 1792).
——, *Poems* (London: Longman & Rees, 1801).
——, *Poetics: or, a Series of Poems, and Disquisitions on Poetry* (2 vols; London: J. Johnson, 1812).
——, *The Complaints of the Poor People of England* (2nd edition; London: J. Ridgway & H. D. Symonds, 1793).
Evans, Evan, *Gwaith y Parchedig Evan Evans*, ed. D. Silvan Evans (Caernarfon: H. Humphreys, 1876).
Evans, Theophilus, *Drych Y Prif Oesoedd*, ed. David Thomas (Cardiff: University of Wales Press, 1955).
Field, Barron, *Memoirs of Wordsworth*, ed. Geoffrey Little (Sydney: Sydney University Press, 1975).
Fields, James T., *Biographical Notes and Personal Sketches with Unpublished Fragments and Tributes from Men and Women of Letters* (London: Sampson Low et al., 1881).
Frend, William, *Peace and Union* (St Ives: P. C. Croft, 1793).
Geirgrawn, Y
Gentleman's Magazine, The
Gerrald, Joseph, *A Convention the only means of saving us from Ruin* (London, 1793).
Gibbs, Warren E., 'An Unpublished Letter from John Thelwall to S. T. Coleridge', *Modern Language Review* 25 (January 1930), 85–90.
Gilpin, William, *Observations on the River Wye, and Several Parts of South Wales, &c. Relative Chiefly to Picturesque Beauty* (London: R. Blamire, 1782).
——, *Observations on the Western Parts of England, Relative Chiefly to Picturesque Beauty* (London: T. Cadell & W. Davies, 1798).
Godwin, William, *An Enquiry concerning Political Justice* (2 vols; London: G. G. & J. Robinson, 1793).
——, *Caleb Williams*, ed. Maurice Hindle (Harmondsworth: Penguin, 1988).
——, *Memoirs of the Author of a Vindication of the Rights of Woman* [with Wollstonecraft's *A Short Residence in Sweden, Norway and Denmark*], ed. Richard Holmes (Harmondsworth: Penguin, 1987).
——, *St. Leon* (4 vols; London: G. G. & J. Robinson, 1799).
Goldsmith, Oliver, *An History of England* (2 vols; London: J. Newbery, 1764).

Gray, Thomas, *A Catalogue of the antiquities, houses, parks, plantations, scenes, and situations in England and Wales*, ed. William Mason (London, 1773).
Grégoire, Henri, *Histoire des Sectes Religieuses* (6 vols; Paris: Baudouin Frères, 1828–45).
Hardy, Thomas, *Memoir of Thomas Hardy, founder of . . . the London Corresponding Society* (London, 1832).
Hazlitt, William, *The Complete Works*, ed. P. P. Howe (21 vols; London: J. M. Dent, 1930–4).
Heath, Charles, *Historical and Descriptive Accounts of the Ancient and Present State of Chepstow Castle* (Monmouth: C. Heath, 1801).
——, *Historical and Descriptive Accounts of the Ancient and Present State of Tintern Abbey* (Monmouth: C. Heath, 1806).
——, *The Excursion Down the Wye from Ross to Monmouth* (Monmouth: C. Heath, 1796, 1799 and 1803 editions).
Holcroft, Thomas, *A Letter to the Right Honourable William Windham* (London: H. D. Symonds, 1795).
——, *The Life of Thomas Holcroft, written by himself*, ed. E. Colby (2 vols; London: Constable & Co., 1925).
Hunt, Leigh, *The Poetical Works*, ed. H. S. Milford (London: Oxford University Press, 1923).
Ireland, Samuel, *Picturesque Views on the River Wye* (London: R. Faulder & T. Egerton, 1797).
Ireland, William Henry, *The Confessions of William Henry Ireland* (London: Thomas Goddard, 1805).
——, *Vortigern, an Historical Tragedy . . . and Henry the Second, an Historical Drama* (London: J. Barker, 1799).
——, *Vortigern: An Historical Play; with an Original Preface* (London: Joseph Thomas, 1832).
Jeffrey, Francis, *Observations on Mr Thelwall's Letter to the Editor of the Edinburgh Review* (Edinburgh, 1804).
——, review of Thelwall's *Poems, Chiefly Written in Retirement*, *Edinburgh Review* 2 (April 1803), 197–202.
Jones, John ('Jac Glan-y-Gors'), *Toriad Y Dydd* (London, 1797).
——, *Seren Tan Gwmmwl* (London: Vaughan Griffiths, 1795).
Jones, Theophilus, *A History of the County of Brecknock* (2 vols; Brecknock: W. & G. North, 1805 and 1809).
Keats, John, *John Keats's Anatomical and Physiological Note Book*, ed. M. B. Forman (Oxford: Oxford University Press, 1934).
——, *The Complete Poems*, ed. John Barnard (2nd edition; Harmondsworth: Penguin, 1977).

———, *The Letters of John Keats 1814–1821*, ed. Hyder E. Rollins (2 vols; Cambridge: Cambridge University Press, 1958).
Lamb, Charles, *Selected Writings*, ed. J. E. Morpurgo (Manchester: Carcanet, 1993).
———, and Lamb, Mary, *The Letters of Charles and Mary Lamb*, ed. E. W. Marrs Jr. (3 vols; Ithaca and London: Cornell University Press, 1975–8).
Landor, Walter Savage, *Imaginary Conversations of Literary Men and Statesmen* (3 vols; London: Taylor & Hessey, 1824).
———, *Letters of Walter Savage Landor, Private and Public*, ed. Stephen Wheeler (London: Duckworth & Co, 1899).
———, *The Complete Works of Walter Savage Landor*, ed. Thomas Earle Welby and Stephen Wheeler (16 vols; London: Chapman & Hall, 1927–36).
Leathart, William Davies, *The Origin and Progress of the Gwyneddigion Society of London* (London: H. P. Hughes, 1831).
Lewis, Samuel, *A Topographical Dictionary of Wales* (3rd edition, 2 vols; London: S. Lewis, 1844).
Malone, Edmond, *An Inquiry into the Authenticity of Certain Miscellaneous Papers* (London: T. Cadell, 1796).
Millingen, J. G., *Recollections of Republican France, from 1790 to 1801* (London: Henry Colburn, 1848).
Milton, John, *Paradise Lost*, ed. Alastair Fowler (London and New York: Longman, 1971).
———, *The Complete Prose Works of John Milton*, ed. Don M. Wolfe et al. (8 vols; New Haven: Yale University Press, 1953–82).
Monmouth, Geoffrey of, *The History of the Kings of Britain*, tr. Lewis Thorpe (Harmondsworth: Penguin, 1966).
Monthly Magazine
Morrison, Alfred, ed., *The Collection of Autograph Letters and Historical Documents formed by Alfred Morrison: The Blessington Papers* (2nd series, 1882–93; London, 1895).
Nennius, *History of the Britons*, ed. A. W. Wade-Evans (London: SPCK, 1938).
Offley, Henry Francis, *Richard Brothers, Neither a Madman nor an Impostor* (London, 1795).
Owen, William ('Sefnyn'), *Y Drych Bradwriaethol, sef Hanes Brad y Cyllill Hirion* (Dolgellau: Richard Jones, 1825).
Paine, Thomas, *Political Writings*, ed. Bruce Kuklick (Cambridge: Cambridge University Press, 1989).
Pennant, Thomas, *A Tour in Wales* (London: Henry Hughes, 1778 and 1781).

Pollin, Burton R., and Burke, Redmond, 'John Thelwall's Marginalia in a Copy of Coleridge's *Biographia Literaria*', *Bulletin of the New York Public Library* 74 (1970), 73–94.

Poole, Edwin, *The Illustrated History and Biography of Brecknockshire* (Brecknock, 1886).

Portal, Abraham, *Vortimer; or, the True Patriot* (London, 1796).

Porter, Jane, *Thaddeus of Warsaw* (London: T. N. Longman & O. Rees, 1803).

Public Characters of 1800–1801 (London, 1801).

(Pughe), William Owen, *The Heroic Elegies and Other Pieces of Llywarç Hen* (London: J. Owen & E. Williams, 1792 [1793]).

Rees, W. J., tr., *The Liber Landavensis, Llyfr Teilo, or the Ancient Register of the Cathedral Church of Llandaff* (Llandovery: William Rees, 1840).

Reflector, The

Reid, W. H., *The Rise and Dissolution of the Infidel Societies in this Metropolis* (London: J. Hatchard, 1800).

Rickword, Edgell, 'Thelwall to Hardy, From a Correspondent', *Times Literary Supplement* (19 June 1953), 402.

Ritchie, Leitch, *The Wye and its Associations: A Picturesque Ramble* (London: Longman, Orme, Brown, Green & Longmans, 1841).

Ritson, Joseph, *The Letters of Joseph Ritson; edited chiefly from originals in the possession of his nephew* (2 vols; London: W. Pickering, 1833).

Rivers, David, *Literary Memoirs of Living Authors* (2 vols; London: R. Faulder, 1798).

Robberds, J. W., ed., *A Memoir of the Life and Writings of the Late William Taylor of Norwich* (2 vols; London: John Murray, 1843).

Roberts, Thomas, *Cwyn yn erbyn Gorthrymder* (London: J. Jones, 1798).

Roberts, Edward ('Iorwerth Glan Aled'), *Brad y Cyllill Hirion* (Rhuthyn: Isaac Clarke, 1853).

Robinson, Henry Crabb, *Diary, Reminiscences, and Correspondence of Henry Crabb Robinson*, ed. Thomas Sadler (3 vols; London: Macmillan & Co., 1869).

——, *Henry Crabb Robinson on Books and their Writers*, ed. Edith J. Morley (3 vols; London: J. M. Dent, 1938).

——, *The Correspondence of Henry Crabb Robinson with the Wordsworth Circle*, ed. Edith J. Morley (2 vols; Oxford: Clarendon Press, 1927).

Roland de la Platière, Marie-Jeanne, *Appeal to Impartial Posterity* (London: J. Johnson, 1795).

Rose, J. Holland, *William Pitt and the Great War* (London: G. Bell, 1911).

Sandford, Elizabeth, *Thomas Poole and his Friends* (2 vols; London: Macmillan, 1888; new edition, Over Stowey: Friarn Press, 1996).

Shakespeare, William, *The Complete Works*, ed. Stanley Wells et al. (Oxford: Clarendon Press, 1994).
Southey, C. C., ed., *Life and Correspondence of Robert Southey* (6 vols; London: Longman et al., 1849–50).
Southey, Robert, *Letters from England*, ed. J. Simmons (Gloucester: Alan Sutton, 1984).
——, *Madoc* (London: Longman, Hurst, Rees & Orme, 1805).
——, *New Letters of Robert Southey*, ed. Kenneth Curry (2 vols; New York: Columbia University Press, 1965).
——, *Selections from the Letters of Robert Southey*, ed. J.W. Warter (4 vols; London: Longman et al., 1856).
——, *Southey's Common-Place Book*, ed. J. W. Warter (4 vols; London: Longman et al., 1849–51).
——, *The Correspondence of Robert Southey with Caroline Bowles*, ed. E. Dowden (Dublin: Hodges & Figgis, 1881).
Stephens, Alexander, ed., *Biographical Anecdotes of the Founders of the French Republic* (2 vols; London: R. Phillips, 1797, 1798).
——, *Memoirs of John Horne Tooke* (2 vols; London, 1813).
Thale, Mary, ed., *Selections from the Papers of the London Corresponding Society, 1792–1799* (Cambridge: Cambridge University Press, 1983).
——, ed., *The Autobiography of Francis Place* (Cambridge: Cambridge University Press, 1972).
Thelwall, Henrietta Cecil, *The Life of John Thelwall* (London: John Macrone, 1837).
Thelwall, John, *A Letter to Francis Jeffray, Esq., on Certain Calumnies and Misrepresentations in the Edinburgh Review* (Edinburgh, 1804).
——, 'A Pedestrian Excursion through Several Parts of England and Wales during the Summer of 1797', *Monthly Magazine* 8 (August 1799), 532–3; 8 (September 1799), 616–19; 8 (November 1799), 783–5; 8 (January 1800), 966–7; 9 (February 1800), 16–18; 9 (April 1800), 228–31; 11 (March 1801), 123–5; 12 (September 1801), 103–6; 12 (October 1801), 198–200; 12 (November 1801), 305–8.
——, *An Address to the Inhabitants of Yarmouth, on the Violent Outrage Lately Committed in their Town* (Yarmouth, 1796).
——, *An Appeal to Popular Opinion against Kidnapping and Murder, Including a Narrative of the Late Atrocious Proceedings at Yarmouth* (London: J. S. Jordan, 1796).
——, *John Gilpin's Ghost* (London: T. Smith, 1795).
——, *On the Moral Tendency of a System of Spies and Informers* (London, 1794).
——, *Peaceful Discussion, and not Tumultuary Violence the Means of Redressing National Grievances* (London, 1795).

Thelwall, John, *Poems, Chiefly Written in Retirement* (Hereford: W. H. Parker, 1801).

——, *Poems Written in Close Confinement in the Tower and Newgate, under a Charge of High Treason* (London, 1795).

——, *Prospectus of a course of Lectures to be delivered . . . in strict conformity with the restrictions of Mr Pitt's Convention Act* (London, 1796).

——, *Reply to the Calumnies, Misrepresentations, and Literary Forgeries, contained in the Anonymous Observations on his Letter to the Editor of the Edinburgh Review* (Glasgow, 1804).

——, *Sober Reflections on the Seditious and Inflammatory Letter of the Rt. Hon. Edmund Burke to a Noble Lord* (London: H. D. Symonds, 1796).

——, *The Daughter of Adoption: A Tale of Modern Times* (4 vols; London: R. Phillips, 1801).

——, *The Natural and Constitutional Rights of Britons to Annual Parliaments, Universal Suffrage, and the Freedom of Popular Association* (London, 1795).

——, *The Peripatetic; or, Sketches of the Heart, of Nature and Society; in a series of Politico-Sentimental Journals* (3 vols; London, 1793).

——, *The Peripatetic*, ed. Judith Thompson (Detroit: Wayne State University Press, 2000).

——, 'The Phenomena of the Wye, during the Winter of 1797–8', *Monthly Magazine* 5 (May 1798), 343–6 and 6 (July 1798), 20–1.

——, *The Politics of English Jacobinism: Writings of John Thelwall*, ed. Gregory Claeys (University Park, PA: Pennsylvania State University Press, 1995).

——, *The Rights of Nature against the Usurpation of Establishments* (London: H. D. Symonds, 1796).

——, *The Speech of John Thelwall, at the second Meeting of the London Corresponding Society . . . at Copenhagen House . . . November 12, 1795* (London 1795).

——, *The Tribune* (3 vols; London, 1795–6).

——, various untitled articles on political, agricultural, financial, and personal matters in the *Monthly Magazine*: 5 (March 1798), 177–9; 5 (May 1798), 343–6; 5 (June 1798), 418–21; 6 (July 1798), 20–1; 6 (November 1798), 323–4; 6 (December 1798), 409; 9 (July 1800), 529–34; 10 (September 1800), 127–30; 13 (May 1802), 344–6; 14 (August 1802), 6–7.

Thompson, Aaron, *The British History, translated into English from the Latin of Jeffrey of Monmouth* (London: J. Bower, 1718).

Tyrrell, James, *The General History of England, as well Ecclesiastical as Civil* (3 vols; London: W. Rogers, 1696–1704).

Universal Magazine of Knowledge and Pleasure

Waring, Elijah, *Recollections and Anecdotes of Edward Williams* (London: Charles Gilpin, 1850).

Warner, Richard, *A Second Walk through Wales, in August and September 1798* (Bath: R. Cruttwell, 1799).
——, *A Walk Through Wales, in August 1797* (Bath: R. Cruttwell, 1798).
——, *Literary Recollections* (2 vols; London, 1830).
——, *War Inconsistent with Christianity* (Bath, 1804).
Warrington, William, *The History of Wales* (London: J. Johnson, 1786).
Wedgwood, Julia, *The Personal Life of Josiah Wedgwood the Potter*, ed. C. H. Herford (London: Macmillan & Co., 1915).
Whitchurch, Samuel, *Elegy on the Death of Mr Thomas Tuppen; with some other Poetical Pieces* (London, 1795).
White, James, *Original Letters, &c. of Sir John Falstaff and His Friends* (London, 1796).
Williams, David, *A Letter to the Body of Protestant Dissenters* (London: J. Almon & J. Wilkie, 1777).
——, *A Plan of Association* (London: G. Kearsly, 1780).
——, *An Apology for Professing the Religion of Nature in the Eighteenth Century of the Christian Æra, addressed to the Right Reverend Dr. Watson, Lord Bishop of Llandaff* (London: J. Ridgway, 1789).
——, *A Liturgy on the Universal Principles of Religion and Morality* (London: T. Payne et al., 1776).
——, *A Treatise on Education* (London: T. Payne et al., 1774).
——, *Claims of Literature* (London: W. Miller, 1802).
——, *Incidents in My Own Life which have been Thought of Some Importance*, ed. Peter France (Brighton: University of Sussex Library, 1980).
——, *Lectures on Education* (3 vols; London: J. Bell, 1789).
——, *Lectures on Political Principles* (London: J. Bell, 1789).
——, *Lessons to a Young Prince by an Old Statesman* (2nd edition; London: H. D. Symonds, 1790).
——, *Letters on Political Liberty* (London: T. Evans, 1782).
——, *Observations sur la dernière constitution de la France* (Paris, 1793).
——, *The History of Monmouthshire* (London: H. Baldwin, 1796).
——, *The Philosopher* (London: T. Becket, 1771).
Williams, Edward, *Gwaith Iolo Morganwg*, ed. Thomas Christopher Evans (Llanuwchllyn: Ab Owen, 1913).
——, *Poems, Lyric and Pastoral* (2 vols; London: J. Nichols, 1794).
——, *Trial by Jury, The Grand Palladium of British Liberty. A Song* (London, 1795).
Williams, G. J., 'Llythyrau ynglŷn ag Eisteddfodau'r Gwyneddigion ac Eisteddfod Corwen, Mai 12 a 13, 1789', *Llên Cymru* 1 (1950), 29–47 and 113–25.

Wollstonecraft, Mary, *Mary* and *The Wrongs of Woman*, ed. Gary Kelly (Oxford: Oxford University Press, 1976).
Wollstonecraft, Mary, *Political Writings*, ed. Janet Todd (Oxford: Oxford University Press, 1994).
——, *The Works of Mary Wollstonecraft*, ed. Marilyn Butler and Janet Todd (7 vols; London: Pickering, 1989).
Wordsworth, Christopher, *Memoirs of William Wordsworth* (2 vols; London: E. Moxon, 1851).
Wordsworth, William, *Lyrical Ballads, 1798*, ed. Thomas Hutchinson (3rd edition; London: Duckworth, 1920).
——, *Lyrical Ballads, and Other Poems, 1797–1800*, ed. James Butler and Karen Green (Ithaca and London: Cornell University Press, 1992).
——, *The Borderers*, ed. Robert Osborn (Ithaca and London: Cornell University Press, 1982).
——, *The Fenwick Notes of William Wordsworth*, ed. Jared Curtis (London: Bristol Classical Press, 1993).
——, *The Letters of William and Dorothy Wordsworth: The Early Years, 1787–1805*, ed. Ernest de Selincourt, rev. Chester L. Shaver (Oxford: Clarendon Press, 1967); *The Middle Years, Part ii, 1812–1820*, ed. Ernest de Selincourt, rev. Mary Moorman and Alan G. Hill (Oxford: Clarendon Press, 1970); *The Later Years, Part i, 1821–1828; Part ii, 1829–1834; Part iii, 1835–1839; Part iv, 1840–1853*, ed. Ernest de Selincourt, rev. Alan G. Hill (Oxford: Clarendon Press, 1978, 1979, 1982 and 1988).
——, *The Pedlar, Tintern Abbey, and The Two-Part Prelude*, ed. Jonathan Wordsworth (Cambridge: Cambridge University Press, 1985).
——, *The Poetical Works*, ed. Ernest de Selincourt and Helen Darbishire (5 vols; Oxford: Clarendon Press, 1940–9).
——, *The Poetical Works of William Wordsworth*, ed. William Knight (8 vols; London: Macmillan, 1896).
——, *The Prelude, 1799, 1805, 1850*, ed. Jonathan Wordsworth, M. H. Abrams and Stephen Gill (New York and London: W. W. Norton & Co., 1979).
——, *The Prelude: The Four Texts*, ed. Jonathan Wordsworth (Harmondsworth: Penguin, 1995).
——, *The Prose Works*, ed. W. J. B. Owen and J. W. Smyser (3 vols; Oxford: Clarendon Press, 1974).
——, *The Salisbury Plain Poems*, ed. Stephen Gill (Ithaca and London: Cornell University Press, 1975).
Yeats, W.B., *The Poems*, ed. Daniel Albright (London: J. M. Dent, 1990).
Young, Arthur, *The Example of France a Warning to Britain* (London: W. Richardson, 1793).

(b) Secondary

Adams, M. Ray, 'Joseph Fawcett and Wordsworth's Solitary', *Publications of the Modern Language Association of America* 48 (1933), 508–28.
——, *Studies in the Literary Backgrounds of English Radicalism* (Lancaster, PA: Franklin and Marshall College Studies, 1947).
Alger, J. G., *Paris in 1789–1794* (London: George Allen, 1902).
Allen, B. Sprague, 'William Godwin's Influence upon John Thelwall', *Publications of the Modern Language Association of America* 37 (1922), 662–82.
Anderson, G. K., 'Popular Survivals of the Wandering Jew in England', in Galit Hasan-Rokem and Alan Dundes, eds., *The Wandering Jew: Essays in the Interpretation of a Christian Legend* (Bloomington, IN: Indiana University Press, 1986), 76–104.
Andrews, Malcolm, *The Search for the Picturesque: Landscape, Aesthetics and Tourism in Britain, 1760–1800* (Aldershot: Scolar Press, 1989).
ap Nicholas, Islwyn, *Iolo Morganwg, Bard of Liberty* (London: Foyle's Welsh Press, 1945).
Averill, James H., 'Wordsworth and "Natural Science": The Poetry of 1798', *Journal of English and Germanic Philology* 77 (1978), 232–46.
Barrell, John, *The Idea of Landscape and the Sense of Place, 1730–1840: An Approach to the Poetry of John Clare* (Cambridge: Cambridge University Press, 1972).
——, *Imagining the King's Death: Figurative Treason, Fantasies of Regicide, 1793–1796* (Oxford: Clarendon Press, 2000).
Bement, Peter, 'Simon Lee and Ivor Hall: A Possible Source', *The Wordsworth Circle* 13, 1 (Winter 1982), 35–6.
Bentley Jr., G. E., *Blake Records Supplement* (Oxford: Clarendon Press, 1988).
——, 'The Triumph of Owen', *National Library of Wales Journal* 24 (1985–6), 248–61.
Betz, Paul, *Romantic Archaeologies* (Baltimore: Albin O. Kuhn Library & Gallery, 1995).
Bloom, Harold, *Poetry and Repression: Revisionism from Blake to Stevens* (New Haven and London: Yale University Press, 1976).
Bodde, Derk, *Shakspere and the Ireland Forgeries* (Cambridge, MA: Harvard University Press, 1930).
Bowen, E. G., *David Samwell* (Cardiff: University of Wales Press, 1974).
Brinkley, Robert A., 'Vagrant and Hermit: Milton and the Politics of "Tintern Abbey"', *The Wordsworth Circle* 16, 3 (Summer 1985), 126–33.
Bromwich, David, *Disowned by Memory: Wordsworth's Poetry of the 1790s* (Chicago and London: University of Chicago Press, 1998).

Bronson, B. H., *Joseph Ritson, Scholar at Arms* (2 vols; Berkeley: University of California Press, 1938).
Carnall, Geoffrey, 'The Monthly Magazine', *Review of English Studies* NS 5 (1954), 158–64.
Carr, Glenda, *William Owen Pughe* (Cardiff: University of Wales Press, 1983).
Carradice, Phil, *The Last Invasion: The Story of the French Landing in Wales* (Pontypool: Village Publishing, 1992).
Carruthers, Gerard, and Rawes, A., eds., *English Romanticism and the Celtic World* (Cambridge: Cambridge University Press, 2002).
Casson, T. E., 'Wordsworth and Theocritus', *Times Literary Supplement* (11 September 1937), 656.
Celoria, Francis, 'Chatterton, Wordsworth and Stonehenge', *Notes and Queries* 221 (March 1976), 103–4.
Cestre, Charles, *John Thelwall: A Pioneer of Democracy in Britain* (London: Swan Sonnenschein & Co., 1906).
Chadwick, Hector Munro, 'Vortigern', *Studies in Early British History* (Cambridge: Cambridge University Press, 1954), 21–46.
Chandler, David, 'A Study of Lamb's "Living Without God in the World"', *Charles Lamb Bulletin* NS 99 (July 1997), 86–101.
——, 'Vagrancy Smoked Out: Wordsworth "betwixt Severn and Wye"', *Romanticism on the Net* 11 (August 1998); http://users.ox.ac.uk/~scat0385/articles.html#11
Chatterton, Thomas, *The Complete Works*, ed. Donald S. Taylor (2 vols; Oxford: Clarendon Press, 1971).
Cobb, Richard and Jones, Colin, *The French Revolution: Voices from a Momentous Epoch, 1789–1795* (London: Simon & Schuster, 1988).
Colley, Linda, *Britons: Forging the Nation, 1797–1837* (London: Vintage, 1996).
Courtney, Winifred, *Young Charles Lamb, 1775–1802* (London: Macmillan, 1982).
Danby, John F., *The Simple Wordsworth: Studies in the Poems, 1797–1807* (London: Routledge & Kegan Paul, 1960).
Davies, David, *The Influence of the French Revolution on Welsh Life and Literature* (Carmarthen: W. Morgan Evans & Son, 1926).
Davies, E. T., *A History of the Parish of Mathern* (2nd edition; Mathern: Mathern PCC, 1990).
Davies, Norman, *God's Playground: A History of Poland* (2 vols; Oxford: Clarendon Press, 1981).
Davies, William Ll., 'David Samwell (1751–1798)', *Transactions of the Honourable Society of Cymmrodorion* (1926–7), 70–133.

Dickstein, Morris, 'Keats and Politics', *Studies in Romanticism* 25 (Summer 1986), 175–81.

Dictionary of National Biography

Dictionary of Welsh Biography down to 1940

Doble, G. M., *Lives of the Welsh Saints*, ed. D. Simon Evans (Cardiff: University of Wales Press, 1971).

Dumville, D. N., 'Sub-Roman Britain: History and Legend', *History* 62 (1977), 173–92.

Dybikowski, J., *On Burning Ground: An Examination of the Ideas, Projects, and Life of David Williams* (Oxford: Voltaire Foundation, 1993).

Ellis, Tecwyn, 'Bardd y Brenin, Iolo Morganwg a Derwyddiaeth', *National Library of Wales Journal* 13 (1963–4), 224–34.

Emsley, Clive, 'The Home Office and its Sources of Information and Investigation, 1791–1801', *English Historical Review* 94 (July 1979), 532–61.

Erdman, David V., *Blake: Prophet Against Empire* (3rd edition; Princeton, NJ: Princeton University Press, 1977).

——, *Commerce des Lumières: John Oswald and the British in Paris, 1790–1793* (Columbia: University of Missouri Press, 1986).

——, 'The Man that was not Napoleon', *The Wordsworth Circle* 12, 1 (Winter 1981), 92–6.

Evans, J. J., *Dylanwad y Chwyldro Ffrengig ar Lenyddiaeth Cymru* (Liverpool: Hugh Evans & Sons, 1928).

——, *Morgan John Rhys a'i Amserau* (Cardiff: University of Wales Press, 1935).

Evans, Thomas, *The Background of Modern Welsh Politics* (Cardiff: University of Wales Press, 1936).

Everest, Kelvin, *Coleridge's Secret Ministry: The Context of the Conversation Poems, 1795–1798* (Hassocks, Sussex: Harvester Press, 1979).

Felsenstein, Frank, *Anti-Semitic Stereotypes: A Paradigm of Otherness in English Popular Culture, 1660–1830* (Baltimore and London: Johns Hopkins University Press, 1995).

Fisher, Peter F., 'Blake and the Druids', *Journal of English and Germanic Philology* 58 (1959), 589–612.

Fletcher, J. Kyrle, 'Iolo Morganwg's List of Subscribers', *Journal of the Welsh Bibliographical Society* 6 (July 1943), 39–41.

Foulkes, Isaac ('Llyfrbryf'), 'John Jones o Lanygors', *Y Geninen* (January 1883), 275–81.

Fulford, Tim, *Landscape, Liberty and Authority: Poetry, Criticism and Politics from Thomson to Wordsworth* (Cambridge: Cambridge University Press, 1996).

Gallop, Geoffrey, 'Ideology and the English Jacobins: The Case of John Thelwall', *Enlightenment and Dissent* 5 (1986), 3–20.

George, Mary Dorothy and Stephens, Frederic George, eds., *Catalogue of Political and Personal Satires Preserved in the Department of Prints and Drawings in the British Museum* (11 vols; London: Trustees of the British Museum, 1870–1954).
Gill, Stephen, *William Wordsworth: A Life* (Oxford: Clarendon Press, 1989).
Goellnicht, Donald C., *The Poet-Physician: Keats and Medical Science* (Pittsburgh: University of Pittsburgh Press, 1984).
Goodwin, Albert, *The Friends of Liberty: The English Democratic Movement in the Age of the French Revolution* (London: Hutchinson, 1979).
Grebanier, Bernard, *The Great Shakespeare Forgery: A New Look at the Career of William Henry Ireland* (London: Heinemann, 1966).
Griffith, John T., *Morgan John Rhys* (Carmarthen: W. M. Evans & Son, 1910).
Haiman, Miecislaus, *Kosciuszko in the American Revolution* (New York: Kosciuszko Foundation, 1975 edition).
——, *Kosciuszko: Leader and Exile* (New York: Polish Institute of Arts & Sciences in America, 1977 edition).
Hamilton, Chloe, 'A Portrait of General Kosciusko by Benjamin West', *Allen Memorial Art Museum Bulletin* 9 (1952), 81–91.
Hampsher-Monk, Iain, 'John Thelwall and the Eighteenth-Century Radical Response to Political Economy', *Historical Journal* 34 (1991), 1–20.
Haraszti, Zoltán, *The Shakespeare Forgeries of William Henry Ireland: The Story of a Famous Literary Fraud* (Boston: Boston Public Library, 1934).
Hartman, Geoffrey, *The Unmediated Vision: An Interpretation of Wordsworth, Hopkins, Rilke, and Valéry* (New York: Harcourt, Brace & World, 1966).
Hayden, John O., 'The Road to Tintern Abbey', *The Wordsworth Circle* 12, 4 (Autumn 1981), 211–16.
Henderson, Andrea K., *Romantic Identities: Varieties of Subjectivity, 1774–1830* (Cambridge: Cambridge University Press, 1996).
Herbert, Trevor and Jones, Gareth Elwyn, eds., *The Remaking of Wales in the Eighteenth Century* (Cardiff: University of Wales Press, 1988).
Hill, Christopher, *Milton and the English Revolution* (London: Faber, 1977).
Holmes, Richard, *Coleridge: Early Visions* (London: Hodder & Stoughton, 1989).
Hone, J. Ann, *For the Cause of Truth: Radicalism in London, 1796–1821* (Oxford: Clarendon Press, 1982).
Hunt, John Dixon, *The Figure in the Landscape: Poetry, Painting, and Gardening during the Eighteenth Century* (Baltimore and London: Johns Hopkins University Press, 1976).

Jacobus, Mary, '"Tintern Abbey" and Topographical Prose', *Notes and Queries* 216 (October 1971), 366–9.

Jarvis, Robin, *Romantic Writing and Pedestrian Travel* (Basingstoke: Macmillan, 1997).

Jenkins, Geraint H., *Facts, Fantasy and Fiction: The Historical Vision of Iolo Morganwg* (Aberystwyth: Centre for Advanced Welsh and Celtic Studies, 1997).

——, *The Foundations of Modern Wales, 1642–1780* (Oxford: Clarendon Press, 1987).

Jenkins, R. T., *Hanes Cymru yn y Ddeunawfed Ganrif* (Cardiff: University of Wales Press, 1931).

Jenkins, R. T. and Ramage, Helen M., *A History of the Honourable Society of Cymmrodorion and of the Gwyneddigion and Cymreigyddion Societies* (London: Honourable Society of Cymmrodorion, 1951).

Johnston, Arthur, 'William Blake and "The Ancient Britons"', *National Library of Wales Journal* 22 (1981–2), 304–20.

Johnston, Kenneth R., *The Hidden Wordsworth: Poet, Lover, Rebel, Spy* (New York and London: W. W. Norton & Co., 1998).

——, 'The Politics of "Tintern Abbey"', *The Wordsworth Circle* 14, 1 (Winter 1983), 6–14.

——, *Wordsworth and 'The Recluse'* (New Haven and London: Yale University Press, 1984).

Jones, David, *Before Rebecca: Popular Protests in Wales, 1793–1835* (London: Allen Lane, 1973).

Jones, Frank Price, *Radicaliaeth a'r Werin Gymreig yn y Bedwaredd Ganrif ar Bymtheg* (Cardiff: University of Wales Press, 1977).

Jones, Myddleton Pennant, 'John Jones of Glan-y-Gors', *Transactions of the Honourable Society of Cymmrodorion* (1909–10), 60–94.

Jones, Whitney R. D., *David Williams: The Anvil and the Hammer* (Cardiff: University of Wales Press, 1986).

Kahan, Jeffrey, *Reforging Shakespeare: The Story of a Theatrical Scandal* (Bethlehem and London: Lehigh University Press, 1998).

Kajencki, Francis Casimir, *Thaddeus Kosciuszko: Military Engineer of the American Revolution* (El Paso, TX: Southwest Polonia Press, 1998).

Kandl, John, 'Private Lyrics in the Public Sphere: Leigh Hunt's *Examiner* and the Construction of a Public "John Keats"', *Keats–Shelley Journal* 44 (1995), 84–101.

Kegan Paul, C., *William Godwin: His Friends and Contemporaries* (2 vols; London: H. S. King, 1876).

Kelly, Gary, *The English Jacobin Novel, 1780–1805* (Oxford: Clarendon Press, 1976).

Kendrick, T. D., *The Druids* (London: Senate Press, 1994).
Kingston, Jeremy, 'Ham Wrote Shakespeare, not Bacon', *The Times* (27 October 1997), 19.
Kirby, D. P., 'Vortigern', *Bulletin of the Board of Celtic Studies* 23 (1968), 37–59.
Legouis, Émile, *The Early Life of William Wordsworth 1770–1798*, tr. J. W. Matthews (New York: Russell & Russell, 1965).
Levinson, Marjorie, *Wordsworth's Great Period Poems: Four Essays* (Cambridge: Cambridge University Press, 1986).
Lewis, Ceri W., *Iolo Morganwg* (Caernarfon: Gwasg Pantycelyn, 1995).
Lewis, Gwyneth, 'Eighteenth-Century Literary Forgeries, with Special Reference to the Work of Iolo Morganwg' (unpublished University of Oxford doctoral thesis, 1991; Bodleian Library, Oxford, MS DPhil c. 8975).
Lewis, Saunders, 'Jack Glan y Gors', *Welsh Outlook* 6 (September 1919), 238–9.
Little, Geoffrey, ' "Tintern Abbey" and Llyswen Farm', *The Wordsworth Circle* 8, 1 (Winter 1977), 80–2.
Liu, Alan, 'Wordsworth and Subversion, 1793–1804: Trying Cultural Criticism', *Yale Journal of Criticism* 2, 2 (1989), 55–100.
——, *Wordsworth: the Sense of History* (Stanford, CA: Stanford University Press, 1989).
Lloyd, Stephen, *Richard and Maria Cosway: Regency Artists of Taste and Fashion* (Edinburgh: Scottish National Portrait Gallery, 1995).
Lucas, E. V., *David Williams, Founder of the Royal Literary Fund* (London: John Murray, 1920).
Lyon, Judson Stanley, *The Excursion: A Study* (New Haven, CT: Yale University Press, 1950).
McCalman, Iain, *Radical Underworld: Prophets, Revolutionaries, and Pornographers in London, 1795–1840* (Oxford: Clarendon Press, 1993).
MacGillivray, J. R., 'Wordsworth and J. P. Brissot', *Times Literary Supplement* (29 January 1931), 79.
McCann, Andrew, *Cultural Politics in the 1790s: Literature, Radicalism, and the Public Sphere* (Basingstoke: Macmillan, 1999).
——, 'Politico-Sentimentality: John Thelwall, Literary Production and Critique of Capital in the 1790s', *Romanticism* 3, 1 (1997), 35–52.
——, 'Romantic Self-Fashioning: John Thelwall and the Science of Elocution', *Studies in Romanticism* 40, 2 (Summer 2001), 215–32.
McGann, J. J., *The Romantic Ideology: A Critical Investigation* (Chicago: University of Chicago Press, 1983).
McLean, Thomas, ' "Transformed, Not Inly Altered": Kosciuszko and Poland in Post-Waterloo Britain', *Keats–Shelley Journal* 50 (2001), 64–83.

McLean, Thomas, '"When hope bade the world farewell": British Responses to the 1794 Kosciuszko Rising', *The Wordsworth Circle* 29, 3 (Summer 1998), 178–85.

McNulty, John Bard, 'Wordsworth's Tour of the Wye: 1798', *Modern Language Notes* 60 (1945), 291–5.

Magnuson, Paul, *Coleridge and Wordsworth: A Lyrical Dialogue* (Princeton: Princeton University Press, 1988).

——, 'The Politics of "Frost at Midnight"', *The Wordsworth Circle* 22, 1 (Winter 1991), 3–11.

——, *Reading Public Romanticism* (Princeton, NJ: Princeton University Press, 1998).

Mair, John, *The Fourth Forger: William Ireland and the Shakespeare Papers* (London: Cobden-Sanderson, 1938).

Manogue, Ralph A., 'Southey and William Winterbotham: New Light on an Old Quarrel', *Charles Lamb Bulletin* NS 38 (April 1982), 105–14.

——, 'The Plight of James Ridgway, London Bookseller and Publisher, and the Newgate Radicals, 1792–97', *The Wordsworth Circle* 27, 3 (Summer 1996), 158–66.

Martin, Peter, *Edmund Malone, Shakespearean Scholar: A Literary Biography* (Cambridge: Cambridge University Press, 1995).

Matthews, E. Gwynn, *Jac Glan-y-Gors a'r Baganiaeth Newydd* (National Eisteddfod of Wales: Llys yr Eisteddfod Genedlaethol, 1995).

Mee, Jon, *Dangerous Enthusiasm: William Blake and the Culture of Radicalism in the 1790s* (Oxford: Clarendon Press, 1992).

Montluzin, Emily Lorraine de, *The Anti-Jacobins, 1798–1800: The Early Contributions to the Anti-Jacobin Review* (Basingstoke: Macmillan, 1988).

Moorman, Mary, *William Wordsworth: A Biography; The Early Years, 1770–1803* (Oxford: Oxford University Press, 1957).

Morgan, Prys, 'From a Death to a View: The Hunt for the Welsh Past in the Romantic Period', in E. Hobsbawm and T. Ranger, eds., *The Invention of Tradition* (Cambridge: Cambridge University Press, 1983), 43–100.

——, 'From Long Knives to Blue Books', in R. R. Davies et al., eds., *Welsh Society and Nationhood: Historical Essays Presented to Glanmor Williams* (Cardiff: University of Wales Press, 1984), 199–215.

——, *Iolo Morganwg* (Cardiff: University of Wales Press, 1975).

——, *The Eighteenth-Century Renaissance* (Llandybïe: Christopher Davies, 1981).

Morris, John, *The Age of Arthur: A History of the British Isles from 350 to 650* (London: Weidenfeld & Nicolson, 1973).

Newlyn, Lucy, *Coleridge, Wordsworth, and the Language of Allusion* (Oxford: Clarendon Press, 1986).

Newlyn, Lucy, '"In City Pent": Echo and Allusion in Wordsworth, Coleridge and Lamb, 1797–1801', *Review of English Studies* NS 32 (November 1981), 408–28.
——, *Paradise Lost and the Romantic Reader* (Oxford: Clarendon Press, 1993).
——, *Reading, Writing, and Romanticism: The Anxiety of Reception* (Oxford: Clarendon Press, 2000).
Noyes, Russell, 'Wordsworth and Burns', *Publications of the Modern Language Association of America* 59 (1944), 813–32.
O'Dea, M. and Whelan, K., eds., *Nations and Nationalisms: France, Britain, Ireland and the Eighteenth-Century Context* (Oxford: Voltaire Foundation, 1995).
Oishi, Kaz, 'Coleridge's Philanthropy: Poverty, Dissenting Radicalism, and the Language of Benevolence', *Coleridge Bulletin* NS 15 (Spring 2000), 56–70.
Oldfield, J. R., *Popular Politics and British Anti-Slavery: The Mobilisation of Public Opinion against the Slave Trade* (Manchester: Manchester University Press, 1995).
Onorato, Richard J., *The Character of the Poet: Wordsworth in The Prelude* (Princeton: Princeton University Press, 1971).
Owen, A. L., *The Famous Druids* (Oxford: Clarendon Press, 1962).
Owen, Bob, 'Jac Glanygors a'r Milisia', *Y Genhinen* (Winter 1952), 1–7.
Parrish, Stephen, *The Art of the Lyrical Ballads* (Cambridge, MA: Harvard University Press, 1973).
Phillips, Geraint, 'Math o Wallgofrwydd: Iolo Morganwg, Opiwm a Thomas Chatterton', *National Library of Wales Journal* 29 (1995–6), 391–410.
Pula, James S., *Thaddeus Kosciuszko: The Purest Son of Liberty* (New York: Hippocrene Books, 1999).
Quinn, David B., 'Wales and the West', in R. R. Davies et al., eds., *Welsh Society and Nationhood: Historical Essays Presented to Glanmor Williams* (Cardiff: University of Wales Press, 1984), 90–107.
Railo, Eino, *The Haunted Castle: A Study of the Elements of English Romanticism* (London: G. Routledge & Sons, 1927).
Reed, Mark, *Wordsworth: The Chronology of the Early Years, 1770–1799* (Cambridge, MA: Harvard University Press, 1967).
——, *Wordsworth: The Chronology of the Middle Years, 1800–1815* (Cambridge, MA: Harvard University Press, 1975).
Richards, H. P., *David Williams* (Cowbridge: D. Brown & Sons, 1980).
Rieder, John, *Wordsworth's Counterrevolutionary Turn: Community, Virtue, and Vision in the 1790s* (Newark: University of Delaware Press, 1997).

Roberts, Daniel Sanjiv, 'Coleridge's Liverpool Connection: An Unpublished Letter from William Roscoe to John Edwards', *Notes and Queries* 244 (December 1999), 455–7.

Rockey, Denyse, 'John Thelwall and the Origins of British Speech Therapy', *Medical History* 23 (1979), 156–75.

——, 'The Logopaedic Thought of John Thelwall, 1764–1834: First British Speech Therapist', *British Journal of Disorders of Communication* 12 (October 1977), 83–95.

Roe, Nicholas, '"Atmospheric Air Itself": Medical Science, Politics and Poetry in Thelwall, Coleridge and Wordsworth', in Richard Cronin, ed., *1798: The Year of the Lyrical Ballads* (Basingstoke: Macmillan, 1998), 185–202.

——, 'Coleridge and John Thelwall: The Road to Nether Stowey', in Richard Gravil and Molly Lefebure, eds., *The Coleridge Connection* (Basingstoke: Macmillan, 1990), 60–80.

——, 'Imagining Robespierre', *Coleridge's Imagination: Essays in Memory of Pete Laver* (Cambridge: Cambridge University Press, 1985), 161–78.

——, *John Keats and the Culture of Dissent* (Oxford: Clarendon Press, 1997).

——, 'Radical George: Dyer in the 1790s', *Charles Lamb Bulletin* NS 49 (January 1985), 17–26.

——, *The Politics of Nature: Wordsworth and Some Contemporaries* (Basingstoke: Macmillan, 1992).

——, *Wordsworth and Coleridge: The Radical Years* (Oxford: Clarendon Press, 1988).

Rose, R. B., 'The "Jacobins" of Liverpool, 1789–1793', *Liverpool Bulletin* 9 (1960–1), 35–49.

Rothstein, Eric, 'Allusion and Analogy in the Romance of *Caleb Williams*', *Toronto University Quarterly* 37 (1967–8), 18–30.

Scrivener, Michael, 'Jacobin Romanticism: John Thelwall's "Wye" Essay and "Pedestrian Excursion"', in Peter J. Kitson, ed., *Placing and Displacing Romanticism* (Aldershot: Ashgate, 2001), 78–92.

——, 'John Thelwall and Popular Jacobin Allegory, 1793–1795', *ELH* 67, 4 (2000), 951–71.

——, 'John Thelwall and the Press', in Stephen C. Behrendt, ed., *Romanticism, Radicalism and the Press* (Detroit: Wayne State University Press, 1997), 120–36.

——, 'John Thelwall and the Revolution of 1649', in Timothy Morton and Nigel Smith, eds., *Radicalism in British Literary Culture, 1650–1830: From Revolution to Revolution* (Cambridge: Cambridge University Press, 2002), 119–32.

——, 'John Thelwall's Political Ambivalence: Reform and Revolution', in Michael T. Davis, ed., *Radicalism and Revolution in Britain, 1775–1848: Essays in Honour of Malcolm I. Thomis* (Basingstoke: Macmillan, 2000), 69–83.

———, review of Gregory Claeys's *The Politics of English Jacobinism: Writings of John Thelwall*, *Romanticism* 3, 1 (1997), 135–8.

———, *Seditious Allegories: John Thelwall and Jacobin Writing* (University Park, PA: Pennsylvania State University Press, 2001).

———, 'The Rhetoric and Context of John Thelwall's "Memoir"', in G. A. Rosso and Daniel P. Watkins, eds., *Spirits of Fire: English Romantic Writers and Contemporary Historical Methods* (Rutherford, NJ: Farleigh Dickinson University Press, 1990), 112–30.

Sellers, Ian, 'William Roscoe, The Roscoe Circle, and Radical Politics in Liverpool, 1787–1807', *Transactions of the Historical Society of Lancashire and Cheshire* 120 (1968), 45–62.

Shankland, Thomas, 'Hanes Dechreuad "Gorsedd Beirdd Ynys Prydain"', *Y Llenor* 3 (1924), 94–102.

Simpson, David, 'Public Virtues, Private Vices: Reading between the Lines of Wordsworth's "Anecdote for Fathers"', in David Simpson, ed., *Subject to History: Ideology, Class, Gender* (Ithaca and London: Cornell University Press, 1991), 163–90.

———, *Wordsworth's Historical Imagination: The Poetry of Displacement* (New York and London: Methuen, 1987).

Solkin, David H., *Richard Wilson: The Landscape of Reaction* (London: Tate Gallery, 1982).

Soule, George, '"Spots of Earth" in *The Excursion*', *Charles Lamb Bulletin* NS 85 (January 1994), 19–24.

Stein, Edwin, *Wordsworth's Art of Allusion* (University Park, PA: Pennsylvania State University Press, 1988).

Stillinger, Jack, *Coleridge and Textual Instability: The Multiple Versions of the Major Poems* (New York and Oxford: Oxford University Press, 1994).

Tatlock, J. S. P., *The Legendary History of Britain: Geoffrey of Monmouth's Historia Regum Britanniae and its Early Vernacular Versions* (Berkeley: University of California Press, 1950).

Taussig, Gurion, 'Idea and Substance: Coleridge, Thomas Poole, and the Gendering of Male Friendship', *Coleridge Bulletin* NS 15 (Spring 2000), 41–55.

Taylor, Clare, 'Edward Williams ("Iolo Morganwg") and his Brothers: A Jamaican Inheritance', *Transactions of the Honourable Society of Cymmrodorion* (1980), 35–43.

Thelwall, Robin, 'The Phonetic Theory of John Thelwall', in R. E. Asher and Eugenie J. A. Henderson, eds., *Towards a History of Phonetics* (Edinburgh: Edinburgh University Press, 1981), 186–203.

Thomas, D. O., *Ymateb i Chwyldro/Response to Revolution* (Cardiff: University of Wales Press, 1989).

Thompson, E. P., 'Disenchantment or Default? A Lay Sermon', in C. C. O'Brien and W. D. Vanech, eds., *Power and Consciousness* (London and New York: University of London Press, 1969), 149–81.

——, 'Hunting the Jacobin Fox', *Past and Present* 142 (1994), 94–140.

——, *The Making of the English Working Class* (Harmondsworth: Penguin, 1991).

Thompson, Judith, 'An Autumnal Blast, a Killing Frost: Coleridge's Poetic Conversation with John Thelwall', *Studies in Romanticism* 36, 3 (Fall 1997), 427–56.

——, '"A Voice in the Representation": John Thelwall and the Enfranchisement of Literature', in Tilottama Rajan and Julia M. Wright, eds., *Romanticism, History, and the Possibilities of Genre: Re-forming Literature 1789–1837* (Cambridge: Cambridge University Press, 1998), 122–48.

——, 'John Thelwall and the Politics of Genre, 1803/1993', *The Wordsworth Circle* 25, 1 (Winter 1994), 21–5.

Thompson, J. M., *English Witnesses of the French Revolution* (Oxford: Basil Blackwell, 1938).

Trott, Nicola, 'The Coleridge Circle and the "Answer to Godwin"', *Review of English Studies* NS 41 (May 1990), 212–29.

Utting, A. R., *Tewdric: Saint and Warrior King* (Mathern: Mathern PCC, 1988).

von Erffa, Helmut, and Staley, Allen, *The Paintings of Benjamin West* (New Haven, CT: Yale University Press, 1986).

von Maltzahn, Nicholas, *Milton's History of Britain: Republican Historiography in the English Revolution* (Oxford: Clarendon Press, 1991).

Walford Davies, Damian, '"G.D." *is* George Dyer', *Notes and Queries* 241 (March 1996), 31.

——, 'Hermits, Heroes and History: Lamb's "Many Friends"', *Charles Lamb Bulletin* NS 97 (January 1997), 9–29.

——, 'Pwy yw "Meirion" y *Monthly Magazine*?', *Llên Cymru* 21 (July 1998), 182–8.

——, '"Some Uncertain Notice": The Hermit of "Tintern Abbey"', *Notes and Queries* 241 (December 1996), 422–4.

——, 'Wordsworth's Blind Beggar and Thelwall's *Poems, Chiefly Written in Retirement*', *Charles Lamb Bulletin* NS 107 (July 1999), 114–16.

Ward, John Powell, 'Wordsworth and Friendship', *Coleridge Bulletin* NS 15 (Spring 2000), 27–40.

Watson, J. R., 'A Note on the Date in the Title of *Tintern Abbey*', *The Wordsworth Circle* 10, 4 (Autumn 1979), 379–80.

Wedd, Mary, '"Tintern Abbey" Restored', *Charles Lamb Bulletin* NS 88 (October 1994), 150–65.

Whalley, George, 'The Bristol Library Borrowings of Southey and Coleridge', *The Library* (5th Series), 4 (1949–50), 114–32.

Whittaker, Jason, *William Blake and the Myths of Britain* (Basingstoke: Macmillan, 1999).

Williams, David, 'A Bibliography of the Printed Works of David Williams (1738–1816)', *National Library of Wales Journal* 10 (1957–8), 121–36.

——, 'A Priest of Nature', *Welsh Review* 5 (1946), 36–41.

——, 'The Missions of David Williams and James Tilly Matthews to England (1793)', *English Historical Review* 53 (1938), 651–68.

Williams, G. J., 'Bywyd Cymreig Llundain yng Nghyfnod Owain Myfyr', *Y Llenor* 18 (1939), 73–82 and 218–32.

——, 'Eisteddfodau'r Gwyneddigion', *Y Llenor* 14 (1935), 11–22 and 15 (1936), 88–96.

——, *Iolo Morganwg* (Cardiff: University of Wales Press, 1956).

——, *Iolo Morganwg a Chywyddau'r Ychwanegiad* (Cardiff: University of Wales Press, 1926).

Williams, Gwyn A., *Artisans and Sans-Culottes: Popular Movements in France and Britain during the French Revolution* (2nd edition; London: Libris, 1989).

——, *Madoc: The Making of a Myth* (London: Eyre Methuen, 1979).

——, 'Romanticism in Wales', in Roy Porter and Mikulás Teich, eds., *Romanticism in National Context* (Cambridge: Cambridge University Press, 1988), 9–36.

——, *The Search for Beulah Land* (New York: Holmes & Meier Publishers, 1980).

——, *The Welsh in their History* (London: Croom Helm, 1982).

Williams, Oswald T., *Undodiaeth a Rhyddid Meddwl* (Llandysul: Gwasg Gomer, 1962).

Williams, W. Philip, 'David Williams, 1738–1816', *Welsh Outlook* 13 (1926), 90–2.

Woof, Robert and Hebron, Stephen, *Towards Tintern Abbey* (Grasmere: Wordsworth Trust, 1998).

Wordsworth, Jonathan, ed., *Bicentenary Wordsworth Studies* (Ithaca and London: Cornell University Press, 1970).

——, *The Music of Humanity* (London: Nelson, 1969).

——, *William Wordsworth: The Borders of Vision* (Oxford: Clarendon Press, 1982).

Worrall, David, *Radical Culture: Discourse, Resistance, and Surveillance, 1790–1820* (New York and London: Harvester Wheatsheaf, 1992).

Wright, Dudley, 'Charles Lamb and George Dyer', *English Review* 39 (September 1924), 390–7.

Wright, Herbert G., 'The Relations of the Welsh Bard Iolo Morganwg with Dr. Johnson, Cowper and Southey', *Review of English Studies* 8 (1932), 129–38.

Wright, Paul, 'Vile Saxons and Ancient Britons: Wordsworth, the Ambivalent Welsh Tourist', in Katie Gramich and Andrew Hiscock, eds., *Dangerous Diversity: The Changing Faces of Wales* (Cardiff: University of Wales Press, 1998), 64–80.

Wu, Duncan, 'The Wordsworth Family Library at Cockermouth: Towards a Reconstruction', *The Library* (6th Series), 14 (1992), 127–35.

——, *Wordsworth's Reading, 1770–1799* (Cambridge: Cambridge University Press, 1992).

——, *Wordsworth's Reading, 1800–1815* (Cambridge: Cambridge University Press, 1995).

Index

Adolphus, John 323
Aikin, John 153, 269 n.10
Alexander I, Tsar of Russia 100
Alfoxden House 27, 38, 187, 211, 230
  Thelwall's visit 79, 81, 90, 200, 201–5, 209, 218, 229, 294, 296, 299, 315
Alfred, King 32, 116, 119
Alger, J. G. 249 n.94
Allen, B. Sprague 276 n.117
Amesbury 83, 199
Analytical Review 42, 247 n.59, 272 n.55
Anderson, G. K. 260 n.112
Anti-Jacobin; or Weekly Examiner 29
Anti-Jacobin Review and Magazine 29, 30, 34, 96
antiquarianism 56, 69, 72, 198, 258 n.82
Arkwright, Richard 311
Arthurian legend 20, 84, 85
Association for Preserving Liberty and Property Against Republicans and Levellers 36, 145
Averill, James H. 277 n.141

Baker, James, *Picturesque Guide through Wales and the Marches* 13, 15, 89
Baker, Sir Richard 309
Barbauld, Anna Laetitia 136, 153
  'Hymn: "Ye are the salt of the earth"' 109

Bardic Jacobinism 6, 72, 135–92
  Coleridge and Edward Williams 167–76
  Edward Williams and the *Gorsedd* 160–7
  Edward Williams in London 136–52
  Edward Williams's *Poems, Lyric and Pastoral* 153–9
  Wordsworth and Edward Williams 176–92
Basaleg (home of Ifor Hael) 187, 188, 189, 278 n.163
Bath
  Blake and 98, 140
  Richard Warner and 96–9, 125, 127–8
  Thelwall at 200, 294, 295, 296, 297
  Wordsworth's visit 124–8, 131, 132–3
battle of Tintern (c.595) 13–16, 20
Beattie, James, *The Minstrel* 184, 185, 252 n.139
Beaupuy, Michel 133
Beddoes, Dr Thomas 282 n.51
Bede, The Venerable 59
Bedford, H. W. 280 n.27
Bement, Peter 187–8
benevolence 35, 36–40, 41, 51–4, 169
Bentley, Thomas 246 n.50
Berkeley, George, Bishop of Cloyne 215, 229

betrayal
  Kosciusko and 128, 232
  Thelwall and 91–4, 232
  Vortigern as model of *see* Vortigern
  Wordsworth and 55–8, 63–9, 78, 79, 92–4, 128, 232
Betz, Paul 248 n.84
Birkbeck, George 322
Blake, William 139, 160, 245 n.34, 262 n.27
  Jerusalem 98, 99, 140
Bloom, Harold 10–11, 58
Bodde, Derk 256 n.48, 257 n.75
Boswell, James 153
Bowdler, Thomas 153
Bowles, William Lisle 102, 153
Bowyer, Robert 27
Braithwaite, G. 318
Brecknockshire
  setting for Thelwall's 'The Fairy of the Lake' 85
  see also Llyswen
Brinkley, Robert A. 11
Brissot de Warville, Jacques-Pierre 9, 22, 24, 25, 29, 31, 153, 248 n.70, 249 n.95
Bristol
  Coleridge at 38
  Edward Williams's connections 136, 147
  Kosciusko at 99, 102–7, 128
  Thelwall at 200, 294, 295–6
British Critic 43
Briton, The 69
Brothers, Richard 150–1, 158, 264 n.49
Browning, Robert 250 n.99
Bürger, Gottfried August 18, 238
Burke, Edmund 72–3, 86, 111, 246 n.54, 264 n.39, 292 n.3
  Observations on a late State of the Nation 324
  Reflections on the Revolution in France 21, 22, 73, 96

Burke, Redmond 264 n.48
Burney, Charles 153
Burney, Fanny 153
Burns, Robert
  'A Bard's Epitaph' 177, 186
  'Man was made to Mourn' 263 n.33
Butler, Charles 323
Butler, Marilyn 247 n.59
Bye-Gones 261 n.7
Byron, George Gordon, Lord 122, 134
  Cain 260 n.111
  Don Juan 122, 265 n.55
  The Age of Bronze 122
  The Vision of Judgement 199

Caldecott, Thomas 73
Caledonian Mercury 316
Calvert, William 57, 58
Cambrian Register, The 42, 165, 166–7
Cambridge Intelligencer 264 n.54
Camden, William 15
Campbell, Alexander 309
Campbell, James Dykes 294 n.1
Campbell, Thomas
  'Lines on Poland' 116
  The Pleasures of Hope 116
Canning, George, 'The New Morality' 29, 30, 33
Cardiganshire, setting for *Simon Lee* 187
Cardon, Anthony 103, 104
Carr, Glenda 274 n.84
Carradice, Phil 255 n.40
Carthew, J. 151
Cartwright, Frances Dorothy 323
Casson, T. E. 277 n.138
Catherine the Great of Russia 100, 113–15, 155–6
Cecil, Henrietta *see* Thelwall, Henrietta Cecil
Celoria, Francis 255 n.25
Cerrig-Enion 232–8

illustration 233
Chadwick, Hector Munro 253 n.13
Chalmers, Alexander 324 n.12
Champion, The 82, 86, 326 n.31
Chartism 325 n.28
Chatterton, Thomas 72, 165, 256 n.62, 269 n.8
  'The Battle of Hastings' 61
Chaucer, Geoffrey 130
Chepstow Castle 89
Chubb, John 82, 280 n.30
Civil and Ecclesiastical Systems of England Defended and Fortified, The 34
Claeys, Gregory 198, 298 n.2
Clarke, Charles Cowden 119
Clarke, William 321
Clayden, P. W. 249 n.95
Cline, Henry 265 n.72
Cobbett, William, *Rural Rides* 195
Coburn, Kathleen 167, 170, 175
Cockburn, Lord 316
Coffman, Ralph J. 251 n.117
Coleridge, Hartley 212–16
Coleridge, Henry Nelson 260 n.115
Coleridge, Samuel Taylor 1, 21, 29, 35, 36, 39, 40, 47, 51, 53, 68, 71–2, 77, 90, 125, 127, 149, 189, 267 n.91, 268 n.100, 298, 302 nn.13,14, 303 n.15, 305 n.21, 311
  grant from Literary Fund 38
  influence of David Williams 7, 9, 27, 41
  poetic dialogue with Thelwall 2, 5, 6, 78, 194, 210–40
  relations with Edward Williams 20, 136, 142, 147, 153, 155, 167–76, 186, 189
  relations with Thelwall 38, 79, 81, 82, 85, 91, 111–12, 155, 168, 173–4, 191–2, 193–4, 195, 201–5, 208–9, 248 n.74, 257 n.64, 280 n.22, 291–2, 294, 296, 299, 300–1, 308, 311 n.4, 315, 317–18, 319

n.7, 327–8
  response to Kosciusko 95, 109–18, 134
WORKS:
  Biographia Literaria 112, 301 n.10, 315, 319 n.7
  Conciones ad Populum 103, 148, 287 n.3
  'Dejection: An Ode' 282 n.61
  'Fears in Solitude' 49, 50–1, 75, 142, 163, 214
  'Frost at Midnight' 212–16, 227, 228, 230, 252 n.144
  'Lay Sermons' 118
  Lectures 1795 111, 112, 173, 185, 248 n.70, 258 n.81, 270 n.22, 276 n.109, 277 n.131, 287 n.3, 289 n.7
  'Letter to Edward Long Fox' 143
  'Letter to Sara Hutchinson' 201, 213
  'Lines on Observing a Blossom on the First of February, 1796' 264 n.46
  'Lines composed while climbing the left ascent of Brockley Coomb' 202, 296 n.3
  'Lines Written at the King's Arms, Ross' 62
  Lyrical Ballads 7, 10, 41, 53, 57, 81, 125, 168, 177–87, 218, 219, 222, 223, 232–8
  'Modern Patriotism' 173–4
  Notebooks 174, 175
  'Ode on the Departing Year' 112, 114–15, 155, 156, 266 n.81
  'On a Late Connubial Rupture in High Life' 18
  'Perspiration: A Travelling Eclogue' 279 n.11
  Poems, 1797 49, 50, 264 n.54
  Poems on Various Subjects 112, 123, 255 n.38, 263 n.39, 276 n.129, 283 n.78
  'Reflections on Entering into

Active Life' 18
'Reflections on Having Left a Place of Retirement' 18, 48–50
'Religious Musings' 12, 127
'Rime of the Ancient Mariner' 91
sonnet to Kosciusko 4, 109–12, 114, 118, 123
sonnet to Thelwall 112
Table Talk 79, 91
'The Dungeon' 6, 89, 219–20
The Fall of Robespierre 112, 113, 123
'The Nightingale' 6, 222, 227, 228
The Plot Discovered 112, 149, 289 n.7
The Statesman's Manual 118
The Watchman 50, 71, 111, 112, 173, 248 n.74, 270 n.22
'This Lime-Tree Bower My Prison' 6, 215, 229–30, 232, 242
'To the Rev. George Coleridge' 201
Coleridge, Sara 201, 229, 294, 296, 315, 318
Colley, Linda 65
Combes, John 287 n.2, 289
Congress of Vienna (1814–15) 101
Cooper, Sir Astley 121–2
Cooper, Bransby Blake 121, 265 n.71
Corfield, P. J. 281 n.44, 283 n.90, 285 n.1
Cosway, Richard 103, 104
Cottle, A. S., *Icelandic Poetry* 308 n.3
Cottle, Joseph 41, 83
The Fall of Cambria 66, 93, 165–6
Courtney, Winifred 248 n.84
Cowbridge, Edward Williams's residence at 164, 273 n.58, 306
Cowper, William 153
Coxe, William
Historical Tour in Monmouthshire, An 15, 245 n.48

Travels in Switzerland 15
Critical Review 184, 250 n.98, 272 n.55
Crompton, Peter 207, 210, 297, 298–305
Cromwell, Oliver 139, 152, 176
Crowe, William, *Lewesdon Hill* 11
Cruttwell, Richard Shuttleworth 99, 102, 131
Currie, James 305 n.21
Curry, Kenneth 255 n.30
Curtis, David 275 n.98

Dafydd ap Gwylim 41, 145, 158–9, 187–9
Danby, John F. 234, 237–8
Danvers, Charles 315
Darwin, Erasmus 277 n.132, 311
Davies, David 258 n.79
Davies, E. T. 13, 244 n.21
Davies, Edward 'Celtic', *The Mythology and Rites of the British Druids* 166
Davies, Roos 281 n.43
Davies, Walter ('Gwallter Mechain') 145, 166, 270 n.28
Davies, William Ll. 274 n.82
De Quincey, Thomas 90, 263 n.29, 320–1
Death of Tewdrig, The (bronze by J. E. and W. M. Thomas) 14
Defence of the Constitution of England, A (1791) 33–4
Defoe, Daniel, *Tour through the Whole Island of Great Britain, A* 60
Demosthenes 311
Derby Society for Political Information 311
Derfel, R. J., *Brad y Llyfrau Gleision* 254 n.15
Dickstein, Morris 116
Doble, G. M. 244 n.16
Doward hills 60, 62, 127
Drayton, Michael 59
Poly-Olbion 61

Dryden, John 313 n.8
Dudley, Sir Henry Bate and Lady Mary 72
Dumville, D. N. 253 n.13
Dundas, Henry, 1st Viscount Melville 150
Dybikowski, J. 245 n.41, 248 n.82, 249 n.86
Dyer, George 9, 16–21, 35, 36–40, 44, 46, 84, 109, 111, 136, 303 n.15, 308–10
  'Address to the Society for establishing a Literary Fund' 38–9
  Complaints of the Poor People of England 35, 189
  Dissertation on the Theory and Practice of Benevolence, A 35, 38, 39, 40, 51–3, 189
  Four Letters on the English Constitution 250 n.108
  Inquiry into the Nature of Subscription to the Thirty-nine Articles, An 35
  Memoirs of Robert Robinson 35
  'On Liberty'('Ode to Liberty') 109
  Poems (1792) 109
  Poems (1801) 38
  Poetics, or, a Series of Poems 16–17

Edinburgh, Thelwall in 316
Edinburgh Review 217, 266 n.80, 277 n.140
Edwards, Edward 281 n.44
Einon Glyd 232
eisteddfodau 145, 160
Ellis, Tecwyn 274 n.82
Enfield, William 18, 42
English Review 42
Erdman, D. V. 29, 98, 140, 249 n.85
Erskine, Thomas 159, 168, 264 n.39, 323 n.7
Erskine, William 316
Estlin, John Prior 136
European Magazine 18

Evans, Chris 281 n.44, 283 n.90, 285 n.1
Evans, Edward 137
Evans, Evan 278 n.164, 278 n.166
  'Llys Ifor Hael' (The Palace of Ifor Hael) 187–8, 189
Evans, J. J. 257 n.79
Evans, Theophilus, *Drych y Prif Oesoedd* (The Mirror of Primitive Ages) 77
Evans, Thomas ('Tomos Glyn Cothi') 136
Everest, Kelvin 282 n.49
Examiner 4, 101, 103, 116–18

Fawcett, Joseph 239
Fenwick, Isabella 238, 239
Field, Barron 31
Fields, James T. 122
Fitzgerald, William Thomas 36, 157
Fletcher, J. Kyrle 273 n.60
Foulkes, Isaac ('Llyfrbryf') 258 n.79
Fox, Charles James 98, 324
Fox, Samuel 311, 314
France, Peter 27
France
  David Williams and 21–2, 24–9, 31–3
  Edward Williams and 150
  Kosciusko and 99
  Sir Astley Cooper and 121
  Wales as mirror of 64–6, 67, 68, 108, 132, 242
  Wordsworth and 12, 24, 26, 27, 28, 29, 31–3, 64–6, 67, 68, 108, 124–5
Franklin, Andrew, *The Wandering Jew, or Love's Masquerade* 90
Franklin, Benjamin 21
Frederick II the Great of Prussia 21
Frederick William II of Prussia 114, 116
Frend, William 36, 40, 111, 251 n.115
Friends of the People 125

Frome, Thelwall at 199–200, 294, 295, 296
Füseli, Henry 70

Ganarew 60, 62
Gardnor, John 18
Gaskell, Mary 329
Geddes, Dr John 269 n.10
Geirgrawn, Y (The Treasury of Words) 76
Gentleman's Magazine, The 36, 99, 101, 107, 136–7, 160, 177, 250 n.99, 262 nn.13,14
Geoffrey of Monmouth 59–60, 61, 62, 75, 83, 84, 92, 309
George III, King 74
George, Prince of Wales 157–9
Gerrald, Joseph 103
  A Convention the only means of saving us from Ruin 34, 323
Gibbon, Edward 273 n.60
Gibbs, Warren E. 251 n.119, 282 n.58, 285 n.1
Gifford, William 34
Gildas 59
Gillray, James 29, 30, 33
Gilpin, William 2, 98
  Observations on the River Wye 10, 16, 126
Glamorganshire Volunteers 149
Godwin, Francis, Bishop of Llandaff 13, 15
Godwin, William 6, 9, 33, 40, 106, 110, 111, 147, 302 n.13
  An Enquiry concerning Political Justice 34–5, 110, 111, 167–87, 190–1, 262 n.28, 314
  Caleb Williams 86–9, 90, 176
  Memoirs of the Author of a Vindication of the Rights of Woman 276 n.116
  St Leon 276 n.116
Goldsmith, Oliver 59, 61
Goodwin, Albert 311

Gordon, George Huntly 66
gorseddau 159, 160–7
gratitude 49–50, 157–9, 167–76, 185, 187–92, 228
Graves, Richard, *The Spiritual Quixote* 176
Gray, James 109
Gray, Thomas 187
  'The Progress of Poesy' 131
Grebanier, Bernard 256 n.48, 257 n.62
Grégoire, Henri 28, 29
Grenville, William Wyndham, Baron 25, 26
Gurney, John 210
Gurney, Joseph 210
Gwernyclepa (home of Ifor Hael) 188, 278 n.163
Gwrtheyrn *see* Vortigern
Gwyneddigion *see* London Gwyneddigion Society
Gwynne, Roderick 281 n.44

Haiman, Mieczyslaus 101, 261 n.11
Hamilton, Chloe 262 n.22
Haraszti, Zoltán 256 n.48, 257 n.62
Harding, S. 97
Hardy, Thomas 26, 27, 79, 142, 143, 210, 281 n.41, 282 n.45, 285 n.1, 308 n.2, 313 n.7, 320, 324
Harmston, Joe 256 n.61
Hartley, David 21, 52, 111, 173, 174, 215
Hartman, Geoffrey 10
Harvey, Daniel Whittle 326 n.32
Haydon, Benjamin Robert 217
Hazlitt, William 80, 106, 118, 262 n.28, 266 n.80, 315, 317, 318
  Lectures on the English Poets 262 n.28
Heath, Charles
  Excursion Down the Wye from Ross to Monmouth 62, 254 n.20, 259 n.89, 263 n.32

Historical and Descriptive Accounts of the Ancient and Present State of Chepstow Castle 15
Historical and Descriptive Accounts of the Ancient and Present State of Tintern Abbey 15–16, 244 n.19
Hébert, Jacques-René 29
Hebron, Stephen 267 n.86, 294 n.1, 298 n.1
Herbert, Trevor 276 n.105
Hereford, Thelwall at 209, 308, 312
Hereford Philanthropic Society 281 n.44
hermit figure 7, 8–54, 56, 128, 194
  Tewdrig 12–16, 40–54
Hill, Alan G. 329 n.5
Hill, Christopher 262 n.27
'Hirlas' 261 n.7
History of Two Acts, The 324
Hofer, Andreas 124
Holcroft, Thomas 29, 33, 35, 40, 79, 109, 110, 111, 176, 248 n.74, 320, 324
Holinshed, Raphael 59, 70, 75, 84, 309
Homer 19
Homfray, Samuel 231–2
Hooper, Thomas 41
Hucks, Joseph 279 n.11
Hume, David, *History of England* 27
Hunt, John Dixon 10
Hunt, Leigh 4, 95, 101, 103, 104, 119
  'To Kosciusko' 116–18
Hutchinson, Thomas 191

Ifor Hael ('Ivor the Generous') 41, 158–9, 187–90
Ireland, Samuel 70, 73, 254 n.20
Ireland, William Henry 59, 165
  Confessions 70, 256 n.47
  Vortigern 69–76, 85
Irish Rebellion 133
Isle of Wight, Wordsworth on 57, 58

jacobinism and radicalism
  David Williams 21–43
  Edward Williams *see* Bardic Jacobinism
  Frome, Bath and Bristol 199–200, 294, 295
  Kosciusko and 108–18
  Liverpool 298–9, 305 n.21, 320–1
  radical benevolence and the Literary Fund 36–40, 41, 51
  Richard Warner 96, 98
  Welsh 76–8
  see also Thelwall, John; Wordsworth, William; Coleridge, Samuel Taylor
Jacobus, Mary 10, 16, 17, 18, 20, 60, 126–7, 255 n.26
Jardine, Alexander 36
Jebb, John 21
Jefferson, Thomas 100
Jeffrey, Francis 217, 222, 277 n.140, 316
  Observations on Mr Thelwall's Letter 281 n.43
Jenkins, Geraint H. 269 n.9
Jenkins, R. T. 257 n.77
Johnson, Joseph 139, 153, 177
Johnson, Samuel 269 n.6
Johnson, William 131–3
Johnston, Kenneth R. 10, 252 n.141
Jones, Edward 145–6, 147
Jones, Gareth Elwyn 276 n.105
Jones, Hugh 140
Jones, John ('Jac Glan-y-Gors') 136, 145, 166
  Seren Tan Gwmmwl (The Cloud-hidden Star) 76–8, 154, 270 n.29
  Toriad y Dydd (The Break of Day) 76
Jones, Myddleton Pennant 258 n.79
Jones, Owen ('Owain Myfyr') 136, 145, 270 n.28
Jones, Robert 12, 58, 63
Jones, Stephen 111

Jones, Theophilus 42, 166–7
    History of the County of Brecknock
    60, 232
Jones, Whitney R. D. 245 n.49, 246
    n.51, 247 n.63, 248 n.82, 250
    n.99, 253 n.2
Jones, Sir William 153
Jordan, Dora 70
Joyce, Jeremiah 320

Kahan, Jeffrey 256 n.48
Kajencki, Francis Casimir 261 n.11
Kandl, John 116–17
Kauffman, Angelica 70
Keats, John 1, 95, 107, 134
    'Ode to a Nightingale' 119–20
    'Sleep and Poetry' 118–22
    'To J. H. Reynolds, Esq.' 45
    'To Kosciusko' 4, 116–18, 122,
    265 n.66
Kelly, Gary 175
Kemble, John Philip 70
Kingston, Jeremy 256 n.61
Kirby, D. P. 253 n.13
Knight, William 184
Kosciusko, Thaddeus 2–3, 4, 6,
    95–134
    Coleridge and 109–18, 123
    portrait by Benjamin West 105
    and the Romantic imagination
    108–24
    Warner's meeting with 98–108,
    129–30
    Wordsworth and 95, 124–34

Lafayette, Marquis de 109
Lafitte, Anne Gédéon, Marquis de
    Pelleport 24
Lake District
    Thelwall visits Wordsworth,
    Coleridge and Southey 315–19, 327
    Wordsworth and Coleridge in 209
Lamb, Charles 29, 36–7, 39, 71, 111,
    210, 229, 230, 231, 250 n.111, 321

Landor, Walter Savage 122
    Imaginary Conversations of Literary
    Men and Statesmen 123
landscape 4, 9, 17, 41, 44–6, 51–3,
    56, 63, 198, 223–4, 228, 241–2,
    315, 319
    see also Nature; picturesque, the
Larevellière-Lépaux, Louis Marie de
    29
Le Brun, Charles-François, Duc de
    Plaisance 25, 249 n.96
Legouis, Émile 191
Levinson, Marjorie 3, 8, 10, 47
Lewis, Blanch 149
Lewis, Ceri W. 269 n.9
Lewis, Gwyneth 164–5, 273 n.62
Lewis, Matthew 90
Lewis, Saunders 258 n.79
Liber Landavensis (Book of Llandav)
    12–13, 15, 20
Literary Fund 21, 26, 29, 34, 35,
    36–40, 51, 53, 157
Little, Geoffrey 259 n.90
Liu, Alan 3, 46–7, 66
Liverpool jacobins 298–9, 305 n.21,
    320–1
Llangynhafal, home of Robert Jones
    12, 58, 63
Lloyd, Charles 29, 38
Lloyd, Stephen 262 n.23
'Llyfrbryf' (Isaac Foulkes) 258 n.79
Llyswen, Brecknockshire
    (Breconshire)
    setting for Thelwall's 'Paternal
    Tears' sequence of poems 210–39,
    242
    Thelwall's invitation to Edward
    Williams to visit 164, 306–7
    Thelwall's residence at 81–3, 84,
    85, 88, 193, 202, 205–10, 298,
    299, 303–4, 313 n.7
    visit by Wordsworth, Dorothy and
    Coleridge 81, 93–4, 208, 219,
    222, 327–8

Index

Loft, Capel 36
London Constitutional Society 143
London Corresponding Society 5, 79, 124, 196, 281 n.44
London Gwyneddigion Society 76, 145
London Philosophical Society 35
Losh, James 18, 40, 61, 124–5, 127–8, 131
Lovell, Mary 315, 318
Lovell, Robert, *Poems* 102
Lucan, *Pharsalia* 200
Lyon, Judson Stanley 279 n.13

MacGillivray, J. R. 31
Mackintosh, James 24
Macpherson, James 165, 308, 309 n.18
Magnus, Olaus 308 n.6
Magnuson, Paul 5, 6, 49, 211, 252 n.144
Mair, John 75, 256 n.48, 257 n.75
Mallet, Paul Henri 309
Malone, Edmond 69, 70, 72–3
Manchester Constitutional Society 168
Manogue, Ralph A. 151
Mant's *Wars of England* 324
Marat, Jean-Paul 150
Margaret Street Chapel, London 28–9, 34, 35
Marten, Henry 89
Martin, James 36
Martin, John 324
Martin, Peter 73
Marxist criticism 205
Mathern 13, 15, 20
Matthews, E. Gwynn 258 n.79
McGann, Jerome J. 3
McLean, Thomas 104, 117–18
Merthyr Rising (1831) 325 n.28
Merthyr Tydfil 231–2
Meurig (son of Tewdrig) 12, 13, 15, 20

Millingen, J. G. 247 n.61
Milton, John 10–11, 59, 69, 239, 304
  History of Britain 255 n.28
  'Il Penseroso' 11, 227
  Paradise Lost 107, 129; Book I 92, 93, 104, 106, 134; Book II 130; Book VII 39, 131; Book XI 11, 108
  Samson Agonistes 226
Miltonic picturesque 11–12, 44, 63, 107–8
Montagu, Basil 38, 238
Montesquieu, Charles-Louis de Secondat, Baron de la Brède et de 21
Monthly Magazine 16–18, 21, 34, 42, 44, 46, 49, 61, 70, 72, 109, 126, 162, 195, 200, 201, 209, 217, 250 n.110, 259 n.100, 279 nn.4,6,7,8, 12,17,18, 280 nn.19,20,21,22,23, 281 n.45, 294, 295 n.2, 299, 303
Moorman, Mary 58, 184, 191
More, Hannah 153
Morgan, John 41, 189
Morgan, Prys 60, 258 n.82, 269 n.9
Morning Chronicle 109, 112, 160, 288
Morning Post 72, 268 n.98, 288, 289
Morris, John 244 n.21
Mortimer, John Hamilton 70
Muir, Thomas 142

Napoleon Bonaparte 47, 100
Nature
  Coleridge and 89, 185, 214, 215, 219, 220, 221, 227, 228, 230, 232, 303 n.15
  David Williams as priest of 21, 28, 34, 44–5
  Edward Williams and 182–3, 184
  Thelwall and 215, 220–5, 231, 232, 303, 327
  Wordsworth and 3, 4, 10, 45–6,

47, 52, 68–9, 81, 89, 182–3, 184, 187, 219, 231, 232
    see also landscape; picturesque, the
Nennius 59, 62, 254 n.17
Nether Stowey 27, 38, 204, 205, 229, 230, 268 n.100
    Thelwall's visit to 79, 81, 112, 193, 200, 201, 209, 218, 294, 296, 299, 327
New Historicism 3, 9, 10, 46, 242
Newlyn, Lucy 106–7, 182, 210–11, 213, 215, 237, 263 n.29
Nichols, John 36, 324
Noble, Mark 176
Noël (French agent) 249 n.96
Noyes, Russell 277 n.139

Offley, Henry Francis 260 n.117
Oldfield, J. R. 275 n.95
Onorato, Richard J. 10, 58
Oracle, The 74
Oswald, John 29, 153, 249 n.85
'Owain Myfyr' see Jones, Owen
Owen, Bob 258 n.79
Owen, Matthew 254 n.23
Owen, William, *Y Drych Bradwriaethol* (The Treacherous Mirror) 254 n.23
Owen, William see Pughe, William Owen

Paine, Thomas 24, 25, 27, 29, 33, 34, 78, 86, 99, 111, 136, 147, 148, 153, 158, 159, 305 n.21
    The Age of Reason 147–9
    The Rights of Man 34, 77
Palmer, Thomas Fysshe 37, 142, 143, 145
Parker, Richard 196
Parrish, Stephen 277 n.139
Paul I, Tsar of Russia 100
Pennant, Thomas 59, 66, 153, 188, 254 n.17
Percy, Thomas 188, 308 n.5, 309

Perry, James 109
Phillips, John 304
Phillips, Richard 303, 310
picturesque, the 2, 9, 10, 11–12, 44–5, 48, 198, 317–18
Pinkerton, J. 309
Pinney, Azariah 27
Piozzi, Hester Lynch 153
Pitt, William, the Younger 27, 36, 77, 79, 99, 101, 108, 113, 114, 119, 143, 146–7, 148, 150–1, 158–9, 172, 195, 196, 208, 211, 261 n.4, 264 n.39, 275 n.98, 286, 288
Pollin, Burton R. 264 n.48
Pontoppidan, Erik 309
Poole, Thomas 79, 193, 202, 205, 229, 268 n.100, 282 n.61
Porson, Richard 110
Portal, Abraham, *Vortimer; or, the True Patriot* 70
Porter, Jane, *Thaddeus of Warsaw* 122
Portland, William Henry Cavendish Bentinck, 3rd Duke of 204, 281 n.44
postcolonial criticism 66
Precious Relics, or the Tragedy of Vortigern Rehears'd 70
Price, Richard 24, 96, 99, 153
Priestley, Joseph 24, 99, 111, 136, 153, 251 n.115, 264 n.39
Pughe, William Owen 61, 136, 145, 160, 161, 162–3, 165, 166, 275 nn.87,88,94
    The Cambrian Biography 165
    The Heroic Elegies and Other Pieces of Llywarç Hen 160–1, 162, 165, 166, 175, 274 n.70
Pula, James S. 261 n.11
Pwll Brochwael (Brockwear) 13, 245 n.42

Quakers 275 n.88, 299, 300
Quarterly Review 260 n.115

Index

Racedown 27, 38, 90, 111
radicalism *see* jacobinism and radicalism
Railo, Eino 260 n.111
Ramage, Helen M. 257 n.77
Rathbone, William 210, 298, 299, 300, 305
Reed, Mark 267 n.86
Reeves, John 36, 140, 145, 146, 147, 154, 157, 271 n.36, 272 n.53
Reflector, The 250 n.108
Reid, William Hamilton 34
Richards, H. P. 247 n.57
Richardson, Samuel 273 n.60
Rickman, John 36, 316
Rickword, Edgell 285 n.1
Rieder, John 203, 243 n.4, 252 n.145, 280 n.28
Rigaud, John Francis 23, 70
Ritchie, Leitch, *The Wye and its Associations* 16
Ritson, Joseph 27, 69
Roberts, Daniel Sanjiv 305 n.21
Roberts, Edward, *Brad y Cyllill Hirion* 254 n.23
Roberts, Thomas, Llwynrhudol, *Cwyn yn erbyn Gorthrymder* (A Complaint against Oppression) 145
Robespierre, Maximilien de 24, 29, 55, 113, 150, 211
Robinson, Henry Crabb 35, 239, 316 n.2
Robinson, Jeffrey 197
Rockey, Denyse 311 n.2
Roe, Nicholas 11–12, 28, 39–40, 44, 51, 52, 56–7, 58, 68, 79, 89, 111, 125, 127–8, 130, 193, 197, 238, 244 n.12, 249 n.94, 252 n.144, 264 n.48, 266 n.72, 283 n.84, 298 n.1
Rogers, Samuel 153, 249 n.95
Roland de la Platière, Jean-Marie 24, 25
Roland de la Platière, Marie-Jeanne 9, 22

Appeal to Impartial Posterity 27–8, 248 n.70
Roscoe, William 298, 305
Rose, J. Holland 285 n.1
Rose, R. B. 305 n.21
Rothstein, Eric 90
Rousseau, Jean-Jacques 21, 273 n.60
Royal Literary Fund *see* Literary Fund
Rushton, Edward 298, 305 n.21
Ryland, William Wynne 70

St Albyn, Mrs 205
Salisbury Plain 58, 60, 63, 83, 199
Sandford, Elizabeth 268 n.100, 280 n.35, 294 n.1
Satan 92–3, 104, 106, 129, 131, 134
Sayers, Frank 309
Scrivener, Michael 196–7, 198, 206, 222, 242, 259 n.93, 279 n.5, 280 n.24
Sellers, Ian 305 n.21
Seneca 303
Seward, Anna 153
Shakespeare, William
  King Lear 11, 75–6
  Othello 19
  Richard II 74
  Vortigern forgery 69–76
Shankland, Thomas 274 n.82
Sharp, William 103, 104
Sheffer, Johannes 308 n.7
Shelley, Percy Bysshe 90, 262 n.27
  Prometheus Unbound 84
Shepherd, William 298, 305, 320–6
Sheridan, Richard Brinsley 70, 264 n.39
Siddons, Sara 170
Simpson, David 205, 278 n.165
Smith, Charlotte 31
Smith, Joseph 298, 300, 305
Society for Constitutional Information 21, 36, 124–5, 143
Society of Friends *see* Quakers
Socrates 303

Southey, Edith 315, 318
Southey, Robert 29, 61, 72, 102, 109, 124, 135, 136, 140, 151, 160, 162, 167, 174, 193, 229, 263 n.39, 275 n.98, 279 n.11, 280 nn.22,33, 283 n.89, 315–16, 317, 318–19, 328
  Annual Anthology 72, 229
  'For the Apartment in Chepstow-Castle where Henry Marten the regicide was imprisoned Thirty Years' 89
  Joan of Arc 200
  Letters from England 28, 103
  Madoc 165–6
  The Fall of Robespierre 112
  Wat Tyler 151
Spenser, Edmund 120
Staley, Walter 103, 262 n.23
Stanislaw II Augustus Poniatowski 100, 123
Stein, Edwin 263 n.33
Stephens, Alexander 323 n.10
Sterne, Laurence, *Tristram Shandy* 302, 304
Stockdale, John 323
Stone, John Hurford 36
Stow, John 309
Strutt, Jedediah 311
Strutt, Joseph 311–14
Stuart, Daniel 72
Surprizing History of the Wandering Jew of Jerusalem with his arrival at Dover this Year 1780, The 90
Sutherland, Thomas 233
Suvorov, Aleksandr Vasilyevich 100, 113, 114, 115

Tacitus 304
Talfourd, Thomas Noon 321
Talleyrand, Charles-Maurice de 136
Tatlock, J. S. P. 254 n.18
Taylor, Clare 273 n.58
Taylor, William 18, 72, 84, 238

Tewdrig Fendigaid (The Blessed), King 2, 12–16, 20, 40–54
  illustration 14
Thelwall, Algernon Sidney 91, 208, 299, 302
Thelwall, John Hampden 91, 212–16, 303, 321
Thelwall, Henrietta Cecil 7
  Letter to William Shepherd 320–6
  Letter to William Wordsworth 217, 327–9
  The Life of John Thelwall 82, 86, 283 n.83, 311 n.2, 321, 322–6, 327, 328–9
Thelwall, John 1, 5, 29, 33, 59, 121, 125, 142, 193–240, 242, 320
  and David Williams 7, 9, 26, 27, 34
  and Edward Williams 136, 143, 164, 306–7
  and Kosciusko 95, 113–16, 134
  Life by Henrietta Cecil Thelwall *see* Thelwall, Henrietta Cecil
  'Pedestrian Excursion' (1797) 79, 81, 83, 164, 194–205, 206, 212, 291, 294–7, 306, 315
  poetic dialogue with Wordsworth and Coleridge 2, 5, 6, 78, 92–4, 194, 210–40
  portrait 80
  relations with Coleridge *see* Coleridge, Samuel Taylor
  relations with Wordsworth *see* Wordsworth, William
  and Vortigern story 78–89
  WORKS:
  'A Pedestrian Excursion' *see above* 'Pedestrian Excursion'
  Appeal to Popular Opinion against Kidnapping and Murder 142
  Effusions *see below* 'Paternal Tears' sequence
  John Gilpin's Ghost 287 n.2
  King Chanticleer, or the Fate of Tyranny 287 n.2

Letter to Francis Jeffray 316
Letters 7; to Edward Williams 164, 306–7; to George Dyer 84, 308–10; to J. Wimpory 291–3; to John Vellum 217–18, 286–9; to Joseph Strutt 311–14; to Peter Crompton 207–8, 210, 298–305; to Susan Thelwall 81, 200, 201–2, 284 n.101, 294–7, 315–19
'Lines, written at Bridgewater' 8, 112, 202–4, 211–12
'Maria. A Fragment' 217, 221, 231
'Ode II' 219
'On Leaving the Bottoms of Glocestershire' 91, 204, 212, 282 n.63, 283 n.88
'On the Prospective Principle of Virtue' 112, 113
'Paternal Tears' sequence 194, 205, 210–40; 'Effusion I. To J–G–' 210, 218, 220, 221; 'Effusion III. On the Banks of the Wye' 223–5; 'Effusion IV. During a severe Indisposition' 223, 226, 227–8; 'Effusion VI. On returning from a Journey to Merthyr Tydfil' 223, 226; 'Effusion VII. On STELLA'S leaving me' 228–32; 'Effusion X. Cerrig-Enion: (Enion's Tomb)' 232–8
Peaceful Discussion, and not Tumultuary Violence the Means of Redressing National Grievances 248 n.74
Poems, Chiefly Written in Retirement 82, 85, 87, 91–2, 210–40, 259 n.97, 277 n.140, 308, 309–10; *see also* 'Prefatory Memoir'
Poems Written in Close Confinement in the Tower and Newgate 219, 220, 221
political lectures 4, 109, 112, 113–14, 115–16, 119, 150, 156, 169–70, 197, 271 n.36, 288–9, 324

'Prefatory Memoir' to *Poems, Chiefly Written in Retirement* 81–3, 84, 85, 86, 87, 88, 89, 194, 195, 200, 205–10, 217, 220, 222, 236, 258 n.85, 281 n.41, 286, 299
Reply to the Calumnies, Misrepresentations, and Literary Forgeries 277 n.140, 281 n.43, 316
Sober Reflections on the Seditious and Inflammatory Letter of . . . Edmund Burke 324
'Sonnet to the Nightingale' 227
'The Cell' 220–1, 231
The Daughter of Adoption 299
'The Fairy of the Lake' 83–6, 89
The Peripatetic 45, 83, 197–8, 239
'The Phenomena of the Wye' 126, 281 n.45
The Rights of Nature 83–4, 291–2, 298 n.2
The Tribune 4, 109, 111, 113, 115, 119, 150, 156, 169, 197, 324
'To the Infant Hampden' 212–16, 217, 283 n.88
Thelwall, Maria 81, 208, 209, 217–18, 228, 232, 235–6, 290, 299, 302
Thelwall, Robin 311 n.2
Thelwall, Susan 'Stella' 81, 200, 201–2, 234–8, 284 n.101, 294–7, 304, 305, 315–19, 320, 328
Thelwall, Weymouth Birkbeck 320, 322 n.3
Theocritus 177
Theophilanthropy 29, 30, 33
Thomas, John Evan 14
Thomas, Thomas 66
Thomas, William Meredyth 14
Thompson, Aaron 59–60, 61, 84, 309
Thompson, E. P. 125, 193, 201, 238, 239–40, 248 n.84, 259 n.97, 285 n.1, 286 n.1, 291 n.1, 294 n.1, 298 n.1, 299, 302 n.14, 306 n.1,

311 n.1, 312 n.5, 314 n.1, 315 n.1, 320 n.1
Thompson, J. M. 247 n.61
Thompson, Judith 5, 91, 212, 216–17, 242
Thomson, James, *The Castle of Indolence* 184
Times, The 73–4, 288
Tintern 12–16, 17, 20, 59, 125–6
Todd, Janet 247 n.59
Tooke, John Horne 26, 27, 79, 136, 142, 143, 153, 320, 323, 324
topographical writing 4, 9, 16–21, 56, 69
tourism 56, 60, 61–2, 96, 198, 241–2
Treason of the Long Knives, The 59, 60, 65, 66, 77–8, 83, 261 n.119
Treason Trials (1794) 26–7, 40, 79, 88, 142–3, 143, 286, 325
Trott, Nicola 276 n.110
True Briton 288
Tryal of M. Margarot, The 323
Two Acts (1795) 79, 112, 199, 271 n.36, 289 n.7, 325 n.26
Tyrrell, James 244 n.21

Unitarianism 111, 136, 147–8, 162, 299, 300–1
Universal Magazine of Knowledge and Pleasure 324
Utting, A. R. 244 n.21

valency, defined 4
Vallon, Annette 57
Vellum, John 88, 202, 207, 217, 286–90, 297, 303, 304, 305, 328
Virgil 313 n.8
Voltaire 21, 34
von Erffa, Helmut 103, 262 n.23
Vortigern 2, 6, 55–6, 59–61, 92, 93, 94, 95, 128, 194
  John Thelwall and 78–89
  as paradigm of betrayal 63–9
  Welsh radicals and 76–8

William Henry Ireland's play 69–76
Wordsworth and 60–9

Wace 254 n.18
Wakefield, Gilbert 36, 37, 136, 145, 147, 299, 301, 320
Wales 2, 241–2
  radicalism 76–8
  Richard Warner and 102, 107, 108, 132
  Thelwall's journey to the Valleys 231–2
  Wordsworth and 64–6, 67, 68, 108
  see also Brecknockshire; Cardiganshire; Llyswen; Tintern; Wye Valley
Walford Davies, Damian 245 n.30, 246 n.49, 275 n.94
Walker, Joseph Cooper 309
Walker, Thomas 168
Walpole, Horace 153
Walsh, James 204
Walters, John 139, 147, 157
Wandering Jews 89–94, 212
Ward, William 311
Waring, Elijah, *Recollections and Anecdotes of Edward Williams* 22, 138, 146–7, 150, 151, 158–9, 162, 268 n.4, 270 n.27, 272 n.50,53, 273 n.58, 275 n.91
Warner, Richard 95–108, 129–34
  portrait by S. Harding 97
  WORKS:
  A Second Walk through Wales 131, 132–3
  A Walk through Wales, in August 1797 16, 60, 96, 98, 99, 102, 108, 125–8
  History of Bath 96, 97
  Literary Recollections 98, 101–3, 131–2, 267 n.91
  Sermon on 'National Blessings' 261 n.4

War Inconsistent with Christianity 98, 140
Warrington, William 59, 254 n.17
Washington, George 24, 99, 124, 153
Watson, J. R. 244 n.18
Watson, Richard, Bishop of Llandaff 20, 153
  Address to the People of Great Britain 37, 301 n.11
  Apology for the Bible 139
Wedgwood, Josiah (the elder) 21
Wedgwood, Josiah (the younger) 21, 299, 300
Wedgwood, Julia 22
Wedgwood, Thomas 21, 299, 300
West, Benjamin 2, 103, 104, 105
Whalley, George 251 n.117
Whitchurch, Samuel
  Elegy on the Death of Mr Thomas Tuppen 264 n.49
  'Farewell to the Year 1794' 111, 112, 113, 114, 115
White, James 71
Widukind 253 n.14
Wilberforce, William 24, 153
Wilkes, John 36
Williams, Ann 170–2
Williams, David (1738–1816) 2, 4, 6, 21–8, 56, 69, 76, 81, 99, 124, 132, 149, 169, 241
  friendship with Edward Williams 136, 158, 162, 271 n.38
  in Gillray's 'New Morality' 29, 30, 33
  influence on Wordsworth 7, 16–21, 22, 26, 27, 28–36, 40–54, 63, 81, 95, 168
  and Literary Fund 21, 26, 29, 34, 35, 36–40, 53
  portrait by J. F. Rigaud 23
  WORKS:
  A Letter to the Body of Protestant Dissenters 249 n.97
  A Liturgy on the Universal Principles of Religion and Morality 21, 28, 162
  A Plan of Association 249–50 n.97
  A Treatise on Education 21, 38, 41
  An Apology for Professing the Religion of Nature . . . addressed to the Right Reverend Dr. Watson, Lord Bishop of Llandaff 20
  Biographical Anecdotes of the Founders of the French Republic 22, 247 n.66, 248 n.70
  Claims of Literature 40
  Incidents in My Own Life which have been Thought of Some Importance 22, 31, 36, 246 nn.50,55, 247 nn.58, 60,62,64,65,67,70, 248 nn.71,73, 75, 250 n.99
  Lectures on Education 24, 169
  Lectures on Political Principles 21, 33, 35
  Lessons to a Young Prince by an Old Statesman 21, 22, 29, 33, 42
  Letters on Political Liberty 21, 22, 33, 248 n.72, 250 n.97
  Observations sur la dernière constitution de la France 21–2, 25
  The History of Monmouthshire 8–9, 16–21, 22, 27, 40–54, 56, 61, 63, 120, 126, 166, 189, 198
  The Philosopher 21, 26, 249 n.97
Williams, David (historian) 25, 249 n.96, 251 n.129, 275 n.92
Williams, Edward ('Iolo Morganwg') 2, 6, 20, 35, 37, 41, 42–3, 77, 84, 135–92, 286, 241, 286, 320
  Bardic Jacobinism 72, 136–53, 160–7
  and Coleridge 20, 167–76
  friendship with David Williams 136, 158, 162, 271 n.38
  portrait 138
  and Thelwall 136, 143, 164, 306–7
  and Wordsworth 168, 176–92

WORKS:
'Apostrophe to Liberty' 160
'Breiniau Dyn' (The Rights of Man) 152
'Epitaph on a Poet' 186
'Gwawr Borau Rhyddid' (The Dawn of Liberty) 152
History of the Ancient British Bards 162, 164
'History of the Druids' 143
Kingcraft versus Christianity 139
'Newgate Stanzas' 151–2
'Ode, Imitated from the Gododin of Aneurin Gwawdrydd' 136
'Ode on converting a Sword into a Pruning Hook' 154, 155–6, 158, 274 n.67
'Ode on the Mythology of the Ancient British Bards' 154, 259 n.103
'On Love' 183
Poems, Lyric and Pastoral 139, 143, 145, 152–9, 160, 164, 165, 167, 170–2, 175, 176–92, 259 n.103, 268 n.3
Salmau yr Eglwys yn yr Anialwch (The Psalms of the Church in the Wilderness) 271 n.38
'Sonnet, To Hope' 273 n.63
'Sonnet, written in 1790, To the Memory of my Mother' 171–2
'The Learned Ignorants' 177–9, 182, 183, 184, 186
'To Ivor the Liberal' 188–90
'To Laudanum' 268 n.3
Trial by Jury, The Grand Palladium of British Liberty. A Song 143, 144
War Incompatible with the Spirit of Christianity 140
'War Song of British Savages' 158
Williams, G. J. 137, 171, 269 n.9, 273 n.58, 276 nn.120,123, 278 n.156
Williams, Gwyn A. 162, 258 n.82, 275 nn.90,92,93

Williams, Helen Maria 249 n.84
Williams, J. 97
Williams, Peter Bailey 166
Williams, Taliesin 270 n.27
Williams, W. Philip 275 n.92
Williams Wynn, C.W. 61
Wimpory, J. 195, 291–3, 297, 300 n.8
Windham, William 27
Winterbotham, William 151–2, 320
Wollstonecraft, Mary 24, 31, 149, 305 n.21
The Wrongs of Woman 82
Woof, Robert 267 n.86, 294 n.1, 298 n.1
Wordsworth, Christopher 249 n.93
Wordsworth, Dora 329
Wordsworth, Dorothy 16, 38, 81, 124, 184, 193, 202, 208, 222, 225, 284 n.103, 296, 317, 327, 328
Wordsworth, Jonathan 58, 277 n.148
Wordsworth, Mary 284 n.103
Wordsworth, Richard 29
Wordsworth, William 1, 3, 15, 21, 38, 39, 40, 51, 53, 149, 268 n.99, 299
and Edward Williams 168, 176–92
experience of betrayal 55–8, 63–9, 78, 79, 92–4, 128, 232
and France 12, 24, 26, 27, 28, 29, 31–3, 64–6, 67, 68, 108, 124–5
influence of David Williams 7, 16–21, 22, 26, 27, 28–36, 40–54, 63, 81, 95, 168
knowledge of Vortigern story 60–2, 68, 70
and Kosciusko 95, 124–34
poetic dialogue with Thelwall 2, 5, 6, 78, 92–4, 194, 210–40
relations with Thelwall 79, 81, 193, 201–5, 206, 207, 208, 209, 294, 296, 315, 316, 317, 327–9
WORKS:
'A Poet's Epitaph' 6, 177–87

'A Slumber did my Spirit Seal' 127
'Advertisement' to 'Guilt and Sorrow' 58
An Evening Walk 18, 177
'Anecdote for Fathers' 81, 205
'Artegal and Elidure' 61, 92, 93
Descriptive Sketches 18, 177, 252 n.139
Ecclesiastical Sketches 61, 64–5
Essays upon Epitaphs 45, 278 n.157
'Expostulation and Reply' 52
Fenwick Notes 187, 284 nn.96,105
'How sweet to walk along the woody steep' 57–8
Letter to the Bishop of Llandaff 20, 28, 47, 66
'Lines Written at a Small Distance from My House' 52, 127
'Lines written in Early Spring' 263 n.33
Lyrical Ballads 7, 10, 41, 53, 57, 81, 125, 168, 177–87, 218, 219, 222, 223, 232–8
'Not useless do I deem' 52, 185–6
'Ode: Intimations of Immortality' 127
'On the Extinction of the Venetian Republic' 130
Poems (1815) 263 n.29
'Preface' to *Lyrical Ballads* 181–2, 183, 207, 237
'Salisbury Plain' 58, 59, 65, 253 n.7
'September 1802' 127
'Simon Lee' 6, 187–92, 263 n.33
'Song for the Wandering Jew' 90–1
'Surprised by Joy' 283 n.65
The Borderers 90, 185, 315
The Convention of Cintra 64–5, 124
'The Convict' 89, 219–20
'The Discharged Soldier' 48, 129–30, 134
The Excursion 239–40, 299, 302 n.14; Book III 94; Book VI 45
'The Idiot Boy' 18
The Prelude 2, 65, 184, 185, 206, 252 n.139
The Prelude (1799) Book I 280 n.25
The Prelude (1805) Book V 278 n.153; Book VI 3, 46–7; Book VII 130; Book VIII 45; Book IX 21, 133–4, 268 n.99; Book X 31–3, 55, 57, 63–4, 145, 150, 163, 278 n.153; Book XI 278 n.153; Book XII 58
The Prelude (1850) Book IV 48; Book X 55, 63; Book XII 185
The Recluse 47, 185, 197, 252 n.142
'The Ruined Cottage' 52, 185
'The Thorn' 6, 18, 232–8
'Thought of a Briton on the Subjugation of Switzerland' 130
'Tintern Abbey' 1, 3, 4, 6, 7, 8–11, 12, 16, 17, 44–51, 52–3, 56–8, 63, 64, 68–9, 79, 81, 89, 90, 92–3, 95, 120–1, 125, 126–8, 168, 187, 192, 194, 222, 223–7, 228, 232, 241, 242, 251 n.122, 327, 328
'To Toussaint L'Ouverture' 130–1
Wraxall, N.W. 324
Wright, Paul 65, 132
Wu, Duncan 61, 244 n.24, 245 n.35, 248 n.77, 250 n.109, 252 n.143, 257 n.67, 261 n.118, 277 n.137, 283 n.76
Wye Valley 2, 4, 9, 15–16, 56, 59–62, 63, 68, 79, 81, 89–94, 124–8, 207, 221–2, 223–4, 228, 241–2
see also Llyswen; Tintern

Yates, John 305 n.21

Yeats, William Butler
  'A Prayer for my Daughter'
  212–13

'Among Schoolchildren' 1